The Right to Reparation in International Law for Victims of Armed Conflict

In this evaluation of the international legal standing of the right to reparation and its practical implementation at the national level, Christine Evans outlines state responsibility and examines the jurisprudence of the International Court of Justice, the Articles on State Responsibility of the International Law Commission and the convergence of norms in different branches of international law, notably human rights law, humanitarian law and international criminal law. Case studies of countries in which the United Nations has played a significant role in peace negotiations and post-conflict processes allow her to analyse to what extent transitional justice measures have promoted state responsibility for reparations, interacted with human rights mechanisms and prompted subsequent elaboration of domestic legislation and reparations policies. In conclusion, she argues for an emerging customary right for individuals to receive reparations for serious violations of human rights and a corresponding responsibility of states.

CHRISTINE EVANS is a staff member of the Office of the United Nations High Commissioner for Human Rights. She holds a Ph.D. in international law from the LSE and an LLM from the Raoul Wallenberg Institute of Human Rights and Humanitarian Law.

The Right to Reparation in International Law for Victims of Armed Conflict

Christine Evans

CAMBRIDGE
UNIVERSITY PRESS

CAMBRIDGE
UNIVERSITY PRESS

University Printing House, Cambridge CB2 8BS, United Kingdom

Cambridge University Press is part of the University of Cambridge.

It furthers the University's mission by disseminating knowledge in the pursuit of education, learning and research at the highest international levels of excellence.

www.cambridge.org
Information on this title: www.cambridge.org/9781107019973

First published 2012

A catalogue record for this publication is available from the British Library

Library of Congress Cataloguing in Publication data

Evans, Christine (E. Christine)
The right to reparation in international law for victims of armed conflict / Christine Evans.
p. cm. – (Cambridge studies in international and comparative law ; 91)
Includes bibliographical references and index.
ISBN 978-1-107-01997-3
1. War reparations. 2. Restorative justice. 3. Reparations for historical injustices 4. Reparation (Criminal justice) I. Title.
KZ6785.E93 2012
340.9–dc23

2011048386

ISBN 978-1-107-01997-3 Hardback

Contents

Acknowledgements

This topic has been a long-standing interest of mine since undertaking volunteer work in 1999 with victims of the armed conflict in Guatemala. The strength of victims of human rights violations and of the advocates who act on their behalf has constituted the major source of inspiration during this research.

This book is based on a Ph.D. thesis successfully defended at the London School of Economics and Political Science (LSE) in November 2010. I wish to express gratitude to Prof. Stanley Cohen for encouraging me to apply to LSE, to Prof. Gerry Simpson for his supervision and to Dr Margot Salomon for her supervision and important guidance during the final stages. I also wish to thank Prof. Manfred Nowak and Prof. Francesca Klug for their invaluable comments in the context of the examination of the thesis.

A warm expression of appreciation to my supervisors at the UN Office of the High Commissioner for Human Rights (OHCHR): Jane Connors and Mercedes Morales for their vital advice and support, without which this project could not have been undertaken. I wish to thank the many colleagues and friends I have had the pleasure of working with and learning from at OHCHR, especially in the Colombia Office (*gracias*) and within the Human Rights Treaties Division and Special Procedures Branch in Geneva. A particularly warm appreciation to Maja Andrijasevic-Boko, Linnea Arvidsson, Therese Björk, Elisabeth da Costa, Helle Dahl Iversen, Joana Miquel Gelabert and Katarina Månsson for many shared smiles and for encouragement over the years. I could not have done this without you. For their friendship and inspiring commitment to human rights work, I also thank: Estelle Askew-Renaut, Carmen Bejarano, Ugo Cedrangolo, Martin Cinnamond, Ellen Colthoff, Claudia de la Fuente, Sara Gustafsson,

Anna-Karin Holmlund, Yasmin Keith Krelik, Danielle Kirby, Diana Losada, Joao Nataf, Nicole Oberholzer, Judy Akot Oder, Krista Oinonen, Santiago Martinez de Orense, Anastasia Panayotidis, Jesus Peña, Laurence Perroud, Björn Pettersson, Carolin Schleker, Karen Sherlock, Marie-Christine Siemerink, Georgina Mendoza Solorio and Anna de la Varga.

A special mention of human rights treaty body members I am grateful to have worked with and learnt from: Dr Agnes Aidoo, Prof. Claudio Grossman, Prof. Helen Keller, Prof. Yanghee Lee, Sir Nigel Rodley, Prof. Fabian Salvioli, Prof. Lucy Smith, Dr Nora Sveass and Mr Jean Zermatten. I would also like to thank Prof. Juan Mendez, UN Special Rapporteur on Torture and Other Cruel, Inhuman or Degrading Treatment or Punishment for his inspirational dedication to advancing human rights.

I would like to extend gratitude to Prof. Gudmundur Alfredsson and the late Prof. Katarina Tomasevski for their teachings and support at the Raoul Wallenberg Institute of Human Rights and Humanitarian Law (RWI) in Sweden. Other colleagues and friends at the RWI whom I wish to acknowledge include: Johannes Eile, Johan Hallenborg, Zophie Landahl, Lena Olsson, Rolf Ring and Ingela Ståhl. A special appreciation to Brian Burdekin for all his insightful advice and encouragement.

I would not have been able to complete this research without the scholarships received from the British Arts and Humanities Research Council (AHRC), the LSE Law Research Studentship, the Judge Rosalyn Higgins Scholarship and the Olive Stone Scholarship. I would also like to thank OHCHR for enabling me to take a period of sabbatical leave in order to complete the thesis. With thanks for the support from the libraries of LSE, RWI, the United Nations Office in Geneva (UNOG) and OHCHR. A special mention of Anthony Donnarumma for all his assistance.

My final expression of gratitude is reserved for my family for all their constant support: Cecilia Engfelt and my parents Alice and Russell Evans.

Table of cases

Permanent Court of International Justice

Factory at Chorzów Case (Germany v. *Poland)*, Jurisdiction, 1927, PCIJ, Ser. A, No. 9 28

Factory at Chorzów Case (Germany v. *Poland)*, Merits, 1928, PCIJ, Ser. A, No. 17 29

International Court of Justice

Corfu Channel Case (United Kingdom v. *Albania)*, Merits, ICJ Report 1949 26

Reparation for Injuries Suffered in the Service of the United Nations, Advisory Opinion of 11 April 1949, ICJ Report 1949 43

Reservations to the Convention on the Prevention and Punishment of the Crime of Genocide, Advisory Opinion, ICJ Report 1951 21

North Sea Continental Shelf Cases, ICJ Reports 1969 40

Barcelona Traction, Light and Power Company Limited, Second Phase, ICJ Report 1970 23

East Timor Case (Portugal v. *Australia)*, ICJ Report 1970 24

Military and Paramilitary Activities in and against Nicaragua Case (Nicaragua v. *United States)*, ICJ Report 1986 40

Gabčikovo-Nagymaros Project Case (Hungary v. *Slovakia)*, ICJ Report 1997 29

Legality of the Threat or Use of Force of Nuclear Weapons, Advisory Opinion, 8 July 1996, ICJ Report 1996 21

Legal Consequences of the Construction of a Wall in the Occupied Palestinian Territory, Advisory Opinion, 9 July 2004, ICJ Report 2004 21, 22, 30, 125

UN human rights treaty bodies: individual communications

Human Rights Committee

Committee against Torture

Committee on the Elimination of Discrimination against Women

UN human rights treaty bodies: general comments

UN human rights treaty bodies: concluding observations

European Court of Human Rights

Inter-American Court of Human Rights

African Commission on Human and Peoples' Rights

Human Rights Chamber for Bosnia and Herzegovina

International Criminal Tribunal for the Former Yugoslavia

Prosecutor v. *Tadić*, Case No. IT-96-21-Y, Judgment, 16 November 1998 89

Prosecutor v. *Furundžija*, Case No. IT-95-17/1-T, Judgment, 10 December 1998 89

Prosecutor v. *Delalić et al.*, Case No. IT-96-21, Judgment, 20 February 2001 90

Prosecutor v. *Nikolić*, Case No. IT-02-60/1, Judgment, 2 December 2003 90

Prosecutor v. *Blagojević and Jokić*, Case No. IT-02-60, Judgment, 17 January 2005 90

International Criminal Tribunal for Rwanda

Prosecutor v. *Akayesu*, Case No. ICTR-96-4-T, Sentence, 2 October 1998 89

Prosecutor v. *Kayishema and Ruzindana*, Case No. ICTR-95-1-T, Sentence, 21 May 1999 89

International Criminal Court

Judgment on Victim Participation in the Investigation Stage of the Proceedings by Appeals Chamber, ICC-01/04-556, 19 December 2008 104

Extraordinary Chambers in the Courts of Cambodia

Kaing Guek Eav (alias Duch), Case 001/18-07-2007/ECCC/TC, Judgment, 26 July 2010 117

Table of treaties

Human rights

Convention on the Prevention and Punishment of the Crime of Genocide, adopted 9 December 1948, GA Res. 260 (III), Part I (A/810) 21, 24, 88

Convention for the Protection of Human Rights and Fundamental Freedoms (ECHR), adopted 4 November 1950, ETS 5, 213 UNTS 221 35–36, 58

International Convention on the Elimination of All Forms of Racial Discrimination (CERD), adopted 21 December 1965, GA Res. 2106 (XX), annex, UN Doc. A/6014 (1966), 660 UNTS 195 19, 24, 35, 138

International Covenant on Civil and Political Rights (ICCPR), adopted 16 December 1966, GA Res. 2200A (XXI), 999 UNTS 171 19, 21, 24, 25, 34, 45

International Covenant on Economic, Social and Cultural Rights (CESCR), adopted 16 December 1966, GA Res. 2200A (XXI), UN Doc. A/6316 (1966), 993 UNTS 3 17, 24, 25, 138

American Convention on Human Rights (ACHR), adopted 22 November 1969, OAS Treaty Ser. No. 36, 1144 UNTS 123 36, 66–68

Convention on the Elimination of All Forms of Discrimination against Women (CEDAW), adopted 18 December 1979, GA Res. 34/180, UN Doc. A/34/46, 1249 UNTS 13 19, 25, 55, 138

African Charter on Human and Peoples' Rights (AChHR), adopted 27 June 1981, OAU Doc. CAB/LEG/67/3 rev. 5, 1520 UNTS 217 36, 76–77, 79

European Convention on the Compensation of Victims of Violent Crimes, adopted 24 November 1983, ETS 116 101

International humanitarian law

International criminal law

General international law

List of abbreviations

ACHPR	African Commission on Human and Peoples' Rights
ACHR	American Convention on Human Rights
CAT	Convention against Torture
CAVR	Commission for Reception, Truth and Reconciliation in East Timor
CEH	Historical Clarification Commission in Guatemala
CRC	Convention on the Rights of the Child
DDR	disarmament, demobilisation and reintegration
ECCC	Extraordinary Chambers in the Courts of Cambodia
ECHR	European Convention on Human Rights
ECtHR	European Court of Human Rights
GA	United Nations General Assembly
IACHR	Inter-American Commission on Human Rights
IACtHR	Inter-American Court of Human Rights
ICC	International Criminal Court
ICCPR	International Covenant on Civil and Political Rights
ICJ	International Court of Justice
ICRC	International Committee of the Red Cross
ICTR	Ad hoc Tribunal for Rwanda
ICTY	Ad hoc Tribunal for Former Yugoslavia
ILC	International Law Commission
MINUGUA	United Nations Human Rights Verification Mission in Guatemala
MoU	Memorandum of Understanding
NGO	non-governmental organisation
NHRI	national human rights institution
OAS	Organization of American States
OAU	Organisation of African Unity

OHCHR	United Nations Office of the High Commissioner for Human Rights
PBF	United Nations Peace-Building Fund
PCIJ	Permanent Court of International Justice
PRSP	Poverty Reduction Strategy Paper
SCSL	Special Court for Sierra Leone
ToR	terms of reference
UDHR	Universal Declaration of Human Rights
UNAMID	African Union and United Nations Hybrid Operation in Darfur
UNAMSIL	United Nations Assistance Mission in Sierra Leone
UNCC	United Nations Compensation Commission
UNDP	United Nations Developments Programme
UNHCR	United Nations High Commissioner for Refugees
UNTAET	United Nations Transitional Administration for East Timor
UNTS	United Nations Treaty Series
UPR	Universal Periodic Review

1 Introduction

1.1 Introduction and context

The rationale for writing this book is the importance of charting the legal standing of the right to reparation for victims of serious violations of human rights and humanitarian law and to explore the challenges associated with the implementation of this right, including the role played by the United Nations (UN) in this regard. This study explores the developing legal norms relating to the rights of victims of serious human rights and humanitarian law violations, identifies implementation gaps in recent international justice accountability initiatives and considers the advancement of the practical implementation of victims' rights, in particular those relating to reparations.

The past few decades have been distinguished by significant advances in the concept of state responsibility for serious violations of human rights and humanitarian law. Progress has been made in various branches of international law and long overdue steps towards implementation have been taken, notably through the development of human rights jurisprudence and the establishment of international criminal tribunals and truth commissions. Based on experiences to date, there is increasing awareness that post-conflict justice initiatives need to be comprehensive, complementary and, in particular, pay due attention to the rights of victims. There is emerging recognition that it is the responsibility of the state to provide justice for victims of armed conflict, and that sustainable justice requires three different components: judicial accountability, truth and reparations.[1] This is reflected in recent

[1] UN Basic Principles and Guidelines on the Right to a Remedy and Reparation for Victims of Gross Violations of International Human Rights Law and Serious Violations of International Humanitarian Law, UN Doc. A/RES/60/147, adopted by the General

developments in general international law and *lex specialis* such as human rights and humanitarian law, as well as post-conflict policy initiatives undertaken by international organisations, primarily the UN. However, due to the tensions surrounding state responsibility to provide reparations, this component of justice continues to be overlooked in favour of what are perceived to be more pressing exigencies to establish accountability and rule of law. This book argues that the rights of victims of serious human rights and humanitarian law violations have traditionally been neglected and that there is a pressing need to promote and apply the emerging norms in order for their rights to be realised and to ensure that a 'tripartite' balance of justice is achieved. Considering the standing individuals have gained in international law, the need to translate consequences of serious violations, such as reparations, in favour of individual victims has become an important aspect of affirming the legitimacy and credibility of the international legal order and human rights standards.

The surge of the human rights movement and the progress made towards universal ratification of human rights instruments over the past few decades has influenced the recognition of individuals as subjects under general international law and their rights versus the state. Both at the international and regional levels, rapidly growing jurisprudence confirms state responsibility to provide reparations for human rights violations caused by state agents or by the failure of states to prevent violations by non-state actors. However, as human rights mechanisms were not designed to deal with large-scale violations in conflict situations, the developing doctrine on redress provided for individual victims of human rights violations stands in stark contrast to the inadequate responses that have thus far been offered in practice to the victims of serious human rights and humanitarian law violations. Victims of ordinary crimes are still more likely to receive redress than those who have suffered serious human rights violations, in particular, when the victims are numerous in the context of an armed conflict. Many victims

Assembly 16 December 2005. UN Principles to Combat Impunity, adopted by the UN Commission on Human Rights in 1997, updated in 2005, UN Doc. E/CN.4/2005/102/Add.1. See also, e.g., C. Bassiouni, 'Accountability for Violations of International Humanitarian Law and other Serious Violations of Human Rights', in C. Bassiouni (ed.), *Post-Conflict Justice* (New York: Transnational Publishers, 2002), p. 26; M. Minow, *Between Vengeance and Forgiveness: Facing History after Genocide and Mass Violence* (Boston, MA: Beacon Press, 1998) and R. Mani, *Beyond Retribution, Seeking Justice in the Shadows of War* (Cambridge: Polity Press, 2002).

of serious violations continue to suffer stigma, social exclusion and re-victimisation as a consequence of the lack of reparations and assistance in order to overcome the impact of armed conflict. Among the victims most affected are women, children and victims of torture and sexual violence. For a majority of these victims, the absence of reparations has impeded their ability to resume their lives and move beyond the trauma they have endured.

Humanitarian law primarily contains provisions relating to the protection of victims, that is, civilians during conflict, but also affirms the duty of responsible parties to pay compensation. Historically, the doctrine in international law on inter-state reparations has to a large extent impeded the ability of victims of conflict to seek reparations. States had the discretion to claim reparations against other states for injuries to their nationals. The defendant state's duties were considered to be owed not to the injured alien, but rather to the alien's national state.[2] However, this doctrine has been challenged at the national level by a number of international redress movements, which in turn have been inspired by the gradual erosion of state immunity in relation to human rights violations. The convergence of human rights and humanitarian law norms that cover the same serious violations, such as, for example, violations of the right to life and acts of torture, exposes gaps as victims are able to seek redress through human rights mechanisms, while humanitarian law fails to provide comparable procedures for implementation.

The recent codification of international criminal law has significantly influenced the discourse on post-conflict justice, while legal research on post-conflict justice has been inspired by the rapid developments in international justice mechanisms. As a result, much focus has been on the accountability of perpetrators, in particular, in the application of universal jurisdiction. Victims have largely remained in the background, analogous to their position in municipal criminal law where reparations are seen as part of civil law, and victims are still primarily perceived according to their capacity as witnesses. However, as awareness of the importance of affirming the rights of victims increases, there is a pressing need to identify gaps in their legal protection as well as effective

[2] I. Brownlie, *Principles of Public International Law* (Oxford: Clarendon Press, 1990), pp. 432–76; A. Cassese, *International Law* (Oxford University Press, 2001), pp. 182–210; P. Malanczuk, *Akehurst's Modern Introduction to International Law* (London: Routledge, 1997), pp. 256–7; D. Shelton, *Remedies in International Human Rights Law* (Oxford University Press, 2005), pp. 56–83.

modalities that can address their situation in practice. The Rome Statute of the International Criminal Court (ICC) establishes new ground by affirming the rights of victims to reparations. Yet the key challenge of how to transform these rights into practice remains, particularly as the coverage of the ICC, and that of its Trust Fund, will be limited by its jurisdiction and capacity to interact with and reach out to victims.

There is a potential problem in focusing on individual responsibility as it may divert attention away from state responsibility. In practical, as well as conceptual, terms, the issue of reparations for victims of armed conflict is difficult to substantiate in terms of individual responsibility. This research argues that there is a need to reinforce the notion that the state carries the principal responsibility for providing redress. Although a state may not have been directly and solely responsible for all violations in question, responsibility can, as is evidenced in international law and succinctly illustrated by case law from the Inter-American human rights system, result from complicity, omission, as well as failure to prevent and demonstrate due diligence.[3] It is submitted that once peace has been achieved and negotiations concluded, the state assumes responsibilities towards the demobilised opponents with respect to, for example, reintegration measures, and, as a logical consequence, should also be responsible to the victims of these former combatants.[4] As is demonstrated by numerous peace agreements, there is recognition that victims are entitled to receive reparations.[5] Examples of such peace agreements are highlighted and explored in Part II of this study. Authorities in post-conflict scenarios need to consider the harm that has been inflicted upon civilians in a non-discriminatory manner

[3] A. Cançado Trindade, 'Complementarity between State Responsibility and Individual Responsibility for Grave Violations of Human Rights: The Crime of State Revisited', in M. Ragazzi (ed.), *International Responsibility Today, Essays in Memory of Oscar Schachter* (Leiden: Martinus Nijhoff, 2005), pp. 253–69. See further references in case law discussed in Chapter 3 and in particular in relation to jurisprudence of the Inter-American Court relating to Guatemala and Colombia, discussed in Part II.

[4] For a thorough discussion see L. Zegveld, *Accountability of Armed Opposition Groups in International Law* (Cambridge University Press, 2002). See also Y. Sooka, 'Dealing with the Past and Transitional Justice: Building Peace through Accountability', *International Review of the Red Cross*, 88(862) (2006), 324–5; P. De Geiff, 'Contributing to Peace and Justice, Finding a Balance between DDR and Reparations', Paper presented at the conference 'Building a Future on Peace and Justice', Nuremberg, 25–27 June 2007.

[5] C. Bell, *Peace Agreements and Human Rights* (Oxford University Press, 2000). See also Report to the Human Rights Council of the Office of the High Commissioner for Human Rights, 'Analytical Study on Human Rights and Transitional Justice', A/HRC/12/18, 6 August 2009 and its Addendum, 'Inventory of Human Rights and Transitional Justice Aspects of Recent Peace Agreements', A/HRC/12/18/Add.1, 21 August 2009.

irrespective of the perpetrators of the acts, and state practice indicates growing recognition of such responsibility.

As noted above, different branches of law are contributing to the development of norms on victims' rights. The convergence of human rights provisions and those related to war crimes under international humanitarian law and international criminal law, for example, the prohibition of extrajudicial executions, torture, racial discrimination and child recruitment, indicate that victims would benefit from claiming their right to receive reparations with reference to different branches of law. There is recognised value in merging the rights of victims currently found in the different strands of international law;[6] however, the adoption of a legally binding instrument that clearly consolidates the rights of victims[7] and the establishment of effective operative redress mechanisms have yet to be realised.

In 2005, the UN Commission on Human Rights adopted, after some fifteen years of drafting negotiations, the UN Basic Principles and Guidelines on the Right to a Remedy and Reparation for Victims of Gross Violations of International Human Rights Law and Serious Violations of International Humanitarian Law (hereafter 'Basic Principles on the Right to Reparation for Victims' or 'the Principles'). The Principles clearly aim to merge international humanitarian and human rights law, and stress the importance of and obligation to implement domestic reparations for victims of conflict. In March 2006, the Principles were adopted by the General Assembly (GA) of the UN, further strengthening their status even though they are formally non-binding.[8] Significantly, the Principles detail the range of components of which reparations

[6] An example, the ICJ *Case Concerning Armed Activities on the Territory of the Congo (Democratic Republic of the Congo* v. *Uganda)*, ICJ Report 2005, affirms the dual and complementary application of human rights and humanitarian law, paras 217–19. Further references on the mutually complementary and reinforcing nature of human rights and humanitarian law: 'Report to the Human Rights Council of the Office of the High Commissioner for Human Rights on the Outcome of the Expert Consultation on the Issue of Protecting the Human Rights of Civilians in Armed Conflict', A/HRC/11/31, 2 June 2009.

[7] T. Meron, 'On the Inadequate Reach of Humanitarian and Human Rights Law and the Need for a New Instrument', *American Journal of International Law*, 77(3) (1983), 589–606; Bassiouni, 'Accountability for Violations of International Humanitarian Law and other Serious Violations of Human Rights', pp. 26–54.

[8] UN Basic Principles and Guidelines on the Right to a Remedy and Reparation for Victims of Gross Violations of International Human Rights Law and Serious Violations of International Humanitarian Law, Preamble, adopted by the UN Commission on Human Rights in 2005, UN Doc. E/CN.4/RES/2005/35 and adopted by the General Assembly on 16 December 2005, UN Doc. A/RES/60/147.

consist: namely, restitution, compensation, rehabilitation, satisfaction and guarantees of non-repetition. The Principles, while still in draft form, were already being referred to in the jurisprudence of numerous human rights treaty bodies, figure in several recently adopted international legal instruments[9] and domestic legislation, and have also been applied by a number of truth commissions, as explored in Part II.[10] As will be explored, the Principles largely reflect already established norms in international law and make an important contribution in unifying and reinforcing them. To a significant extent, the Principles draw upon the Articles on State Responsibility adopted by the International Law Commission (ILC) in 2001.[11] This study examines the different elements of reparations and identifies aspects that are deemed to be the most essential by those victims who remain particularly vulnerable after armed conflict. As noted by Nowak and MacArthur: 'usually, victims of torture are not primarily interested in monetary compensation but in other means of reparation which are better suited to restore their dignity and humanity'.[12]

Although reparations are clearly a state responsibility, the UN plays a considerable role in promoting the rights of victims in conflict mediation and post-conflict peace-building. The authority of the UN, empowered by its Charter with the duty to maintain international peace and security in conformity with the principles of justice and international law, faces a major challenge in promoting normative standards on victims' rights in its operative work. The expanded role of the UN in peacekeeping missions,[13] and in post-conflict justice initiatives

[9] The Rome Statute of the International Criminal Court (ICC) contains an implicit reference to the principles in Article 75; they are also explicitly mentioned in the International Convention on the Protection of All Persons from Enforced Disappearance, Article 24 (adopted 20 December 2006, entered into force 23 December 2010).

[10] For example, the truth commissions in South Africa and Sierra Leone, as underlined by Ms Yasmin Sooka, former Commissioner in the South African and Sierra Leone TRCs during 'Workshop to Combat Impunity and Provide Reparations' at OHCHR Geneva on 19 September 2005. See also Shelton, *Remedies in International Human Rights Law*, p. 350.

[11] Draft Articles on Responsibility of States for Internationally Wrongful Acts, Report of the International Commission 2001, 53rd session contained in the Official Records of the General Assembly, 56th session, Supplement No. 10, UN Doc. A/56/10, ch. IV.E.I.

[12] M. Nowak and E. McArthur, *The United Nations Convention against Torture, A Commentary* (Oxford University Press, 2008), p. 483.

[13] Report of the Secretary-General to the General Assembly, 'Investing in the United Nations, for a Stronger Organisation worldwide', released 7 March 2006, UN Doc. A/60/692 details that: 'in the first 44 years of the history of the UN, only 18 peacekeeping missions were set up. In the 16 years since 1990, 42 new missions have been authorised', para. 4.

undertaken over the past fifteen years, underlines its position that state responsibility towards victims should not be abandoned during accountability and reconciliation processes. This study explores the role of the international community, and notably the UN, in ensuring victims' rights in peace negotiations and the establishment and operation of, as well as follow-up to, transitional justice mechanisms. As expressed by Kofi Annan in his 2005 reform proposal, 'we must move from an era of legislation to an era of implementation'.[14] While emphasis during past decades has been on the development of norms and standards in the realm of human rights, today attention should be placed on the importance of ensuring that rights are effectively put into practice.

1.2 Aim and objectives of the study

The overall aim of this study is to analyse the international legal standing of the right to reparation for victims of serious human rights and humanitarian law violations, and to assess the degree of practical implementation of that right at the national level through case studies on post-conflict and transitional justice measures. The central objective is to chart and evaluate developments in law, based on comprehensive analysis of provisions and jurisprudence, as well as in practice, in order to substantiate arguments in favour of an emerging customary right for individuals to receive reparations for serious violations of human rights and the corresponding responsibility of states.

Although research on reparations has gained increased attention, considerable research has been compartmentalised and focused on either redress in human rights,[15] international humanitarian law[16] or international criminal law.[17] This study rather promotes the position that victims benefit from a reparations concept that merges provisions, especially since the prohibition of the most serious human rights

[14] Report of the Secretary-General to the General Assembly, 'In Larger Freedom, Towards Development, Security and Human Rights for All', UN Doc. A/59/2005, 25 March 2005, para. 132.

[15] Shelton, *Remedies in International Human Rights Law.*

[16] A. MacDonald, 'Rights to Legal Remedies for Victims of Serious Violations of IHL', Doctoral thesis, Queen's University of Belfast, 2003; L. Zegveld, 'Remedies for Victims of Violations of International Humanitarian Law', *International Review of the Red Cross*, 85 (2003), 497–526.

[17] F. McKay, 'Are Reparations Appropriately Addressed in the ICC Statute?', in D. Shelton (ed.), *International Crimes, Peace and Human Rights: The Role of the International Criminal Court* (New York: Transnational Publishers, 2000), pp. 163–78.

violations coincide with provisions in international humanitarian law and international criminal law. The focus on these synergies follows as a natural consequence of increased convergence and cross-referencing regarding victims' rights between the different branches of law. As Bassiouni notes; 'if the victim is our concern and interest, then legal distinctions and technicalities surrounding various classifications of crimes should be re-conceptualised ... such distinctions are of little significance to victims in their quest for redress'.[18] The right of individuals to receive reparations for serious violations is an indispensable corollary to an effective remedy for the violations suffered. The study focuses on the reparations aspects of victims' rights rather than on their right to access to justice and their right to a legal remedy. The objective is to apply a victim-oriented approach by using as a key evaluation tool the comprehensive concept of the victims' right to reparations established in the UN Basic Principles on the Right to Reparation for Victims, rather then referring to the polarised 'truth versus justice' discourse, which until the Basic Principles were adopted tended to dominate in assessments of post-conflict and transitional justice initiatives.[19]

Parallel to legal developments, it is pertinent to scrutinise how actual post-conflict measures on the ground have managed to incorporate victims' rights elements and to what extent this has been achieved by initiatives constructed to promote retributive, transitional or restorative justice. There is a lacuna as the concept of state responsibility has evolved, alongside an emerging customary right to receive reparations, yet in practice a national legal framework and forum to which victims can submit claims commonly remains lacking. Thus, the right cannot be effectively guaranteed. This book aims to assess the degree to which concrete measures have been taken to bridge this gap. The research contrasts legal norms with state practice by exploring a number of case studies of countries recently emerged or emerging from conflict, in

18 C. Bassiouni, 'International Recognition of Victims Rights', *Human Rights Law Review*, 6 (2006), 204–5.

19 See, e.g., R. Rotberg and D. Thompson (eds), *Truth v. Justice, The Morality of Truth Commissions* (Princeton University Press, 2000); P. Akhavan 'Beyond Impunity: Can International Justice Prevent Future Atrocities?', *American Journal of International Law*, 95(7) (2002), 7–31; A. Barahona de Brito, C. Gonzalez Enriquez and P. Aguilar (eds), *The Politics of Memory, Transitional Justice in Democratizing Societies* (Oxford University Press, 2001); A. J. McAdams (ed.), *Transitional Justice and the Rule of Law in New Democracies* (University of Notre Dame Press, 1997); N. Kritz (ed.), *Transitional Justice: How Emerging Democracies Reckon with Former Regimes*, 3 vols (Washington, DC: US Institute of Peace Press, 1995); A. Rigby, *Justice and Reconciliation after Violent Conflict* (Boulder, CO: Lynne Rienner, 2001).

which the UN plays or has played a significant role in peace negotiations, the establishment of transitional justice mechanisms and in their follow-up. The impact of specific provisions on reparations in peace agreements and mandates of UN-supported transitional justice initiatives is examined.

The establishment of numerous truth commissions has sparked considerable interest in their restorative value, in particular, among scholars in the field of political science, sociology and psychology. However, only recently has the contribution of truth commissions become recognised among legal scholars as having a complementary, rather than alternative, function.[20] Approaches to post-conflict analysis have tended to be short-sighted and have failed to pay due consideration to an aspect crucial for the victims: namely, the right to reparation. Therefore, this study sets out from the perspective of the victims, for whom the absence of reparations undermines the concept of justice. The second part of the book assesses the role of the UN in relation to transitional justice mechanisms, both courts and truth commissions, and the degree to which these have managed to influence the national discourse and promote state responsibility and responsiveness to victims' claims for reparations. When applicable, the contributions of international commissions of inquiry are also considered.

Specifically, this study discusses state practice and the extent to which truth commissions have provided a basis for subsequent elaboration of domestic legislation and comprehensive reparations measures. The book furthermore considers to what extent truth commissions have played, and will continue playing, a significant role in promoting the practical implementation of the right to reparation for victims of armed conflict. The case studies aim at identifying which factors are decisive in promoting the right in practice. For this reason, the case studies document the interplay between transitional justice processes and human rights mechanisms, both international and regional, and to what extent these have promoted state responsibility effectively. Finally, the case studies

[20] R. Goldstone, 'Advancing the Cause of Human Rights: The Need for Justice and Accountability', in S. Power and G. Allison, *Realising Human Rights, Moving from Inspiration to Impact* (New York: St. Martin's Press, 2000), pp. 195–221; C. Stahn, 'United Nations Peace-building, Amnesties and Alternative Forms of Justice: A Change in Practice', *International Review of the Red Cross*, 84(845) (2002), 191–205; W. Schabas, 'The Relationship between Truth Commissions and Courts: The Case of Sierra Leone', Paper presented at conference on the 'Inter-Relationship between Truth Commissions and Courts', Galway, 4 October 2002; R. Zacklin, 'The Failings of Ad Hoc International Tribunals', *Journal of International Criminal Justice*, 2 (2004), 541–5.

analyse the degree of engagement and support by the international community, along with geopolitical factors, as these provide key elements in prompting states to recognise and assume their responsibilities vis-à-vis victims of serious human rights violations. With a view towards the future, suggestions for concrete measures, such as the creation of trust funds, are identified and put forward.

1.3 Structure and outline

1.3.1 Part I

The first chapter of Part I explores the customary nature of human rights and humanitarian law, outlines the basic premise of state responsibility in relation to violations and identifies the general international norms that establish the obligation to provide reparations. The convergence of norms and legal sources is documented by reference to the status of reparations in relation to individuals, as demonstrated in jurisprudence from the International Court of Justice, the Articles on State Responsibility of the ILC,[21] as well as in provisions in humanitarian and human rights instruments. The influence of international human rights law on general international law is particularly highlighted. The study furthermore examines international standards that are formally non-binding, with emphasis on the Basic Principles on the Right to Reparation for Victims, as these illustrate an emerging fusion in international law in favour of victims. The chapter acknowledges some of the reservations expressed in relation to the status of the right to reparation and notes how such concerns are counteracted by developments in international law.

The second chapter studies in further detail developments in the area of reparations on the basis of the international and regional human rights systems. The chapter charts the evolving concept of reparations for serious human rights violations through a comparative study of case law under the international and regional human rights systems. Focus is set on cases that illustrate elements of reparations for serious human rights violations relating to restitution, no repetition, compensation, satisfaction and rehabilitation, according to the elements as affirmed in the Basic Principles on the Right to Reparation for Victims. Consideration is also given to the operative challenges faced

[21] Draft Articles on Responsibility of States for Internationally Wrongful Acts, A/56/10, ch. IV.E.I.

by international courts and human rights mechanisms and the rules of procedure that regulate their practice.

The third chapter of Part I provides an overview of the gradual incorporation of reparations provisions in international criminal law. In particular, the chapter studies the lack of attention for victims in the ad hoc tribunals (ICTY for the former Yugoslavia and ICTR for Rwanda), the unsuccessful attempts to create compensation mechanisms for the ad hoc tribunals and the impetus behind the groundbreaking provisions in the Rome Statute of the International Criminal Court. Some reflection is also made in relation to victims in the hybrid international tribunals (Sierra Leone, East Timor and Cambodia). Finally, the chapter also traces some of the major influences on this branch of law, such as the victimology movement, as well as restorative justice theory and feminist legal critique.

1.3.2 Part II

Building on Part I on legal standards and reparations provisions in different branches of international law, Part II applies the affirmed right of victims to reparations as a yardstick to assess the realisation of the right in practice. Thus, the objective is to contrast the situation *de jure* and the situation *de facto* in a number of countries in different regions by considering state practice and how actual post-conflict measures on the ground have managed to incorporate victims' rights elements, in particular, the right to reparation.

Transitional justice measures, such as truth commissions, have provided important impetus to the promotion of the right to reparation by creating forums for large-scale claims from victims of armed conflict. Truth commissions have permitted a comprehensive assessment of the impact violations have had on victims and, through a victim participatory process, proposed recommendations for large-scale reparations. International commissions of inquiry have in a similar manner, albeit on a reduced scale, documented violations in situations of unrest and armed conflict and recommended reparations for victims.

Part II explores aspects of reparations over the course of the decade 1999–2009 in four case studies: Guatemala, Sierra Leone, East Timor and Colombia.[22] The case studies represent different geographic regions that

[22] The selection of two case studies from Latin America is due to a number of factors. Primarily, because it represents the region where the most interesting procedural, legal and political developments have taken place at the national level and where the regional human rights system has played a particularly important role in promoting reparations for victims. Second, it is the region where the author has personal experience and was able to access primary materials in Spanish.

have suffered armed conflict and where the UN has played a significant role in promoting transitional justice initiatives. Given the key role of the UN in advocating for greater state responsibility vis-à-vis victims, the second part of this research studies to what extent it has been possible to provide reparations in practice through UN-supported transitional justice processes and which factors have been decisive in promoting state responsibility and responsiveness to victims' claims for reparations. Brief mention is made of the role of the Security Council, in particular, the unique reparations measures that formed part of the United Nations Compensation Commission and of the challenges to date of addressing reparations for victims in Darfur.

The selected case studies consider the issue of reparations in peace agreements, as well as in statutes of transitional justice mechanisms, notably truth commissions, and in their final reports. The impact of truth commission reports is analysed and the degree to which there has been the political will to implement the recommendations of such reports. The case studies note the national developments that have taken place with regard to legislation and policies on reparations and explore practical challenges in developing reparations programmes. When concrete reparations measures have been adopted, consideration is given to which push-and-pull factors were applicable in the national circumstances, such as the degree to which international and regional human rights mechanisms have influenced national reparations policies. The strength and influence of civil society and victims' organisations is assessed. The degree to which UN peacekeeping presences or other UN entities, in particular, the Office of the High Commissioner for Human Rights, have focused and followed up on reparations is studied. Furthermore, the case studies consider the relationship between different transitional justice initiatives such as truth commissions and international criminal tribunals and courts.

In conjunction with the case studies, particular consideration is given to reports and resolutions of the UN relating to a number of entities, including the Secretary-General, the Security Council, the General Assembly, the Office of the High Commissioner for Human Rights and the Human Rights Council (former Commission on Human Rights). The case studies draw upon personal field experience, informal conversations and interviews conducted with victims, NGO representatives, academics, UN human rights colleagues, International Committee of the Red Cross (ICRC) delegates, ICC and other international tribunal staff, as well as government officials. To date, the author has undertaken human rights work with victims of armed conflict in Guatemala and Colombia. The study reflects materials and developments up to early 2011.

A key aim of this book is to identify ways whereby the discrepancies between standards and implementation can be addressed by drawing on good practices, while also acknowledging shortcomings. The case studies identify the reparations measures provided or deemed to be a priority in future programmes and victims in which categories are most likely to be favoured or excluded. Furthermore, the case studies observe the obligations of non-state actors and study the degree of responsibility assumed by states for such violations. The overall aim is to consider to what extent state practice converges with legal norms and supports the argument that the right to reparation is attaining customary status in international law.

1.4 Definition of key concepts

There is a common misconception that reparations are synonymous with monetary compensation. Although compensation is a common component of reparations, the concept of reparations has evolved and now covers a wide range of measures. The various elements that reparations consist of have been affirmed in recent years in the International Law Commission's Draft Articles on State Responsibility (2001) and in the Basic Principles on the Right to Reparation for Victims (2005).

As will be further explored in the first section of this research, *reparations* consist of five key elements, namely: restitution, compensation, rehabilitation, satisfaction (disclosure of the truth) and guarantees of non-repetition. *Remedy* in this context is a general term and refers to access to legal remedies as well as to reparations. In this study, the term reparations will be used as it is generally understood to comprise the aspects aside from access to justice.[23] *Redress* is most commonly the noun that describes the action involved, but may also be used as a synonym for remedies.

[23] Different terminology is used by leading scholars and advocates who use different terms when referring to the same concept, e.g., Dinah Shelton uses the term 'remedies' when referring to reparations (Shelton, *Remedies in International Human Rights Law*), while the NGO 'Redress' prefers the term 'reparations'. See www.redress.org and also discussion in McKay, 'Are Reparations Appropriately Addressed in the ICC Statute?', pp. 163–78. Both terms are reflected in the title of the 2005 UN Basic Principles on the Right to a Remedy.

The concept of *victim* applied in this study is drawn from the Basic Principles on the Right to Reparation for Victims, as it offers a clear and comprehensive definition consistent with human rights norms and jurisprudence from the international as well as regional level. Accordingly:

> victims are persons who individually or collectively suffered harm, including physical or mental injury, emotional suffering, economic loss or substantial impairment of their fundamental rights . . . also includes the immediate family or dependants of the direct victim and persons who have suffered harm in intervening to assist victims in distress or to prevent victimization.[24]

International humanitarian law does not define the concept of victim. The Rome Statute of the International Criminal Court does not contain a definition of victims; however, this is defined in the Rules of Procedure, Rule 85.[25] The author notes that certain victims' organisations prefer the term *survivor* rather than the term *victim*, as an indication of their active resilience in overcoming the violence perpetrated against them. However, this study refers to the term *victim* for legal reasons, without prejudice to other terms, such as survivors, which may be preferred in different contexts.

[24] UN Basic Principles and Guidelines on the Right to a Remedy and Reparation for Victims of Gross Violations of International Human Rights Law and Serious Violations of International Humanitarian Law, UN Doc. A/RES/60/147, para. 8.

[25] Rule 85 states: 'For the purposes of the Statute and the Rules of Procedure and Evidence:

(a) "Victims" means natural persons who have suffered harm as a result of the commission of any crime within the jurisdiction of the Court;

(b) Victims may include organizations or institutions that have sustained direct harm to any of their property which is dedicated to religion, education, art or science or charitable purposes, and to their historic monuments, hospitals and other places and objects for humanitarian purposes.'

Part I

Responsibility and legal standards

'If the country in which genocide was committed is not to be held responsible for reparations, who is?'

Official Comments on Article XIII of the Draft Convention on the Crime of Genocide, p. 48, UN Doc. E/447, prepared 26 June 1947 by the UN Secretary-General upon request by the General Assembly.

Article XIII stated: 'When genocide is committed in a country by the government in power and by sections of the population, and if the government fails to resist it successfully, the State shall grant to the survivors of the human group that is a victim of genocide redress of a nature and in an amount to be determined by the United Nations.'

Article XIII was eliminated during the final stages of the political negotiations on the treaty. The Genocide Convention as approved by the General Assembly on 9 December 1948 regrettably contains no provision on reparations.

2 State responsibility, the legal order and the development of legal norms for victims

2.1 Introduction

The aim of this chapter is to give an overview of the shift that has taken place in the international legal order, particularly since the Second World War. International law is developed between states, based upon the principle of sovereignty and, as such, has been dictated largely by the interests of states rather than individuals. In the past, claims for individual compensation could be lodged only through inter-state complaints.[1] There was no obligation on the state whose nationals had been injured to present claims against other states. In fact, there was no impediment against states being able to waiver their claims without any consultation with the victims concerned.[2] Mechanisms were not available for individuals to seek redress for violations committed by their own state. Over the past sixty years, a considerable shift has taken place whereby treaty law, jurisprudence and customary law have been developed affirming the right of the individual against the state, clearly recognising the individual as a subject of international law.[3]

Particularly in the field of international human rights law, states have voluntarily ratified numerous treaties and consented to the establishment of mechanisms, whereby individuals have been given procedural standing to present claims against the state. However, the position of the individual under general international law is more complicated and interlinked with recognition of respect for human rights and humanitarian law as legitimate concerns for the world community as customary

[1] Brownlie, *Principles of Public International Law*, pp. 432–76; Cassese, *International Law*, pp. 182–210; Shelton, *Remedies in International Human Rights Law*, pp. 48–9.

[2] Brownlie, *Principles of Public International Law*, pp. 457–73, 580–94.

[3] Bassiouni, 'International Recognition of Victims Rights', pp. 203–79.

law. In this chapter, the standards affirming victims' rights in different branches of law will be identified, and the relationship between general international law and *lex specialis*, in particular, that of humanitarian and human rights law, is explored.

2.2 Recognition of human rights in customary law

The 1945 Charter which established the United Nations marked a turning point in international law as it identified universal protection of human rights as one of the principal objectives of the organisation, as stated in Articles 1(3) and 55. Article 56 of the Charter obliges members of the organisation to pledge themselves to 'take joint and separate action in cooperation with the organisation for the achievement of the purposes set forth in Article 55'. The Charter, although recognising state sovereignty, created the Security Council and authorised it to undertake measures to maintain international peace and security. The Charter placed human rights as a legitimate concern for the international community, set in motion the gradual development of normative standards on human rights, and sowed the seeds for human rights supervisory mechanisms.

The Charter also established the International Court of Justice (ICJ) as the principal judicial organ of the United Nations. The ICJ reflects traditional international law and is a forum in which only states can present claims against other states.[4] In this sense, individuals can benefit from reparations only if they are able to present a claim through their own state against another. Should the case be favourably decided, the victims still depend upon the goodwill of state authorities to distribute reparations to individual beneficiaries.

Article 38 of the Statute of the ICJ states that it shall apply from the following sources:

> a. International conventions, whether general or particular, establishing rules expressly recognised by the contesting States;
> b. International custom, as evidence of a general practice accepted by law;
> c. The general principles of law as recognised by civilised nations;
> d. . . . judicial decisions and the teachings of the most highly qualified publicists of various nations, as subsidiary means for the determination of rules of law.

[4] The Statute of the ICJ (Articles 65–8) also establishes that principal UN organs may request Advisory Opinions.

Historically, the ICJ was somewhat reluctant in referring to human rights instruments in its decisions.[5] However, during the past two decades, the court has come to play a significant role in advancing recognition of human rights and humanitarian law as general principles and customary law, based on the provision in Article 38(b) of its Statute.

Human rights law has developed as a separate branch of law built on recognition of the individual as a subject under international law, and the state as the responsible entity to guarantee the rights of all people within its territory. The foundations of human rights law are established in the UN Charter and the Universal Declaration of Human Rights (UDHR). During the past four decades, nine international core human rights treaties have entered into force, six of which have been adhered to by more than 75 per cent of states.[6] The number of ratifications of human rights conventions, including optional protocols, has drastically increased, from a total of 243 ratifications in 1980, to 553 in 1990, 926 in 2000 and 1,885 by 1 April 2011. It is essential to underline that states have agreed voluntarily to be bound by the obligations contained in the relevant treaties upon ratification or accession. The extensive support and practice among states of committing themselves to human rights instruments and engaging with monitoring mechanisms significantly informs the evolving concept of customary law and the recognition of human rights therein.[7]

Humanitarian law has been developed as a separate branch of law and was originally based on customary norms that date further back than human rights law.[8] The core of humanitarian law was established

[5] R. Higgins, 'The International Court of Justice and Human Rights', in K. Wellens (ed.), *International Law: Theory and Practice* (The Hague: Kluwer Law International, 1998), pp. 691–705; R. Higgins, *Problems and Process, International Law and How We Use It* (Oxford: Clarendon Press, 1994), pp. 95–110; R. Higgins, 'The International Court of Justice and the European Court of Human Rights: Partners for the Protection of Human Rights', Speech in Strasbourg at ceremony marking the 50th Anniversary of the European Court of Human Rights, 30 January 2009.

[6] As of 1 April 2011, all states have adhered to at least one of the core human rights conventions and 75 per cent of all states have ratified or acceded to six or more core human rights conventions: CERD, 174; ICCPR, 167; ICESCR, 160; CAT, 147; CEDAW, 186; CRC, 193; CMW, 44; CRPD, 98 (EIF 3 May 2008); and CPPED, 25 (EIF 23 December 2010). Source: UN Office of Legal Affairs, see http://treaties.un.org.

[7] For further discussion see Higgins, *Problems and Process*, pp. 30–1; O. Schacter, *International Law in Theory and Practice* (Dordrecht: Martin Nijhoff, 1991), pp. 334–8; B. Lepard, *Customary International Law: A New Theory and Practical Applications* (Cambridge University Press, 2010), pp. 191–207.

[8] For an overview of the development of international humanitarian law, see F. Kalshoven and L. Zegveld, *Constraints on the Waging of War, An Introduction to IHL* (Geneva: ICRC, 2001).

by the four Geneva Conventions in 1949, which have now been universally ratified by all 192 states. The principal difference between human rights law and humanitarian law is that the latter applies only in times of armed conflict, is binding upon all parties, including non-state actors, and that the majority of its provisions apply exclusively in international conflict. Only Common Article 3 of the Geneva Conventions and the Additional Protocol II apply in internal armed conflict. The language used in humanitarian law is primarily focused on the regulation of combat methods and the protection of civilians, and, *prima facie*, does not address individual rights. It should, however, be recognised that human rights and humanitarian law are intricately interlinked by the nature of their principal concern: the protection of human beings.[9] The ICJ has affirmed that application of human rights and humanitarian law can be dual and complementary.[10] More recent instruments of humanitarian law, such as the two Additional Protocols (1977) to the Geneva Conventions, make explicit references to human rights.[11] Conversely, certain human rights instruments contain clear references to humanitarian law, such as the Convention of the Rights of the Child (1989) and its Optional Protocol on the Involvement of Children in Armed Conflict (2000). Jurisprudence by human rights bodies refers increasingly to the importance of, and interrelation with, humanitarian law.[12]

There are a number of areas where human rights law and humanitarian law overlap. Some key points of convergence are found in basic prohibitions of extrajudicial executions, torture and cruel, inhuman and degrading treatment, discrimination on the grounds of race, sex,

[9] For further discussion see R. Provost, *International Human Rights and Humanitarian Law* (Cambridge University Press, 2002); M. Sassoli, 'The Victim-oriented Approach of International Humanitarian Law and of the International Committee of the Red Cross', in C. Bassiouni, *International Protection of Victims, Nouvelle Etudes Penales*, Association International de Droit Penal (Toulouse: Eres Publications, 1988), pp. 147–80.

[10] *Armed Activities on the Territory of the Congo Case (Democratic Republic of the Congo* v. *Uganda)*, ICJ Report 2005. Further references on the mutually complementary and reinforcing nature of human rights and humanitarian law see Report to the Human Rights Council of the Office of the High Commissioner for Human Rights on the Outcome of the Expert Consultation on the Issue of Protecting the Human Rights of Civilians in Armed Conflict, A/HRC/11/31, 2 June 2009.

[11] Protocol I, Article 72 and Protocol II, Preamble. Further detail and analysis in T. Meron, *Human Rights in Internal Strife, Their International Protection* (Cambridge: Grotius Publications, 1987).

[12] References to IHL by human rights bodies is further noted in Chapter 3 on jurisprudence. See also: C. Droege, 'Elective Affinities? Human Rights and Humanitarian Law', *International Review of the Red Cross*, 90(871) (2008), 501–48.

language or religion, slavery and the right to a fair trial.[13] All the above violations are addressed by Common Article 3 and are considered to constitute grave breaches of the Geneva Conventions. Conversely, the above-mentioned rights are established as non-derogable by the Human Rights Committee.[14]

The concept of customary law, as envisaged in Article 38(b) of the ICJ Statute, implies that certain provisions in international law are binding upon all without the need for ratification. Already in 1951, the ICJ had proclaimed in its Advisory Opinion on Reservations to the Genocide Convention that: 'the principles underlying the Convention are principles which are recognised by civilised nations as binding on States, even without any conventional obligation'. The ICJ thereby established a clear landmark in the development of general principles and customary international law.[15] Furthermore, it has been established through the 1996 ICJ Advisory Opinion on the Legality of the Threat or Use of Force of Nuclear Weapons[16] with regard to the Hague and Geneva Conventions that:

> a great many rules of humanitarian law applicable in armed conflict are so fundamental to the respect of the human being ... these are to be observed by all States whether or not they have ratified the conventions that contain them because they constitute intransgressible principles of international customary law.

This position was restated in the 2004 ICJ Advisory Opinion on the Legal Consequences of the Construction of a Wall in the Occupied Palestinian

13 Meron, 'On the Inadequate Reach of Humanitarian and Human Rights Law', pp. 589–606. Further discussion on overlaps of provisions and critique of inconsistencies in their development, see S. Ratner, 'The Schizophrenias of International Criminal Law', *Texas International Law Journal*, 33 (1998), 237–57.

14 The Human Rights Committee is the body of independent experts that monitors implementation of, and interprets, the International Covenant on Civil and Political Rights. Although not explicitly listed as non-derogable, the provision on non-discrimination as well as the provisions on detention and the right to a fair trial are considered non-derogable by the Human Rights Committee, see CCPR General Comment No. 29, CCPR/C/21/Rev.1/add.11, 2001, paras 8–16. F. Hampson, 'The Relationship between International Humanitarian Law and Human Rights Law from the Perspective of a Human Rights Body', *International Review of the Red Cross*, 90(871) (2008), 549–72.

15 *Reservations to the Convention on the Prevention and Punishment of the Crime of Genocide*, Advisory Opinion, ICJ Report 1951, para. 15. Discussed in Higgins, 'The International Court of Justice and Human Rights', p. 695; C. Tomuschat, *Human Rights, Between Idealism and Realism* (Oxford University Press, 2008), pp. 192–3.

16 *Legality of the Threat or Use of Force of Nuclear Weapons*, Advisory Opinion, 8 July 1996, ICJ Reports, para. 79. Further discussion in V. Chetail, 'The Contribution of the International Court of Justice to International Humanitarian Law', *International Review of the Red Cross*, 85(850) (2003), 235–69.

Territory.[17] In 1995, the ICTY affirmed in the Tadić Case that rights recognised under customary law entail obligations on all states irrespective of the ratification status of a specific country or whether the breach occurred during internal or international conflict.[18] Numerous scholars including Greenwood, Cassese, Bassiouni and Schabas recognise the significant growth of customary international law by jurisprudence from a number of international tribunals and by codification in new instruments, which serve to expand the concept and status of serious violations of humanitarian law.[19] Specifically, the Rome Statute of the International Criminal Court reinforces the status of the prohibitions contained in the fundamental guarantees paragraphs of the Additional Protocols to the Geneva Conventions,[20] which cover, for example, child recruitment and sexual crimes.[21] Schabas notes that 'the definitions of crimes set out in Articles 6–8 [of the Rome Statute] ... correspond in a general sense to the state of customary international law'.[22]

In 2005, the ICRC published an extensive international study of state practice, conducted over a period of eight years, in relation to humanitarian law and asserted the existence of twelve fundamental guarantees for the protection of civilians, concluding that they have attained status as customary law and, therefore, are applicable in all armed conflict, whether international or internal. The introduction to the study explains that relevant practice under human rights law has been included in the study because in principle, human rights law continues to apply during armed conflicts. While the ICRC did not purport to assess customary human rights law,

[17] *Legal Consequences of the Construction of a Wall in the Occupied Palestinian Territory*, Advisory Opinion, 9 July 2004, ICJ Reports, para. 157.

[18] ICTY, *Tadić Case* (Interlocutory Appeal), Judgment, 2 October 1995, para. 97. T. Meron, 'The Continuing Role of Custom in the Foundation of International Humanitarian Law', *The American Journal of International Law*, 90(2) (1996), 238–49.

[19] C. Greenwood, 'International Humanitarian Law', in F. Kalshoven (ed.), *The Centennial of the First International Peace Conference* (The Hague: Kluwer Law, 2000), para. 5.2; Cassese, *International Law*; Tomuschat, *Human Rights, Between Idealism and Realism*, p. 253; C. Bassiouni, *Post-Conflict Justice* (New York: Transnational Publishers, 2002). pp. 10–30; W. Schabas, *An Introduction to the International Criminal Court*, 3rd edn (Cambridge University Press, 2007), pp. 84–7.

[20] Additional Protocol I, para. 75; Additional Protocol II, para. 4.

[21] For further analysis of sexual crimes in humanitarian law, see R. Dixon, 'Rape as a Crime in International Humanitarian Law. Where to From Here?', *European Journal of International Law*, 13(3) (2002), 697–719 and L. May, *Crimes Against Humanity, A Normative Account* (Cambridge University Press, 2005), pp. 96–111.

[22] Schabas, *An Introduction to the International Criminal Court*, p. 85.

nevertheless references to human rights law were included to 'support, strengthen and clarify analogous principles in international humanitarian law'.[23]

In 1969, the concept of *jus cogens* was established by the Vienna Convention on the Law of Treaties, defining it as:

a peremptory norm of general international law is one which is ... accepted and recognised by the international community of States as a whole as a norm from which no derogation is permitted and which can be modified only by a norm of general international law having the same character ... if a new peremptory norm of general international law emerges, any existing treaty which is in conflict with the norm becomes void and terminates.[24]

Although there is some dispute among legal scholars about the interpretation of *jus cogens*, it is generally understood to entail breaches which are considered to be an affront to the entire world community and carry a high level of acceptance of customary law.[25] Shortly after the term *jus cogens* was created, the ICJ applied a mirror term by the creation of obligations *erga omnes*, which are applicable at all times without derogation. As stated by the ICJ in the *Barcelona Traction Case*, 1970:[26]

an essential distinction should be drawn between the obligations of a State towards the international community as a whole, and those arising vis-à-vis another State in the field of diplomatic protection. By their very nature the former are the concern of all States. In view of the importance of the rights involved, all States can be held to have a legal interest in their protection; they are obligations *erga omnes*.

Such obligations derive, for example, in contemporary international law, from the outlawing of acts of aggression, and of genocide, as also from the principles and rules concerning the basic rights of the human being, including protection from slavery and racial discrimination.

[23] J-M. Henckaerts and L. Doswald-Beck, *Customary International Humanitarian Law*, 3 vols (Cambridge University Press, 2005). The study originated from recommendations by an international conference and an intergovernmental group of experts for the protection of war victims (1993 and 1995).

[24] Vienna Convention on the Law of Treaties, 1969, United Nations, Treaty Series, vol. 1155, p. 331, Articles 53, 64.

[25] For further discussion on the criteria for consideration as *jus cogens* norms see Brownlie, *Principles of Public International Law*, pp. 509–17; May, *Crimes Against Humanity* and C. Bassiouni, 'International Crimes: *Jus Cogens* and *Obligatorio Erga Omnes*', *Law and Contemporary Problems*, 59 (1996), 63–74.

[26] *Barcelona Traction, Light and Power Company Limited*, Second Phase, ICJ Reports 1970, para. 33.

The ICJ has repeatedly referred to the concept of *erga omnes* in several cases; however, it has not put forward an exhaustive list of obligations.[27] The lack of defined obligations *erga omnes* is partially due to the evolving nature of international law and the careful assessment required of the norms that may be considered customary. Undeniably, the sensitive legal, as well as political, implications that an expanded understanding of customary law has on state responsibility require due consideration. It is, however, significant that the ICJ stated as early as 1970 that obligations *erga omnes* cover rules concerning 'the basic rights of the human being'.[28] It is particularly worth recalling that the case was decided at a time when little international human rights law was codified and thus drew examples largely from international humanitarian law. The situation today is, however, quite the contrary due to the rapid expansion of human rights treaty law and the considerable recognition and use of human rights norms to complement humanitarian law.

The International Convention on the Elimination of All Forms of Racial Discrimination (CERD) entered into force in 1969, and although the two principal human rights treaties, the International Covenants on Economic, Social and Cultural Rights (ICESCR) and the International Covenant on Civil and Political Rights (ICCPR), were opened for ratification in 1966, neither entered into force until 1976. As previously mentioned, the number of states parties to the core human rights treaties has rapidly increased during the past two decades and now ratification or accession by a majority of states has been reached for six of the core treaties. As noted by some scholars, the customary recognition of human rights provisions has been questioned due to an insufficient number of ratifications. Meron, writing in 1983, noted that the difficulty of affirming customary status of human rights treaties, compared with the Geneva Conventions (1949) and the Hague Regulations (1907), was partly due to the low number of states parties to human rights instruments (CERD at the time had the highest number of ratifications at 115, while the Geneva Conventions enjoyed 152 states parties).[29]

[27] *East Timor Case (Portugal v. Australia)* ICJ Reports 1970, p. 3; *Application of the Convention on the Prevention and Punishment of the Crimes of Genocide, Preliminary Objections*, ICJ Reports 1996, pp. 595, 616.

[28] Further analysis see G. Gaja, 'Obligations *Erga Omnes*, International Crimes and *Jus Cogens*, A Tentative Analysis of Three Related Concepts', in J. Weiler, A. Cassese and M. Spinedi (eds), *International Crimes of States, A Critical Analysis of the ILC's Draft Article 18 on State Responsibility* (Berlin: Walter de Gryter, 1998), pp. 151–60.

[29] Meron, 'On the Inadequate Reach of Humanitarian and Human Rights Law', pp. 589–606.

Of importance is thus that today five (CERD, ICCPR, ICESCR, CEDAW and CRC) of the core human rights treaties have acquired well over 152 states parties, that is, the number of ratifications by which the Geneva Conventions were considered to have attained customary status. Although scholars recognise the impact of human rights law in general international law, they tend to be careful in defining and delimiting specific human rights provisions as customary norms.[30] Meanwhile, the Human Rights Committee affirmed in 2001 that 'the category of peremptory norms extends beyond the list of non-derogable provisions in Article 4, para. 2' (of the ICCPR).[31] As noted above, considerable evolution has taken place regarding the extent to which human rights obligations invoke state responsibility in international law. Analogous serious violations that are enshrined in both humanitarian and human rights law have gained recognition in customary law, yet there is reluctance to define such violations in exact detail in order not to unduly restrict the perceived coverage of such protection and to allow for continuous developments in this area.

Having noted some of the interpretations of state responsibility in relation to human rights obligations, we now turn to the International Law Commission (ILC), established by the General Assembly (GA) in 1947 to promote the progressive development of international law and its codification. Already in 1949, the importance of reaching a legal definition of state responsibility had been identified as one of the principal areas of work for the ILC.[32] As noted by Brownlie, the ILC, although

[30] B. Simma and P. Alston, 'The Sources of Human Rights Law: Custom, *Jus Cogens* and General Principles', *Australian Yearbook of International Law*, (1988–9), 82–108; Malanczuk, *Akehurst's Modern Introduction to International Law*, pp. 220–1; Tomuschat, *Human Rights, Between Idealism and Realism*, pp. 34–5: 'there exists today broad agreement to the effect that many of the rules enunciated in the UDHR have crystallized as customary law, in particular the right to life, the prohibition of torture, which is the reverse side of a right to physical integrity, the protection of personal freedom and the prohibition of discrimination on racial grounds'; Cassese, *International Law*, p. 372; D. Orentlicher, 'Settling Accounts: The Duty to Prosecute Human Rights Violations of a Prior Regime', in N. Kritz (ed.), *Transitional Justice: How Emerging Democracies Reckon with Former Regimes*, 3 vols (Washington, DC: US Institute of Peace Press, 1995), pp. 375–415. Orentlicher had already noted in the mid-1990s that: 'Although publicists disagree about the range of human rights protected by customary law, there is general agreement that customary law prohibits torture, disappearances, and extra-legal executions and that these prohibitions are peremptory norms.' An exception is, however, provided by Leper, *Customary International Law*.

[31] CCPR General Comment No. 29, CCPR/C/21/Rev.1/add.11, 2001, para. 11.

[32] J. Crawford, *The International Law Commission's Articles on State Responsibility; Introduction, Text and Commentaries* (Cambridge University Press, 2002), p. 1.

formally integrated by independent experts, reflects a variety of political standpoints and thus its agreed drafts provide a realistic basis for acceptable and recognised legal obligations.[33]

The issue of state responsibility proved so contested that it took four decades of drafting before the ILC could adopt its Articles on State Responsibility in 2001.[34] The same year, the ILC recommended that the GA take note of the Articles; however, consensus remains lacking within the ILC as well as the GA regarding the possibility of codifying state responsibility in an international convention.[35] Nevertheless, already prior to their formal adoption, the Articles were widely cited in several ICJ cases and advisory opinions, as well as in international and regional human rights jurisprudence.

The Articles of the ILC define state responsibility as arising from a breach of an international obligation, and it is important to underline that such liability might arise from action as well as from omission (Article 2); a principle that has been developed by human rights jurisprudence, but derives from precedents in general international law, such as the ICJ *Corfu Channel Case* of 1949.[36] Chapter 3, Article 40 of the ILC Articles on State Responsibility establishes a distinction with regard to particularly serious breaches:

> 1. This chapter applies to the States responsibility which is entailed by a serious breach by a State of an obligation arising under a peremptory norm of general international law.
> 2. A breach of such an obligation is serious if it involves a gross or systematic failure by the responsible State to fulfil the obligation.[37]

The official Commentaries to the ILC Articles cite the prohibitions established as *jus cogens* norms by the ICJ; however, they also stress that: 'the examples given may not be exhaustive ... the Vienna Convention contemplates that new peremptory norms of general international law may

33 Brownlie, *Principles of Public International Law*, p. 30.

34 ILC, Draft Articles on Responsibility of States for Internationally Wrongful Acts, 2001, extract of ICL Report to the GA, A/56/10, ch. IV.E.1.

35 J. Crawford and S. Olleson, 'The Continuing Debate on a UN Convention on State Responsibility', *International and Comparative Law Quarterly*, 54 (2005), 959–71.

36 *Corfu Channel Case (United Kingdom v. Albania)*, Merits, ICJ Report 1949. The case is discussed at length by Brownlie, *Principles of Public International Law*, pp. 432–72 and cited in the ILC, Commentaries on the Draft Articles on Responsibility of States for Internationally Wrongful Acts, 2001 (extract of ICL to the GA, A/56/10, ch.IV.E.2), Article 2, para. 4.

37 ILC, Draft Articles on Responsibility of States for Internationally Wrongful Acts, Article 40.

come into existence through the processes of acceptance and recognition by the international community of States as a whole'.[38]

James Crawford, the ILC Special Rapporteur on State Responsibility, restated this position in his account of the *travaux preparatoires*, noting that the ILC deliberately avoided defining the coverage of peremptory norms in order to keep interpretation open for inclusion of other breaches of international law which carry serious consequences.[39] Furthermore, the reference to peremptory norms provided an acceptable solution, while the proposal to mention state crimes was eliminated as it obstructed completion of the project.[40]

Regarding coverage of the Articles on State Responsibility, Article 33 sets forth that the obligations of the responsible state, depending on the circumstances, may be owed to other states and to the international community, and are without prejudice to any right that might accrue directly to any person or entity other than a state. Importantly, the official Commentaries clarify that:

> an internationally wrongful act may involve consequences in the relations between the State responsible for that act and persons or entities other than States. This follows from Article 1, which covers all international obligations of the State and not only those owed to other States. Thus State responsibility extends, for example, to human rights violations and other breaches of international law where the primary beneficiary of the obligation is not a State.[41]

Although the ILC Articles recognise state responsibility towards individuals, this recognition is subtle, especially in view of the fact that human rights law represents one of the branches of law where codification and adherence has been exceptionally strong during the past two decades, as discussed above. The timidity of the provisions in the Articles highlights

[38] ILC, Commentaries on the Draft Articles on Responsibility of States for Internationally Wrongful Acts, Article 40, para. 6.

[39] Crawford, *The International Law Commission's Articles on State Responsibility*, pp. 37–8.

[40] Crawford, *The International Law Commission's Articles on State Responsibility*, pp. 16–20. According to US ILC member Rosenstock 'rejection of proposals concerning so-called crimes of states ... reflected members' recognition that such proposals simply would not fly'. For further context of the controversy see R. Rosenstock, 'The ILC and State Responsibility', *American Journal of International Law*, 96 (2002), 792–7; E. Wyler, 'From State Crime to Responsibility for Serious Breaches of Obligations under Peremptory Norms of General International Law', *European Journal of International Law*, 13(5) (2002), 1147–60; P.-M. Dupuy, 'A General Stocktaking of the Connections between the Multilateral Dimension of Obligations and Codification of the Law of Responsibility', *European Journal of International Law*, 13(5) (2002), 1053–81.

[41] ILC, Commentaries on the Draft Articles on Responsibility of States for Internationally Wrongful Acts, Article 28, para. 3.

the tensions surrounding the notion of state responsibility in general international law compared with *lex specialis*, such as human rights. However, the Articles on state responsibility contain a provision in Article 55, which confirms the maxim *lex specialis derogate legi generali*, that is, specialised law takes precedence over general law, thereby ensuring that human rights law will not be displaced by the less defined provisions set forth by the ILC.[42] A subsequent study by the ILC in 2006 on challenges relating to fragmentation of international law stated that: 'fragmentation and diversification account for the development and expansion of international law in response to the demands of a pluralistic world'.[43] This can be interpreted as recognition of the influence of human rights on general international law.

Having set out the basic provisions of state responsibility in relation to violations of human rights, we proceed to review the specific provisions in international human rights humanitarian and criminal law that affirm the right to reparation and consider the legal shifts that have taken place in favour of individuals in this regard.

2.3 Recognition in general international law of individuals as beneficiaries of reparations

The principle in international law affirming the obligation to provide reparation dates back many years. Already in 1927 and 1928, the Permanent Court of International Justice (PCIJ), the predecessor of the ICJ, had stated in the *Factory at Chorzów Case* that:

> It is a principle of international law and even a general conception of law that any breach of an engagement involves an obligation to make reparation in an adequate form ... reparation is the indispensable complement of a failure to apply a convention and there is no necessity for this to be stated in the convention itself.[44]

> reparation must, as far as possible, wipe out all the consequences of the illegal act and re-establish the situation which would, in all probability, have existed if that act had not been committed. Restitution in kind, or, if this is not possible, payment of a sum corresponding to the value which a restitution would

[42] ILC, Commentaries on the Draft Articles on Responsibility of States for Internationally Wrongful Acts, Article 55, paras 1–6.

[43] ILC, 'Fragmentation of International Law: Difficulties Arising from the Diversification and Expansion of International Law', Report of the Study Group of the International Law Commission, A/CN.4/L.702, 2006, p. 5.

[44] *Factory at Chorzów Case (Germany* v. *Poland)*, Jurisdiction, 1927, PCIJ, Ser. A, No. 9, p. 21.

bear ... such are the principles which should serve to determine the amount of compensation due for an act contrary to international law.[45]

The dictum established in the sentence of the PCIJ in the *Factory at Chorzów Case* has been widely cited and reaffirmed in a number of judgments of the ICJ, including the *Gabčikovo-Nagymaros Project Case*,[46] the more recent *Case Concerning Armed Activities on the Territory of the Congo*[47] and in numerous international and regional human rights case law.[48]

As seen above, the *Factory at Chorzów Case* deals only with two forms of reparations: namely, restitution and compensation. These components historically constituted the basic foundations for the concept of reparations, which has in turn been furthered due to interpretations in human rights jurisprudence in particular. In cases of serious violations of human rights, it clearly is impossible to achieve *restitutio in integrum*, that is, re-establish the situation that existed before the wrongful acts.

As already noted, historically, general international law viewed reparations as an inter-state measure. However, the convergence of a number of developments in international law over the past decades has produced important shifts that have come to be recognised in general international law. A number of these have been identified in the previous section: namely, the affirmation of state responsibility in relation to certain fundamental human rights through the advancement of multiple treaty provisions in humanitarian as well as human rights law. Several of these have acquired recognition as customary law, and, in some cases, even as peremptory norms that the world community has a common interest in protecting. The ILC Articles on State responsibility adopted in 2001 support this affirmation. The Articles define reparation as consisting of the following components: guarantees of non-repetition (Article 30); restitution (Article 34); compensation (Article 36); and satisfaction (Article 37). Although human rights are not specifically referred to in the ILC Articles, the official Commentaries to Article 33 assert that:

[45] *Factory at Chorzów Case (Germany* v. *Poland)*, Merits, 1928, PCIJ, Ser. A, No. 17, p. 47.

[46] *Gabčikovo-Nagymaros Project Case (Hungary* v. *Slovakia)*, ICJ Report 1997, p. 7, paras 149–52.

[47] *Armed Activities on the Territory of the Congo Case (Democratic Republic of the Congo* v. *Uganda)*, ICJ Report 2005, p. 82, para. 259.

[48] Examples include *Papamichalopoulos* v. *Greece* (Article 50), ECtHR, Ser. A, No. 330-B, 1995, para. 36; *Velásquez Rodríguez*, IACtHR, Ser. C, No. 4, 1989, pp. 26–7, 30–1. See further references in Chapter 3 on human rights jurisprudence.

When an obligation of reparation exists towards a State, reparation does not necessarily accrue to that State's benefit. For instance, a State's responsibility for the breach of an obligation under a treaty concerning the protection of human rights may exist towards all the other parties to the treaty, but the individuals concerned should be regarded as the ultimate beneficiaries and in that sense as the holders of the relevant rights.[49]

The ILC Articles were greeted with a generally positive reception by human rights scholars. However, the references to the rights of the individual in relation to human rights violations are subtle and figure only in the Commentaries rather than in the actual Articles. This sparked criticism, in particular, when considering the practical challenges that persist in defining reparations during reconciliation efforts and the pressing need to define state responsibility in this area.[50]

Additional affirmation of the acceptance of the right of individuals to reparations in general international law can be found in the ICJ Advisory Opinion on Legal Consequences of the Construction of a Wall in the Occupied Palestinian Territory of 2004,[51] which affirmed the duty of Israel to provide restitution and compensate individuals and 'all natural and legal persons having suffered any form of material damage as a result of the wall's construction'. Regrettably, the ICJ *Bosnia Genocide Case* of 2007 provided significantly less clarity on state obligations to provide reparations and has been criticised for backtracking and creating inconsistency in the jurisprudence of the court.[52]

With the recognition of human rights as *jus cogens*, individuals appear as rights bearers and subjects in general international law. The logical consequence of such recognition implies that there is a clear need to translate consequences of breaches, such as reparations, in favour of individual victims. The provision of reparations remains primarily a state responsibility and closing the gap between international legal standards and their application represents a key challenge to the international legal order and to the human rights regime.

[49] ILC, Commentaries on the Draft Articles on Responsibility of States for Internationally Wrongful Acts, Article 33, para. 3.

[50] D. Shelton, 'Righting Wrongs: Reparations in the Articles on State Responsibility', *The American Journal of International Law*, 96(4) (2002), 833–56.

[51] *Legal Consequences of the Construction of a Wall in the Occupied Palestinian Territory*, Advisory Opinion, 9 July 2004, ICJ Report, paras 145, 152–3.

[52] *Application of the Genocide Convention Case (Bosnia and Herzegovina* v. *Serbia and Montenegro)*, ICJ Report 2007. Case discussed in P. Gaeta (ed.), *The Genocide Convention, A Commentary* (Oxford University Press, 2009), pp. 364–73.

Although general international law has been slow to embrace individuals as direct beneficiaries of reparations, the concept of reparations has itself undergone changes and expanded to comprise a number of aspects. Again, the move towards a comprehensive perception of reparations is due largely to human rights law codification and jurisprudence. In addition, support has also come from reinterpretations and analysis of provisions in humanitarian and international criminal law.

2.4 Reparation in international humanitarian law

References to reparations in international humanitarian law can be traced to Article 3 of the 1907 IV Hague Convention, wording which is repeated in Article 91 of the Additional Protocol I to the Geneva Conventions.[53] It states that:

> A Party to the conflict which violates the provisions of the Conventions or of this Protocol shall, if the case demands, be liable to pay compensation. It shall be responsible for all acts committed by persons forming part of its armed forces.

The official ICRC Commentary[54] gives some further guidance on the interpretation of the provisions. In line with general international law, the Article is construed on the presumption that it be exercised through an intra-state mechanism. The ICRC Commentary, however, gives little guidance as to how states should ensure that non-state parties to a conflict fulfil the obligation of paying compensation. Given the current extent of internal armed conflicts involving non-state entities, this illustrates a major lacuna in international humanitarian law.

It is important to observe that the Commentary affirms that state responsibility may also be incurred by omission when due diligence to prevent violations from taking place has not been demonstrated and, once they have occurred, repression of the acts has not been ensured.[55] Furthermore, Article 91 makes specific reference to coverage of all provisions of the Geneva Conventions. A weak point is that no corresponding provision exists in the Additional Protocol II.

53 E-C. Gillard, 'Reparation for Violations of International Humanitarian Law', *International Review of the Red Cross*, 85(851) (2003), 529–53.

54 1977 Protocol Additional I to the Geneva Conventions, ICRC Commentary to Article 91, paras 3645–61.

55 1977 Protocol Additional I to the Geneva Conventions, ICRC Commentary to Article 91, para. 3660.

Furthermore, the official Commentary provides no clear explanation as to why the term *compensation* figures rather than the more comprehensive term *reparation*, which would have been consistent with the jurisprudence of the ICJ. Nevertheless, the Commentary explains that the term compensation, generally perceived to be a reference to monetary redress, in this context comprises the obligation to ensure restitution to the extent possible in addition to financial compensation.

While a conservative interpretation of Article 91 fails to recognise it as a source of rights in favour of individuals,[56] several scholars, including Kalshoven and Greenwood, have made important contributions to broaden the interpretation of Article 91. They have based their arguments on the *travaux preparatoires* of the 1907 Hague Convention IV, which indicate that the provision was not intended to be confined to claims between states, but was to be conceived as creating a direct right to compensation for individuals.[57] The debate on the reinterpretation of Article 91 stems in part from the redress movement against the Japanese government in the 1990s, during which both scholars submitted legal advice on the right to reparation.[58] Furthermore, it has been noted that the establishment of the United Nations Compensation Commission (UNCC) by the Security Council in 1991 following the Iraq war demonstrated state responsibility in relation to reparations for violations of humanitarian law.[59] The influence of different international and national redress movements and the role of the UN in relation to state practice are further explored in subsequent chapters.

[56] Provost, *International Human Rights and Humanitarian Law*, pp. 47–56. Provost nevertheless makes the point that while expressing reservations regarding the right to reparation in humanitarian law, certain such violations are 'coextensive with violations of non-derogable human rights, for which there is undoubtedly a right to a remedy and that the complementarity of human rights and humanitarian law ensures that the victims will not be left without a right to reparation for their injuries', p. 49. See also C. Tomuschat, 'Reparation for Victims of Grave Human Rights Violations', *Tulane Journal of International and Comparative Law*, 10 (2002), pp. 178–9.

[57] Greenwood, 'International Humanitarian Law', p. 250; F. Kalshoven, 'State Responsibility for Warlike Acts of the Armed Forces', *International and Comparative Law Quarterly*, 40 (1991), 827, 830. This argument is also supported by L. Zegveld, 'Remedies for Victims of Violations of International Humanitarian Law', pp. 497–526; Gillard, 'Reparation for Violations of International Humanitarian Law', pp. 529–53 and R. Pisillo Mazzeschi, 'Reparation Claims by Individuals for State Breaches of Humanitarian Law and Human Rights: An Overview', *Journal of International Criminal Justice*, 1 (2003), 339–47.

[58] S. Hae Bong, 'Compensation for Victims of Wartime Atrocities, Recent Developments in Japan's Case Law', *Journal of International Criminal Justice*, 3 (2005), 189.

[59] A. Gattini, 'The UN Compensation Commission: Old Rules New Procedures on War Reparations', *European Journal of International Law*, 13(1) (2002), 161–81.

Although the implications of reparation provisions in humanitarian law are still being explored and the implementation thereof largely remains lacking, some scholars have stated that provisions on reparations have attained customary law status and, consequently, states cannot absolve themselves or other states for liability with respect to grave breaches.[60] Kalshoven and Zegveld state that: 'the rule of responsibility, including the liability to pay compensation, has acquired a much broader scope. Although formally written for the Conventions and the Protocol as treaties, it is not too daring to regard it as applicable to the whole of international humanitarian law, whether written or customary.'[61]

Of considerable importance is that the ICRC has specifically affirmed, in its 2005 in-depth study of customary international humanitarian law previously cited, that state responsibility for reparations has become established as a customary norm both in international and non-international armed conflicts.[62] A weak aspect of humanitarian law, however, is its lack of enforcement and monitoring mechanisms. Recent developments in international criminal courts and tribunals, further explored in Chapter 4, provide avenues for certain victims. Henckaerts notes that the renewed interest in the relationship between humanitarian law and human rights law relates to victims' ongoing search for a forum in order to obtain remedies for violations of their rights during armed conflict.[63]

2.5 Reparation in international human rights law

In contrast to humanitarian law, provisions on remedies and reparations are key features in all human rights instruments, which establish a multitude of legally binding and quasi-judicial enforcement mechanisms. Some scholars have argued that breaches of humanitarian law

[60] Kalshoven and Zegveld, *Constraints on the Waging of War*, p. 147; Zegveld, 'Remedies for Victims of Violations of International Humanitarian Law'; M. Sassoli, 'The Victim-oriented Approach of International Humanitarian Law', pp. 1165–6.

[61] Kalshoven and Zegveld, *Constraints on the Waging of War*, p. 147.

[62] Henckaerts and Doswald-Beck, *Customary International Humanitarian Law*, Rule 150: 'A State responsible for violations of international humanitarian law is required to make full reparation for the loss or injury caused.'

[63] J-M. Henckaerts, 'Concurrent Application of International Humanitarian Law and Human Rights Law: A Victim Perspective', in R. Arnold and N. Quenivet (eds), *International Humanitarian Law and Human Rights Law, Towards a New Merger in International Law* (Leiden: Martinus Nijhoff, 2008). pp. 237–67.

could be addressed through human rights mechanisms in view of the lack of enforcement mechanisms in humanitarian law.[64] Human rights jurisprudence has played an important role in defining different forms of reparations and has provided considerable guidance on the development of non-monetary forms of remedies.

The origins of reparations in human rights law stem from the adoption of the UDHR in 1948, as Article 8 states that:

> Everyone has the right to an effective remedy by the competent national tribunals for acts violating the fundamental rights granted him by the constitution or by law.

The International Covenant on Civil and Political Rights (ICCPR) echoes the provision above as a legally binding norm in Article 2(3a): 'any person whose rights or freedoms as herein recognized are violated shall have an effective remedy'. In addition, Articles 9(5) and 14(6) provide a right to compensation for unlawful arrest, detention and conviction. The Human Rights Committee has given considerable interpretation of the content of the concept 'effective remedy' in its decisions in cases of individual petitions, general comments on the interpretation of treaty provisions and also in its concluding observations of state party reports. This is further explored in Chapter 3 on jurisprudence by human rights bodies.

In 2004, the Human Rights Committee adopted its General Comment No. 31 on the Nature of the General Legal Obligation Imposed on States Parties to the Covenant, largely inspired by the adoption of the ILC Draft Articles on State Responsibility in 2001 and the then draft Basic Principles on the Right to Reparation for Victims. The General Comment makes the link between the terms 'remedy' and 'reparation' explicit by stating that:

> Article 2, paragraph 3 requires that States Parties make reparation to individuals whose Covenant rights have been violated. Without reparation to individuals whose rights have been violated, the obligation to provide an effective remedy, which is central to the efficacy of article 2, paragraph 3, is not discharged. The Committee notes that, where appropriate, reparation can involve restitution, rehabilitation and measures of satisfaction, such as public apologies, public memorials, guarantees of non-repetition and changes in relevant laws and practices, as well as bringing to justice the perpetrators of human rights violations.[65]

[64] These include Greenwood, Pisillo, Hampson, Zegveld and Droege, see above.

[65] CCPR General Comment No. 31, The Nature of General Legal Obligation Imposed on States Parties to the Covenant, CCPR/C/21/Rev.1/Add.13, 2004, para. 16.

Other human rights treaty provisions, such as Article 14 of the Convention against Torture (CAT),[66] Article 6 of the Convention on the Elimination of All Forms of Racial Discrimination (CERD), Article 39 of the Convention of the Rights of the Child (CRC) and Article 24(4) of the International Convention for the Protection of All Persons from Enforced Disappearance (CPPED),[67] affirm the right to reparation in different forms. The CPPED provides a particularly important contribution as its entry into force in 2010 provided a comprehensive definition of reparations in a legally binding instrument. Article 24(4), (5) established the following:

> Each State Party shall ensure in its legal system that the victims of enforced disappearance have the right to obtain reparation and prompt, fair and adequate compensation. The right to obtain reparation ... covers material and moral damages and, where appropriate, other forms of reparation, such as: (a) restitution, (b) rehabilitation, (c) satisfaction, including restoration of dignity and reputation; (d) guarantees of non-repetition.

As will be explored in Chapter 3, the above-mentioned human rights treaties have monitoring mechanisms that have the competence to undertake state party reviews and, with the exception of CRC,[68] receive individual complaints, pending the recognition of the state party, and recommend reparations.

2.6 Reparation provisions in regional human rights instruments

The first provision establishing the competence to emit legally binding case decisions figures in the European Convention on Human Rights (ECHR), which entered into force in 1953. Article 13 of the

[66] Convention against Torture and Other Cruel, Inhuman or Degrading Treatment or Punishment, Article 14: 'Each State Party shall ensure in its legal system that the victim of an act of torture obtains redress and has an enforceable right to fair and adequate compensation, including the means for as full rehabilitation as possible. In the event of the death of the victim as a result of an act of torture, his dependants shall be entitled to compensation.'

[67] International Convention for the Protection of All Persons from Enforced Disappearance, Article 24(4): 'Each State Party shall ensure in its legal system that the victims of enforced disappearance have the right to obtain reparation and prompt, fair and adequate compensation.'

[68] An open-ended Working Group was, however, established by the Human Rights Council in 2009 in order to explore possibilities for a complaints mechanism under the CRC. In February 2011, negotiations for a draft Optional Protocol to the CRC on communications were concluded by the Working Group and submitted to the 17th session of the Human Rights Council, with a request for its submission to the General Assembly for adoption.

ECHR affirms the right to an effective remedy, and Article 41 establishes that the court shall afford just satisfaction if internal law in the state party allows only partial reparation to be made. The jurisprudence of the European Court of Human Rights (ECtHR) has been conservative in its interpretation of an effective remedy and just satisfaction, and has largely limited its interpretation to monetary forms of reparations.[69] This is likely explained by the nature of the claims, which during the first decades of the ECtHR did not involve serious human rights violations relating to armed conflict. However, the jurisprudence has undergone significant developments, particularly over the past decade.

The American Convention on Human Rights (ACHR), which entered into force on 18 July 1978, provides another legally binding and enforceable complaint mechanism at the regional level. Article 25 of the ACHR affirms the right to a legal remedy, and Article 63 of the ACHR specifies the right to a remedy and fair compensation. From its inception, the Inter-American Court on Human Rights (IACtHR) took a creative approach to reparations and sought to interpret the concept as broadly as possible.

Unlike the other international and regional human rights instruments referred to previously, the African Charter contains no clear provision on individual complaints and lacks a general reference to the right to a remedy for violations. This has limited the ability of the African Commission on Human and Peoples' Rights (ACHPR) to address reparations. However, the situation is likely to change once the African Court on Human and Peoples' Rights, established by the Protocol to the Charter, becomes fully operational as Article 27 of the Protocol contains a broad provision regarding reparations. The jurisprudence from the international and regional human rights systems will be further discussed and compared in Chapter 3.

2.7 Basic principles on the right to reparation for victims

As outlined above, the international and regional human rights mechanisms have contributed to an expanded concept of reparations for victims of serious human rights violations. Their work has also

[69] M. Nowak, 'The Right to Reparation for Victims of Gross Human Rights Violations', in G. Ulrich and L. Krabbe Boserup (eds), *Human Rights in Development, Yearbook 2001* (The Hague: Kluwer Law International, 2002), pp. 277–308.

benefited from a number of UN non-binding standards, which reinforce and assist in defining the notion of remedies and reparations.[70] The Declaration of Basic Principles of Justice for Victims of Crime and Abuse of Power (1985) primarily focused on victims of ordinary crimes; it does, however, contain provisions on victims who have suffered harm 'through acts or omissions that do not yet constitute violations of national criminal laws but of internationally recognised norms relating to human rights'. The Declaration provided scarce guidance on operative aspects, and also stated that national legislation should be enacted and enforced in order to allow victims access to remedies, including restitution, compensation and assistance.

The Basic Principles on Reparation for Victims, which were developed during a fifteen-year period prior to their adoption in 2006, provide a crucial benchmark, as they synthesise and define the areas of reparations as consisting of restitution, compensation, rehabilitation, satisfaction and guarantees of non-repetition.[71]

The Principles aim to reflect the normative connection between international humanitarian and human rights law, and stress the importance of, and obligation to, implement domestic reparations for victims of armed conflict. The Principles explicitly state in the preamble that they: 'identify mechanisms, modalities, procedures and methods for the implementation of existing legal obligations under international human rights and international humanitarian law, which are complementary though different as to their norms'. The Principles do not define what exactly gross human rights violations and serious humanitarian law violations are, leaving this definition open to interpretation and forthcoming legal developments. As previously noted, the Principles, even when still in draft, have been referred to in jurisprudence by numerous human rights bodies, they figure in several recently

[70] Examples of UN non-binding standards which relate to reparations include: 1985 Declaration of Basic Principles of Justice for Victims of Crime and Abuse of Power, A/RES/40/34; 1997 Revised Final Report on the Question of the Impunity of Perpetrators of Human Rights Violations (Joint principles), E/CN.4/Sub.2/1997/20/Rev.1; 2005 Updated Principles on Action to Combat Impunity, E/CN.4/2005/102/Add.1.

[71] For a comprehensive commentary and description of the *travaux preparatoires* of *the Basic Principles* see T. van Boven, 'Victims' Rights to a Remedy and Reparation: The New United Nations Principles and Guidelines', in C. Ferstman, M. Goetz and A. Stephens (eds), *Reparations for Victims of Genocide, War Crimes and Crimes against Humanity, Systems in Place and Systems in the Making* (Leiden: Martinus Nijhoff, 2009), pp. 19–40 and Bassiouni, 'International Recognition of Victims Rights', pp. 203–79.

adopted legal instruments[72] and, as will be explored in Part II of this book, have been applied by a number of truth commissions.[73] A key provision in the Basic Principles is contained in paragraph 16, which affirms that: 'States should endeavour to establish national programmes for reparation and other assistance to victims in the event that the party liable for the harm suffered is unable or unwilling to meet their obligation.' This provision is particularly important for the practical implementation of the Basic Principles, as will be illustrated in the subsequent case studies.

The finalisation of the Principles was delayed for a number of reasons; among them the debate on historical reparations for slavery and colonialism, as well as the political controversies that occurred in conjunction with the World Conference against Racism, held in Durban in 2001.[74] The finalisation of the Principles was achieved primarily thanks to the persistence of two independent experts, Theo van Boven and Cherif Bassiouni, who prepared and presented various versions. The UN Office of the High Commissioner for Human Rights (OHCHR) convened a series of consultations in Geneva for states and non-governmental organisations (NGOs) in 2002, 2003 and 2004.[75]

In December 2005, the Principles were adopted by the GA of the UN, which further strengthened their status in international law, although they are formally non-binding. The Principles make an important contribution by defining remedies for human rights violations. To a significant extent, the Basic Principles draw upon the Draft Articles on State Responsibility adopted by the ILC in 2001.

The various mandate-holders who have acted as the UN Special Rapporteur on Torture, Sir Nigel Rodley, Theo van Boven, Manfred Nowak and Juan Méndez, have consistently expressed strong support for the Principles, both throughout their elaboration and subsequent to their formal adoption.[76] Van Boven, the Special Rapporteur on Torture between 2001 and 2004,

[72] The Rome Statute of the ICC contains an indirect reference to forthcoming principles in Article 75; they are also mentioned in the International Convention on the Protection of all Persons from Forced Disappearances, adopted in December 2006.

[73] See examples of Truth Commissions citing the Principles in Part II of this book.

[74] Van Boven, 'Victims' Rights to a Remedy and Reparation', pp. 19–40.

[75] Report to the Commission on Human Rights on the First Consultative Meeting on the Draft Principles in 2002, UN Doc. E/CN.4/2003/63; Report to the Commission on Human Rights on the Second Consultative Meeting on the Draft Principles in 2003, UN Doc. E/CN.4/2004/57; Report to the Commission on Human Rights on the Third Consultative Meeting on the Draft Principles in 2004, UN Doc. E/CN.4/2005/59.

[76] Special Rapporteur on Torture and Other Cruel, Inhuman or Degrading Treatment or Punishment, Sir Nigel Rodley, Report to the General Assembly 2000, UN Doc. A/55/290; Special Rapporteur on Torture and Other Cruel, Inhuman or Degrading Treatment or

played a particularly important role as he provided the original impetus towards the development of the Principles through the groundbreaking study he undertook in 1992 on 'The question of the right to restitution, compensation and rehabilitation for victims of gross violations of human rights and fundamental freedoms' while a member of the Subcommission on Prevention of Discrimination and Protection of Minorities.[77]

2.8 A customary right to reparation?

Based on the above overview, which arguably indicates extensive recognition of the right of the individual to reparation in human rights and humanitarian law, as well as under general international law, it appears reasonable to state that this right has acquired a degree of recognition as forming part of customary law. Certain scholars consider the right already well-grounded in customary law,[78] while others identify it as an emerging rule.[79] Furthermore, it has been asserted that individual reparation claims, based on Article 14 of CAT, can be presented without territorial restrictions.[80]

Punishment, Theo van Boven, Report to the General Assembly 2003, UN Doc. A/58/120; Special Rapporteur on Torture and Other Cruel, Inhuman or Degrading Treatment or Punishment, Theo van Boven, Report to the General Assembly 2004, UN Doc. A/59/324; Special Rapporteur on Torture and Other Cruel, Inhuman or Degrading Treatment or Punishment, Manfred Nowak, Report to the Human Rights Council 2007, UN Doc. A/HRC/4/33; Special Rapporteur on Torture and Other Cruel, Inhuman or Degrading Treatment or Punishment, Juan E. Méndez, Report to the Human Rights Council 2011, UN Doc. A/HRC/16/52.

77 Report presented to the Commission on Human Rights, UN Doc. E/CN.4/Sub.2/1993/8.

78 Shelton, *Remedies in International Human Rights Law*, p. 238; Kalshoven and Zegveld, *Constraints on the Waging of War*, p. 147; Bassiouni, 'International Recognition of Victims' Rights', p. 217: 'Treaty based and customary law reflect the principle that States' nationals and aliens should have the right to a remedy for violations committed within a State's territory.' See also C. Bassiouni, 'Accountability for Violations of International Humanitarian Law and other Serious Violations of Human Rights'; International Commission of Jurists (together with fifteen other NGOs and Foundations including Amnesty International, the Association for the Prevention of Torture, the International Federation for Human Rights, the Redress Trust and the World Organisation Against Torture), Joint Written Statement at the Commission on Human Rights, 2005.

79 Pisillo Mazzeschi, 'Reparation Claims by Individuals for State Breaches of Humanitarian Law and Human Rights', pp. 339–47; J. Gardam and M. Jarvis, *Women, Armed Conflict and International Law* (The Hague: Kluwer Law International, 2001), pp. 87–92; Droege, 'Elective Affinities?', pp. 501–48; Provost, *International Human Rights and Humanitarian Law*, p. 44.

80 C. K. Hall, 'The Duty of States Parties to the Convention against Torture to Provide Procedures Permitting Victims to Recover Reparations for Torture Committed Abroad', *The European Journal of International Law*, 18(5) (2008), 921–37.

The ICRC Customary Law study explores some of the general principles established by the ICJ regarding the criteria for assessing rules and practice as customary. The ICRC study notes the position of the ICJ in the *North Sea Continental Shelf Cases*:

Although the passage of only a short period of time is not necessarily, or of itself, a bar to the formation of a new rule of customary international law on the basis of what was originally a purely conventional rule, an indispensable requirement would be that within the period in question, short though it might be, State practice, including that of States whose interests are specially affected, should have been extensive and virtually uniform in the sense of the provision invoked and should moreover have occurred in such a way as to show a general recognition that a rule of law or general obligation is involved.[81]

Regarding the criteria for virtually uniform practice, the ICJ stated in the *Nicaragua Case* that:

The Court does not consider that, for a rule to be established as customary, the corresponding practice must be in absolute rigorous conformity with the rule. In order to deduce the existence of customary rules, the Court deems it sufficient that the conduct of States should, in general, be consistent with such rules and that instances of State conduct inconsistent with a given rule should generally be treated as breaches of that rule, not as indications of the recognition of a new rule.[82]

The above criteria for assessing customary law are applied throughout this study, which charts considerable state practice, both in intergovernmental settings and at the national level, and emphasises the *opinio juris* of 'States whose interests are specially affected' in relation to state responsibility to provide reparation for serious violations. Simma and Paulus note that '*opinio juris* may be deduced from the conclusion of treaties or voting records in international fora, up to the point where practice and *opinio juris* cannot be clearly distinguished from each other. This allows for the rather rapid development of international law.'[83]

While there is overwhelming support in the international legal community for the right to reparation for individuals, Tomuschat offers a dissenting opinion.[84] While not disputing the right to reparation *per se*,

[81] North Sea Continental Shelf Cases, ICJ Reports 1969, p. 43.

[82] *Military and Paramilitary Activities in and against Nicaragua Case* (*Nicaragua* v. *United States*), ICJ Report 1986, p. 98.

[83] B. Simma and A. L. Paulus, 'The Responsibility of Individuals for Human Rights Abuses in Internal Conflicts: A Positivist View', *American Journal of International Law*, 93(2) (1999), 307.

[84] Public lecture by Prof. Tomuschat at the Graduate Institute of International and Development Studies, HEI, Geneva, 10 December 2009; Tomuschat, *Human Rights, Between Idealism and Realism*, pp. 293–317; Tomuschat, 'Darfur – Compensation for the Victims',

he denies that it is an individual right, rather claiming it should be conceptualised collectively. Among his arguments, he claims, *inter alia*, that reparation provisions in human rights treaties do not provide a right as they depend on discretionary incorporation into national law and he refers to state immunity.[85] Tomuschat gives an incomplete description of human rights provisions and refers critically to jurisprudence by human rights courts, which he at times describes in terms such as 'erratic' or 'sweeping' and based on a 'misunderstanding'.[86]

As for the claim that human rights are discretionary and dependent on the national order, the Vienna Convention on the Law of Treaties of 1969 clearly established in Article 27 that: 'A party may not invoke the provisions of its internal law as justification for its failure to perform a treaty.' The ILC has underlined the irrelevance of internal law as a justification for failure to comply with international obligations, stating that: 'the responsible State may not rely on the provisions of its internal law as justification for failure to comply with its obligations ... '[87] The Human Rights Committee and the European Court of Human Rights are unequivocal with regard to the duty of the state to ensure that its domestic legal system complies with applicable international human rights obligations.[88] Higgins has eloquently and affirmatively stated:

Journal of International Criminal Justice, 3 (2005), 579–89. There is a certain irony to the conservative stance of Tomuschat, given the fact that he has contributed significantly to advancing the right to reparation in practice through the role he played in Guatemala, where he co-chaired the UN Truth Commission, as is explored in Part II of this book.

85 Tomuschat, *Human Rights, Between Idealism and Realism.*

86 Tomuschat, 'Reparation for Victims of Grave Human Rights Violations', pp. 157–84: 'one may conclude that the jurisprudence of the Inter-American Court is predicated on a basic misunderstanding', at p. 166.

87 ILC, Articles on Responsibility of States for Internationally Wrongful Acts, adopted 2001, Article 32: 'Irrelevance of internal law – The responsible State may not rely on the provisions of its internal law as justification for failure to comply with its obligations under this part.'

88 CCPR, General Comment No. 31 on The Nature of the General Legal Obligation Imposed on States Parties to the Covenant, para. 13: 'Article 2, paragraph 2, requires that States Parties take the necessary steps to give effect to the Covenant rights in the domestic order. It follows that, unless Covenant rights are already protected by their domestic laws or practices, States Parties are required on ratification to make such changes to domestic laws and practices as are necessary to ensure their conformity with the Covenant. Where there are inconsistencies between domestic law and the Covenant, Article 2 requires that the domestic law or practice be changed to meet the standards imposed by the Covenant's substantive guarantees.' The Committee of Ministers of the Council of Europe (which supervises the execution of the judgments of the European Court of Human Rights in accordance with Article 46), *Monitoring of the Payment of Sums*

> Once it is recognised that obligations are owed to individuals, then there is no reason or logic why the obligation should be owed only to foreign nationals. It becomes unsustainable to regard the treatment of one's own nationals as matters falling essentially within domestic jurisdiction ... Human rights cannot be given or withdrawn at will by any domestic legal system, that system is not the source of the right. International human rights law is the source of the obligation albeit the obligation is reflected in the content of the domestic law.[89]

Furthermore, the ILC Articles on Diplomatic Protection adopted in 2006 specifically note that a state should hand over compensation to their own nationals, should a state raise a claim against another on the basis of diplomatic protection.[90]

2.9 Conclusions

To sum up this chapter, the initial section identified certain core human rights violations, which have in common that they figure both in human rights law as well as humanitarian law, are non-derogable and have been widely acknowledged as carrying status as customary law, which makes them universally applicable without treaty adherence. In some cases, certain core human rights are even considered to form part of *jus cogens* norms.

Subsequently, the chapter documented that reparations are a legally inseparable corollary to human rights violations, which by definition constitute violations whereby the state is responsible towards the individual. Human rights law contains specific references to reparation as a right. Basis for the individual right to reparation can also be found in humanitarian law and international criminal law. Until recently, individuals who were primarily perceived as victims of humanitarian law

Awarded by Way of Just Satisfaction, 15 January 2009, para. 4: 'The Committee of Ministers has regularly pointed out that the obligation to abide by the judgments of the Court is unconditional, a State cannot rely on specificities of its domestic legal system to justify failure to comply with the obligations by which it is bound under the Convention.'

89 Higgins, *Problems and Process, International Law and How We Use It*, pp. 96–7.

90 ILC, Draft Articles on Diplomatic Protection, adopted 2006, Article 19: 'A State entitled to exercise diplomatic protection according to the present draft Articles, should: (c) Transfer to the injured person any compensation obtained for the injury from the responsible State subject to any reasonable deductions'; ILC, Commentaries on the Draft Articles on Diplomatic Protection, 2006, Official Records of the General Assembly, 61st session, Supplement No. 10 (A/61/10). Article 19, para. 8: 'public policy, equity and respect for human rights support the curtailment of the States discretion in the disbursement of compensation'; ILC, 'Seventh Report on Diplomatic Protection by Special Rapporteur John Dugard', A/CN.4/567, 2006, paras 93–103.

breaches received little redress, while victims who argued their cases as human rights violations stood a slightly better chance of receiving reparations. With the gradual advent of international criminal courts and tribunals, more avenues are available for victims. Hopefully, recognition of victims as a beneficiary under different but complementary branches of law will contribute to advancing gradual implementation of their rights.

The convergence of norms and legal sources that explore and define the nature of reparations in relation to individuals is demonstrated in jurisprudence from the ICJ, the Articles on State Responsibility of the ILC, humanitarian law and human rights instruments, both legally binding and non-binding, as well as human rights jurisprudence and international criminal law (to be further explored in subsequent chapters) and the ICRC Customary Law Study. All these elements support the argument that state responsibility for reparations in favour of individuals has acquired certain customary standing.

Already in 1949, Judge Álvarez of the International Court of Justice had declared that three essential factors have to be taken into account in the development of international law, namely: 'the general principles of the new international law, the legal conscience of the peoples and the exigencies of contemporary international life'.[91] In retrospect, the relevance of this affirmation appears ever more pertinent.

[91] *Reparation for Injuries Suffered in the Service of the United Nations*, Advisory Opinion, 11 April 1949, Individual Opinion of Judge Álvarez, ICJ Report 1949.

3 Human rights jurisprudence on reparations, international and regional

3.1 Introduction

This chapter explores the concept of reparations for serious human rights violations through a comparative study of jurisprudence and its evolution within the international and regional human rights systems. The overview permits the identification of specific contributions from the different regions towards developing a broader notion of reparations. The chapter is structured according to the separate systems, whereby case law is identified as it highlights and expands on different components of reparations. The jurisprudence of the Inter-American human rights system has provided particularly important contributions in this field. Focus is set on cases that illustrate elements of reparations for serious human rights violations, in particular, violations involving torture, disappearances and extrajudicial executions. Where possible, examples are drawn from countries involved in armed conflict and, if available, from the countries that are the focus in the case studies in Part II of this study. The aim is to chart the elements of reparations as affirmed in the ILC Articles on State Responsibility and the UN Basic Principles on the Rights to Reparation for Victims: namely, restitution, compensation, rehabilitation, satisfaction and guarantees of non-repetition.

Restitution measures seek to restore the victim to the situation prior to the violation, something that in most cases of serious violations is impossible. However, restitution may involve return to one's place of residence, restoration of liberty and return of property. Compensation should be provided for economically assessable damage, proportional to the gravity of the violations and, for example, include consideration for loss of material assets and income, physical and mental harm and suffering, and costs for legal assistance. Rehabilitation involves providing assistance for medical and psychological care and may also include legal and social services. Satisfaction is a broad term which is commonly conceived of as covering a series of measures, including investigations and sanctions against perpetrators, protection of witnesses and the victim's relatives, searching for the whereabouts of the disappeared, public disclosure of the truth about violations, and official recognition of state responsibility, along with public apologies and commemorations to victims. Finally, reparation measures that seek to guarantee non-repetition include, for example, review and reform of laws that allow violations, institutional reform of the military ensuring it is under civilian control and accountability, as well as human rights and humanitarian law training for police and armed forces.

The chapter notes some of the differences in the provisions regarding reparations in international and regional human rights instruments, and highlights variations and certain inconsistencies in the awards of remedies. An attempt is made to identify some of the remaining challenges in order to advance a more coherent approach in international law to reparations for victims of gross human rights violations. In order to limit the chapter, national case law has been excluded. Ultimately, the chapter seeks to reaffirm the position that individual victims and their right to comprehensive reparations have gained enhanced legal standing in international law. A significant obstacle remains, however, in transforming the standards into practice in situations of armed conflict, particularly as international human rights instruments and mechanisms were not originally developed to address claims stemming from large-scale serious violations of human rights.

3.2 The international human rights treaty body system

As noted in Chapter 2, several international human rights treaties contain references to remedies and compensation; however, the language used in these provisions varies and the interpretations of them have developed gradually. The Covenant on Civil and Political Rights (ICCPR) provides a reference to the right to an 'effective remedy' in Article 2(3).[1] The remedy

[1] Article 2(3) of the ICCPR states:
Each State Party to the present Covenant undertakes:
(a) To ensure that any person whose rights or freedoms as herein recognized are violated shall have an effective remedy, notwithstanding that the violation has been committed by persons acting in an official capacity;

is to be determined by 'competent authorities' and there is no precise indication of what a remedy entails other than it should 'develop the possibilities of judicial remedy'. However, the state party is obliged to 'ensure that the competent authorities shall enforce such remedies when granted'. The Covenant refers to the word 'compensation' only in the context of unlawful arrest, detention and conviction in Articles 9(5) and 14(6).

The Human Rights Committee was established by Article 28 of the Covenant to oversee its implementation at the national level.[2] The Committee has given considerable interpretation of the content of the concept of a remedy in its decisions on individual petitions, as well as in Concluding Observations in relation to periodic state party reports and in General Comments on the interpretation of treaty provisions.[3] While the Committee does not have the competence to issue legally binding judgments, it adopts decisions, referred to as 'views', upon analysis of petitions from individuals who claim to have suffered violations in states that have ratified the Optional Protocol of the Covenant.[4] Among the key admissibility criteria, the petitioner must prove prior exhaustion of domestic remedies. The Optional Protocol entered into force in 1976. The Committee had by mid 2010 registered 1,960 individual complaints concerning 84 states parties and adopted views on 731 petitions, including 589 in which violations of the Covenant were found, while 557 petitions were declared inadmissible.[5]

The Committee affirms that state responsibility to comply stems from the legally binding obligations adhered to in the Covenant; however,

(b) To ensure that any person claiming such a remedy shall have his right thereto determined by competent judicial, administrative or legislative authorities, or by any other competent authority provided for by the legal system of the State, and to develop the possibilities of judicial remedy;
(c) To ensure that the competent authorities shall enforce such remedies when granted.

[2] The Human Rights Committee is a quasi-judicial body of eighteen independent international expert members who meet three times a year in Geneva or in New York.

[3] M. Nowak, *UN Covenant on Civil and Political Rights, CCPR Commentary*, 2nd edn (Kehl: N. P. Engel, 2005); S. Joseph, J. Schultz and M. Castan, *The International Covenant on Civil and Political Rights: Cases, Material and Commentary*, 2nd edn (Oxford University Press, 2004). Further detailed and updated information on the work of the Human Rights Committee can be found on the official web page of OHCHR at: www.ohchr.org/english/bodies/hrc/index.htm.

[4] As of 1 April 2011, the CCPR Optional Protocol had 113 state parties. Updated information on ratification status is available at the United National Treaty Bodies Collection at the UN Office of Legal Affairs at: http://www.untreaty.un.org.

[5] Annual Report of the Human Rights Committee to the General Assembly, 2010, UN Doc. A/65/40.

there is no formal enforcement mechanism.[6] This has had a negative impact on the implementation of the decisions, which in a majority of cases has remained inadequate.[7] The Committee is seeking to develop follow-up mechanisms and requests states parties to provide information within ninety days on the measures taken to implement the Committee's views.[8] The UN High Commissioner for Human Rights and the UN Special Rapporteur on Torture encourage compliance with treaty body jurisprudence; however, such efforts are not systematic. There is no formal relationship between the human rights treaty bodies and the political body, the Human Rights Council. The absence of such a relationship, which may have prompted compliance, has been noted as a significant limitation on the effectiveness of the system.[9]

With regard to Article 2(3), the Committee, when finding violations of the right to life (Article 6) and of the prohibition against torture (Article 7), commonly uses standard language and concludes that the victim has a right to an effective remedy, including compensation, and that the state party is under an obligation to prevent similar events from occurring again in the future. At times, the Committee uses other terms such as 'adequate reparation' or 'full reparation'; however, the terms are applied inconsistently. As a measure of acknowledgement and satisfaction for the victims, the Committee has gradually developed a practice of explicitly requesting that the state party publish the Committee's Views upon the finding of violations.[10] It is a considerable weakness that the Committee has rarely explored in detail the implications of what an

[6] CCPR General Comment No. 31, The Nature of General Legal Obligation Imposed on States Parties to the Covenant, UN Doc. CCPR/C/21/Rev.1/Add.13, 2004. Further discussion in G. Echeverria, 'Redressing Torture, a Genealogy of Remedies and Enforcement', Torture (IRCT Journal), 16(3) (2006), 152–81.

[7] Open Society Justice Initiative, *From Judgment to Justice, Implementing International and Regional Human Rights Decisions* (New York, 2010), p. 119.

[8] M. Schmidt, 'Follow-up Procedures to Individual Complaints', in G. Alfredsson, J. Grimheden, B. Ramcharan and A. de Zayas (eds), *International Human Rights Monitoring Mechanisms* (The Hague: Kluwer Law International, 2001), pp. 201–15; A. de Zayas, 'The Examination of Individual Complaints by the United Nations Human Rights Committee under the Optional Protocol of the CCPR', in G. Alfredsson, J. Grimheden, B. Ramcharan and A. de Zayas (eds), *International Human Rights Monitoring Mechanisms* (The Hague: Kluwer Law International, 2001), pp. 67–121. Both authors recognise the difficulties in conducting follow-up on cases and the lack of responsiveness among states parties, however, they point to examples indicating improvements.

[9] Open Society Justice Initiative, *From Judgment to Justice*, p. 135.

[10] *Kurbonov* v. *Tajikistan*, No. 1208/2003, Final Views, 16 March 2006, para. 9; *Medjnoune* v. *Algeria*, No. 1297/2004, Final Views, 14 July 2006, para. 11; *Mulezi* v. *Democratic Republic of Congo*, No. 962/2001, Final Views, 8 July 2004, para. 8.

effective remedy entails in individual cases, nor how the state party should proceed in order to prevent reoccurrence of similar violations.

The Committee had already stated in *Rodríguez* v. *Uruguay*,[11] a case of torture and arbitrary detention in 1984 during the military dictatorship, that amnesties for gross human rights violations are incompatible with the obligations under the Covenant. The Committee specifically urged 'the State party to take effective measures (a) to carry out an official investigation into the author's allegations of torture, in order to identify the persons responsible for torture and ill-treatment and to enable the author to seek civil redress; (b) to grant appropriate compensation to Mr Rodríguez; and (c) to ensure that similar violations do not occur in the future'. The Committee clearly stated in its early jurisprudence that the anguish suffered by family members of victims of disappearances constitutes a violation of torture in itself (see *Quinteros* v. *Uruguay*).[12]

In the case of *Bautista* v. *Colombia*[13] regarding the disappearance, torture and killing in 1987 of a member of a radical left-wing group (M-19), by members of the armed forces, the Committee went one step further by noting that disciplinary measures against the military officials and the award of a compensatory claim by an administrative tribunal were insufficient. The Committee insisted that the state party should expedite criminal proceedings leading to the prompt prosecution and conviction of the persons responsible: 'because purely disciplinary and administrative remedies cannot be deemed to constitute adequate and effective remedies within the meaning of Article 2, paragraph 3 of the Covenant, in the event of particularly serious violations of human rights'. The body of Nydia Bautista was identified in 1990 and the family suffered death threats for pursuing the case, thus the Committee also noted in its decision that the state party was under an obligation to provide appropriate protection for members of the victim's family.

In the case of *Laureano* v. *Peru*,[14] regarding a girl disappeared in 1992, presumably by army officials who had threatened her family and previously detained the girl on suspicion of being a member of the guerrilla group the Shining Path, the Committee determined that the state had failed its positive duty to protect the life of the victim and confirmed its

[11] *Rodríguez* v. *Uruguay*, No. 322/1988, Final Views, 9 August 1994, para. 14.
[12] *Quinteros* v. *Uruguay*, No. 107/1981, Final Views, 21 July 1983, para. 14.
[13] *Bautista* v. *Colombia*, No. 563/1993, Final Views, 27 October 1995, paras 8.2, 10. Case also discussed in Nowak, *UN Covenant on Civil and Political Rights*, p. 65.
[14] *Laureano* v. *Peru*, No. 540/1993, Final Views, 16 April 1996, paras 8.2–11.

previous jurisprudence in considering that the suffering imposed upon her family through the disappearance constituted torture.

In *Jegatheeswara* v. *Sri Lanka*, a case relating to a suspected Tamil Tiger (LTTE) sympathiser disappeared by the army in 1990, the Committee commented in further detail upon the suffering by family members:

> Moreover, noting the anguish and stress caused to the author's family by the disappearance of his son and by the continuing uncertainty concerning his fate and whereabouts, the Committee considers that the author and his wife are also victims of violation of Article 7 of the Covenant. The Committee is therefore of the opinion that the facts before it reveal a violation of Article 7 of the Covenant both with regard to the author's son and with regard to the author's family.[15]

The case is noteworthy because of its admissibility *ratione temporis* as the disappearance took place prior to the accession by Sri Lanka to the Optional Protocol in 1997. The decision to admit the case was based upon the position that continuing violations of the Covenant may take place after the entry into force. Furthermore, in its decision on remedies the Committee added as an extra element the right of the family to receive information relating to the investigations of the case: 'the State party is under an obligation to provide ... a thorough and effective investigation into the disappearance and fate of the author's son, his immediate release if he is still alive, adequate information resulting from its investigation, and adequate compensation'. Similar language has been used in several cases relating to disappearances such as *El Hassy* v. *Libya*[16] and *Sharma* v. *Nepal*.[17] In the case of *Sankara* v. *Burkina Faso*,[18] the Committee found a violation of Article 7 due to suffering caused to the victim's wife and children because of the uncertainty about the circumstances of Mr Sankara's death and the precise location where his remains were buried. The Committee affirmed that the state party was required to officially recognise the burial place and provide compensation for the anguish suffered by the family.

With regard to cases where violations of torture have been found, the Committee has only occasionally specified the obligation of the state party to provide medical assistance.[19] Curiously, the Committee took

[15] *Jegatheeswara* v. *Sri Lanka*, No. 950/2000, Final Views, 31 July 2003, paras 9.5, 6.2, 11.

[16] *El Hassy* v. *Libya*, No. 1422/2005, Final Views, 24 October 2007.

[17] *Sharma* v. *Nepal*, No. 1469/2006, Final Views, 28 October 2008.

[18] *Sankara* v. *Burkina Faso*, No. 1159/2003, Final Views, 28 March 2006, para. 14.

[19] Examples of cases where the petitioners were found to be victims of torture; however, no mention is made in the decisions regarding medical attention and rehabilitation: *Isidore Kanana* v. *Zaire*, No. 366/1989, Final Views, 8 November 1993; *Rodríguez* v. *Uruguay*,

this position in *Setelich* v. *Uruguay* and *Izquierdo* v. *Uruguay*,[20] decided back in the early 1980s; however, it has rarely repeated the demand. The victims in the above cases were at the time of the decisions still in detention. Yet it is undisputed that victims of torture generally require not only immediate medical attention, but also rehabilitation for prolonged periods after the violations have taken place. Therefore, it is a significant omission that reference to medical attention and rehabilitation is largely absent in jurisprudence of the Committee.

One explanation why attention to remedies in the jurisprudence of the Human Rights Committee is deficient is likely due to the absence of consultations with the victim regarding remedies during the consideration of the complaint. The model form for complaints that the petitioner is required to use contains no references to whether remedies are requested by the victim. Discussions are ongoing within the Committee regarding the need to develop more precise remedies in decisions; however, progress in this area remains blocked due to a lack of consensus in the Committee over support for such change.[21] Until progress is made in this area, follow-up on implementation of remedies will remain severely challenged due to lack of clarity regarding the measures the state needs to undertake in order to comply with the decision.

In addition to receiving individual communications, the Human Rights Committee reviews state party reports on the implementation at the national level. In accordance with Article 40 of the Covenant, all states parties should submit a report within one year of the entry into force of the Covenant and thereafter whenever the Committee so requests, usually every four years. These reports are subsequently reviewed in a public session by the Committee, which contrasts the information with that contained in alternative reports from UN entities as well as NGOs and publicly available material, and subsequently adopts Concluding Observations on the situation in the state under scrutiny.[22] Regarding the interpretation of remedies for serious violations which

No. 322/1988, Final Views, 9 August 1994; *Ndong Bee* v. *Equatorial Guinea*, Nos 1152/2003 and 1190/2003, Final Views, 30 November 2005.

[20] *Setelich* v. *Uruguay*, No. 63/1979, Final Views, 28 October 1981, para. 21; *Izquierdo* v. *Uruguay*, No. 73/1980, Final Views, 1 April 1982, para. 10.

[21] Report of the Inter-Committee Meeting working group on follow-up to concluding observations, decisions on individual complaints and inquiries, HRI/ICM/2011/3-HRI/MC/2011/2, 4 May 2011, para. 51.

[22] Updated information regarding the periodic reviews of state party reports by the Human Rights Committee, available on OHCHR's web page at: www.ohchr.org/english/bodies/hrc/index.htm.

occur in the context of armed conflict, the Committee has explored this in detail in several Concluding Observations, for example, in its review of Bosnia and Herzegovina (2006):

The Committee notes with concern that the fate and whereabouts of some 15,000 persons who went missing during the armed conflict (1992 to 1995) remains unresolved. It reminds the State party that the family members of missing persons have the right to be informed about the fate of their relatives, and that failure to investigate the cause and circumstances of death, as well as to provide information relating to the burial sites of missing persons increases ... suffering inflicted to family members and may amount to a violation of Article 7 of the Covenant (Arts 2(3), 6 and 7).

The Committee went on to issue detailed recommendations regarding satisfaction:

The State party should take immediate and effective steps to investigate all unresolved cases of missing persons and ensure without delay that the Institute for Missing Persons becomes fully operational ... It should ensure that the central database of missing persons is finalized and accurate, that the Fund for Support to Families of Missing Persons is secured and that payments to families commence as soon as possible.[23]

The above extract relating to Bosnia and Herzegovina provides an interesting example of a broader interpretation of remedies, in particular, satisfaction, by affirming the right of family members of victims to truth and knowledge of past violations and by proposing concrete measures to be taken by the state party.

The Committee noted further examples of remedies in the periodic review of the Central African Republic (2006) and notably invoked the congruence of serious violations under human rights and humanitarian law, affirming that the state party should:

ensure in all circumstances that victims of serious violations of human rights and international humanitarian law are guaranteed effective remedy, which is implemented in practice, including the right to as full compensation and reparations as possible ... act swiftly to implement recommendations of 'national dialogue' on establishment of a truth and reconciliation commission ... provide detailed information in next report on complaints filed ... and on reparations paid to victims over past three years ... improve training provided to law enforcement personnel.[24]

[23] CCPR Concluding Observations on Bosnia and Herzegovina, November 2006, CCPR/C/BIH/CO/1, para. 14.

[24] CCPR Concluding Observations on Central African Republic, July 2006, CCPR/C/CAF/CO/2, paras 8, 12. As another example, in the Concluding Observations

As noted in Chapter 2, in 2004 the Human Rights Committee clarified its position on reparations in a General Comment No. 31 on the Nature of the General Legal Obligation Imposed on States Parties to the Covenant,[25] which affirmed that reparation is a central part of an effective remedy and reiterated the components of reparation: restitution, compensation, rehabilitation, measures of satisfaction and guarantees of non-repetition.[26] The above-quoted General Comment also clearly sets out the positive obligations of the state as enshrined in the Covenant: 'There may be circumstances in which a failure to ensure Covenant rights as required by Article 2 would give rise to violations by States Parties of those rights, as a result of States Parties' permitting or failing to take appropriate measures or to exercise due diligence to prevent, punish, investigate or redress the harm caused by such acts by private persons or entities.'[27] The General Comment entrenched the position taken by the Committee in individual decisions and Concluding Observations, particularly in relation to cases of disappearances.

To sum up, the Committee is giving gradual interpretation of the provision establishing the right to an effective remedy. As demonstrated above, in relation to individual petitions, the Human Rights Committee maintains a narrow interpretation of Article 2(3) and remedies have not been developed in line with the elements set out in the General Comment of 2004. While the Committee lacks a mandate to order financial awards in individual cases, other components of reparations, such as concrete measures for satisfaction and rehabilitation, should be further explored in its jurisprudence. Nonetheless, a broader approach

on the Democratic Republic of the Congo (2006), the Committee also affirmed the importance of investigations and effective reparations for victims, March 2006, CCPR/C/COD/CO/3, para. 16.

25 CCPR General Comment No. 31, The Nature of General Legal Obligation Imposed on States Parties to the Covenant, UN Doc. CCPR/C/21/Rev.1/Add.13, 2004, para. 16. The General Comment is further discussed in Shelton, *Remedies in International Human Rights Law*, p. 117.

26 CCPR/C/31/Rev.1/Add.13, para. 16: 'Article 2, paragraph 3 requires that States Parties make reparation to individuals whose Covenant rights have been violated. Without reparation to individuals whose rights have been violated, the obligation to provide an effective remedy, which is central to the efficacy of article 2, paragraph 3, is not discharged . . . the Committee considers that the Covenant generally entails appropriate compensation. The Committee notes that, where appropriate, reparation can involve restitution, rehabilitation and measures of satisfaction, such as public apologies, public memorials, guarantees of non-repetition and changes in relevant laws and practices, as well as bringing to justice the perpetrators of human rights violations.'

27 CCPR/C/31/Rev.1/Add.13, para. 8. Further discussion in A. Clapham, *Human Rights Obligations of Non-State Actors* (Oxford University Press, 2006), pp. 328–32.

has been taken in its Concluding Observations adopted upon review of periodic state party reports. The Committee will hopefully reconsider the conservative approach to reparation it has taken to date in view of more progressive developments by other treaty bodies.

The Committee against Torture, established by Article 17 of the Convention with the same name, has given further interpretation to the concept of reparations, specifically with regard to the need for rehabilitation for victims. Article 14(1) of the Convention clearly sets out that:

> Each State Party shall ensure in its legal system that the victim of an act of torture obtains redress and has an enforceable right to fair and adequate compensation, including the means for as full rehabilitation as possible. In the event of the death of the victim as a result of an act of torture, his dependants shall be entitled to compensation.

The Committee against Torture may consider complaints from individuals for violations that have occurred within the jurisdiction of states parties that have made a declaration under Article 22 of the Convention. By mid 2010, the Committee had registered 420 petitions concerning 30 states parties and had issued decisions on 164 petitions,[28] that is, its jurisprudence is significantly less than that of the Human Rights Committee. The Committee against Torture, similarly to the Human Rights Committee, seldom explores the concept of reparations in detail in its decisions on individual cases. However, the Committee took a particular position in the case of *Kepa Urra Guridi* v. *Spain*, decided in 2005, regarding torture inflicted upon an ETA suspect in 1992. While certain compensation had already been paid to the victim, the Committee against Torture stated that:

> Article 14 of the Convention not only recognizes the right to fair and adequate compensation but also imposes on States the duty to guarantee compensation for the victim of an act of torture ... compensation should cover all the damages suffered by the victim, which includes, among other measures, restitution, compensation, and rehabilitation of the victim, as well as measures to guarantee the non-repetition of the violations, always bearing in mind the circumstances of each case.[29]

[28] Annual Report of the Committee against Torture to the General Assembly, 2010, UN Doc. A/65/44.

[29] *Kepa Urra Guridi* v. *Spain*, No. 212/2002, Final Views, 17 May 2005, para. 6.8. It should be noted that the case probably contains a mistake that has arisen during translation, the original case having been drafted in Spanish; the second and third reference to compensation should likely read reparation. The origin of the terminological confusion is the discrepancy between the two language versions of the Convention, English (uses

However, despite the language in Article 14 of the Convention, the Committee against Torture has generally applied a relatively conservative approach in its jurisprudence and avoided elaborating on the concept of rehabilitation.

The Committee against Torture, also in a manner analogous to that of the Human Rights Committee, reviews periodic state party reports and adopts Concluding Observations on the implementation at the national level of the rights enshrined in the Convention.[30] The Committee has provided further analysis of different components of reparations in its Concluding Observations, for example, upon reviewing Sri Lanka in 2005 it noted 'with concern the absence of a reparation programme, including rehabilitation, for the many victims of torture committed in the course of the armed conflict. The State party should establish a reparation programme, including treatment of trauma and other forms of rehabilitation, and provide adequate resources to ensure its effective functioning.'[31] Subsequent to the adoption of the UN Basic Principles on the Right to Reparation for Victims in 2005, the Committee has made explicit reference to these in its Concluding Observations on Colombia in 2009, whereby it called for the Principles to be taken into account in the establishment of a comprehensive national reparations programme.[32] The Committee against Torture is currently in the process of drafting a General Comment on Article 14 which will provide further guidance and its interpretation of reparations.

In a parallel initiative to the Convention against Torture, the UN General Assembly created the Voluntary Fund for Victims of Torture in 1981.[33] The mandate has remained the same over the past three decades: it specifically refers to humanitarian assistance rather than reparation and rehabilitation. The Fund was established in recognition of the

the term compensation) and Spanish (uses the term reparation). See further discussion regarding the significance of the case in Nowak and McArthur, *The United Nations Convention against Torture*, pp. 453, 481–2.

30 For updated information about the periodic reviews of state party reports by the Committee Against Torture, see OHCHR's web page at: www.ohchr.org/english/bodies/cat/index.htm.

31 CAT Concluding Observations on Sri Lanka, November 2005, CAT/C/LKA/CO/2, para. 16.

32 CAT Concluding Observations on Colombia, November 2009, CAT/C/COL/CO/4, para. 24.

33 The Fund was established by GA resolution 36/151 of 16 December 1981. *Report of the Secretary-General on the United Nations Voluntary Fund for Victims of Torture*, A/63/220, 5 August 2008. Further information about the United Nations Voluntary Fund for Victims is available on the web page of the UN Office of the High Commissioner for Human Rights (which acts as the Secretariat of the Fund) at: www.ohchr.org/EN/Issues/Pages/TortureFundMain.aspx.

importance of providing assistance for victims. However, the use of the term humanitarian assistance is a clear indication that the Fund does not assume responsibility for reparation as this duty lies with the state.

Over the years, the activities of the Voluntary Fund for Victims of Torture have expanded, and in 2010 it allocated approximately $10 million to 250 projects providing direct assistance for victims through NGOs in some seventy countries. The type of assistance provided may be psychological, medical, social, legal or, to some extent, economic. The Fund thus has a unique mandate in the UN system to provide direct assistance to victims. The Fund operates independently of the Committee against Torture, yet both the Committee and Special Rapporteur on Torture consistently encourage states to support the Voluntary Fund. The UN Special Rapporteur has even suggested that a mechanism might be devised to hold accountable those states in which torture is systematic and widespread in order that they may live up to their obligations under Article 14, and that such states might be required to contribute adequate funds to the Voluntary Fund.[34]

The Convention on the Elimination of All Forms of Discrimination against Women (CEDAW), unlike most other human rights treaties, does not contain a clear provision on the right to a remedy. However, this has not hindered the Committee from applying a progressive interpretation to the issue. The Optional Protocol to the Convention entered into force in 2000 and created the possibility for the Committee to receive petitions. The jurisprudence of the Committee deserves mention as it identifies specific remedies. In *Vertido* v. *Philippines* (2010), a case relating to discrimination by the judiciary in a rape case, the Committee recommended that the state party should provide the victim with appropriate compensation commensurate to the gravity of the violation, and also take specific measures to review and expedite legal proceedings involving rape, including review of its legislation and the conduct of regular training on the Convention for judges, lawyers and law enforcement officers.[35]

The Convention on the Rights of the Child (CRC) and its Optional Protocols on children in armed conflict and on the sale of children contain specific references to reparations. Article 39 of the CRC reads:

[34] UN Special Rapporteur on Torture Manfred Nowak, Oral Statement to the 4th session of the Human Rights Council, 26 March 2007.

[35] *Vertido* v. *Philippines*, No. 18/2008, Final Views, adopted 22 September 2010, para. 8.9.

States Parties shall take all appropriate measures to promote physical and psychological recovery and social reintegration of a child victim of: any form of neglect, exploitation, or abuse; torture or any other form of cruel, inhuman or degrading treatment or punishment; or armed conflicts.[36]

The CRC and its Protocol relating to armed conflict both contain cross-references to the applicability of humanitarian law.[37] While the Committee on the Rights of the Child cannot yet receive individual communications,[38] it issues Concluding Observations, similar to other treaty bodies, upon review of the periodic reports of states parties. Following the review of states currently undergoing armed conflict, the Committee has stressed aspects relating to reparations; for example, in the 2006 Concluding Observations on Colombia, the state party was urged to: 'Substantially increase the resources for social reintegration, rehabilitation and reparations available to demobilized child soldiers as well as for child victims of landmines.'[39]

A comprehensive concept of reparations has been gradually developed through the jurisprudence of human rights treaty bodies and has been supported by soft law texts such as the Basic Principles on the Right to Reparation for Victims. Importantly, the entry into force in December 2010 of the International Convention for the Protection of all Persons from Enforced Disappearance (CPPED) for the first time established the right to truth and a comprehensive definition of reparations in a legally binding instrument.[40] The Convention clearly reaffirms a holistic concept of reparations and specifies the same five elements as the Basic Principles.[41] The Convention will be monitored by a Committee and in

[36] Full text of the Convention on the Rights of the Child and its Optional Protocols and updated information on periodic reviews available on the web page of OHCHR at: www.ohchr.org/english/bodies/crc/index.htm.

[37] CRC, Article 38, Optional Protocols on Children in Armed Conflict, Preamble and Article 5.

[38] An open-ended Working Group was, however, established by the Human Rights Council in 2009 in order to explore the possibilities for a complaints mechanism under the CRC. In February 2011, negotiations for a draft Optional Protocol to the CRC on communications were concluded by the Working Group and submitted to the 17th session of the Human Rights Council, with a request for its submission to the GA for adoption.

[39] CRC Concluding Observations on Colombia, June 2006, CRC/C/COL/CO/3, para. 81.

[40] On 1 April 2011, the CPPED had twenty-five states parties. It entered into force on 23 December 2010, one month following the 20th ratification or accession. For the text and updated status of ratification of the Convention on Disappearances, see the UN Office of Legal Affairs (OLA) web page at: http://treaties.un.org.

[41] International Convention on Disappearances, Article 24(4), (5): 'Each State Party shall ensure in its legal system that the victims of enforced disappearance have the right to

time its jurisprudence will most likely provide significant contributions to the evolving concept of reparations.

To sum up, the treaty bodies of the international system for human rights protection have explored the concept of reparations for serious violations to a varying degree. Although individual decisions from treaty bodies are not legally enforceable *per se*, they would benefit from providing more specific guidance on what an effective remedy and reparations entail. To date, the decisions have tended to focus on procedural aspects of access to justice rather than on concrete interpretations of reparations. Despite the relevant General Comment adopted by the Human Rights Committee in 2004, the concept of reparations therein has yet to be fully reflected in the jurisprudence of the Committee. In particular, the areas of rehabilitation, satisfaction and guarantees of non-repetition remain underexplored. The more specific language in Article 14 of the Convention against Torture has allowed for some further detailed jurisprudence. However, the various treaty bodies provide a more comprehensive analysis of remedial measures in their Concluding Observations adopted upon the periodic review of states parties' reports. Importantly, both the individual decisions and the Concluding Observations of the treaty bodies affirm positive obligations on the state by exploring its responsibility, including for actions not directly attributable to state agents. A principal challenge facing the international system is the lack of effective monitoring and follow-up of compliance with treaty body jurisprudence at the national level. Among the proposals to address this problem it has been suggested, including by Nowak and Scheinin, that a World Court for Human Rights be established.[42]

3.3 The European system for human rights protection

As noted in Chapter 2, the Council of Europe created the first human rights system with the faculty to deliver legally binding and enforceable judgments on remedies. These provisions figure in the European

obtain reparation and prompt, fair and adequate compensation. The right to obtain reparation referred to in paragraph 4 of this Article covers material and moral damages and, where appropriate, other forms of reparation such as: (a) Restitution; (b) Rehabilitation; (c) Satisfaction, including restoration of dignity and reputation; (d) Guarantees of non-repetition.'

[42] M. Nowak, 'The Need for a World Court of Human Rights', *Human Rights Law Review*, 7(1) (2007), 251–9; J. Kozma, M. Nowak and M. Scheinin, *A World Court of Human Rights – Consolidated Statute and Commentary* (Vienna: Neuer Wissenschaftlicher Verlag, 2010).

Convention on Human Rights (ECHR), which entered into force in 1953.[43] Individuals who have exhausted all domestic remedies can file complaints directly with the European Court of Human Rights (ECtHR) (since the entry into force of Protocol 11 in 1998, previously the European Commission of Human Rights was the first instance) and all states parties undertake not to hinder the exercise of this right in any way.[44]

Article 13 of the ECHR affirms the right to an effective remedy and declares that:

> Everyone whose rights and freedoms as set forth in this Convention are violated shall have an effective remedy before a national authority notwithstanding that the violation has been committed by persons acting in an official capacity.

Interpretation of Article 13 is done in conjunction with Article 41 of the ECHR which establishes that:

> If the Court finds that there has been a violation of the Convention or the Protocols thereto, and if the internal law of the High Contracting Party concerned allows only partial reparation to be made, the Court shall, if necessary, afford just satisfaction to the injured party.

The jurisprudence by the ECtHR relating to the above Articles has been much debated, and scholars agree that Article 13 has been one of the most challenging Articles of the Convention to interpret, which in turn has resulted in certain inconsistencies in the practice of the ECtHR.[45]

[43] The official web page of the European Court of Human Rights at: www.echr.coe.int/echr.

[44] European Convention for the Protection of Human Rights and Fundamental Freedoms, Article 34: 'The Court may receive applications from any person, non-governmental organisation or group of individuals claiming to be the victim of a violation by one of the High Contracting Parties of the rights set forth in the Convention or the protocols thereto. The High Contracting Parties undertake not to hinder in any way the effective exercise of this right.' All references to Article numbers refer to the Convention as amended after Protocol 11 entered into force in 1998 (replacing the Commission with a single instance of a full-time Court).

[45] C. Ovey and R. White, *The European Convention on Human Rights*, 3rd edn (Oxford University Press, 2002), pp. 386–95; D. Harris, M. O'Boyle and C. Warbrick, *Law of the European Convention on Human Rights* (London: Butterworths, 1995), p. 443; D. Gomien, *Short Guide to the European Convention on Human Rights*, 2nd edn (Strasbourg: Council of Europe Publishing, 1998), pp. 124–7. P. Van Dijk and G. Van Hoof, *Theory and Practice of the European Convention on Human Rights* (The Hague: Kluwer Law International, 1998), p. 697 cites the partly dissenting opinion of judges Matscher and Farinha in the *Malone Case*, judgment 2 August 1984, p. 41; 'Article 13 constitutes on of the most obscure clauses in the Convention and its application raises extremely complicated problems of interpretation. This is probably the reason why, for approximately two decades, the Convention institutions avoided analysing this provision, for the most part advancing barely convincing reasons.'

These difficulties are partly due to a lack of clarity in the drafting of the provisions and also to the ECtHR's traditionally restrictive interpretation of them.[46] The ECtHR has battled with concepts such as what constitutes an effective remedy and to what extent national authorities should be given the discretion to ensure the effectiveness of a remedy.[47]

For decades, the ECtHR focused on the right to access a remedy rather than taking a position on what constitutes an effective remedy. Furthermore, the interpretation of Article 41, which indicates that the ECtHR shall afford just satisfaction 'if necessary', has been criticised, among others by Judge Higgins, as it has been interpreted in jurisprudence as optional and that the judgment in itself may afford satisfaction for victims.[48] In a dissenting opinion, Judge Bonello stated that: 'I consider it wholly inadequate and unacceptable that a court of justice should "satisfy" the victim of a breach of fundamental rights with a mere handout of legal idiom.'[49] As noted by Shelton, the narrow interpretation of the Convention has hampered the evolution of remedies in the European system, and to some degree undermined the remedial purpose of the Articles in question.[50] Part of the explanation of the initial conservative approach to remedies can be explained by the pioneering role of the European human rights system and that it did not at first envisage the individual as the primary focus, but rather retained an inter-state traditional approach.[51] It should also be noted that the European system, in contrast to other regional human rights systems in

[46] Nowak, *UN Covenant on Civil and Political Rights*; M. Nowak, 'The Right of Victims of Gross Human Rights Violations to Reparation', in F. Coomans (ed.), *Rendering Justice to the Vulnerable* (The Hague: Kluwer Law International, 2000), pp. 203–24; Shelton, *Remedies in International Human Rights Law*, pp. 195, 197, 200.

[47] *Leander* v. *Sweden*, ECtHR, Judgment, 26 March 1987, para. 84. The case is discussed in Harris, O'Boyle and Warbrick, *Law of the European Convention on Human Rights*, pp. 456–8 and G. Dutertre, *Key Case Law Extracts European Court of Human Rights* (Strasbourg: Council of Europe Publishing, 2003), p. 353. Further discussion on the concept of an effective remedy also in Nowak, 'The Right to Reparation for Victims of Gross Human Rights Violations', p. 288 and Ovey and White, *The European Convention on Human Rights*, p. 390.

[48] Judge Rosalyn Higgins has criticised this practice: 'the intention is not that a party has to rest content with the judgment as his satisfaction. In spite of the unclear terminology, the intention is exactly the opposite – that the Court shall itself be able to assist by providing, if necessary, for just satisfaction', cited in Shelton, *Remedies in International Human Rights Law*, p. 195, further discussion pp. 257–60.

[49] Judge Bonello in *Nikolova* v. *Bulgaria*, ECtHR, Judgment, 25 March 1999, cited by Mowbray, *Cases and Materials on the European Convention on Human Rights*, pp. 730–2.

[50] Shelton, *Remedies in International Human Rights Law*, p. 197.

[51] Shelton, *Remedies in International Human Rights Law*, p. 200.

the Americas and Africa, was not initially confronted with large numbers of cases relating to serious violations, such as to the right to life.

However, significant changes have taken place with the expansion of the number of states parties, the reform and creation of the full-time court in 1998 and the increasing number of cases received relating to serious human rights violations, including in the context of armed conflict. In 1996, the ECtHR for the first time issued a sentence finding state officials directly responsible for torture (Article 3) in the case of *Aksoy* v. *Turkey*. The case represented a groundbreaking shift in the jurisprudence of the ECtHR as it finally defined that: 'the notion of an effective remedy entails, in addition to the payment of compensation where appropriate, a thorough and effective investigation capable of leading to the effective identification and punishment of those responsible and including effective access for the complainant to the investigatory procedure'.[52] In 1994, the applicant was killed, allegedly for bringing the claim to the ECtHR. His father continued his application, and for the first time the ECtHR awarded the full amount claimed, including £25,000 for non-pecuniary damages.[53]

During the 1990s, the Convention was ratified by an additional twenty states parties and the expansion eastwards significantly increased the number of cases filed. The number of annual applicants rose from 5,900 in 1998 to 27,000 in 2003, and during 2010 the number of applicants was 61,300.[54] The latter figure is higher than the number of cases registered during the system's first thirty years of existence. The ECtHR issued 180 judgments during its first thirty years, while in 1999 alone the court emitted almost as many (177).[55] During 2010, six states accounted for two-thirds of the case load as the majority of the judgments were against Russia (28.9 per cent), Turkey, Romania, Ukraine, Italy and Poland. Compared with the international human rights system, the efficiency and resources available at the regional level speak for themselves. During 2010, the ECtHR issued as many judgments (1,499) as the Human Rights Committee has emitted decisions during its entire existence.

[52] *Aksoy* v. *Turkey*, ECtHR, Judgment, 18 December 1996, para. 98. The victim, resident in south-east Turkey, was detained in 1992 upon suspicion of belonging to the PKK (Partiya Karerên Kurdistan, Workers' Party of Kurdistan) and was tortured by police during a two-week period.

[53] Case discussed in Mowbray, *Cases and Materials on the European Convention on Human Rights*, pp. 87–90; Shelton, *Remedies in International Human Rights Law*, p. 297.

[54] European Court of Human Rights, *Annual Reports 2008, 2009 and 2010*; The European Court of Human Rights, *Some Facts and Figures 1959–2008*.

[55] Shelton, *Remedies in International Human Rights Law*, p. 198.

Through the number of cases filed in the European system relating to serious violations of human rights, including the right to life and prohibition against torture, the ECtHR has gradually evolved its jurisprudence in the area of remedies. In 1993, a seventeen-year-old girl in south-east Turkey was detained together with her family upon suspicion of belonging to the PKK. She was subsequently raped and subjected to torture at the hands of state security forces. The case, *Aydin* v. *Turkey*, was decided in 1997 and marked the first time that rape was explicitly defined as torture by the ECtHR. The ECtHR further criticised the lack of a thorough and effective investigation into the allegation of rape in custody and that the victim was not examined by competent, independent medical professionals.[56]

In yet another Turkish case, *Mahmut Kaya* v. *Turkey*, the ECtHR commented upon the positive obligations of the state to prevent violations and demonstrate due diligence, including in the context of armed conflict. The ECtHR took the position that although it could not be established beyond doubt whether state agents were directly involved in the killing, it was clear that the state party was aware of the threats against the victim and failed to take preventive action and conduct a criminal investigation subsequent to the events.[57] The decision marks a progressive shift in the ECtHR's position on the positive obligations of the state to prevent violations, notably compared with its restrictive interpretation in the decision of the case *Osman* v. *United Kingdom*.[58]

Regarding the consideration of family members of victims who have suffered serious violations, the ECtHR is more likely to recognise parents rather than siblings as having suffered in cases of disappearances and

[56] *Aydin* v. *Turkey*, ECtHR, Judgment, 25 September 1997. Case discussed in Mowbray, *Cases and Materials on the European Convention on Human Rights*, pp. 91–2 and Nowak, 'The Right to Reparation for Victims of Gross Human Rights Violations', p. 288. Case summaries available at Utrecht Law School (SIM) Database: http://www.sim.law.uu.nl/SIM/Dochome.nsf?Open.

[57] *Mahmut Kaya* v. *Turkey*, ECtHR, Judgment, 28 March 2000. Case discussed in Mowbray, *Cases and Materials on the European Convention on Human Rights*, pp. 62–5 and in Clapham, *Human Rights Obligations of Non-State Actors*, p. 365. In 1993, a medical doctor in south-east Turkey left home to treat a wounded member of the PKK. Six days later he was found murdered, shot in the head with his hands tied. Prior to the killing, the victim had expressed concern over surveillance by state agents. In 1998, a government report, containing details of state-sponsored extrajudicial killings in the region, was made public.

[58] *Osman* v. *United Kingdom*, ECtHR, Judgment, 28 October 1998. Case discussed in Mowbray, *Cases and Materials on the European Convention on Human Rights*, pp. 60–2; Dutertre, *Key Case Law Extracts*, pp. 30–2; Clapham, *Human Rights Obligations of Non-State Actors*, pp. 361–5.

extrajudicial killings. While the ECtHR issued only nominal non-pecuniary damages to the brothers (applicants) in the cases *Mahmut Kaya* v. *Turkey* and *Çakici* v. *Turkey*,[59] they recognised the mother of the victim in the disappearance case *Kurt* v. *Turkey*[60] as an indirect victim of a violation of Article 3 due to the anguish she had suffered not knowing the fate of her son. The ECtHR, somewhat ambiguously, stated that:

> the Kurt case does not establish a general principle that a family member of a disappeared person is thereby a victim of treatment contrary to Article 3. Whether a family member is such a victim will depend on the existence of special factors which gives the suffering of the applicant a dimension and character distinct from the emotional distress which may be regarded as inevitably caused to relatives of a victim of a serious human rights violation.[61]

The position of the ECtHR regarding claims from family members of victims does not clearly state what 'special factors' are required to fulfil the criteria of secondary victimisation. Clearly, such special factors were excluded in the decision of the case *McCann and Others* v. *United Kingdom*,[62] one of the ECtHR's most criticised judgments, where despite finding violations of the right to life, family members of the three suspected IRA terrorists killed were denied any damages. Also, in *Güleç* v. *Turkey*[63] the ECtHR controversially reduced the damages awarded to the family of a fifteen-year-old boy killed in a demonstration, apparently based on presumption that his presence at the demonstration indicated a mitigating factor in relation to state responsibility. Nevertheless, despite inconsistencies in the jurisprudence, the ECtHR has set important precedents by establishing the right of family members to know the fate of disappeared persons and by considering this as an additional violation.[64]

In a case relating to serious violations in Chechnya, *Khashiyev and Akayeva* v. *Russia*, several family members of the applicants had been extrajudicially executed by Russian Army forces in 2000. In the judgment emitted in 2005, the ECtHR: 'recalled its case law in this area and

[59] *Çakici* v. *Turkey*, ECtHR, Judgment, 8 July 1999.

[60] *Kurt* v. *Turkey*, ECtHR, Judgment, 25 May 1998.

[61] *Çakici* v. *Turkey*, paras 98–9, noted in Dutertre, *Key Case Law Extracts*, pp. 80–1.

[62] *McCann and Others* v. *United Kingdom*, ECtHR, Judgment, 27 September 1995. Case discussed in Shelton, *Remedies in International Human Rights Law*, pp. 264–5.

[63] *Güleç* v. *Turkey*, ECtHR, Judgment, 27 July 1998. Case discussed in Shelton, *Remedies in International Human Rights Law*, p. 304.

[64] Y. Naqvi, 'The Right to the Truth in International Law, Fact or Fiction?', *International Review of the Red Cross*, 88(862) (2006), p. 257.

the need, in cases involving State agents or bodies, to ensure their accountability for deaths occurring under their responsibility. The obligations under Article 2 could not be satisfied merely by awarding damages. The investigation had to be timely, effective and not to be dependent for its progress on the initiative of the survivors or the next of kin.[65]

In the case of *Isayeva* v. *Russia*, also decided by the ECtHR in 2005, the applicant complained of indiscriminate bombing of a village in Chechnya in 2000. The ECtHR stated regarding the aerial bombings that:

> using this kind of weapon in a populated area, outside wartime and without prior evacuation of the civilians, was impossible to reconcile with the degree of caution expected from a law-enforcement body in a democratic society ... the use of indiscriminate weapons stood in flagrant contrast with this aim and could not be considered compatible with the standard of care prerequisite to an operation of this kind involving the use of lethal force by State agents.[66]

It is interesting to note that while the applicants invoked humanitarian law (Common Article 3 and II Additional Protocol) in their claim, the ECtHR made no specific reference to this in the judgment and simply stated 'while the situation that existed in Chechnya at the relevant time called for exceptional measures by the State ... no state of emergency had been declared and no derogation has been entered under Article 15 of the Convention'. With regard to reparations, the case provides an unusual example as the applicant was awarded pecuniary damages for the loss of earnings of her deceased son, upon whom she was financially dependent. In contrast, in subsequent case law of 2008, *Korbely* v. *Hungary*, the ECtHR made explicit references to humanitarian law.[67]

As noted above, the ECtHR has played an important role in developing human rights jurisprudence as it was the first such institution to issue legally binding decisions. The system has developed, from initially being rather conservative, to responding to a rapidly escalating, almost

[65] *Khashiyev and Akayeva* v. *Russia*, ECtHR, Judgment, 24 February 2005.

[66] *Isayeva* v. *Russia*, ECtHR, Judgment, 24 February 2005. Case discussed in N. Lubell, 'Challenges in Applying Human Rights Law to Armed Conflict', *International Review of the Red Cross*, 87(860) (2005), 742–4. As a result of the attack, the son and three nieces of the applicant were killed. It was also alleged that in total some 150 people died during the bombing, many internally displaced fleeing from other parts of Chechnya. A national criminal investigation, opened in September 2000, confirmed the applicant's version of events. The national investigation was, however, closed in 2002; the actions of the military were found to have been legitimate in the circumstances, as a large group of illegal fighters had occupied the village.

[67] *Korbely* v. *Hungary*, ECtHR, Judgment, 19 September 2008.

exploding, number of complaints. Critics, including Nowak, have noted the reluctance of the ECtHR to define and expand the concept of *just satisfaction* in conjunction with Article 13.[68] The reticence to award damages and the position that judgments alone provide satisfaction for victims have been overturned during the past decade as the ECtHR has been faced with a rapidly growing number of cases involving serious human rights violations, many in the context of internal armed conflict. The ECtHR has drawn upon principles of humanitarian law, as noted above, and developed jurisprudence clearly affirming the positive obligations of the state, including when the violations may not be directly attributable to state agents. While the ECtHR now routinely awards both pecuniary and non-pecuniary damages, as well as compensation for legal costs, it has rarely ventured into awarding other types of reparations. Controversially, non-pecuniary damages vary depending on the ECtHR's assessment of the victim's moral conduct and, in the case of deceased victims, of his or her relationship with the family member presenting the claim.[69] To date, the ECtHR has in no case specifically awarded rehabilitation for victims of torture. Nevertheless, in 2010 the ECtHR issued a judgment which may indicate a step forward in this direction; in the case *Danev* v. *Bulgaria*,[70] the court emphasised that the adverse effects of unlawful detention on a person's psychological condition could persist even after release and critiqued the state for having refused to provide reparations.

Only exceptionally has the ECtHR resorted to restitution of property as a measure of reparations.[71] The *travaux preparatoires* of the Convention indicate that the ECtHR does not have the faculty to review legislation and overturn national judgments.[72] The ECtHR, however, has affirmed

[68] Nowak, *UN Covenant on Civil and Political Rights*, p. 74; Shelton, *Remedies in International Human Rights Law*, pp. 238, 280; L. Loucaides, 'Reparation for Violations of Human Rights under the European Convention and *Restitutio in Integrum*', *European Human Rights Law Review*, 2 (2008), 182–92; Redress, *Enforcing Reparations, Enforcement of Awards for Victims of Torture and Other International Crimes* (London: The Redress Trust, 2006), p. 30.

[69] Notably in the case, *McCann and Others* v. *United Kingdom*, ECtHR, Judgment, 27 August 1995. Discussed in Shelton, *Remedies in International Human Rights Law*, pp. 197, 264–5, 303–4 and L. Wildhaber, 'Article 41 and Just Satisfaction in the European Convention on Human Rights', *Baltic Yearbook of International Law*, 3 (2003), 6, 13 and also in Mowbray, *Cases and Materials on the European Convention on Human Rights*, pp. 35–50.

[70] *Danev* v. *Bulgaria*, ECtHR, Judgment, 2 October 2010.

[71] *Papamichalopoulos* v. *Greece*, ECtHR, Judgment, 31 October 1995, discussed in Shelton, *Remedies in International Human Rights Law*, pp. 199, 238.

[72] Shelton, *Remedies in International Human Rights Law*, p. 281; Ovey and White, *The European Convention on Human Rights*, p. 394.

the obligation of the state to conduct effective investigations, *ex officio* if necessary, in order to establish accountability and inform complainants about investigation efforts undertaken.

The principal challenge currently facing the ECtHR is the booming number of cases filed and the fact that many of them essentially refer to similar circumstances and types of violation. The ECtHR in principle does not accept collective claims or *actio popularis*,[73] however, it will be forced to address the quickly growing burden of cases. In many of the Turkish cases, the applicants requested the ECtHR to identify systematic practices, yet it generally responded with a standard phrase that: 'it did not find it necessary to determine whether the failings identified are part of a practice adopted by the authorities'.[74] However, in 2004 the Committee of Ministers, which oversees the execution of judgments in accordance with Article 46 of the Convention, requested the ECtHR to identify systemic problems and the source of such problems in order to assist states in finding necessary remedial measures.[75] The ECtHR has since sought to apply a 'pilot judgment procedure', which aims to identify human rights violations that affect large numbers of applicants and suggest effective domestic remedies in order to reduce the backlog of cases.[76] This approach may gradually orient the ECtHR towards ordering reparations that have a policy impact[77] in order to assert guarantees of non-repetition of violations.

Two recent measures will contribute to expediting the ECtHR's processing of applications. In 2009, it adopted a priority policy according to

[73] Van Dijk and Van Hoof, *Theory and Practice of the European Convention on Human Rights*, p. 46.

[74] *Mahmut Kaya* v. *Turkey*, ECtHR, Judgment, 28 March 2000, para. 128.

[75] Shelton, *Remedies in International Human Rights Law*, p. 284. Recommendation No. 6 (2004) from the Committee of Ministers; further detailed and updated information can be found at the Committee of Ministers' web page for the supervision of execution of judgments at: www.coe.int/T/E/Human_rights/execution.

[76] E. Fribergh, Registrar, European Court of Human Rights, Presentation at Stockholm Colloquy, 9 June 2008: 'the Court identifies the shortcoming in the legal order – the systemic problem – that is the cause of the violation which affects a whole class of individuals. The specific feature of the PJP is that instead of dealing with each individual case, the Court singles out one or a small number of applications for priority treatment and adjourns all other applications until the pilot case has been decided ... the Court gives advice to the Government on how to solve the systemic problem. The basic idea is that the Court should be dispensed from dealing with all the follow-up cases, which would be dealt with through a new domestic remedy introduced as a result of the implementation of the pilot judgment.'

[77] Wildhaber, 'Article 41 and Just Satisfaction in the European Convention on Human Rights', p. 17.

the importance and urgency of the case applications; and, in June 2010, Protocol No. 14 entered into force, increasing the ECtHR's capacity by introducing smaller judicial formations, thereby freeing up more judicial time to devote to cases considered to be of greater legal importance or urgency.[78]

In contrast with other human rights systems, the implementation rate of judgments in the European system is considerably higher. The Committee of Ministers is an important strength as it is a political body with a specific mandate, in accordance with Article 46 of the European Convention, to monitor the domestic compliance with judgments.[79]

In 2008, a Human Rights Trust Fund was established at the Council of Europe with the aim of assisting states in the full and timely execution of judgments. However, the Human Rights Trust Fund does not provide assistance for individual victims, but rather supports activities to implement the ECtHR's judgments through promotion of the rule of law and the compatibility of national legislation and administrative practices with the Convention.[80]

3.4 The Inter-American system for human rights protection

The jurisprudence of the Inter-American human rights system has, without doubt, developed the most innovative jurisprudence on reparations. The American Convention on Human Rights (ACHR), which entered into force on 18 July 1978, established the second legally binding and enforceable complaints mechanism at the regional level. Article 25 of the ACHR affirms the right to a legal remedy,[81] and Article 63 specifies the right to reparation:

[78] European Court of Human Rights, *Annual Report*, 2010.

[79] Open Society Justice Initiative, *From Judgment to Justice, Implementing International and Regional Human Rights Decisions*, pp. 33–61.

[80] Committee of Ministers, *Supervision of the Execution of Judgments*, 2nd Annual Report, 2008, see the official web page of the Human Rights Trust Fund of the Council of Europe at: www.coe.int/humanrightstrustfund.

[81] Article 25 of the American Convention:

1. Everyone has the right to simple and prompt recourse, or any other effective recourse, to a competent court or tribunal for protection against acts that violate his fundamental rights recognized by the constitution or laws of the state concerned or by this Convention, even though such violation may have been committed by persons acting in the course of their official duties.
2. The States Parties undertake:
   a. to ensure that any person claiming such remedy shall have his rights determined by the competent authority provided for by the legal system of the state
   b. to develop the possibilities of judicial remedy; and
   c. to ensure that the competent authorities shall enforce such remedies when granted.

63(1). If the Court finds that there has been a violation of a right or freedom protected by this Convention, the Court shall rule that the injured party be ensured the enjoyment of his right or freedom that was violated. It shall also rule, if appropriate, that the consequences of the measure or situation that constituted the breach of such right or freedom be remedied and that fair compensation be paid to the injured party.

Upon comparison, Article 63 of the ACHR is more explicit than Article 41 of the European Convention, which merely contains vague reference to just satisfaction. The *travaux preparatoires* indicate that early draft versions of the ACHR contemplated financial compensation only as a measure of reparation. However, during the negotiation process of the Convention, the Guatemalan delegation proposed that it be expanded. Finally, the ACHR contains references to the obligation to ensure future respect for the exercise of the violated right, and to the award of remedies as well as compensation.[82] This language, whereby remedies are referred to as separate from compensation, has allowed the Inter-American Court of Human Rights (IACtHR) to interpret the concept of remedies in a creative manner, bearing in mind the particular characteristics of the region. The motivation to expand the concept of remedies stems from the nature of the violations in the region. Among the cases that have reached the IACtHR, there have been few surviving victims amid the applicants. The military dictatorships that plagued the region resulted in high incidences of cases relating to torture, disappearances and extrajudicial executions. Several of the recent judgments of the IACtHR refer to massacres, notably in Guatemala and Colombia.[83] Due to the nature of the violations, restitution has often been impossible. Relatives of the victims have generally been more interested in receiving reparations in the form of satisfaction measures in order to restore the dignity of the victims, who were often discredited by the authorities and accused of being subversives.

[82] J. Pasqualucci, 'Victim Reparations in the Inter-American Human Rights System: A Critical Assessment of Current Practice and Procedure', *Michigan International Law Journal*, 1(18) (1996), pp. 8–12; see also Shelton, *Remedies in International Human Rights Law*, p. 217.

[83] Examples of cases include: *Plan de Sánchez Massacre* v. *Guatemala*, IACtHR, Judgment, 29 April 2004, Ser. C, No. 105; *Mapiripán Massacre* v. *Colombia*, IACtHR, Judgment, 15 September 2005, Ser. C, No. 134; *Pueblo Bello Massacre* v. *Colombia*, IACtHR, Judgment, 31 January 2006, Ser. C, No. 140; *Ituango Massacre* v. *Colombia*, IACtHR, Judgment, 1 July 2006, Ser. C, No. 148.

Two human rights monitoring bodies interpret the ACHR, a Commission as the first instance, which has the competence to investigate, recommend friendly settlements and, as a final resort, refer cases to the IACtHR, which emits legally binding judgments and monitors their implementation. All complaints must be submitted to the Commission as the IACtHR has no faculty to receive cases directly. The Commission pre-dates the Convention and had already started to receive individual communications in 1965.[84] The IACtHR came into existence in 1979.[85] Unlike the Council of Europe, where member states are *ipso facto* parties to the European Convention on Human Rights, this is not the case in the Organization of American States (OAS). To date the Convention has been ratified by twenty-five states parties, of which twenty-two have recognised the jurisdiction of the IACtHR.[86] Canada and the United States are notably absent among the states parties to the Convention.

The jurisprudence of the IACtHR has tended to link remedies for violations directly to the general provision on state responsibility set forth in Article 1 of the Convention.[87] This is in contrast to the Human Rights Committee and the European Court of Human Rights, which have interpreted violations primarily in conjunction with Article 2(3) of the Covenant and Article 13 of the European Convention. Furthermore, the IACtHR has adopted a standard phrase in much of its jurisprudence affirming that: 'Article 25 is one of the basic pillars not only of the American Convention but of the very rule of law and of a democratic society'.[88]

Unlike the ECtHR, which operates full-time since its reform, the IACtHR meets only in a limited number of sessions during the year, often around ten weeks. The human resources available within the two systems vary considerably, as the ECtHR in addition to having full-time

84 C. Cerna, 'The Inter-American Commission on Human Rights', in D. Harris and S. Livingstone (eds), *The Inter-American System of Human Rights* (Oxford: Clarendon Press, 1998), pp. 65–114.

85 A. Cançado Trindade, 'The Operation of the Inter-American Court of Human Rights', in D. Harris and S. Livingstone (eds), *The Inter-American System of Human Rights* (Oxford: Clarendon Press, 1998), pp. 133–49.

86 OAS web page with links to both the Inter-American Commission on Human Rights and the Inter-American Court of Human Rights at: www.oas.org/OASpage/humanrights.htm.

87 Nowak, 'The Right to Reparation for Victims of Gross Human Rights Violations', p. 281.

88 *Loayza Tamayo* v. *Peru*, IACtHR, Judgment (Reparations), 27 November 1998, Ser. C, No. 42, para. 169; *Blake* v. *Guatemala*, IACtHR, Judgment, 22 January 1999, para. 63. Discussed in Shelton, *Remedies in International Human Rights Law*, p. 140.

judges also has approximately six times as many staff.[89] During the IACtHR's first decade of existence it only emitted twenty judgments; however, since 2005 it has decided around fifteen cases per year and many of the cases have related to collective victims' claims. In order to expedite the number of cases, both courts have moved towards including their decision on reparations within the main judgment rather than as a subsequent separate stage of proceedings. Within the Inter-American system, Advisory Opinions of the IACtHR have played an important role in the interpretation of the obligations contained in the Convention. This possibility also exists in the European system, but has not been a prominent feature.[90]

While the European system has developed a legal aid programme and the ECtHR awards successful applicants the recovery of legal costs, this was not initially applied in the Inter-American system despite the starker socio-economic realities in the region. The IACtHR presumed that the Commission, when bringing the case to the court, would act on behalf of the victims and failed to see the importance of independent representation for victims, especially at the reparations stage. This was, however, amended in 1998 when the IACtHR adopted new Rules of Procedure, which also allowed for the presence of victims during the reparations stage of proceedings.[91]

Already in the first judgment of the IACtHR emitted in 1988, *Velásquez Rodríguez* v. *Honduras*, relating to the disappearance of a university student in 1981, the much-cited dictum had been established by affirming positive obligations of the state:

The obligation of the States Parties is to 'ensure' the free and full exercise of the rights recognised by the Convention to every person subject to its jurisdiction ... As a consequence of this obligation, the States must prevent, investigate and punish any violation of the rights recognised by the Convention and, moreover, if possible attempt to restore the right violated and provide compensation as warranted for damages resulting from the violation ... Reparation of harm brought about by the violation of an international obligation consists in full restitution (*restitutio in integrum*), which includes the restoration of the prior situation, the reparation of the consequences of the violation, and

[89] C. Heyns, D. Padilla and L. Zwaak, 'A Schematic Comparison of Regional Human Rights Systems', *African Human Rights Law Journal*, 5(2) (2005), 308–20.

[90] Van Dijk and Van Hoof, *Theory and Practice of the European Convention on Human Rights*, p. 690.

[91] Shelton, *Remedies in International Human Rights Law*, pp. 378–9; Pasqualucci, 'Victim Reparations in the Inter-American Human Rights System', p. 47.

indemnification for patrimonial and non-patrimonial damages, including emotional harm.[92]

The IACtHR set important precedents in its early jurisprudence with regard to reparations, for example, in *Aloeboetoe et al.* v. *Suriname*.[93] In the judgment, the court, in addition to financial compensation to relatives, also awarded measures of a collective nature, including the setting up of a school and a medical dispensary, which previously were unavailable in the rural area of the tribe.[94]

In the case of *Loayza Tamayo* v. *Peru*,[95] a university professor was arbitrarily detained in 1993 upon suspicion of collaborating with the Shining Path (guerrilla group). She was sentenced in a military trial by faceless judges and subjected to torture. In the judgment the IACtHR expanded on the spectrum of reparations. In addition to pecuniary and moral damages, it ordered the state to provide restitution by reinstating her in her teaching position at the university, to provide support for medical rehabilitation, to publicly apologise in the major newspapers in order to clear her name, and to bring its anti-terrorist legislation in line with the provisions of the Convention.[96] Furthermore, the judgment invented the concept of *proyecto de vida* (life plan), which seeks to establish compensation for damages to the victim's professional and personal development.[97] The concept has been difficult to define and has rarely been resorted to in subsequent jurisprudence.[98] Nevertheless, it may be noted that the ECtHR has applied similar reasoning judgments in relation to the loss of earnings of victims, for example, as seen above in *Isayeva* v. *Russia*.

[92] *Velásquez Rodríguez* v. *Honduras*, IACtHR, Judgment, 29 July 1988, Ser. C, No. 4, paras 166–7; *Velásquez Rodríguez* v. *Honduras*, IACtHR, Judgment (Reparations), 21 July 1989, Ser. C, No. 7, para. 26.

[93] *Aloeboetoe et al.* v. *Suriname*, IACtHR, Judgment (Reparations), 10 September 1993, Ser. C, No. 15. The case involved the killing by the army of members of a maroon tribe (descendants of African slaves that live traditionally in the jungle), in total six men and a minor. In 1988, they were beaten in front of the community, taken away, forced to dig their own graves and executed.

[94] Shelton, *Remedies in International Human Rights Law*, pp. 244–5.

[95] *Loayza Tamayo* v. *Peru*, IACtHR, Judgment (Reparations), 27 November 1998, Ser. C, No. 42.

[96] J. Pasqualucci, *The Practice and Procedure of the Inter-American Court of Human Rights* (Cambridge University Press, 2003), p. 248.

[97] A. Carrillo, 'Justice in Context: The Relevance of Inter-American Human Rights Law and Practice to Repairing the Past', in P. De Greiff (ed.), *The Handbook of Reparations* (Oxford University Press, 2006), pp. 504–38.

[98] Shelton, *Remedies in International Human Rights Law*, pp. 314–16.

Among later jurisprudence, the IACtHR has been presented with the challenge of deciding cases relating to massacres involving large numbers of victims. The atrocities of the case *Massacre Plan de Sánchez* v. *Guatemala*[99] occurred in a Mayan indigenous village during the civil war in 1982. As part of the scorched earth policy applied by the military dictatorship at the time, the village was surrounded by the army and paramilitary units (PAC) and around 280 people were executed, many of whom were women and children. The children were saved until last and forced to watch the atrocities. The massacre was one of 626 massacres documented by the United Nations Truth Commission in Guatemala (CEH), which is further discussed in Part II of this book. The CEH report, published in 1999, estimated that approximately 200,000 people were killed during the armed conflict in Guatemala. Furthermore, the report noted that the vast majority of victims had been indigenous and concluded that the state had conducted a policy of genocide.[100] The above case presented the IACtHR with a very particular challenge of awarding fair reparations and also highlights the difficulties faced by victims of similar violations who had been unable to litigate their case. The case set an important precedent by recognising the community as beneficiary of collective reparations and by recognising that there may be individuals who could not be identified among the victims.[101] The IACtHR ordered in its judgment in 2004 that the state, in addition to compensation, should undertake a series of measures aimed at achieving restitution, rehabilitation and satisfaction through acknowledgement. The measures included a public act of recognition in the village, translation of the Convention and judgment into indigenous languages, the provision of free medical and psychological services, and in particular to undertake efforts to promote indigenous culture by the establishment of an educational institution. As for restitution, the state was requested to ensure that all survivors from the village be guaranteed a decent standard of living with access to clean water. In a concurring opinion attached to the judgment, Judge Cançado Trindade affirmed that the nature of

[99] *Plan de Sánchez Massacre* v. *Guatemala*, IACtHR, Judgment, 29 April 2004, Ser. C, No. 105.

[100] The United Nations Guatemalan Truth Commission report (1999) is available at: http://shr.aaas.org/guatemala/ceh/report/english/toc.html.

[101] C. Sandoval-Villalba, 'The Concepts of "Injured Party" and "Victim" of Gross Human Rights Violations in the Jurisprudence of the Inter-American Court of Human Rights: A Commentary on their Implications for Reparations', in C. Ferstman, M. Goetz and A. Stephens (eds), *Reparations for Victims of Genocide, War Crimes and Crimes against Humanity, Systems in Place and Systems in the Making* (Leiden: Martinus Nijhoff, 2009), pp. 243–82.

the violations indicated an aggravated responsibility of the state,[102] however, the judgment omits reference to the genocide charge presented in the UN Truth Commission report.[103] Due to the affirmation of genocide by the Truth Commission, the state was reluctant to assume responsibility for the Plan de Sánchez massacre, but gradually relented.[104] Following the judgment, the vice president visited the village, paid his respects at the mass exhumation site and apologised directly to the community. Parts of the judgment were translated into the local Mayan language, Achí.[105]

Regarding compensation, the Guatemalan State basically complied with the order of the IACtHR and paid US$25,000 for each of the 236 victims, in total an amount of US$5.9 million. Unfortunately, the payment of such a large sum to individual members of the indigenous community resulted in significant divisions within the community and with neighbouring villages. Unprepared to receive such sums, some victims, many of them illiterate, squandered the amount and others were victims of attacks, probably because the state had published information on how the payments would be realised. To avoid this scenario, in subsequent cases relating to indigenous communities the IACtHR attempted to resort to measures such as the establishment of trust funds.

During the past few years, the Guatemalan State has adopted a policy of friendly settlements for a significant number of cases, and in 2003 established a national programme for reparations as a way to ward off cases being brought to the Inter-American human rights system. The national reparations programme, one of the recommendations of the UN Truth Commission, is further discussed in Part II. While the amounts foreseen by the national reparations programme are significantly less than those awarded by the IACtHR, the experience in Guatemala highlights the nexus between the regional human rights system and its

102 Judge Cançado Trindade's concurring opinion is available at the end of the judgment (Spanish only), available at: www.corteidh.or.cr/docs/casos/articulos/seriec_116_esp1.doc.

103 K. Dill, 'Reparation and the Elusive Meaning of Justice in Guatemala', in B. Johnston and S. Slyomovics (eds), *Waging War, Making Peace, Reparations and Human Rights* (Walnut Creek, CA: Left Coast Press, 2009), pp. 183–204.

104 M. Mersky and N. Roht-Arriaza, '"Case Study Guatemala" in Due Process of Law Foundation', *Victims Unsilenced: The Inter-American Human Rights System and Transitional Justice in Latin America* (Washington, DC: DPLF, 2007), pp. 7–32.

105 F. La Rue, Speech at Conference on Reparations in the Inter-American System, American University, Washington, 6 March 2007, published in *American University Law Review*, 56 (2007), 1459–63.

impact on the overall policy of the state regarding reparations. While this development is largely very positive, the discrepancies between the amounts awarded for the same type of serious violations will continue to pose a challenge in the future and it is likely to result in friction between victims due to their unequal treatment.

In another case involving a massacre in Colombia, *Mapiripán Massacre* v. *Colombia*,[106] the IACtHR established that the state party was responsible for the extrajudicial executions of some forty-nine people, although the actual killings were perpetrated by paramilitaries (AUC). The AUC surrounded the village of Mapiripán during six days in 1997 and proceeded to identify suspected guerrilla collaborators, who were executed, dismembered and whose bodies were thrown in the river. The IACtHR found proof that the military had collaborated and deliberately failed to prevent or stop the massacre, having assisted in the transportation of the paramilitaries to the village and disregarded the pleas for help by civilian authorities during the first days of the massacre. The IACtHR in its judgment of 2005 raised serious concerns over the lack of investigations into the case and the extensive delay caused by remitting it to the military justice system, which was clearly unsuitable to conduct an impartial investigation. Furthermore, the IACtHR made reference to the Justice and Peace Law 975 of 2005 (discussed in detail in Chapter 10). While the IACtHR declined to make an express assessment of the law, it nevertheless underlined the incompatibility of amnesties with international human rights obligations for serious violations.[107] Regarding reparations, in addition to financial compensation, the IACtHR ordered the state party to pay particular attention to the rights of relatives of the victims by ensuring proper identification of all victims, to provide adequate medical and psychological assistance for their families, and to offer a public apology as well as a remembrance monument and human rights training for members of the military. The case provided an important precedent regarding the responsibility of the state to demonstrate due diligence and assume its positive obligations to protect and prevent violations, even in the context of armed conflict. Finally, the concurring separate opinion of Judge Cançado Trindade underlined the complementarity of state responsibility and international criminal responsibility of individuals, no doubt hinting at the 'warning letter'

[106] *Mapiripán Massacre* v. *Colombia*, IACtHR, Judgment, 15 September 2005, Ser. C, No. 134.

[107] D. Rodriquez Pinzon, Speech at Conference on Reparations in the Inter-American System, American University, Washington, 6 March 2007, published in *American University Law Review*, 56 (2007), 1390–6.

sent to the Colombian government by the International Criminal Court in early 2005 against the backdrop of the concurrent negotiations with the paramilitaries.[108]

The above two cases relating to massacres illustrate some of the challenges in providing redress when many victims have suffered similar violations to the cases brought before the IACtHR. While in the European system the repetition of resembling cases is a major concern, nevertheless the ECtHR has considerably better capacity to deal with the rising number of cases. In the Inter-American system it is simply not feasible for many victims to present their claims nor is there capacity to process a large influx of cases. Some observers have suggested that the creation of a claims fund for victims under the auspices of the IACtHR might be an option to obtain better equity; however, this proposal has not yet been developed.[109]

As regards the application of international humanitarian law, the Inter-American system has taken an ambivalent position. The Inter-American Commission has referred to international humanitarian law in several cases that have subsequently been referred to the IACtHR. However, in the final judgments the IACtHR has declined to confirm the reference to this branch of law other than as a tool of interpretation or in passing in separate opinions of the judges.[110] In the case of *Las Palmeras* v. *Colombia*,[111] relating to the extrajudicial execution of six civilians, who were later dressed in military uniforms by the army and presented as subversives killed in combat, the state party opposed the reference to humanitarian law. However, judges Cançado Trindade and Pacheco-Gómez noted in a separate opinion attached to the judgment that humanitarian law offers parallel duties to human rights law and that these simply reinforce the obligations by which the state party has to abide. Thus, the Inter-American human rights system has explored the notion of state responsibility in situations of armed conflict by drawing from principles of international humanitarian law, and has made

[108] Judge Cançado Trindade's concurring opinion is available at the end of the judgment (Spanish only), available at: www.corteidh.or.cr/docs/casos/articulos/seriec_134_esp1.doc.

[109] Pasqualucci, 'Victim Reparations in the Inter-American Human Rights System', p. 23.

[110] C. McCarthy, 'Human Rights and the Laws of War under the American Convention on Human Rights', *European Human Rights Law Review*, 6 (2008), pp. 762–80.

[111] *Las Palmeras* v. *Colombia*, IACtHR, Judgment, 6 December 2001, Ser. C, No. 90. Case discussed in Lubell, 'Challenges in Applying Human Rights Law to Armed Conflict', p. 742 and in Pisillo Mazzeschi, 'Reparation Claims by Individuals for State Breaches of Humanitarian Law and Human Rights', p. 343.

important contributions to the notion of responsibility resulting from omission to prevent as well as complicity with non-state actors.[112]

One aspect that differs from the European system is the approach to the non-pecuniary damage inflicted upon relatives of victims. While the ECtHR has applied certain criteria and at times exercised judgment with respect to the level of suffering of relatives,[113] the IACtHR on the contrary has taken a more generous approach, whereby the suffering of family members of victims does not require proof or an assessment of the moral character of the victims.[114]

As noted above, the IACtHR has from its inception taken a very creative approach to reparations and has sought to interpret the concept as broadly as possible. It has attempted to specify concrete reparations with particular emphasis on aspects of satisfaction and guarantees of non-repetition. Particular attention has been paid to ordering concrete reparations measures in favour of victims, such as remembrance monuments, public apologies and provision of access to education and medical services. Consequently, the IACtHR has played a significant role in developing jurisprudence in relation to reparations and has extensively widened the concept, which only later gained recognition as a comprehensive concept within the UN human rights system.

Furthermore, the IACtHR has taken into account socio-economic realities and cultural considerations, in particular, the relevance of reparations for victims of large-scale violations in the context of armed conflict, and has paid particular attention to the vulnerability of minorities and indigenous peoples. The IACtHR has developed innovative measures to provide collective redress, for example, in relation to claims from indigenous peoples who have suffered serious human rights violations.[115] Reparations may be distributed through tripartite trust funds and the IACtHR itself seeks to monitor compliance with judgments and can, in accordance with Article 65 of the Convention, submit a report to the General Assembly of the Organization of American States specifying cases in which the state has not complied with its judgments. However,

[112] See discussion in Zegveld, 'Remedies for Victims of Violations of International Humanitarian Law', pp. 497–526.

[113] Shelton, *Remedies in International Human Rights Law*, p. 242.

[114] Pasqualucci, *The Practice and Procedure of the Inter-American Court of Human Rights*, p. 268.

[115] *Aloeboetoe et al.* v. *Suriname*, IACtHR (Reparations), Ser. C, No. 15, 1993; *Mayagna Awas Tingni* v. *Nicaragua*, IACtHR, Ser. C, No. 79, 2001; *Yakye Axa Indigenous Community* v. *Paraguay*, IACtHR (Reparations), Ser. C, No. 142, 2006; *Moiwana Community* v. *Suriname*, IACtHR (Reparations), Ser. C, No. 145, 2006.

it remains a weakness that the Inter-American system lacks an entity to explicitly supervise the execution of judgments, such as the Committee of Ministers of the Council of Europe.

3.5 The African system for human rights protection

The human rights system in Africa is the youngest of the regional mechanisms. The African Charter on Human and Peoples' Rights entered into force in 1986 and the African Commission on Human and Peoples' Rights (ACHPR) was established in 1987 within the framework of the Organisation of African Unity (in 2001 transformed into the African Union (AU)).[116] In January 2004, the Protocol on the African Court and Peoples' Rights entered into force; however, the court only became gradually operational in 2009.

Unlike the other international and regional human rights instruments referred to previously, the African Charter contains no clear provision on individual complaints and lacks a general reference to the right to a remedy for violations. Nonetheless, the Commission has interpreted the provision on 'communications other than those of States parties' in Article 55 of the Charter to refer to the possibility of receiving complaints from individuals and NGOs.[117] Furthermore, the African Charter, unlike the United Nations human rights treaties and the European Convention on Human Rights, contains no specific provision regarding individual victim requirement (i.e., that the applicant must be directly affected by the violation). This has permitted NGOs, both national and international, to submit cases to the African Commission and has allowed for the review of cases relating to large-scale human rights abuses. In practice, the Commission has tended to combine various complaints that allege related violations in the same country.

The Commission emits its recommendations on cases in conjunction with the publication of its annual session report; however, according to

[116] C. Heyns (ed.), *Compendium of Key Human Rights Documents of the African Union* (Pretoria University Law Press, 2005); R. Murray, *Human Rights in Africa: From OAU to AU* (Cambridge University Press, 2004). Further information can be found at the official web page of the African Commission on Human and Peoples' Rights: www.achpr.org.

[117] O. Umozurike, 'The Complaint Procedures of the African Commission on Human and Peoples' Rights', in G. Alfredsson, J. Grimheden, B. Ramcharan and A. de Zayas (eds), *International Human Rights Monitoring Mechanisms* (The Hague: Kluwer Law International, 2001), pp. 713–30; F. Viljoen, 'Admissibility under the African Charter', in M. Evans and R. Murray (eds), *The African Charter on Human and Peoples' Rights, the System in Practice 1986–2000* (Cambridge University Press, 2002), pp. 61–99.

Article 59 of the African Charter, the cases remain confidential until approval has been given by the AU Assembly of Heads of State and Government.[118] The recommendations are quasi-judicial in nature, analogous to those of the United Nations treaty bodies, such as the Human Rights Committee.[119] It is significant that by mid 2010, the Commission had only issued sixty decisions in total. The Commission has affirmed in its decisions that it expects the states parties to comply with its findings and recommendations, yet the compliance rate remains poor.[120]

The issue of reparations has so far received insufficient attention in the jurisprudence of the African Commission and the approach has been incoherent.[121] Alarmingly, in some cases where serious human rights violations have been found, no reparations figure at all.

In an early case, *Commission Nacionale des Droits de l'Homme et des Libertés* v. *Chad*,[122] decided in 1995, the Commission found numerous cases of extrajudicial killings, disappearances and torture. The state argued that violations had taken place in the context of armed conflict and were the responsibility of parties other than the state. The Commission, however, affirmed that while it 'could not be proved that violations were committed by government agents, the government had a responsibility to secure the safety and the liberty of its citizens, and to conduct investigations into murders'. The decision set an important precedent in affirming the positive duty of the state to prevent violations by non-state actors[123] and is consistent with jurisprudence of the international treaty bodies and two other regional human rights systems above discussed. The Commission also noted that the African Charter has no derogation clause 'thus, even a civil war in Chad cannot be used as an excuse for the State violating or permitting violations of rights'. The decision

118 N. Udombana, 'So Far So Fair: The Local Remedies Rule in the Jurisprudence of the African Commission of Human and Peoples' Rights', *American Journal of International Law*, 97(1) (2003), pp. 1–37.

119 G. Naldi, 'Reparations in the Practice of the African Commission on Human and Peoples' Rights', *Leiden Journal of International Law*, 14 (2001), p. 684.

120 Udombana, 'So Far So Fair', pp. 1–37.

121 Naldi, 'Reparations in the Practice of the African Commission on Human and Peoples' Rights', pp. 681–93; Open Society Justice Initiative, *From Judgment to Justice*, pp. 93–115.

122 *Commission Nationale des Droits de l'Homme et des Libertés* v. *Chad*, Communication 74/92, decided 18th Ordinary Session October 1995, 9th Annual Activity Report.

123 C. Heyns, 'Civil and Political Rights in the African Charter', in M. Evans and R. Murray (eds), *The African Charter on Human and Peoples' Rights, the System in Practice 1986–2000* (Cambridge University Press, 2002), p. 148; Clapham, *Human Rights Obligations of Non-State Actors*, pp. 433–4.

concluded that there have been serious and massive violations of human rights in Chad, however, it was completely silent regarding the duty of the state to guarantee non-repetition and reparation measures.

In the case *Organisation Mondiale Contre la Torture and Others* v. *Rwanda*,[124] decided in 1996, the Commission combined several complaints documenting a series of different violations, primarily relating to ethnically motivated massacres and extrajudicial killings by armed state forces between 1989 and 1992. While the Commission concluded findings of serious or massive violations, the decision contains no reference to victims' right to reparation and only 'urged the government of Rwanda to adopt measures in conformity with the decision', without providing any guidance on what such measures should entail. This example is paradigmatic in illustrating the African regional human rights system's failure to address reparations and its inability to thereby influence the discourse on reparations at the national level.[125]

In 1999, the Commission decided a series of combined communications in *Amnesty International and Others* v. *Sudan*.[126] The complaints described numerous serious violations that took place in different parts of the country, primarily between 1989 and 1993. Among the violations figured cases of extrajudicial and summary execution, torture and discrimination on the basis of religion.[127] The Commission concluded that the government had been sufficiently aware of the situation prevailing within its territory as well as the content of its international obligations and that despite the civil war: 'civilians in areas of strife are especially vulnerable and the state must take all possible measures to ensure that

124 *Organisation Mondiale Contre la Torture and Association Internationale des Juristes Democrates, International Commission of Jurists, Union Africaine des Droits de l'Homme* v. *Rwanda*, Communications 27/89, 49/91 and 99/93, decided 20th Ordinary Session, October 1996, 10th Annual Activity Report.

125 'Contrary to the important impact of the regional human rights protection mechanisms in several European and Latin American cases, it may be concluded that, in the case of Rwanda, the regional level has had no impact at all in terms of reparations', in H. Rombouts and S. Vandeginste, 'Reparation to Victims in Rwanda: Caught between Theory and Practice', in K. De Feyter, S. Parmentier, M. Bossuyt and P. Lemmens (eds), *Out of the Ashes, Reparation for Victims of Gross and Systematic Human Rights Violations* (Antwerp: Intersentia, 2005), p. 319.

126 *Amnesty International, Comite Loosli Bachelard, Lawyers Committee for Human Rights, Association of Members of the Episcopal Conference of East Africa* v. *Sudan*, Communications 48/90, 50/91, 52/91, 89/93, decided 26th Ordinary Session, November 1999, 13th Annual Activity Report.

127 For a critical discussion of the case see R. Murray, 'Current Developments, Recent Decisions of the African Commission on Human and Peoples' Rights', *South African Journal on Human Rights*, 17 (2001), 146–56.

they are treated in accordance with international humanitarian law'. The reference to humanitarian law is novel, however, the Commission did not explore further on the implications of this affirmation. The Commission finally, rather flatly, recommended: 'strongly to the government of Sudan to put an end to the violations in order to abide by its obligations under the African Charter'. Given the gravity of the violations found, it is highly questionable that the Commission did not provide further details and orientation in relation to the obligations of the state party to prevent, ensure non-repetition and provide reparations for the victims.

The case *Malawi African Association and Others* v. *Mauritania*,[128] constitutes a significant leap forward with regard to reparations for serious human rights violations in the African regional system. The complaints again consist of a range of massive violations relating, for example, to extrajudicial executions, disappearances, torture and slavery. In the decision of 2000, the Commission declared that grave and massive human rights violations took place between 1989 and 1992 and recommended a series of concrete reparations measures, including: the establishment of an independent inquiry into disappearances; the replacement of identity cards and reparations for people forcibly expelled; appropriate measures to ensure payment of a compensatory benefit to widows and other beneficiaries of victims of violations; the carrying out of an assessment of degrading practices with a view to identifying the deep-rooted causes and putting into place a strategy aimed at their eradication; and measures to effectively enforce the abolition of slavery. The case stands out as a positive example among the regional jurisprudence in its detailed list of reparations measures.[129] Regrettably, the case has not yet managed to establish a model for comprehensive reparations by the African Commission as subsequent jurisprudence has reverted to more spartan decisions.[130] Nevertheless, given the focus on systematic human rights violations in the African

[128] *Malawi African Association, Amnesty International, Ms Sarr Diop, Union Interafricaine des Droits de l'Homme and RADDHO, Collectif des Veuves et Ayants-droit and Association Mauritanienne des Droits de l'Homme* v. *Mauritania*, Communications 54/91, 61/91, 98/93, 164–96/97 and 210/98, decided 27th Ordinary Session, May 2000, 13th Annual Activity Report.

[129] Murray, 'Current Developments, Recent Decisions of the African Commission on Human and Peoples' Rights', p. 169.

[130] For example, in *African Institute for Human Rights and development (on behalf of Sierra Leonian refugees in Guinea)* v. *Republic of Guinea*, Communication 249/2002, decided 36th Ordinary Session, December 2004, 20th Activity Report (the decision is ambivalent, although it recognises massive violations there is no conclusive affirmation of the

system, the Commission in the *Malawi African Association and Others* v. *Mauritania* demonstrated its potential to interpret reparations in a broad manner so as to respond to the seriousness of the violations.

In the jurisprudence of a more recent case, the *Association of Victims of Post Electoral Violence & Interrights* v. *Cameroon*,[131] relating to post-election violence in 1992, the Commission held that victims should receive fair and equitable compensation; however, it added the caveat that the amount be fixed 'in accordance with applicable laws'.[132] The victims are thereby forced to revert to the national judicial system, which for two decades had proved itself unable to address the case.

As a distinction between the African system and other regional systems and that of the United Nations treaty body system, one can make the following observation: namely, that the African Commission initially adopted a particularly conservative approach to the issue of reparations. Early jurisprudence by the African Commission simply failed to consider reparations. The language of the African Commission is significantly weaker than that of, for example, the Human Rights Committee, which consistently affirms the individual's right to a remedy.[133] Yet the African Commission, when faced with numerous cases of serious human rights violations, has taken an innovative approach to exploring policy-oriented and collective reparations measures. Furthermore, the African Commission has openly cited humanitarian law in its jurisprudence, indicating a progressive approach to using this branch of law as a reference tool. The challenge, on the other hand, remains in relation to implementation and, in particular, to enforce collective and policy-oriented recommendations for reparations at the individual level, a particular challenge as the victims are not identified.

At the practical level, a major challenge to the effectiveness of the African Commission has been the lack of resources of its Secretariat, which consists of a small group of professional legal staff. The Commissioners, eleven in total, meet at the sessions of the Commission, which

rights of victims, yet there is a brief recommendation that a Commission be established to assess losses by victims).

131 *Association of Victims of Post Electoral Violence & Interrights* v. *Cameroon*, Communication 272/2003, decided at the 46th Ordinary Session, November 2009, 27th Activity Report.

132 J. Biegon and M. Killander, 'Human Rights Developments in the African Union during 2009', *African Human Rights Law Journal*, 10 (2010), 212–28.

133 Naldi, 'Reparations in the Practice of the African Commission on Human and Peoples' Rights', p. 692.

normally take place twice a year.[134] The Commission has gradually dedicated further attention to the challenges in enforcing and following-up on recommendations at the national level. In November 2006, the Commission adopted a resolution specifically requesting states parties to provide information on implementation of recommendations and affirming that the Commission intends to compile reports on compliance.[135]

In 2004, the Protocol establishing the African Court of Human and Peoples' Rights entered into force.[136] During 2009, the court was set up in Tanzania, a great distance from the Commission, which is based in the Gambia. Concern has been raised over the delays in establishing the court[137] and over the decision to merge it with the Court of Justice of the African Union.[138] Regarding admissibility of cases, the court will act as a second instance in a manner analogous to that of the Inter-American human rights system.[139] Only in exceptional cases will petitioners be able to file cases directly to the court, pending whether the state party in question deposited a declaration to this effect upon ratification of the Protocol.[140]

Lack of clarity remains regarding the future relationship between the Commission and the court[141] and some fears have been expressed over

[134] Heyns Padilla and Zwaak, 'A Schematic Comparison of Regional Human Rights Systems', pp. 308–20.

[135] Resolution on the Importance of the Implementation of the Recommendations of the African Commission on Human and Peoples' Rights by States Parties, adopted by the African Commission at its 40th Ordinary Session in Banjul, 29 November 2006, available at: www.achpr.org/english/resolutions/resolution102_en.html.

[136] Fifteen state party ratifications were required for the Protocol to enter into force. As of 1 May 2011, twenty-five out of fifty-three states in Africa had ratified the Protocol to the Charter.

[137] R. Murray, 'Recent Developments in the African Human Rights System 2007', *Human Rights Law Journal*, 8(2) (2008), 356–76.

[138] This will occur when the Protocol on the Statute of the African Court of Justice and Human Rights, adopted by the Assembly of the African Union on 1 July 2008, enters into force.

[139] D. Padilla, 'An African Human Rights Court: Reflections from the Perspective of the Inter-American System', *African Human Rights Law Journal*, 2(2) (2002), 185–94.

[140] Article 34(6) of the Protocol. Further discussion in A. Pieter van der Mei, 'The New African Court on Human and Peoples' Rights; Towards an Effective Human Rights Protection Mechanism for Africa?', *Leiden Journal of International Law*, 18 (2005), 112–29.

[141] J. Sarkin, 'The Role of Regional Systems in Enforcing State Human Rights Compliance: Evaluating the African Commission on Human and Peoples' Rights and the New African Court of Justice and Human Rights with Comparative Lessons from the Council of Europe and the Organization of American States', *Inter-American and European Human Rights Journal*, 1(2) (2008), 199–242.

the referral power of cases, which potentially could end up as a legal ping pong on politically sensitive cases.[142] On a positive note, the Protocol contains some very progressive provisions, for example, allowing the court to apply as sources of law, in addition to the Charter, 'any other relevant human rights instrument'.[143] Finally, it has been noted that Article 27 of the Protocol contains what might be considered one of the most progressive and broadest provisions regarding reparations: 'If the Court finds that there has been violation of a human or peoples' rights, it shall make appropriate orders to remedy the violation, including the payment of fair compensation or reparation', potentially allowing the future court to play a pioneering role in this respect.[144] Major challenges, however, persist in the African human rights system, principal among them being inadequate political will to place human rights as a priority. Notably, in the transition from the Organisation of African Unity to the African Union, the Constitutive Act of 2000 failed to recognise the African Commission on Human and Peoples' Rights as one of the principal organs, which in turn reflects the inadequate importance given to human rights protection in the region.

3.6 Conclusions

The comparison of jurisprudence of the international and regional human rights systems reveals that the approach to reparations varies considerably depending on the applicable provision on reparations as well as the mandate and interpretation given by the relevant committee, court or commission. Clearly, the regional human rights courts wield great advantages in their authority to order legally binding judgments; this has resulted in a significantly high compliance rate on reparations compared with the United Nations treaty bodies. Although the jurisprudence contains variations, there is convergence within the international and regional systems on key points, such as the affirmation of positive obligations of the state and the responsibility to prevent and protect against violations, including those committed by non-state actors in the

[142] Articles 5 and 6 of the Protocol. Further discussion in E. De Wet, 'The Protection Mechanism under the African Charter and the Protocol on the African Court of Human and Peoples' Rights', in G. Alfredsson, J. Grimheden, B. Ramcharan and A. de Zayas (eds), *International Human Rights Monitoring Mechanisms* (The Hague: Kluwer Law International, 2001), pp. 713–30.

[143] Article 7 of the Protocol.

[144] Shelton, *Remedies in International Human Rights Law*, p. 226.

context of armed conflict. As demonstrated in Chapter 2, this is consistent with, and has most likely supported, the position taken by the International Law Commission in its 2001 Articles on State Responsibility.

In cases where violations have occurred in the context of armed conflict, the analysis in the jurisprudence shows increasing recognition of, and reference to, principles of international humanitarian law. As demonstrated in Chapter 2, this reinforces the legal argument for reparations as it unites claims under the two branches of law. Furthermore, consideration of humanitarian law principles, such as distinction and proportionality, would assist in determining the responsibility of the state in preventing and responding to attacks that result in civilian casualties.

The international and regional systems also differ regarding whether they consider individual or collective reparations measures. The United Nations treaty body system considers both aspects; while the decisions on individual petitions tend to take a restrictive approach, a more collective policy-oriented approach is applied in the recommendations contained in Concluding Observations. The European human rights system is faced with a sharp increase in cases, of which an increasing number have occurred in the context of armed conflict. While the European Court of Human Rights has traditionally been conservative with regard to reparations, it is important to acknowledge the precedent-setting role of the ECtHR and that it over time has developed an extensive and more victim-oriented jurisprudence. The ECtHR is gradually moving towards emitting policy-oriented judgments in order to address the overlap and backlog of cases. The Inter-American human rights system has been of key importance due to its demonstrated focus on ordering detailed and specific reparations measures in favour of victims and their relatives. The Inter-American Court of Human Rights has played a leading role in expanding the concept of reparations regarding satisfaction and guarantees of non-repetition and its recent jurisprudence has established groundbreaking collective measures, which take into account the socio-economic conditions of the victims. Such measures are clearly deemed to be of particular importance for victims of serious human rights violations in the context of armed conflict. The African human rights system is still developing its position with regard to reparations; the Commission initially lacked consideration for reparations, however, jurisprudence indicates a gradual shift and the court, which is just becoming operational, has the potential to offer a broad and innovative approach to reparations for victims.

The jurisprudence reviewed in the present chapter indicates the significant jurisprudential progress made towards ordering comprehensive victim-oriented reparations measures; however, it also points towards the need to further develop, clarify and consolidate the concept of reparations. While the provisions on remedies in the different instruments vary, the interpretation of them by the various treaty bodies, courts and commissions would benefit from harmonisation and by drawing on each other's best practices. Certain concerns have been expressed over the current development of divergent jurisprudence on reparations.[145] In view of the backlog of cases confronting both the international and regional systems, it is submitted that particular consideration should be given to addressing collective claims, which would allow the identification of systematic practices and underscore state responsibility to cease violations, comply with remedies and ensure non-repetition. Nevertheless, it is important that a policy-oriented approach to reparations in jurisprudence should complement, but not substitute, individualised awards in order to retain focus on the victims directly affected and ensure that they are ultimately recognised as beneficiaries. It is essential that reparations measures be developed as victim-oriented, comprehensive and specific as possible. The principal challenge for all the human rights systems is ensuring a high compliance rate among states parties. In order to do so, judgments must contain detailed reparation awards, as this allows for follow-up on the implementation at the national level and, most importantly, lies in the interest of furthering the rights of victims of serious human rights violations. While the responsibility to provide reparations principally remains the duty of the state, it may be argued that the international community bears positive obligations to assist developing states in fulfilling their responsibilities, and therefore consideration should be given to the establishment of trust funds within the regional human rights systems to support the effective implementation of reparation measures.

The standards established by the international and regional human rights systems provide the norm-setting basis for Part II on the practical challenges involved in the implementation of reparations in countries that have endured armed conflict. Identification of specific linkages between human rights mechanisms and standards will be made in

[145] A. Cutter Patel, Deputy Director of the International Centre for Transitional Justice (ICTJ), Interview in ICTJ Newsletter, *Transitions*, January 2010, available at: www.ictj.org.

relation to transitional and post-conflict justice initiatives. Chapter 4, the final chapter in Part I, explores the gradual development of the right to reparation in international criminal law. In particular, the influences of human rights law are highlighted, as these have provided key impetus towards the recent recognition and gradual implementation of victims' rights.

4 Reparations in international criminal law

4.1 Introduction

The objective of this chapter is to chart the origins and the gradual development of reparation provisions in international criminal law and consider their contribution to the standing and rights of victims of armed conflict in international law.

Until the adoption of the Rome Statute of the International Criminal Court, the rights of victims in international criminal proceedings were largely marginalised. Reparation provisions in international criminal law have evolved at a slower pace than corresponding rights in human rights law. This development can partly be explained by the significant influence of municipal criminal law in the evolution of this sphere in international law. While it has been argued that international criminal law can now provide the bite that international human rights law has lacked,[1] one notes that from a victim's perspective, experiences seeking reparations to date have been more successful on the basis of human rights law. Expectations are high that the emerging practice of the International Criminal Court (ICC) and its Trust Fund will provide a radical shift in favour of victims. However, it is submitted that responsibility for reparations should maintain an element of state responsibility, as those considered to have carried the greatest responsibility for serious violations may have exercised functions of state authority. There are inherent dangers in shifting responsibility from states towards individuals, as this may ultimately leave victims without redress. While the shift towards recognising victims and their right to reparation in international criminal law is welcome and positive, ideally this should operate alongside measures to establish state responsibility vis-à-vis victims.

[1] G. Simpson, *Law, War and Crime* (Cambridge: Polity Press, 2007), p. 57.

Following a largely chronological order, the chapter identifies the gradual incorporation of reparation provisions in international criminal law. In particular, the chapter studies the provisions and practice of the International Criminal Tribunals for the Former Yugoslavia (ICTY) and Rwanda (ICTR), and the impetus that resulted in the groundbreaking provisions in the Rome Statute of the ICC. Consideration is given to the influences prompting the recognition of victims' rights in international criminal law, which are traced to human rights law, the victimology movement, feminist interpretations of international law, as well as restorative justice theory and practice. Albeit delayed, the right of victims to claim reparations has now been established in international criminal law. This recognition largely took place due to influences from international and regional human rights treaties and jurisprudence, and, furthermore, sought inspiration from the development of the Basic Principles on the Right to Reparation for Victims.[2] The chapter identifies which elements of reparations have been addressed to date in the practice of international criminal law. Due to purposes of delimitation, procedural aspects of victim participation and witness protection are largely excluded. These aspects have been dealt with extensively by other authors.[3]

The chapter builds upon previous chapters and completes Part I on legal standards, which provides an overview of reparation provisions in different branches of international law and considers the current status of victims and their rights.

4.2 Origins of reparation provisions in international criminal law

Reparation provisions in international criminal law reflect a recent development. Their incorporation can in part be explained by growing

[2] UN Basic Principles and Guidelines on the Right to a Remedy and Reparation for Victims of Gross Violations of International Human Rights Law and Serious Violations of International Humanitarian Law, UN Doc. A/RES/60/147.

[3] Academic literature which addresses aspects of victim protection and participation includes, e.g.: H. Friman, 'The International Criminal Court and the Participation of Victims: A Third Party to the Proceedings?', *Leiden Journal of International Law*, 22 (2009), 485–500; C. McLaughlin, 'Victim and Witness Measures of the International Criminal Court: A Comparative Analysis', *The Law and Practice of International Courts and Tribunals*, 6 (2007), 189–220; D. Tolbert and F. Swinnen, 'The Protection of, and Assistance to, Witnesses at the ICTY', in H. Abtahi and G. Boas (eds), *The Dynamics of International Criminal Justice* (Leiden: Martinus Nijhoff, 2006), pp. 193–229; G. Sluiter, 'The ICTR and the Protection of Witnesses', *Journal of International Criminal Justice*, 3 (2005), 962–76; E. Haslam, 'Victim Participation at the International Criminal Court: A Triumph of Hope over Experience', in D. McGoldrick, P. Rome and E. Donnelly (eds), *The Permanent International Criminal Court, Legal and Policy Issues* (Oxford: Hart Publishing, 2004), pp. 315–34.

attention to victims within national criminal justice systems and also as a reaction to criticism of the manner in which victims' concerns were considered by the ICTY and the ICTR.[4]

When seeking to trace victims' provisions in international criminal law, it should be noted that the Nuremberg and Tokyo Charters did not even mention victims.[5] The Convention on the Prevention and Punishment of the Crime of Genocide obliges states parties to provide effective penalties, but is silent with regard to victims. Nevertheless, it is significant that the *travaux preparatoires* of the Convention, notably the draft Convention on the Crime of Genocide prepared by the Secretariat of the UN Secretary-General in 1947, contemplated a specific provision on reparation.[6] Draft Article XIII stated:

> When genocide is committed in a country by the government in power and by sections of the population, and if the government fails to resist it successfully, the State shall grant to the survivors of the human group that is a victim of genocide redress of a nature and in an amount to be determined by the United Nations.

Furthermore, the Official Comments on the Draft Convention by the Secretariat of the UN state: 'If the country in which genocide was committed is not to be held responsible for reparations, who is?'[7] The draft provision on reparation remained in early 1948; it was, however, lost in the final political negotiation process.[8] While the Genocide Convention, as adopted in December 1948, ultimately failed to contain a provision on redress and reparation, it is nevertheless significant

[4] L. Zegveld, 'Victims' Reparations Claims and International Criminal Courts, Incompatible Values?', *Journal of International Criminal Justice*, 8 (2010), 79–111; E. Stover, *The Witnesses, War Crimes and the Promise of Justice in the Hague* (Philadelphia, PA: University of Pennsylvania Press, 2005); Haslam, 'Victim Participation at the International Criminal Court', pp. 315–34.

[5] S. Zappala, *Human Rights in International Criminal Proceedings* (Oxford University Press, 2003), p. 220.

[6] Draft Convention on the Crime of Genocide, UN Doc. E/447, prepared 26 June 1947 by the Secretary-General upon request by the General Assembly. Among the states that supported the inclusion of a provision on reparation for victims were the United Kingdom, France, Belgium and Syria. The Official Comments on the Draft distinguished between criminal and civil state responsibility.

[7] The Official Comments by the Secretariat of the UN, contained in the Draft Convention on the Crime of Genocide, UN Doc. E/447, p. 48.

[8] See the French version of the Draft Convention; reparations still figured in Article 7, presented 9 February 1948, UN Doc. E/623/Add.1. The Genocide Convention as adopted in the General Assembly on 9 December 1948 contains no provision on reparations. See further discussion in W. Schabas, *Genocide in International Law, the Crime of Crimes* (Cambridge University Press, 2000), p. 400; H. Abtani and P. Webb, *The Genocide Convention, the Travaux Preparatoires*, vol. 1 (Leiden: Martinus Nijhoff, 2008).

that the notion of state responsibility for reparations had significant international support already in the late 1940s.

4.3 Reparations and the ad hoc international tribunals

Following the standstill in international criminal law during nearly half a century following the International Military Tribunals after the Second World War, the creation of the Statutes of the International Criminal Tribunals for Former Yugoslavia in 1993 and Rwanda in 1994 failed to provide significant progress in the recognition of victims. Nevertheless, the experiences of victims in the ad hoc Tribunals have provided an impetus for advocacy towards recognition of victims' rights.

The objectives of the ad hoc Tribunals are referred to in the preambles of the Security Council resolutions creating their Statutes.[9] In the case of the ICTY, Security Council Resolution 827 of 1993 states that the Tribunal was established for 'the sole purpose of prosecuting persons responsible for serious violations' and to 'contribute to ensuring that violations are halted and effectively redressed'. Security Council Resolution 955 of 1994 establishing the ICTR echoes the above, but also states that among the aims of the prosecutions is 'contribution to the process of national reconciliation'.

The judgments of the ICTY and the ICTR contain ample references to the purposes of sentencing. Curiously, each judgment contains a separate analysis of applicable principles and purposes of punishment. The majority of sentences indicate that the primary objectives of the Tribunals are deterrence and retribution, as illustrated in the cases of *Prosecutor* v. *Tadić* and *Prosecutor* v. *Akayesu*.[10] Certain judgments of the Tribunals also state that one of the aims of sentencing is reconciliation, such as in the case of *Prosecutor* v. *Furundžija*.[11] References have been

[9] Security Council Resolution 827, adopted on 25 May 1993, S/RES/827 and Security Council Resolution 955, adopted on 8 November 1994, S/RES/955. Available at the official web page of the ICTY at: www.un.org/icty and the official web page of the ICTR at: www.ictr.org.

[10] *Prosecutor* v. *Tadić*, Case No. IT-96-21-Y, Judgment, 16 November 1998, para. 21; *Prosecutor* v. *Kayishema and Ruzindana*, Case No. ICTR-95-1-T, Sentence, 21 May 1999, para. 2; *Prosecutor* v. *Akayesu*, Case No. ICTR-96-4-T, Sentence, 2 October 1998, para. 19. See further discussion in W. Schabas, *An Introduction to the International Criminal Court*, 2nd edn (Cambridge University Press, 2004), p. 164 and also in R. Dixon and K. Khan, *Archbold, International Criminal Courts, Practice, Procedure and Evidence* (London: Sweet & Maxwell, 2005), p. 484.

[11] *Prosecutor* v. *Furundžija*, Case No. IT-95-17/1-T, Judgment, 10 December 1998, para. 288.

made to the rehabilitation of offenders as a purpose of sentencing, however, the degree to which the ICTY in particular has recognised this as a stated aim has varied and it has been affirmed that 'the rehabilitative purpose of sentencing will not be given undue prominence'.[12]

Victims are generally given scant recognition in the exploration of purposes of punishment, however, in some judgments retribution is described as 'the expression of condemnation of grave violations of fundamental human rights ... it is also recognition of the harm and suffering caused to the victims'.[13] The lack of consistency in the formulation of principles relating to the objectives of punishment is regrettable.[14] Undeniably, all the cases brought before the ad hoc Tribunals involve victims of serious violations, and it would have been important to provide equal recognition of justice for victims in a standard formulation on the objectives of the Tribunals.

A closer review of the Statutes of the ICTY and the ICTR reveals that references to victims are scarce. Generally, references to victims in the Statutes of the ad hoc Tribunals refer primarily to their relevance as witnesses and as passive contributors to the proceedings. Article 15 of the Statute of the ICTY (mirrored by Article 14 of the ICTR) mentions that the protection of victims and witnesses should be taken into account in the adoption of Rules of Procedure. Article 20(1) of the Statute of the ICTY (which corresponds to Article 20(1) of the ICTR Statute) establishes that trials be conducted with 'full respect for the rights of the accused and due regard for the protection of victims and witnesses'. It appears thus as if the rights of the accused are given priority as they must be 'fully respected', whereas for victims the proceedings are merely required to show 'due regard'. The difficult balancing of rights of the accused versus witnesses has caused significant controversy in the Tribunals and protective measures in favour of witnesses, especially victims of sexual violence, have been challenged by the defence, while at the same time criticised by human rights lawyers for their inadequacy.[15] As recognised by the former

12 Earlier judgments of the ICTY made restrictive references to rehabilitation, e.g., *Prosecutor* v. *Delalić et al.*, Case No. IT-96-21, Judgment, 20 February 2001, para. 806. Citation from *Prosecutor* v. *Blagojević and Jokić*, Case No. IT-02-60, Judgment, 17 January 2005, paras 814–25.

13 *Prosecutor* v. *Nikolić*, Case No. IT-02-60/1, Judgment, 2 December 2003, para. 86.

14 R. Cryer (ed.), *An Introduction to International Criminal Law and Procedure* (Cambridge University Press, 2007), pp. 395–6, contains further discussion on inconsistencies in the current purposes of sentencing.

15 For contrasting views regarding measures undertaken for witness protection refer to F. Mumba, 'Ensuring a Fair Trial Whilst Protecting Victims and Witnesses – Balancing of

President Jorda of the ICTY, victims have largely been considered as 'object-matter or an instrument' in the proceedings of the ad hoc Tribunals.[16]

There is no direct reference to reparations in the Statutes other than restitution. The Tribunals have no faculty to award compensation, but may decide on cases relating to restitution. Article 24(3) of the Statute of the ICTY (mirrored by Article 23(3) of the Statute of the ICTR) reads: 'in addition to imprisonment, the Trial Chamber may order the return of any property and proceeds acquired by criminal conduct, including by means of duress, to their rightful owner'. The use of the term restitution, however, does not indicate state responsibility. According to the Statutes, states are responsible only insofar as they should enforce orders between individuals. As described in the Rules of Procedure and Evidence (RPE) Rule 105, which is common to both Tribunals, the request for restitution cannot be initiated by the victim, but must be presented by the Prosecutor or the Chamber. Disappointingly, the Tribunals have been unwilling to use their authority to order restitution, including in cases where it was clearly established that property was illegally taken from victims.[17]

In the drafting process of the RPE of the Tribunals, some attempt was made to address the issue of compensation. However, as noted by Cassese, this possibility was compromised due to the absence of a corresponding provision in the Statutes.[18] Rule 106 of the RPE provides that the Registrar of the Court shall transmit judgments detailing convictions to relevant national authorities and that the judgment shall be considered final and binding as to the criminal responsibility of the convicted perpetrator. The same Rule further states that it is up to the victims themselves to claim compensation before national courts 'pursuant to the relevant national legislation'.

Interests', in R. May (ed.), *Essays on ICTY Procedure and Evidence* (The Hague: Kluwer Law International, 2001), pp. 359–71; C. Chinkin, 'The Protection of Victims and Witnesses', in K. McDonald and S. Goldman (eds), *Substantive and Procedural Aspects of International Criminal Law* (The Hague: Kluwer Law International, 2000), pp. 451–77; Sluiter, 'The ICTR and the Protection of Witnesses', pp. 962–76; Tolbert and Swinnen, 'The Protection of, and Assistance to, Witnesses at the ICTY', pp. 193–229.

16 C. Jorda and J. Hemptinne, 'The Status and Role of the Victim', in A. Cassese, P. Gaete and J. Jones (eds), *The Rome Statute of The International Criminal Court* (Oxford University Press, 2002), pp. 1387–419.

17 S. Malmström, 'Restitution of Property and Compensation to Victims', in R. May (ed.), *Essays on ICTY Procedure and Evidence* (The Hague: Kluwer Law International, 2001), pp. 373–84.

18 A. Cassese, *International Criminal Law* (Oxford University Press, 2003), p. 429.

Morris and Scharf examined the *travaux preparatoires* of the ICTY and the considerations presented during the negotiations of the provisions relating to restitution and compensation.[19] Among the arguments used to justify the exclusion of reparation provisions was the wording of the Security Council Resolution establishing the Tribunal for the 'sole' purpose of prosecution. It was feared that dealing with cases involving restitution and compensation would distract the Tribunal by forcing it to operate as a claims commission and thereby 'divert' its limited resources. Security Council Resolution 827, which created the ICTY, does, however, note that the work of the Tribunal 'shall be carried out without prejudice to the right of the victims to seek, through appropriate means, compensation for damages incurred as a result of violations of international humanitarian law'. The resolution gives no indication to what the term 'through appropriate means' refers, but it is worthwhile noting that at the time it was considered a possibility that the Security Council establish another body for restitution claims. Morris and Scharf affirm that 'the prosecution and punishment of individuals responsible for war crimes does not relieve the State of its responsibility for the violations of international law and its obligation to provide compensation'.[20]

The mandates and proceedings of the ad hoc Tribunals reveal numerous deficiencies. Importantly, the lack of recognition of the rights of victims stands out in disharmony with developments in international law, both in general international law and human rights law, as documented in the previous chapters. Proceedings of the ad hoc Tribunals cite richly from human rights law concerning the right to a fair trial and in relation to the rights of the accused, however, they omit the application of human rights law in the area of victims' rights. Leaving victims at the mercy of their domestic legal systems renders them dependent on whether the national legislation foresees the possibility of compensation claims. Domestic legislation and political policy thus determine whether victims have access to present their claims. As a consequence, redress may be available to some victims but not others. To date, there are few, if any, reports of domestic claims being successful as they depend on the national legal and institutional framework, whether resources can actually be extracted from the perpetrator of the violations, as well as the

[19] V. Morris and M. Scharf, *An Insider's Guide to the International Criminal Tribunal for the Former Yugoslavia* (New York: Transnational Publishers, 1995), pp. 283–9.

[20] Morris and Scharf, *An Insider's Guide to the International Criminal Tribunal for the Former Yugoslavia*, p. 288.

political goodwill of the specific state to assume responsibility.[21] Stateless victims are left entirely without any recourse.

The approach of the Tribunals thus results in discriminatory treatment of victims depending on their nationality and origins. Most disconcertingly, the provisions of the Tribunals recognise the right to restitution for victims of property theft, but in contrast provide no recourse or right to remedies for victims of serious human rights violations who have survived genocide and torture.[22]

There were attempts to modify the mandates of the ad hoc Tribunals. These initiatives were largely undertaken in view of the credibility challenge facing the Tribunals due to their restricted ability to recognise victims' rights; criticism raised by victims' groups and the successful incorporation of provisions for victims' rights in the Rome Statute of the International Criminal Court. In November 2000, the Prosecutor, del Ponte, strongly advocated for the creation of a Claims Commission to compensate victims in an address in the Security Council affirming that:

> it is regrettable that the Tribunals' statutes ... make only a minimum of provision for compensation and restitution to people whose lives have been destroyed ... my office is having considerable success in tracing and freezing large amounts of money in the personal accounts of the accused. Money that could very properly be applied by the courts to the compensation of the citizens who deserve it ... I would therefore respectfully suggest to the Council that the present system falls short of delivering justice to the people of Rwanda and the former Yugoslavia, and I would invite you to give serious and urgent consideration to any change that would remove this lacuna.[23]

In a parallel move, also in November 2000, the President of the ICTY, Jorda, presented a report to the Security Council through the Secretary-General of the United Nations.[24] The report specifically expressed concern over the Tribunal's lack of authority to deal with compensation for victims. The report concluded that 'in order to bring about reconciliation in the former Yugoslavia and to ensure the restoration of peace, it is necessary that persons who were the victims of crimes that fall within the jurisdiction of the Tribunal receive compensation for their injuries'.

[21] Malmström, 'Restitution of Property and Compensation to Victims', pp. 373–84.

[22] I. Bottigliero, *Redress for Victims of Crimes under International Law* (Leiden: Martinus Nijhoff, 2004), p. 202.

[23] Address by the Prosecutor of the ICTY/ICTR, Carla del Ponte, to the Security Council on 21 November 2000, ICTY Press Release issued on 24 November 2000, JL/P.I.S./542-e.

[24] Letter dated 2 November 2000 from the Secretary-General to the President of the Security Council, UN Doc. S/2000/1063, 3 November 2000.

The report noted the general trend towards recognising a right to compensation in international law not only to states, but also to individuals based on state responsibility and reached the conclusion that victims of crimes over which the Tribunal has jurisdiction are entitled to benefit from a legal right to compensation. The report focused on financial compensation and deliberately avoided discussion of other forms of remedies, such as rehabilitation, stating that such measures would require further study.

In support of the position that individual victims have a right to compensation, the report cited the UN Declaration of Basic Principles of Justice for Victims of Crime and Abuse of Power (1985)[25] and the then draft UN Basic Principles on the Right to Reparation for Victims,[26] discussed in previous chapters, as well as the relevant provisions established in the Rome Statute of the International Criminal Court, to be discussed below. The report advised against amending the Tribunal's Statute and Rules and Procedure in order to incorporate a compensation mechanism as this would imply several practical difficulties, which would affect the length of the trials. However, the President of the ICTY advocated for the creation by the Security Council of another body that could operate as an international compensation commission. The President of the ICTR, Pillay, also submitted a letter to the Security Council through the Secretary-General in support of the creation of a compensation scheme or trust fund for victims in Rwanda.[27] Regrettably, no such measure was adopted by the Security Council nor was an official response received.

Despite the obstacles outlined above, it is noteworthy that both ad hoc Tribunals set up Victims and Witness Support Units, established by Rule 34 of the RPEs. The units, which are located in the Registry on the basis of its neutrality, provide advice, assistance and protection arrangements during the trial period; however, they operate with scarce resources[28]

[25] UN Declaration of Basic Principles of Justice for Victims of Crime and Abuse of Power, UN Doc. A/RES/40/34, adopted by the General Assembly, 29 November 1985.

[26] UN Basic Principles and Guidelines on the Right to a Remedy and Reparation for Victims of Gross Violations of International Human Rights Law and Serious Violations of International Humanitarian Law, UN Doc. A/RES/60/147.

[27] Letter dated 14 December 2000 from the Secretary-General to the President of the Security Council, UN Doc. S/2000/1198, 15 December 2000.

[28] T. Ingadottir, F. Ngendahayo and P. Sellers, 'The Victims and Witnesses Unit', in T. Ingadottir (ed.), *The International Criminal Court: Recommendations on Policy and Practice* (New York: Transnational Publishers, 2003), p. 5; Stover, *The Witnesses, War Crimes and the Promise of Justice in The Hague*, p. 129.

and have few means of ensuring follow-up and the long-term safety of witnesses upon the completion of prosecution.[29] While the RPEs of the two ad hoc Tribunals coincide in the majority of their text, it should be noted that Rule 34 provides an exception. In the case of the ICTR, the Rule was amended in 1998 to extend the mandate of the Victims and Witness Support Unit to: 'ensure that they receive relevant support, including physical and psychological rehabilitation, especially counselling in cases of rape and sexual assault; and to develop short-term and long-term plans for the protection of witnesses who have testified before the Tribunal and who fear a threat to their life, property or family.'

In the case of the ICTY, Rule 34 merely refers to the mandate to provide counselling and support, and there is no mention of physical and psychological rehabilitation or the duty to develop long-term plans for the protection of victims. ICTR has thus to be noted for its attempt to address certain urgent and practical needs of victims, in particular, in relation to victims of sexual violence and their access to rehabilitation measures. Such measures were undertaken in response to the outcry from victims and witnesses, especially those who found themselves HIV positive with no access to medical attention, while such was provided for defendants. However, as documented by De Brouwer,[30] the ICTR made some progress in providing medical assistance, including anti-retroviral treatment, for victims who had appeared as witnesses. Certain efforts were also made to sustain assistance following the trial. While the initiative taken to afford rehabilitation measures for victims of sexual violence is commendable, its weakness lies in its limited application as only victims who provide testimony qualify for assistance.[31] Also, it is worth noting that the medical assistance programme for victims and witnesses was only established several years after the ICTR became operational and following considerable critique of the discrepancies in relation to medical assistance for the accused vis-à-vis their victims.

There has been only limited research documenting the experiences of victims and witnesses in international criminal proceedings. Stover, following extensive interviews in the former Yugoslavia with witnesses who had previously testified in the ICTY, concluded that a majority of them

29 Tolbert and Swinnen, 'The Protection of, and Assistance to, Witnesses at the ICTY'.

30 A. De Brouwer, 'Reparation to Victims of Sexual Violence: Possibilities at the International Criminal Court and the Trust Fund for Victims and Their Families', *Leiden Journal of International Law*, 20 (2007), 207–37.

31 Ingadottir, Ngendahayo and Sellers, 'The Victims and Witnesses Unit', p. 29.

resisted a definition of justice that focused solely on the punishment of suspected war criminals ... justice had to include an array of social and economic rights for the persecuted, including the right to move about freely and without fear, the right to have the bodies of loved ones returned for proper burial and the right to receive adequate treatment for the psychological trauma as a result of witnessing wartime atrocities.[32]

The findings of the study indicated that while a majority of witnesses described their experiences at the ICTY as positive, nevertheless 'by and large, war crimes trials are generally ill-suited for the sort of expansive and nuanced story-telling so many witnesses yearn to engage in'.[33]

Further reflections on the results of the Tribunals recognise their shortcomings and the need for accountability mechanisms that take victims' concerns into account. Zacklin states:

Criminal Courts exist for the purpose of establishing individual accountability, not to uncover the fates and remains of loved ones. Nor is it their purpose to provide an official history. To the extent that a historical record is integral to individual trials it might be said that this is incidental to the work of the ICTY but it is not its primary purpose. Even less so is the awarding of compensation for victims ... The hope was that the establishment of the ICTY would promote reconciliation. There is little evidence to date that this is the case. Clearly, the Tribunal itself is not sufficient to promote reconciliation. Additional mechanisms, such as functioning national courts and truth commissions are needed.[34]

Although initiatives existed and continue to exist for the setting up of a truth commission in former Yugoslavia, in particular in Bosnia, such plans have to date not prospered. A main reason was the strong opposition by the ICTY to the proposal of a truth commission, especially during the late 1990s.[35] Debate, however, remains ongoing and victims groups have continued to advocate for the establishment of an independent truth commission.[36] Other transitional justice mechanisms

32 Stover, *The Witnesses, War Crimes and the Promise of Justice in The Hague*, pp. 119–20.
33 Stover, *The Witnesses, War Crimes and the Promise of Justice in The Hague*, pp. 129, 134.
34 Zacklin, 'The Failings of Ad Hoc International Tribunals', pp. 541–5.
35 Stover, *The Witnesses, War Crimes and the Promise of Justice in The Hague*, pp. 115–17. The proposal for a truth commission in Bosnia was initiated by Jacob Finci, head of Bosnia's small Jewish community. However, during the years 1998–2002 the ICTY vigorously opposed the proposal. While the ICTY has abandoned its opposition, financial funds and political impetus for a truth commission remain lacking. P. Hayner, *Unspeakable Truths: Confronting State Terror and Atrocity, How Truth Commissions around the World are Challenging the Past and Shaping the Future* (New York: Routledge, 2001), pp. 207–9.
36 J. N. Clark, 'The Limits of Retributive Justice, Findings of an Empirical Study in Bosnia and Hercegovina', *Journal of International Criminal Justice*, 7 (2009), 463–87.

have, however, played an important role in advancing victims' rights in the region, notably the Human Rights Chamber for Bosnia Herzegovina, which was set up by the Dayton Peace Agreement in 1995 and remained in existence until 2003. The Human Rights Chamber had unique features, as it acted as an international human rights court (based on the European Convention on Human Rights) in a national setting and enjoyed a broad mandate to award reparations, in accordance with Article XI(1) of the Dayton Agreement.[37] The Human Rights Chamber played a particularly important role in reaffirming the right of relatives of those disappeared and, while excluded *ratione temporis* to decide on cases that occurred during the war, was able to set significant precedents for the right to truth and collective reparations, notably in the '*Srebrenica Disappearance Case*'.[38] While still in draft form at the time, the Basic Principles on the Right to Reparation for Victims were relied upon in the reparation decisions of the Human Rights Chamber.

Nor did initiatives for a truth commission prosper in Rwanda, where domestic political emphasis and donor attention were placed on the *gacaca* trials. A national reconciliation commission was established; however, it lacked investigatory functions and instead conducted public awareness campaigns on peace and unity.[39] A limited and controversial reparations programme was set up in 1998, which focused primarily on educational grants and has been criticised for giving priority for ethnic Tutsi victims.[40] Furthermore, strongly critical observations have been made regarding the disproportionate amounts spent by the international community on disarmament, demobilisation and reintegration (DDR)

[37] M. Nowak, 'Reparations by the Human Rights Chamber for Bosnia Herzegovina', in K. De Feyter, S. Parmentier, M. Bossuyt and P. Lemmens (eds), *Out of the Ashes, Reparation for Victims of Gross and Systematic Human Rights Violations* (Antwerp: Intersentia, 2005), pp. 245–88. Article XI(c) of the Dayton Peace Agreement mandated the Human Rights Chamber to address in its judgments 'What steps shall be taken by the State party to remedy such breach, including orders to cease and desist, monetary relief (including pecuniary and non-pecuniary injuries), and provisional measures.'

[38] *Selimović and 48 Others* v. *RS*, CH/01/8365 *et al.*, decision of 7 March 2003 is known as the '*Srebrenica Disappearance Case*'.

[39] In Rwanda the government established a National Unity and Reconciliation Commission in 1999, however, its function is not investigatory but rather public promotion of peace, culture and unity. See J. Sarkin, 'The Necessity and Challenges of Establishing a Truth and Reconciliation Commission in Rwanda', *Human Rights Quarterly*, 21(3) (1999), 767–823; M. Drumbl, 'Restorative Justice and Collective Responsibility: Lessons For and From the Rwandan Genocide', *Contemporary Justice Review*, 5(1) (2002), pp. 5–22; E. Neuffer, *The Key to My Neighbour's House, Seeking Justice in Bosnia and Rwanda* (London: Picador, 2002).

[40] Rombouts and Vandeginste, 'Reparation to Victims in Rwanda', pp. 309–41.

programmes, detainees and genocide trials in contrast to the lack of reparations for survivors in Rwanda.[41]

In conclusion, the overall attention given to victims' rights in proceedings of the ad hoc Tribunals has been inadequate and mainly focused on urgent protection measures for witnesses, rather than more long-term considerations for victims and their right to reparation. Lack of adequate outreach programmes and sustained protection measures both in the ICTY and the ICTR has left victims in doubt about the value of international criminal justice. In the debate on the compatibility of measures taken to protect witnesses versus the rights of the accused, considerable attention has been dedicated to the applicable minimum human rights standards guaranteeing a fair trial.[42] In this context, it is remarkable that the corresponding rights of victims of serious human rights violations have not been equally invoked. Given the significant developments in human rights law with regard to the right of victims to seek redress, it is regrettable that such provisions were not reflected in the Statutes and Rules of Procedure of the ad hoc Tribunals. Although the establishment of responsibility by the Tribunals relates to that of individuals rather than states, clearly the violations and the suffering of the victims in cases under international criminal law are equal to that of victims who present cases of serious violations to human rights mechanisms. Progress made in one branch of international law, in particular, in the realm of human rights, should have been transferred into international criminal law.

Despite the deficient attention to victims' rights in the Statutes and Rules of Procedure of the ad hoc Tribunals, the experiences drawn from their operation nevertheless presented important precedents which influenced the creation of the International Criminal Court. The challenges faced by the Tribunals due to their restrictions regarding victim participation and redress provided important lessons in order to construct a concept of justice for serious violations that recognises victims' rights. As concluded by Jorda, the former President of the ICTY, reparations for those who have suffered such harm is a '*sine qua non* for the establishment of a deep-rooted and lasting peace'.[43]

[41] L. Waldorf, 'Goats and Graves: Reparations in Rwanda's Community Courts', in C. Ferstman, M, Goetz and A. Stephens (eds), *Reparations for Victims of Genocide, War Crimes and Crimes against Humanity, Systems in Place and Systems in the Making* (Leiden: Martinus Nijhoff, 2009), pp. 515–39; De Geiff, 'Contributing to Peace and Justice'.

[42] Mumba, 'Ensuring a Fair Trial Whilst Protecting Victims and Witnesses – Balancing of Interests', pp. 359–71; Chinkin, 'The Protection of Victims and Witnesses', pp. 451–77.

[43] Jorda and Hemptinne, 'The Status and Role of the Victim', p. 1398.

4.4 Reparations in the Rome Statute of the International Criminal Court

The provisions of the Rome Statute of the International Criminal Court represent a significant landmark for the affirmation of the rights of victims of serious violations in international law. The preamble of the Statute gives recognition that 'during this century millions of children, women and men have been victims of unimaginable atrocities that deeply shock the conscience of humanity'.[44] For the first time, victims were acknowledged as stakeholders in international criminal proceedings and numerous Articles in the Statute relating to victim participation and protection, as well as their right to reparation, bear evidence to this effect.

Importantly, for the first time an international court was provided with the authority, at its own discretion, to award reparations in favour of victims. Article 75 of its Statute states that:

> 1. The Court shall establish principles relating to reparations to, or in respect of, victims, including restitution, compensation and rehabilitation ...
>
> 2. The Court may make an order directly against a convicted person specifying reparations ... Where appropriate, the Court may order that the award for reparations be made through the Trust Fund provided for in Article 79.

It should, however, be noted that the original draft of the Statute presented in 1994 by the International Law Commission (ILC)[45] did not contain specific references to reparations, apart from a vague reference to the possibility of creating a trust fund for victims. Rather, the inclusion of reparations provisions occurred during the preparatory negotiation meetings, 'PrepComs', due to the pressure from NGOs, who were particularly anxious that the weaknesses of the ad hoc Tribunals should not be repeated and fixed in international law. NGOs formed a coalition working group specifically on victims' rights and strongly advocated for the incorporation of principles of human rights law and restorative justice. Yet, in the draft Statute, upon which the Rome negotiations were initiated, the Article relating to reparations was still in square

[44] Available at the official web page of the ICC at: www.icc-cpi.int.

[45] See further details of the *travaux preparatoires* of the ILC in relation to the Statute of the ICC at: www.un.org/law/ilc and full text of the Draft Statute as adopted by the ILC in 1994 at: http://untreaty.un.org/ilc/texts/instruments/english/draft%20Articles/7_4_1994.pdf.

brackets due to the lack of consensus and support among states.[46] Certain states opposed the inclusion of a mandate to order reparations by arguing that, similar to the situation in conjunction with the creation of the ad hoc Tribunals, such a provision would distract from the main purpose of the ICC: that is, to prosecute.

Originally, the term that figured in the draft text was 'compensation', echoing the language of the RPE of the ad hoc Tribunals. However, NGOs advocated for the inclusion of the more comprehensive term 'reparations', which eventually prevailed, as did specific references to 'restitution, compensation and rehabilitation'. Ultimately, the inclusion of the final text in the Article on reparations was possible thanks to the political will displayed during the negotiations by certain states, notably the United Kingdom and France.[47]

Major debates took place regarding whether reparations would be considered as part of the penalty, and whether reparation orders from the ICC could be aimed not only at convicted individuals but also at states. However, in both cases there was an overall lack of support for the endorsement of such provisions.[48] States were wary of the potential inclusion of state responsibility in the context of reparations and the exclusion of such references was a compromise to ensure the approval of Article 75. Robertson has noted that states suffering from 'human rights amnesia' deliberately declined to allow the ICC to order reparations against governments and that: 'this omission reflects one of the key weaknesses in the current philosophy behind the international justice movement, which denies the existence of collective responsibility in order to fasten upon the blameworthy individual. Where crimes against humanity are concerned, the two are not mutually exclusive.'[49]

Nevertheless, Article 25(4) of the Statute affirms that 'no provision in this Statute relating to individual criminal responsibility shall affect the responsibility of States under international law'. As noted by Muttukumaru, the Statute 'does not diminish any responsibilities assumed by States under other treaties and will not – self-evidently – prevent the Court

[46] C. Muttukumaru, 'Reparations to Victims', in S. Lee (ed.), *The International Criminal Court: The Making of the Rome Statute, Issues, Negotiations, Results* (The Hague: Kluwer Law International, 1999), pp. 262–70.

[47] D. Donnat-Cattin, 'Article 75', in O. Triffterer (ed.), *Commentary on the Rome Statute of the International Criminal Court – Observers' Notes, Article by Article* (Baden Baden: Nomos Verlag, 1999), pp. 965–78.

[48] McKay, 'Are Reparations Appropriately Addressed in the ICC Statute?', pp. 163–78.

[49] G. Robertson, *Crimes Against Humanity, The Struggle for Global Justice*, 2nd edn (London: Penguin, 2002), p. 386.

from making its attitude known through its judgments in respect of State complicity in a crime'.[50] In this context, it is pertinent to recall the wording of the ILC in its Articles on State Responsibility, specifically in Article 5, which affirms that the conduct of a person who has status as an organ of state or of a person 'empowered by the law of that State to exercise elements of the governmental authority shall be considered an act of the State under international law'.[51]

Given the likely coincidence between state and individual responsibility for the crimes within the jurisdiction of the ICC, which is 'limited to the most serious crimes of concern to the international community', it is inevitable that the debate on state responsibility in relation to the ICC will continue and gain increased importance.[52] As there are potential future overlaps between the jurisdiction of the ICC and human rights mechanisms, this aspect must be given further consideration, especially given the likelihood that convicted individuals may seek to avoid responsibility by claiming that they lack funds to pay reparations. In this context, it should also be noted that there is considerable state practice relating to the payment of reparations to victims of violent crimes when the offender is without resources or not identified. At the regional level, a treaty has existed within the Council of Europe since the 1980s, which affirms state responsibility on the basis of equity and social solidarity.[53] Furthermore, the UN Basic Principles of Justice for Victims of Crime and Abuse of Power state that: 'In cases where the Government under whose authority the victimizing act or omission occurred is no longer in existence, the State or Government successor in title should provide restitution to the victims ... When compensation is not fully available from the offender or other sources, States should endeavour to provide financial compensation.'[54]

[50] Muttukumaru, 'Reparations to Victims', p. 268.

[51] Articles on Responsibility of States for Internationally Wrongful Acts, adopted in 2001 by the International Law Commission.

[52] For example, see discussion by A. Nollkaemper, 'Concurrence between Individual Responsibility and State Responsibility in International Law', *International and Comparative Law Quarterly*, 2(3) (2003), 615–30.

[53] European Convention on the Compensation of Victims of Violent Crimes, CETS, 116, adopted 24 November 1983, and entered into effect in 1988. On 1 May 2011 the treaty had twenty-five states parties, see http://conventions.coe.int/Treaty/en/Treaties/Html/116.htm. Further discussion in Zappala, *Human Rights in International Criminal Proceedings*, pp. 230–1.

[54] UN Declaration of Basic Principles of Justice for Victims of Crime and Abuse of Power, General Assembly Resolution 40/34 adopted on 29 November 1985, Articles 11 and 12.

The mention in Article 75(1) of the Rome Statute of the establishment of 'principles relating to reparations' was intended as an indirect reference to the UN Basic Principles of Justice for Victims of Crime and Abuse of Power and the then draft UN Basic Principles on the Right to Reparation.[55] Yet, as the latter were still under negotiation in the former Commission on Human Rights, the reference was deliberately vague with a view to their future adoption. The language was used to defer to the definitions contained in the UN Principles regarding the concepts of victims and reparations. The Rules of Evidence and Procedure and the Regulations of the Court do not establish or expand on specific 'principles relating to reparations'. This would appear to confirm the acceptance of the UN principles as the standard to be applied by the ICC. Their practical elaboration will be developed over time through jurisprudence. By mid 2011, no case had yet been concluded and thus no reparation orders issued by the ICC.[56] In November 2009, the ICC adopted its official overall strategy in relation to victims; it specifically affirms that it draws on the UN Basic Principles of Justice for Victims of Crime and the Basic Principles on the Right to Reparation.[57]

While the Statute does not provide a definition of who is a victim, Article 75 nevertheless speaks of 'reparations to, or in respect of, victims'. This signals recognition of family members and successors of victims and is consistent with jurisprudence of human rights mechanisms as explored in Chapter 3.[58] Rule 85 of the Rules of Procedure and Evidence defines victims as 'natural persons who have suffered harm as a result of the commission of any crime within the jurisdiction of the Court'.[59] Furthermore, organisations or institutions, dedicated to religion, art, science, charitable or humanitarian purposes, as well as historic monuments and hospitals may also be considered as victims.

[55] UN Declaration of Basic Principles of Justice for Victims of Crime and Abuse of Power. Further discussion in McKay, 'Are Reparations Appropriately Addressed in the ICC Statute?', p. 174.

[56] G. Bitti and G. Gonzalez Rivas, 'The Reparations Provisions for Victims Under the Rome Statute of the International Criminal Court', in International Bureau of the Permanent Court of Arbitration (ed.), *Redressing Injustices Through Mass Claims* (Oxford University Press, 2006), p. 311.

[57] International Criminal Court, Report of the Court on the Strategy in Relation to Victims, 10 November 2009, ICC-ASP/8/45, para. 6. See discussion in Redress, 'Victims' Central Role in Fulfilling the ICC's Mandate', Paper for the 8th Assembly of States Parties, The Hague, 18–26 November 2009, available at: www.redress.org.

[58] Donnat-Cattin, 'Article 75', p. 969.

[59] ICC Rules of Procedure and Evidence, Adopted by the Assembly of States Parties, New York, 3–10 September 2002, Official Records ICC-ASP/1/3.

According to Rule 97(1) of the Rules of Procedure, awards can be determined on 'an individualized basis or, where it deems it appropriate, on a collective basis or both', thus the ICC has considerable discretion and flexibility to decide how it chooses to approach the matter of reparations. The ICC should 'apply applicable treaties and the principles and rules of international law, interpretation of law' and 'must be consistent with internationally recognized human rights' according to Article 21 of the Statute. The reference to human rights in the Statute is an important recognition of victims' rights as jurisprudence on redress in international and regional human rights systems, as explored in Chapter 3, has significantly contributed to developing the concept of reparations.[60] Furthermore, Rule 86 of the Rules of Procedure establishes as a general principle that 'organs of the Court in performing their functions under the Statute or the Rules, shall take into account the needs of all victims and witnesses in accordance with Article 68 [protection], in particular, children, elderly persons, persons with disabilities and victims of sexual or gender violence'. This principle underlines that the ICC must ensure that special consideration is given to vulnerable persons in their proceedings. Article 43(6) of the Statute provides for a Victims and Witnesses Unit within the Registry of the court, which is responsible for protection and counselling and should have staff with expertise in trauma, including sexual violence. Thus, the Unit was created as a statutory body, unlike the Victims and Witnesses Units of the ad hoc Tribunals, which were established as an afterthought by the Rules of Procedure and Evidence.[61] A Victims Participation and Reparations Unit, located within the Registry, was also established to advise victims and enable them to submit applications to the court. Furthermore, in 2005 the ICC established the Office of Public Council for Victims as an independent entity to provide support and assistance to victims and their legal representatives, including in relation to reparations.[62]

Among the most controversial provisions of the Rome Statute is Article 68(3), which states that 'where the personal interests of victims are affected, the Court shall permit their views and concerns to be presented and considered at stages of the proceedings determined to be appropriate by the Court'. The ICC has already drawn on human

60 Bitti and Gonzalez Rivas, 'The Reparations Provisions for Victims under the Rome Statute of the International Criminal Court', p. 312.

61 Ingadottir, Ngendahayo and Sellers, 'The Victims and Witnesses Unit', pp. 1–33.

62 Report of the International Criminal Court to the General Assembly of the United Nations 2006, A/61/217.

rights standards and jurisprudence in its various decisions on victim participation.[63] The introduction of the right to victim participation in international criminal law was a novelty that continues to be contested, the practical implications of which have raised considerable concern both inside and outside the court. As could be expected given the situations under investigation, large numbers of victims have filed requests to participate in various stages of the proceedings: by the end of 2009 some 1,800 individual applications had been submitted. By late 2010, approximately 450 victims had, through their legal representatives, participated in the investigations into the situation in the Democratic Republic of the Congo (*Prosecutor* v. *Lubanga* and *Prosecutor* v. *Katanga and Chui*).[64] Questions regarding at which stage and how victims may participate continue to be debated and, while there is recognition of the importance of victim participation, there are also legitimate fears that it may delay proceedings.[65] It is likely that some victims file to participate in the early stages of the proceedings out of concern that they may not otherwise be considered at the reparations stage. However, the application form for victims issued by the ICC in 2010 clearly sets out that victims may request to participate in proceedings and submit an application for reparations as parallel processes independently of each other.

A relevant observation is that the victim is defined as a person who has suffered harm due to 'a crime within the Court's jurisdiction': that is, the definition does not hinge on the crime already under investigation or decided by the ICC. Commentators have noted that this could be interpreted as affecting the presumption of innocence of the accused.[66] However, victims' ability to resort to reparations provisions is subject to considerable restrictions. Although the victim does not have to refer to a specific investigation in his or her reparation claim,[67] nevertheless, the

[63] Zegveld, 'Victims' Reparations Claims and International Criminal Courts', p. 101.

[64] Report of the International Criminal Court to the General Assembly of the United Nations, 2007/2008, A/63/323; Report of the International Criminal Court to the General Assembly of the United Nations, 2008/2009, A/64/356; Report of the International Criminal Court to the General Assembly of the United Nations, 2009/2010, A/65/313; Redress, 'Victims' Central Role in Fulfilling the ICC's Mandate'; ICC Investigation into the Situation in the Democratic Republic of the Congo, ICC-01/04, including *Prosecutor* v. *Lubanga*, ICC-01/04-01/06 and *Prosecutor* v. *Katanga and Chui*, ICC-01/04-01/07.

[65] Friman, 'The International Criminal Court and the Participation of Victims', pp. 485–500; Judgment on Victim Participation in the Investigation Stage of the Proceedings by Appeals Chamber, ICC-01/04-556, 19 December 2008.

[66] Jorda and Hemptinne, 'The Status and Role of the Victim', p. 1403.

[67] Bitti and Gonzalez Rivas, 'The Reparations Provisions for Victims under the Rome Statute of the International Criminal Court', pp. 312–14.

request for reparations must ultimately be linked to criminal proceedings against the person responsible for the harm. Reparation orders can be issued only once a case is decided. Should the defendant be acquitted there may be no reparations for the victims.[68] Given the experiences of international tribunals so far it appears unlikely that the reparation provisions, although groundbreaking, will live up to the expectations of victims and NGOs. The complexity of the cases before the ICC result in proceedings that last several years and eventual reparation orders are dependent on whether there is a conviction.

4.5 International Criminal Court Trust Fund for Victims

An additional challenge for the ICC relates to the implementation of the reparation orders as these are made against individuals. Experiences from international tribunals indicate that the defendants often claim indigence.[69] As state responsibility is not reflected in the Rome Statute, it was deemed necessary to provide the ICC with an alternative means to ensure reparations for victims, who would otherwise be dependent on the financial solvency of the perpetrator.[70] In this context, Article 79 of the Statute foresaw the creation of a Trust Fund by the Assembly of States Parties for the benefit of victims and their families. The Trust Fund for Victims was formally created in 2002 when the Rome Statute entered into force; it is independent from the ICC and is managed by the Assembly of States Parties. The Statute does not detail how it will be financed other than stating that the ICC may order money and other property collected through fines and forfeiture (Article 109) to be transferred to the Trust Fund. The Assembly of States Parties has subsequently defined that the Trust Fund may receive voluntary contributions from governments, international organisations, individuals, corporations and other entities.[71]

As defined in Rule 98 of the Rules of Evidence and Procedure, the ICC may depend on the Trust Fund in several ways. It can order that an award against a convicted person be deposited through the Fund, which in turn shall forward it to the individual victim. The ICC may

[68] Bitti and Gonzalez Rivas, 'The Reparations Provisions for Victims under the Rome Statute of the International Criminal Court', pp. 312–14.

[69] Schabas, *An Introduction to the International Criminal Court*, p. 175.

[70] Jorda and Hemptinne, 'The Status and Role of the Victim', p. 1408.

[71] Bitti and Gonzalez Rivas, 'The Reparations Provisions for Victims under the Rome Statute of the International Criminal Court', pp. 315–16.

also resort to the Trust Fund when the 'number of the victims and the scope, forms and modalities of reparations makes a collective award more appropriate'. Furthermore, the ICC can, in consultation with the Trust Fund, order an award for reparations to an intergovernmental, international or national organisation approved by the Fund. The ICC has discretion to decide whether to order awards for victims, and it should also be noted that the court may act on its own initiative without a specific request from a victim. This is important, particularly in situations where it is clear that many victims cannot approach the court for practical reasons, such as the remote geographic location of the communities affected. The official web page of the Fund states that 'unless ordered by the Court to award reparations to individuals, the Trust Fund favours reparations activities which are directed at groups, based on similarities in their claims or situations'.[72] The Trust Fund can act only in situations where the ICC has jurisdiction. However, the Fund is formally independent of the court and may assist victims independently of ongoing investigations, as long as its activities are not inconsistent with the rights of the accused to a fair and impartial trial.[73]

The Regulations of the Trust Fund were adopted in 2005, a Board of Directors (*pro bono*) was appointed, and in early 2007 the Trust Fund became operational. The activities of the Trust Fund have to date been undertaken within the framework of Article 50(a)(i) of the Regulations of the Trust Fund, which enables it to undertake measures on its own accord 'when the Board of Directors considers it necessary to provide physical or psychological rehabilitation or material support for the benefit of victims and their families'. Such measures, known as general assistance rather than reparations, target victims of the situations before the ICC regardless of whether the harm they suffered stems from particular crimes charged by the Prosecutor in a specific case. Those activities are based on voluntary contributions to the Fund rather than on seized assets from the accused. In January 2008, the Trust Fund notified the Pre-Trial Chambers of its intention to carry out activities in the Democratic Republic of the Congo and Uganda; these were in turn approved by the Chambers once it was deemed that they would not 'pre-determine

[72] Information about the Trust Fund at the web site of the International Criminal Court, including Resolution IStruct-ASP/4/Res. 3, Regulations of the Trust Fund for Victims, adopted 3 December 2005, available at: www.icc-cpi.int/Menus/ICC/Structure+of+the+Court/Victims.

[73] Resolution ICC-ASP/4/Res. 3, Articles 48, 50.

any issue to be determined by the Court'.[74] By the end of 2010, some thirty-four projects were approved and being implemented in partnership with local NGOs, grass-roots organisations and women's associations. The majority of the projects provided rehabilitation assistance and counselling for victims and also contributed to creating livelihood opportunities, such as micro-credit projects, for survivors. Many of the projects specifically target women and children in their interventions. The Trust Fund for Victims estimated that by late 2010, some 70,000 persons were benefiting directly from such assistance and that some further 270,000 family members would benefit indirectly through improved well-being and reduced stigma.[75] In 2008, the Fund had a budget of €1,650,000 and made the remarkable observation that the cost per victim beneficiary was less than €5. By 2010, the total amount of contributions received by the Fund was €5.8 million.[76]

As noted by Redress, local victims' organisations report on positive reactions to the projects and 'for many, the work of the Trust Fund in providing assistance to victims under its "other mandate" might be the most tangible impact they might experience from the ICC'.[77] As previously noted, the activities carried out by the Trust Fund to date are regarded as a form of general humanitarian assistance rather than reparation measures, which from a legal point of view have to be formally awarded by the ICC.[78] Nevertheless, this distinction is likely to be of limited relevance to victims whose urgency is grave and whose lives simply cannot be resumed without immediate assistance. While not negating that compensation will remain an important element of reparations for victims, the direct impact of assistance focused on rehabilitation and access to basic health, education and livelihood opportunities enables victims to overcome stigma in their communities and equips them, in a gender- and child-sensitive manner, with tools to look to the future. Such results cannot be achieved by financial compensation alone. In 2010, the Trust Fund undertook an in-depth survey

[74] Report of the International Criminal Court to the General Assembly of the United Nations 2007/2008, A/63/323, paras 18 and 27.

[75] The Trust Fund web page at: http://trustfundforvictims.org/projects.

[76] The Trust Fund for Victims, Programme Progress Report, Autumn 2010.

[77] Redress, 'Report on the Impact of the Rome Statute System on Victims and Affected Communities', 22 March 2010, p. 15.

[78] E. Kristjansdottir, 'International Mass Claims Processes and the ICC Trust Fund for Victims', in C. Ferstman, M. Goetz and A. Stephens (eds), *Reparations for Victims of Genocide, War Crimes and Crimes against Humanity, Systems in Place and Systems in the Making* (Leiden: Martinus Nijhoff, 2009), p. 175.

among 2,600 of the project beneficiaries in the Democratic Republic of the Congo and Uganda; the results confirm the urgency required in ensuring the provision of rehabilitation measures as a majority of victims indicated it to be their priority concern. The survey also indicated the accentuated social stigma, poor mental health and reduced quality of life that survivors of sexual violence face, confirming the importance of gender considerations in reparations and assistance measures.[79]

The establishment and operation of the Trust Fund of the ICC drew inspiration from the United Nations Voluntary Fund for Victims of Torture, which was established by the General Assembly in 1981.[80] In 2010, the Voluntary Fund provided direct assistance for victims through NGOs in some seventy countries. There is a need to ensure that the two funds exchange information about their activities due to the potential overlap of their mandates. Furthermore, it may also be necessary to coordinate information exchanges between trust funds established by regional human rights mechanisms and, in the future, with national reparation programmes, which, as indicated in Part II, are increasingly being established and sometimes linked to recommendations issued by truth commissions.

Concerns have been raised regarding the financial means available to the Trust Fund of the ICC.[81] As the ICC and the Trust Fund are not part of the United Nations, they are not provided funds through the regular budget of the UN. A future challenge faced by the Trust Fund will be its ability to sustain funding, especially once the ICC starts to issue orders for reparations as these are likely to be in favour of large numbers of victims and involve considerable sums. To date, the majority of the voluntary funding for the Trust Fund has come from governments. By the end of 2010, although the Trust Fund had only been operational for three years, contributions had been received from twenty-five states.

[79] The Trust Fund for Victims, Programme Progress Report.

[80] The Fund was established by General Assembly Resolution 36/151 of 16 December 1981. Information about the United Nations Fund for Victims is available at the web page of the UN Office of the High Commissioner for Human Rights (acts as the Secretariat of the Fund) at: www.ohchr.org/EN/Issues/Pages/TortureFundMain.aspx. Report of the Secretary-General on the United Nations Voluntary Fund for Victims of Torture, A/63/220, 5 August 2008. See previous references to the Voluntary Fund in Chapter 3.

[81] T. Ingadottir, 'The Trust Fund of the ICC', in D. Shelton (ed.), *International Crimes, Peace and Human Rights: The Role of the International Criminal Court* (New York: Transnational Publishers, 2000), pp. 149–61; S. Garkawe, 'Victims and the International Criminal Court: Three Major Issues', *International Criminal Law Review*, 3 (2003), 345–67.

Among the numerous difficult issues that remain to be resolved, the ICC must clarify how it intends to assess reparations claims, to what degree these will be done on an individual or collective basis and which standards of proof will be applied.[82] The latter aspect has considerable practical implications as certain victims will have had limited access to formal education, which, even with the aid of legal representation, will impact on their ability to present their claims. Furthermore, many of the victims come from areas where civil registries and birth registration are lacking, as are medical facilities in order to document sexual violence; this in turn has a deleterious effect on the possibilities that victims have to present relevant documentation and supporting evidence. It has been observed that before the ICC starts issuing reparation orders, it would be advisable that it refer to and incorporate lessons learnt from previous mass claims processes. Notable among these was the United Nations Claims Commission (UNCC) and the experiences of the UNCC in relation to reparations are explored in Chapter 6 on practical measures supported by the UN in order to transfer standards into reality.

It is important to acknowledge the novelty of the creation of a trust fund linked to international criminal proceedings. However, as outlined above, the reactions of victims and their organisations with regard to the reparations regime of the ICC are likely to be marred by disappointment due to their high expectations. Among the challenging issues relating to reparations that the ICC will be faced with are delays in concluding prosecutions, the inability to ensure enforcement of reparations against individual perpetrators, restrictions due to the limited jurisdiction, inadequate funding of the Trust Fund and lack of outreach and information access for the victims most in need.[83] The ICC will also have to define how to address the situation of numerous victims who carry the dual identity of perpetrators, such as children who have been recruited and used in hostilities.

Nevertheless, the ICC, in particular through the Trust Fund, can play a vital role in reaching out to victims and putting true meaning into

[82] C. Ferstman and M. Goetz, 'Reparations before the International Criminal Court: The Early Jurisprudence on Victim Participation and its Impact on Future Reparations Proceedings', in C. Ferstman, M. Goetz and A. Stephens (eds), *Reparations for Victims of Genocide, War Crimes and Crimes against Humanity, Systems in Place and Systems in the Making* (Leiden: Martinus Nijhoff, 2009), pp. 313–50.

[83] G. Greco, 'Victims' Rights Overview under the ICC Legal Framework: A Jurisprudential Analysis', *International Criminal Law Review*, 7 (2007), 531–47; Redress, 'Report on the Impact of the Rome Statute System on Victims and Affected Communities'.

the terms justice and reconciliation for victims by providing them with the practical means of resuming their lives. Through the Trust Fund, projects can be carried out in a collective manner and reach victims who are unable or reluctant to approach the ICC personally.[84] Importantly, through the Trust Fund assistance can be delivered as an interim measure pending the outcome of investigations and can be tailored in consultation with affected communities in order to correspond with their needs. These activities, many of which focus on rehabilitation, will be a crucial complement to formal reparation orders, which are more likely to focus on financial compensation. The ICC and the Trust Fund have the opportunity to develop further the complementing concepts mentioned in the Rome Statute of 'restitution, compensation and rehabilitation' as the practical implementation of reparations will require a creative approach towards developing measures that are deemed relevant and appropriate by the victims themselves. Furthermore, the jurisprudence of the ICC will probably prompt impetus at the national level to establish reparations programmes. Such programmes will be essential to avoid discrimination among victims and ensure that as many as possible can benefit from reparations, while they at the same time provide an important recognition of state responsibility vis-à-vis the victims.

The perceived injustices and blatant discrepancies in the treatment of defendants compared with victims and witnesses by the ad hoc Tribunals have provided fundamental lessons on the importance of not ignoring the tragic reality of the victims. Although faced with high expectations, the reparations regime of the ICC can provide a turning point in international criminal law by vindicating its credibility among those most concerned: the victims themselves.

4.6 Steps backwards? The Special Panels for Serious Crimes in East Timor, the Special Court for Sierra Leone and the Extraordinary Chambers in the Courts of Cambodia

Regrettably, the provisions regarding victims' rights in the statutes of the hybrid criminal justice initiatives in East Timor, Sierra Leone and Cambodia did not follow the precedent of the Rome Statute of the International Criminal Court. Rather, they were largely modelled on the ad hoc tribunals for former Yugoslavia and Rwanda. However, despite the limited provisions on victims' rights in the respective statutes, the hybrid courts have managed

[84] Shelton, *Remedies in International Human Rights Law*, p. 236.

to incorporate some practical elements in their operative work. This shift has been prompted following pressure from victims' and human rights organisations. While largely neglected in the courts in East Timor and Sierra Leone, the issue of reparations is receiving greater attention in conjunction with the ongoing prosecutions in Cambodia.

4.6.1 *East Timor*

The establishment of the Special Panels for Serious Crimes was unprecedented, as the UN at the time was fully responsible for the transitional administration in East Timor. Following the violence of the referendum regarding independence on 25 October 1999, the Security Council adopted Resolution 1272 under Chapter VII of the UN Charter, whereby the peacekeeping mission UNTAET was given total administrative and executive authority in the territory, including for the administration of justice.[85]

In June 2000, UNTAET established the Special Panels for Serious Crimes through Regulation No. 2000/15.[86] Unlike subsequent hybrid courts, the legal basis of the Special Panels stemmed from the authority of UNTAET, as there was no state counterpart with whom the UN could negotiate a bilateral treaty.[87] While other ad hoc courts were specifically mandated to focus on those carrying the greatest responsibility, this was not the case in East Timor and resulted in an unclear prosecution strategy that included mid- and low-level perpetrators. The prosecutions were established within the local Dili courts and each panel was staffed by two international judges and one national judge. The process faced the significant challenge of simultaneously establishing and training an East Timorese judiciary. Investigations, initially conducted by the human rights unit of UNTAET, were transferred to a Serious Crimes Unit (SCU) within the Public Prosecutor in mid 2000. The SCU was established and operated separately from the panels. In this sense, the Serious Crimes process in East Timor differed significantly from other ad hoc courts, which were created as one institution.[88]

85 Security Council Resolution on the Situation in East Timor, S/RES/1272, adopted 25 October 1999; S. Chesterman, 'East Timor', in M. Berdal and S. Economides (eds), *United Nations Interventionism 1999–2004* (Cambridge University Press, 2007), pp. 192–216.

86 UN Doc. UNTAET/REG/2000/15, adopted 6 June 2000.

87 C. Reiger, 'Hybrid Attempts at Accountability for Serious Crimes in East Timor', in N. Roht-Arriaza and J. Mariezcurrena (eds), *Transitional Justice in the Twenty-First Century, Beyond Truth versus Justice* (Cambridge University Press, 2006), p. 149.

88 C. Reiger and M. Wierda, 'The Serious Crimes Process in Timor Leste: In Retrospect', *Prosecution Case Studies Series*, International Center for Transitional Justice, March 2006, pp. 11–13.

The Regulation No. 2000/15, which established the Special Panels, did contain specific reference (section 24) to witness protection, mentioning specifically measures for sexual and gender-based violence and violence against children. It also mentioned (section 25) the possibility of setting up a Trust Fund for victims:

> A Trust Fund may be established by decision of the Transitional Administrator in consultation with the National Consultative Council for the benefit of victims of crimes within the jurisdiction of the panels, and of the families of such victims. The panels may order money and other property collected during fines, forfeiture, foreign donors or other means to be transferred to the Trust Fund.

The Trust Fund for victims foreseen in the 2000/15 regulation was, however, never established.[89] Rather, the issue of reparations was left for the Truth Commission to address, as will be further explored in Part II of this book.

The experience of the panels indicates a significant discrepancy between legal provisions and practice in reality. The Serious Crimes process in East Timor was completely under-funded given its task and lacked earmarked funding. Furthermore, establishing accountability for past crimes was merely one of several competing priorities of UNTAET.[90] The Serious Crimes Panels faced considerable criticism for numerous aspects of their operative work. Having to operate in four languages was a major obstacle and caused serious mistakes.[91] Considerable critique has pointed to a lack of due process and violations of rights of the accused, many of whom were provided with inadequate defence assistance.[92] Despite provisions to the contrary, no witness protection measures were provided during the prosecutions.[93] Incidents such as that of a rape victim, who was due to testify and was forced to travel for hours on

[89] S. Linton, 'Putting Things into Perspective: The Realities of Accountability in East Timor, Indonesia and Cambodia', *Maryland Series in Contemporary Asian Studies*, School of Law, University of Maryland, No. 3, 2005, pp. 75–6.

[90] Chesterman, 'East Timor', pp. 192–216.

[91] D. Cohen, 'Indifference and Accountability: The United Nations and the Politics of International Justice in East Timor', *East West Center Special Report*, No. 9, June 2006, pp. 26–9.

[92] S. Linton, 'Cambodia, East Timor and Sierra Leone: Experiments in International Justice', *Criminal Law Forum*, 12 (2001), 226–30; Reiger and Wierda, *The Serious Crimes Process in Timor Leste*; Cohen, 'Indifference and Accountability', pp. 26–9.

[93] In contrast to the Special Court in Sierra Leone, which had a witness protection unit of some fifty-five specialised staff, the issue of witness protection in East Timor was assigned to a single person, see D. Cohen, 'Hybrid Justice in East Timor, Sierra Leone and Cambodia: Lessons Learnt and Prospects for the Future', *Stanford Journal of International Law*, 43(1) (2007), 21.

public transport with the alleged perpetrator, are indicative of the lack of sensitivity towards victims. Due to poor preparedness and coordination within the panels, victims were forced to repeatedly recount distressing accounts of atrocities without any psychosocial support and endure multiple exhumations of relatives' graves.[94]

The Serious Crimes investigations in East Timor were discontinued in early 2005. The process was characterised by a lack of ownership within both the UN and East Timorese authorities, and this was particularly notable in the context of the Wiranto indictment.[95] The prosecutions largely lacked support from the civilian population, as people questioned the lack of focus on those who carried the greatest responsibility, the end result being a high conviction rate of mid-level perpetrators, while the majority of the indicted, including those carrying the greatest responsibility, remained sheltered in an uncooperative Indonesia. Furthermore, the Serious Crimes process lacked an outreach programme to explain its objectives to the population and its relationship with victims' organisations was poor.[96] Chapter 9 in Part II of this book explores in further detail the relationship between the prosecutions, the Truth Commission (CAVR) and that of other transitional justice initiatives for East Timor, and, in particular, considers the implications for the issue of reparations.

4.6.2 *The Special Court for Sierra Leone*

Following a request from the Security Council, an agreement between the United Nations and the government of Sierra Leone established the hybrid Special Court for Sierra Leone in January 2002.[97] The Statute of the Court (Article 16) established a Victims and Witnesses Unit within its Registry. Article 19 provides for possible restitution: 'the Trial Chamber may order the forfeiture of the property, proceeds and any assets

[94] Cohen, 'Hybrid Justice in East Timor, Sierra Leone and Cambodia', p. 18; Reiger, 'Hybrid Attempts at Accountability in Timor Leste', p. 160; S. Katzenstein, 'Hybrid Tribunals: Searching for Justice in East Timor', *Harvard Human Rights Journal*, 16 (2003), 261.

[95] Reiger, 'Hybrid Attempts at Accountability in Timor Leste', pp. 160–1; S. De Bertodano, 'East Timor: Trials and Tribulations', in C. Romano, A. Nollkaemper and J. Kleffner (eds), *Internationalized Criminal Court, Sierra Leone, East Timor, Kosovo and Cambodia* (Oxford University Press, 2004), pp. 84–6.

[96] Reiger, 'Hybrid Attempts at Accountability in Timor Leste', pp. 159–60.

[97] Security Council Resolution, S/RES/1315, 14 August 2000, 'requested the Secretary-General to negotiate an agreement with the Government of Sierra Leone to create an independent special court' – unlike the previous ad hoc tribunals set up by the Security Council under Chapter VII of the UN Charter. See official web page of the Special Court for Sierra Leone at: www.sc-sl.org.

acquired unlawfully or by criminal conduct, and their return to their rightful owner or to the State of Sierra Leone'. The reference to restitution echoes from the ad hoc tribunals and the absence of a clear reparations provision for victims has been noted as a major failing.[98] Furthermore, as all defendants charged by the Special Court have so far declared themselves indigent, restitution efforts seem unlikely.[99] To date, none of the judgments of the Special Court address issues of restitution.

In 2007, an in-depth survey was conducted with 200 witnesses who had testified to the court. The majority indicated that their expectations had not been met and that they had expected some financial support and, in particular, assistance with medical care and education for their children.[100] Yet the court has demonstrated little interest in offering victims more than mere information regarding its mandate and in certain instances it has provided protection measures for witnesses.[101]

As a point of controversy, Article 17 of the Statute provided jurisdiction over children above the age of fifteen. Although the Statute potentially allowed for the accountability of children, it also provided certain recognition that they simultaneously remain victims, without specifically referring to the term, by including reference to rehabilitation and reintegration measures. The court chose not to exercise its jurisdiction over children, but rather, in accordance with its mandate, to focus investigations on those bearing the greatest responsibility for serious violations.[102]

Part of the explanation for why reparations were not considered in the drafting of the Statute of the Court was related to the Lomé Agreement of 1999, which made unclear references to the creation of a Special Fund for War Victims. After a delay of a decade, the fund was finally set up in December 2009 with support from the United Nations Peace-building Fund. However, funding sustainability and the willingness of the state to

98 A. MacDonald, 'Sierra Leone's Shoestring Special Court', *International Review of the Red Cross*, 84 (2002), 121–42.

99 Cohen, 'Hybrid Justice in East Timor, Sierra Leone and Cambodia', pp. 1–38.

100 Special Court for Sierra Leone, 'Best-Practice Recommendations for the Protection and Support of Witnesses, An Evaluation of the Witness and Victims Section', 2008.

101 Seventh Annual Report of the President of the Special Court for Sierra Leone, June 2009–May 2010 and Sixth Annual Report of the President of the Special Court for Sierra Leone, June 2008–May 2009.

102 See detailed analysis in International Crisis Group Briefing, 'The Special Court for Sierra Leone, Promises and Pitfalls of a "New Model"', *Africa Briefing*, No. 16, 4 August 2003; S. Horovitz, 'Transitional Criminal Justice in Sierra Leone', in N. Roht-Arriaza and J. Mariezcurrena (eds), *Transitional Justice in the Twenty-First Century, Beyond Truth versus Justice* (Cambridge University Press, 2006), pp. 43–69.

assume responsibility for its continued operation remains unclear.[103] Chapter 8 of this book explores in further detail the issue of reparations in relation to the Lomé Peace Agreement and the Truth Commission in Sierra Leone, and how the relationship between, and the parallel operation of, the Special Court and the Truth Commission were perceived from the perspective of victims.

4.6.3 *Cambodia*

In Cambodia, protracted negotiations between the United Nations and the government of Cambodia resulted in an agreement in 2003, followed by a law in 2004 establishing the Extraordinary Chambers in the Courts of Cambodia (ECCC).[104] Victims do not figure in the legislation other than in a vague reference that notes that they are entitled to protection measures. Although the law contains a provision on restitution in Article 39, it excludes reference to individuals: 'the Court may order the confiscation of personal property, money, and real property acquired unlawfully or by criminal conduct. The confiscated property shall be returned to the State.' Thus, the language fails to provide a basis for restitution to victims.

Although the law contains no reference to a victims unit, nevertheless such a Victim Support Section was established by the Internal Rules.[105] The Internal Rules contain innovative provisions regarding victims as they, for the first time in an international criminal court, can be formally recognised as civil parties in a case.[106] This allows victims to request representation by a lawyer and participate actively during the various stages of the criminal proceedings. The degree of participation of victims has proven to be one of the more contested features of

103 P. Hayner, 'Negotiating Peace in Sierra Leone, Confronting the Justice Challenge', Study of the Humanitarian Dialogue project 'Negotiating Justice', December 2007, pp. 1–37; International Center for Transitional Justice (M. Suma and C. Correa), Report and Proposals for the Implementation of Reparations in Sierra Leone, December 2009.

104 Law on the Establishment of the Extraordinary Chambers, with inclusion of amendments as promulgated on 27 October 2004 (NS/RKM/1004/006); the law revised previous legislation from 2001. Official web page of the Extraordinary Chambers in the Courts of Cambodia at: www.eccc.gov.kh/english. L. Barria and S. Roper, 'Providing Justice and Reconciliation: The Criminal Tribunals for Sierra Leone and Cambodia', *Human Rights Review*, October–December (2005), pp. 4–25.

105 ECCC Internal Rules, 5th revised version, February 2010.

106 ECCC Internal Rules, Rule 23; see also ECCC Press Release, 'Historic Achievement in International Criminal Law, Victims of the Khmer Rouge Crimes Fully Involved in Proceedings of the ECCC', 4 February 2008, available at: www.eccc.gov.kh/english.

the ECCC.[107] Furthermore, the Internal Rules establish that victims' associations may assist civil parties.[108]

Despite the lack of references to reparations in the 2004 national legislation establishing the ECCC, mention of reparations was inserted in the Internal Rules. Rule 23 states that civil parties, that is, victims, can seek collective and moral reparations and that these shall be awarded against and be borne by convicted persons. Reference to compensation in the Rules is, however, omitted. The Internal Rules further specify that awards may include publishing the judgment in the news or funding of a non-profit activity or service that is intended for the benefit of victims or other appropriate forms of reparation.[109] Information on the ECCC official web page suggests that reparations could entail memorials and the establishment of mental health clinics. The Victim Support Section conducted a survey in 2010 to identify the preferences of all civil applicants in the first two cases in the ECCC. Key priorities indicated by victims were physical and mental health facilities and educational measures, while the delivery of justice was ranked to have less importance.[110]

Reparations in the context of the ECCC raise several problematic issues. Individuals cannot claim reparations and financial compensation cannot be awarded. In any case, the Internal Rules note that reparations are to be borne by convicted persons, which, based on claims of indigence of defendants in other international criminal courts, raises doubts over the viability of successful reparation claims. Furthermore, it should be noted that reparations figure only in the Internal Rules and not in the agreement between the Cambodian government and the UN, nor in the national legislation creating the ECCC. The legal basis for reparations is thus not particularly solid. There is growing recognition that unless concrete measures are taken to ensure the availability of funds for the implementation of reparations, it is unlikely that they will ever materialise. This has led to calls among NGOs for the establishment of a trust fund for victims, based on that of the International Criminal Court;[111]

[107] ECCC Press Release, 'Trial Chamber Issues Reasoned Decision Defining Civil Party Rights During Trial Proceedings', 13 October 2009, available at: www.eccc.gov.kh/english.

[108] ECCC Internal Rules, Rule 23 quarter; 'Victim Associations'.

[109] ECCC Internal Rules, Rule 23 quarter; 'Victim Associations'. See also Zegveld, 'Victims' Reparations Claims and International Criminal Courts', p. 99.

[110] ECCC Press Release, 'Victims Support Section Convenes Roundtable Discussion on Broader Support to Victims', 15 September 2010, available at: www.eccc.gov.kh/english.

[111] Redress, 'Considering Reparations for Victims of the Khmer Rouge Regime', Discussion Paper, November 2009.

the Cambodian government has not, however, indicated support for such an initiative. Regrettably, the first case decided by the ECCC further undermined expectations among victims as the judgment essentially dismissed the majority of the claims of the civil parties, which included requests for medical care and the construction of memorials.[112]

4.7 Contributing factors to the shift in the focus on victims' rights within international criminal law

In order to contextualise further the development of reparations provisions in criminal law as set out above, one should consider some of the influences that have contributed to improved focus on victims. Without doubt, the primary influence can be traced from human rights law and jurisprudence, which has been explored in detail in Chapter 3. However, it should also be acknowledged that other movements in law and related disciplines, such as criminology, sociology and political science, have had a significant impact. Among these, the role played by the victimology movement, restorative justice initiatives and feminist critique of international humanitarian and criminal law will be briefly touched on.

4.7.1 Victimology

The victimology movement originated in the 1970s and was developed, largely by criminologists, in response to the general disregard for victims of crime within national justice systems.[113] The movement was also linked to the increasing crime rates in many developed countries and the discontent among victims of crime regarding their treatment in the criminal procedure. The objectives of the movement were to visualise and strengthen the position of victims of crime by stressing the need for victims' services and lobbying for the right to compensation. Among the outcomes of the victimology movement were the establishment of victim support networks and government programmes for compensation for victims of crime, primarily in developed countries.

While the movement assisted in highlighting the vulnerability of individual victims and their lack of standing in criminal procedure, it

[112] *Kaing Guek Eav, alias Duch*, Case 001/18-07-2007/ECCC/TC, Judgment, 26 July 2010, paras 635–75.

[113] P. Rock (ed.), *Victimology* (Aldershot: Dartmouth Publishing, 1994); R. Elias, *The Politics of Victimization, Victims, Victimology and Human Rights* (Oxford University Press, 1986); C. Hoyle and R. Young, *New Visions of Crime Victims* (Oxford: Hart Publishing, 2002). For further information see: www.worldsocietyofvictimology.org.

may also be noted that the focus was on victims of ordinary crimes. Scant attention was paid to victims of human rights violations.[114] This in turn is reflected in the Declaration of Basic Principles of Justice for Victims of Crime and Abuse of Power adopted in 1985.[115] The Declaration is divided into two sections; as the title indicates, one part deals with victims of (ordinary) crimes and the second part with victims of abuse of power. The first part on ordinary crime is notably more elaborated and sets out specific provisions on access to justice, restitution, compensation and social assistance, while the provisions relating to victims of human rights violations (i.e., abuse of power) are significantly shorter.[116]

4.7.2 *Restorative justice*

Related to the victimology movement was the development of restorative justice theory, which started during the 1980s and 1990s. Restorative justice, like victimology, seeks to affirm the status of the victims and their rights. However, restorative justice is based on a larger picture as it seeks to take into account and consider the interests of the victim, the offender as well as the community. In essence, restorative justice questions traditional retributive criminal justice, which has as its primary objective the maintenance of the rule of law and punishment of the offender. Rather, restorative justice argues that successful resolution of crime requires analysis of the impact on all involved parties and their active participation in the process.[117] A description by practitioners states that: 'Restorative justice is a theory of justice that emphasizes repairing the harm caused or revealed by criminal behaviour. It is best accomplished through cooperative processes that include all stakeholders.'[118]

Proponents of restorative justice underline the need for a value shift away from retribution and stress the importance of mediation between victims and perpetrators in order to identify the harm caused. Perhaps not surprisingly, the theory largely stems from juvenile justice initiatives

[114] Elias, *The Politics of Victimization*.

[115] UN Declaration of Basic Principles of Justice for Victims of Crime and Abuse of Power, General Assembly Resolution 40/34, adopted 29 November 1985 (see also previous mention in this chapter in relation to the Rome Statute of the International Criminal Court).

[116] E. Fattah (ed.), *Towards a Critical Victimology* (London: St. Martin's Press, 1992), p. 402.

[117] H. Zehr, *Changing Lenses: A New Focus for Crime and Justice* (Scottsdale, PA: Herald Press, 1990); H. Zehr, *The Little Book of Restorative Justice* (Intercourse, PA: Good Books, 2002); J. Braithwaite, *Restorative Justice and Responsive Regulation* (Oxford University Press, 2002).

[118] 'What is Restorative Justice?', May 2005, available at: www.restorativejustice.org/intro.

in developed countries. The origins of restorative justice have also been traced to indigenous peoples' traditions in North America and New Zealand.

By the 1990s, restorative justice became associated with transitional justice initiatives as it was attributed by Desmond Tutu as a principle guiding the work of the Truth Commission in South Africa.[119] This in turn triggered interest among restorative justice proponents to 'export' their theory to countries where serious human rights violations had occurred.[120] The theory has subsequently gained appeal among certain governments seeking non-retributive measures to deal with human rights violations and to eschew accountability. There is a danger that states see restorative justice as an escape route to avoid complying with their human rights obligations, which may result in undue amnesties and, in situations where perpetrators still exercise control, risk of the lives of victims. Such aspects will be further explored in the case studies, notably that of Colombia, in Part II of this book.

The incorporation of elements of restorative theory in post-conflict justice mechanisms may be positive and contribute to a broader and more comprehensive concept of justice. However, although restorative justice theory supports the rights of victims and sets important focus on their right to reparation, caution is advised against presenting restorative justice as an alternative to formal justice. In 2002, the United Nations adopted Basic Principles on the use of restorative justice programmes.[121] While the preamble states that 'restorative justice does not prejudice the right of States to prosecute alleged offenders', regrettably there is no mention of human rights law or the obligation of the state to ensure accountability for human rights violations. Furthermore, the Principles call for the provision of technical assistance to developing countries in order to promote restorative justice programmes. Again, this highlights the dangers involved in trying to export restorative justice to countries where the ordinary justice system remains inadequate. The tendency to promote restorative justice as an alternative,

[119] R. A. Wilson, *The Politics of Truth and Reconciliation in South Africa, Legitimising the Post-Apartheid State* (Cambridge University Press, 2001), p. 25; Minow, *Between Vengeance and Forgiveness*, pp. 81–2.

[120] Braithwaite, *Restorative Justice and Responsive Regulation*, ch. 6. As an example, the International Symposium on Restorative Justice in Colombia was held in Cali, Colombia, 9–12 February 2005 (attended by author).

[121] Basic Principles on the Use of Restorative Justice Programmes in Criminal Matters, Resolution 2002/12, adopted by the United Nations Economic and Social Council, 24 July 2002, E/RES/2002/12.

rather than as a complementary measure, may result in diminished accountability and thus contribute to a climate of impunity.[122]

4.7.3 *Feminist critique*

To conclude this chapter, some final reflections will be made on the role that feminist critique has played in promoting a focus on victims in international criminal law. As the enforcement of international criminal law is based on provisions of international humanitarian law, the use of discriminatory terminology in the latter has provoked significant criticism.[123] As noted by Gardam and Jarvis: 'the regime of special protection of women during armed conflict reveals a picture of women that is drawn exclusively on the basis of their perceived weakness, both physical and psychological, and their sexual and reproductive functions'.[124] International humanitarian law, including the 1977 Protocols Additional to the Geneva Conventions, is particularly conservative in its provisions relating to sexual violence. Rape is described as an attack on the honour of the women, a form of indecent assault and as an outrage upon personal dignity. Askin notes that: 'this mischaracterization of sexual violence as a violation of the victim's dignity or honour stigmatizes the victim by inferring that she is somehow dishonoured, defiled or shamed by the sexual violence committed against her'.[125] Furthermore, women are referred to as being in need of protection, rather than in language indicating the prohibition of violations against them.[126]

Analysis and critique of the application of international criminal law and its treatment of female victims of violations was triggered by the operation and jurisprudence of the ICTY and the ICTR. Gender-based crimes were widespread in the conflicts under the jurisdiction of the tribunals, and prosecutors were faced with the challenge of applying terms from international humanitarian law that were discriminatory

122 See discussion in D. Roche, *Accountability in Restorative Justice* (Oxford University Press, 2003); D. Roche, 'Gluttons for Restorative Justice', *Economy and Society*, 32(4) (2003), 630–43.

123 J. Gardam and H. Charlesworth, 'Protection of Women in Armed Conflict', *Human Rights Quarterly*, 22 (2000), 148–66.

124 Gardam and Jarvis, *Women, Armed Conflict and International Law*, pp. 93–7.

125 K. Askin, 'Women's Issues in International Criminal Law: Recent Developments and the Potential Contribution of the ICC', in D. Shelton (ed.), *International Crimes, Peace and Human Rights: The Role of the International Criminal Court* (New York: Transnational Publishers, 2000), pp. 47–63.

126 Gardam and Charlesworth, 'Protection of Women in Armed Conflict', p. 159.

against women. Nevertheless, the ad hoc Tribunals ultimately provided important recognition of crimes of sexual violence, notably by defining rape as torture, by acknowledging that the rape of a single woman can constitute an international crime and by establishing that rape can be considered as a crime against humanity.[127]

While the jurisprudence of the ad hoc Tribunals provided recognition of violations particularly against women, it also served to underline the importance of reparations for victims by exposing the hardships of female survivors and the inadequacies of international criminal law in this regard.[128] The experiences of the female victims in the ad hoc Tribunals galvanised support for the inclusion of gender-sensitive victims' provisions during the negotiations of the Rome Statute of the International Criminal Court.[129] In 2000, the Security Council passed Resolution 1325 on Women, Peace and Security, which calls for the inclusion of the special needs of women and girls and for rehabilitation, reintegration and post-conflict construction.[130] In 2009, the Security Council in Resolution 1888 specifically addressed the issue of sexual violence and armed conflict and underlined the importance of access to health care, psychosocial support, legal assistance and socio-economic reintegration for victims.[131] However, a lack of gender-sensitive implementation of rehabilitation and reparations measures for victims still remains a key challenge. In 2007, an international meeting of civil society and gender experts in Kenya adopted the Nairobi Declaration on the Rights of Women and Girls to a Remedy and Reparation with the aim of supporting the recently adopted UN Basic Principles on the Right to Reparation for Victims, while encouraging further consideration of gender aspects in their implementation.[132] Furthermore, the UN Special Rapporteur on Violence against Women

[127] C. Chinkin and H. Charlesworth, 'Building Women into Peace, the International Legal Framework', *Third World Quarterly*, 27(5) (2006), 937–57; Askin, 'Women's Issues in International Criminal Law', pp. 47–63.

[128] Gardam and Charlesworth, 'Protection of Women in Armed Conflict', p. 157; H. Charlesworth, 'Feminist Methods in International Law', *American Journal of International Law*, 93(2) (1999), 379–94.

[129] Women's Caucus for Gender Justice and The Women's Initiatives for Gender Justice, see www.iccwomen.org.

[130] Security Council Resolution 1325 on Women, Peace and Security, 31 October 2000; Chinkin and Charlesworth, 'Protection of Women in Armed Conflict', p. 938.

[131] Security Council Resolution 1888 on Sexual Violence and Armed Conflict, 30 September 2009.

[132] V. Couillard, 'The Nairobi Declaration: Redefining Reparations for Women Victims of Sexual Violence', *International Journal of Transitional Justice*, 1 (2007), 444–53.

conducted a thematic study on reparations in 2010 in order to emphasise gender aspects of reparations.[133]

Women and children remain the most affected by violence in armed conflicts and generally suffer the continued social stigma after having been victims of sexual violence. At the national level, women's organisations have been particularly active in placing reparations on the public agenda in numerous post-conflict contexts.[134] The case studies in Part II provide some further illustration of the role played by women's organisations in this regard.

4.8 Conclusions

This chapter has explored the gradual recognition of victims' right to reparation in international criminal law. The consideration given to victims in this branch of international law has been deficient and inconsistent. This in turn relates to its corresponding analogies with municipal criminal law with regard to the status of victims and witnesses, who traditionally have been considered peripheral to the objectives of criminal justice. As demonstrated in the chapter, shifts towards a more victim-oriented international criminal law have, however, taken place in the past two decades due to significant impetus from, in particular, the human rights movement and women's organisations.

The Statutes and Rules of Procedure of the ad hoc Tribunals, the ICTY and the ICTR, lacked reference to provisions on reparations other than brief mention of restitution, which remained inoperative and deferred compensation claims to national courts. The treatment of victims and witnesses during the proceedings of the tribunals has been subject to criticism. The disproportionate attention given to perpetrators and the continued disregard for victims in the aftermath of armed conflict has raised considerable concerns over the credibility and legitimacy of the kind of justice offered by international criminal law. Objections that were raised in the past, notably by prosecutors, that any assistance for victims, including basic medical attention, would place due process at risk cannot be sustained when contrasted to the momentous impact serious violations have on victims. Victims whose lives have been shattered and who require medical services cannot place their lives on hold

133 Special Rapporteur on Violence Against Women, Rashida Manjoo, Report to the Human Rights Council 2010, UN Doc. A/HRC/14/22.

134 R. Rubio-Marín, *What Happened to the Women? Gender and Reparations for Human Rights Violations* (New York: Social Science Research Council, 2006).

awaiting lengthy legal proceedings. The neglect of victims in transitional justice processes serves to undermine efforts to promote reconciliation.

The adoption of the Rome Statute of the International Criminal Court in 1998 signalled a momentous change, whereby victims and their rights were given prominent recognition. For the first time, the role of victims as participants in proceedings was acknowledged and their right to reparation was defined in a comprehensive manner as consisting of restitution, compensation and rehabilitation. Although still in draft form at the time, the Basic Principles on the Right to Reparation for Victims provided a foundation for the recognition of victims' rights during the adoption of the Rome Statute and the development of the Rules of Evidence and Procedure of the ICC.

The innovative creation of the Trust Fund of the ICC, which acts independently of investigations and the stage of proceedings of the court, illustrates how concrete measures can be undertaken in order to reach victims. Although reparations cannot be formally awarded until the ICC issues a conviction, nevertheless the Trust Fund has provided assistance for victims in the form of rehabilitation and livelihood opportunities. Such measures are likely to have a considerable, positive impact on changing the situation for victims, rather than rendering them dependent on protracted international criminal proceedings. In societies where armed conflict has largely affected poor and vulnerable groups in society, reparations are an indispensable element of transitional justice in order for victims to be able to re-establish their situation, resume their lives and participate on an equal footing in society. As indicated in several surveys with victims, practical measures such as access to medical and psychosocial services as well as education are primary concerns among victims.

While the progress made with regard to victims' rights in the ICC is remarkable, numerous tensions and unresolved challenges remain. Among them are the divergent interests of victims versus the need for expediency in the criminal justice process. Irrespective of the recognition given to victim participation, it is unlikely that international criminal proceedings will ever provide an adequate forum for victims to relate their experiences. While certain victims experience closure when testifying, others conclude that they are considered secondary to the interests and the objectives of the court. Extensive victim participation can delay proceedings, and sentences against individuals cannot comprehensively address the questions relating to institutional and state responsibility that victims wish to explore.

Reparation awards against convicted individuals are unlikely to be effectively implemented without a degree of recognition of state responsibility, which may be concurrent for those carrying the greatest responsibility for the crimes committed. As demonstrated by human rights mechanisms, state responsibility may also result from failure to show due diligence and prevent violations. From the perspective of victims, being able to present evidence against a specific individual, attend international trial proceeding and await the outcome of proceedings is something few victims of serious violations are able to undertake. As is illustrated, for example, in the current ICC investigations in relation to Sudan, the concurrent application of state responsibility and international criminal law will have to be given further consideration.

Without disregarding the crucial role of judicial accountability, it should be recognised that many victims perceive the concept of justice as being alien unless accompanied by reparations. The establishment of trust funds for victims, notably of the ICC, shows recognition of the importance that the right to reparation be implemented. Ideally, such trust funds should be operated with some allocations by the state where the violations took place and in tandem with national reparation programmes. Trust funds also offer an opportunity for the international community to demonstrate its commitment to, and solidarity with, the situation of the victims. Regrettably, despite the precedent-setting example of the Trust Fund of the ICC, similar initiatives have not been consistently established in other situations where hybrid criminal justice initiatives have been undertaken.

While important progress has been made with regard to victims' rights and reparations in international criminal justice, significant challenges remain in order to prove that victims are no longer an afterthought and to ensure that their rights are effectively enjoyed not only in law, but also in practice.

5 Conclusions Part I – legal state of play: convergence of international law and reparation as an individual legal right with customary recognition

Historically, international law viewed reparations as an inter-state measure. However, the convergence of a number of developments in international law over the past decades has produced important shifts. Part I of this book has identified the fundamental changes in state responsibility through the advancement of multiple treaty provisions in human rights law. Significant changes have also taken place in international humanitarian law and international criminal law, whereby victims' rights have gained recognition. Increasing cross-references and linkages between different branches of international law, in particular, in relation to the rights of the individual and the significant increase in state party ratifications of human rights treaties, voluntarily undertaken over the past few decades, are all indicative of such shifts. Furthermore, the establishment of numerous human rights monitoring mechanisms, at the international and regional level, points towards a global acceptance by states of human rights obligations and responsibilities vis-à-vis the individual. Several provisions on human rights have acquired recognition as customary law and, in some cases, even as peremptory norms that the world community has a common interest in protecting. The jurisprudence of the International Court of Justice (ICJ) and the Articles on State Responsibility adopted by the International Law Commission (ILC) in 2001[1] support this affirmation. Furthermore, both the ICJ[2] and the ILC have provided significant normative impetus regarding reparations in general international law.

[1] 'Articles on Responsibility of States for Internationally Wrongful Acts', Report of the International Commission, UN Doc. A/56/10, ch. IV.E.I.

[2] In particular. the case *Legal Consequences of the Construction of a Wall in the Occupied Palestinian Territory*, Advisory Opinion, 9 July 2004, ICJ Report, paras 145, 152–3.

The logical consequence of the recognition of human rights as *jus cogens* implies that individuals appear as rights bearers or subjects in general international law. Having afforded individuals such standing in international law, the need to translate consequences of breaches, such as reparations, in favour of individual victims becomes apparent. The right of individuals to receive reparations for serious violations is an indispensable corollary in order to provide an effective remedy for the violations suffered. As noted by Higgins: 'rights suppose a correlative obligation on the part of the State ... without a remedy, a right may be but an empty shell'.[3] State responsibility entails positive duties and may also be incurred when the state has omitted or failed to demonstrate due diligence to prevent violations.

The concept of reparations has gradually evolved and consolidated through specific provisions in numerous treaties, in particular, those of human rights, but also in humanitarian and criminal law. The dual and complementary nature of human rights and humanitarian law provisions has been affirmed, notably by the ICJ,[4] as well as by several UN bodies, such as the General Assembly and the Human Rights Council. As noted in preceding chapters, the specific language on reparations in different treaties may vary in detail, however, it is significant that such provisions exist in all major human rights treaties. Considerable jurisprudence at the international as well as regional level confirms a growing consensus regarding the elements and importance of reparations for the individual victim of serious human rights violations. State compliance with reparations awards varies; however, within regional human rights systems where supervisory or follow-up mechanisms exist (Europe and the Americas), compliance rates are relatively high.

The ICRC, following a lengthy and comprehensive study on state practice in relation to humanitarian law, concluded in 2005 that state responsibility to provide reparations has attained customary status.[5] While provisions regarding reparations for victims have developed at a slower pace in international criminal law, the importance of the

[3] Higgins, *Problems and Process, International Law and How We Use It*, p. 99.

[4] *Armed Activities on the Territory of the Congo Case (Democratic Republic of the Congo* v. *Uganda)*, ICJ Report 2005. For further references on the mutually complementary and reinforcing nature of human rights and humanitarian law see 'Outcome of the Expert Consultation on the Issue of Protecting the Human Rights of Civilians in Armed Conflict', Report to the Human Rights Council of the Office of the High Commissioner for Human Rights, A/HRC/11/31, 2 June 2009.

[5] Henckaerts and Doswald-Beck, *Customary International Humanitarian Law*.

groundbreaking reparation provisions, notably Articles 75 and 79, in the Rome Statute of the International Criminal Court (1998) and the creation of its Trust Fund cannot be underestimated. Although the ad hoc Tribunals, the ICTY and the ICTR, largely disregarded victims and their rights in the criminal procedure, considerable recognition is given to victims in the provisions of the Rome Statute, and the Trust Fund has proceeded to provide assistance for victims independently of investigations of the court.

The adoption of the Basic Principles on the Right to Reparation for Victims in 2005 following fifteen years of negotiations, provided yet another important benchmark, as these reflect the normative connection between international humanitarian and human rights law and synthesise and define the areas of reparations as consisting of restitution, compensation, rehabilitation, satisfaction and guarantees of non-repetition.[6] While formally non-binding, the Principles reflect already established norms in international law. The status of the Principles is strengthened by the fact that they have already been widely cited and referred to, including when they were still in draft form, in jurisprudence by numerous human rights bodies. Furthermore, they figure in several recently adopted legal instruments and, as will be explored in Part II, have been referred to by a number of truth commissions and in national legislation in several countries. It is therefore submitted on the basis of the findings set forth in Part I of this book that state responsibility to provide reparations in favour of individuals has acquired a certain customary standing.

While the legal basis for claiming the right to reparation for victims of serious human rights violations has become firmly entrenched, the preceding chapters acknowledge some of the challenges that have arisen and that remain in order to assert that the right can be effectively exercised in practice. The major challenge continues to be that of implementation. While human rights mechanisms have increased their efficiency, expanded their jurisprudence in the realm of reparations and sought to undertake measures to monitor compliance by states, such mechanisms were not designed to address large numbers of victims in conflict situations. This worrisome lacuna needs to be addressed; the concept of state responsibility is maturing, alongside a customary right

[6] UN Basic Principles and Guidelines on the Right to a Remedy and Reparation for Victims of Gross Violations of International Human Rights Law and Serious Violations of International Humanitarian Law, UN Doc. A/RES/60/147.

to receive reparations, yet it remains all too common that a national legal framework and forum to which victims can submit claims is lacking. While the provision of reparations remains primarily a state responsibility, the gap between international legal standards and their application represents a challenge to the international legal order and the international organisations entrusted with the promotion of human rights. The establishment of various trust funds for victims, both at the international and regional level, provides avenues for victims to present claims. However, their sustainability depends on voluntary funding by the international community and ultimately their impact is dependent on their ability to invoke the responsibility of concerned states and harmonise efforts with broader national measures to address reparations.

Jurisprudence on reparations by human rights courts and entities set important precedents and standards; however, major challenges are visible in their limited and stretched capacity to monitor compliance by states. Comprehensive measures are required to be undertaken at the national level in order to ensure that the number of beneficiaries is expanded and that the most vulnerable victims are identified and prioritised when it comes to redress claims. Transitional justice initiatives have gradually incorporated more emphasis on the rights of victims and sought to promote the adoption of national legislation and reparations programmes to that end. Part II of this book proceeds to explore such efforts, undertaken in collaboration with, and with support of, the United Nations in a number of countries that have faced armed conflict in order to compare and contrast the right to reparation and its application and enforcement in practice.

Part II

Transferring standards into reality

In honouring the victim's right to benefit from remedies and reparation, the international community keeps faith with the plight of victims, survivors and future human generations, and reaffirms the international principles of accountability, justice and the rule of law.

UN Basic Principles and Guidelines on the Right to a Remedy and Reparation for victims of Gross Violations of International Human Rights Law and Serious Violations of International Humanitarian Law, UN Doc. A/RES/60/147.

6 The role of the UN and the promotion of victims' rights and reparations in practice

6.1 Introduction to transitional justice mechanisms and truth commissions

Building on Part I on legal standards and reparation provisions in different branches of international law, Part II seeks to apply the affirmed right of victims to reparations as a yardstick to assess the realisation of the right in practice. Transitional justice measures, such as truth commissions, have provided important impetus to the promotion of the right to reparation by creating forums for large-scale claims from victims of armed conflict. Truth commissions have permitted an assessment of the impact that violations have had on victims and, through a victim participatory process, proposed recommendations for comprehensive reparations. Therefore, the second part of this book explores the situation *de jure* as well as *de facto* by considering how actual post-conflict measures on the ground have managed to advance this right in practice. An overall aim is to consider to what extent state practice supports the argument that the right to reparation is attaining customary status in international law.

Part II explores the aspects of reparations in four case studies (Guatemala, Sierra Leone, East Timor and Colombia) from different geographic regions that have endured armed conflict and where the UN has played a significant role in promoting transitional justice initiatives. Given the key role of the UN in advocating for greater state responsibility vis-à-vis victims, focus is on the extent to which it has been possible to provide reparations in practice through UN-supported transitional justice processes, and on which factors have been decisive in promoting state responsibility and responsiveness to victims' claims for reparations. This first chapter of Part II briefly introduces the notions of transitional justice and truth commissions. Furthermore, mention is made of the unique reparation measures that formed part of the United Nations Compensation Commission and of subsequent efforts by the Security Council to address reparations in Sudan.

Just to recap, Chapter 2 of Part I identified state responsibility in international law to provide victims of grave or serious human rights violations with reparations. As noted in Chapter 3 on human rights jurisprudence, the concept of reparations has benefited vastly from the expansion of case law of human rights bodies, both international and regional, during recent decades. Yet the main challenge remains in the limited applicability of such case law in countries where serious human rights and humanitarian law violations have taken place. International human rights courts and bodies, while important standard-setters, were not conceived of for the purpose of dealing with large-scale claims, and generally national enforcement mechanisms are poor. Thus, the impact of human rights jurisprudence is restricted due to the limited number of beneficiaries and the lack of systematic follow-up at the country level.

With regard to international criminal law, as noted in Chapter 4, reparations have been considered only to a very limited extent in retributive accountability measures. The ad hoc Tribunals, ICTY and ICTR, largely disregarded victims and their rights in the criminal procedure. This has been addressed by the considerable recognition given to victims in the provisions of the Rome Statute of the International Criminal Court; however, the practical implementation of these rights remains to be proven. Positive steps have nevertheless been taken by the Trust Fund of the ICC, which has proceeded to provide assistance for victims independently of investigations by the ICC. The Extraordinary Chambers in the Courts of Cambodia (ECCC) contributed to the recognition of victims' rights in international criminal law by allowing them to participate as a party during the proceedings and to present collective claims through associations of victims; however, its first judgment was disappointing and in practice to date the ECCC has done little to advance the right to reparation.

While the different branches of law over time have provided the essential legal framework for victims' right to reparation, their practical impact on the ground for the most affected victims has been limited. Meanwhile, the UN has been present on the ground in numerous conflict and post-conflict situations through peace mediation and peacekeeping operations. The UN, vested by the Charter with the authority and duty to maintain international peace and security in conformity with the principles of justice and international law, has faced, and continues to face, major challenges in promoting normative standards for victims in its operative work. The expanded role of the UN in peacekeeping missions,[1] and in post-conflict justice initiatives undertaken over the past fifteen years, underlines the importance played by the organisation in ensuring that state responsibility towards victims should not be abandoned during accountability and reconciliation processes.

In seeking new modalities to deal with the complex legacy of accountability in post-conflict countries, numerous countries have implemented transitional justice measures. As the rule of law and institutional judicial structures generally collapse during armed conflict, the UN has often been called upon to provide assistance in rebuilding their credibility. Transitional justice measures have commonly been linked to peace agreements and to a varying and increasing degree involved the UN in their establishment and operation. According to the United Nations:

> the notion of transitional justice . . . comprises the full range of processes and mechanisms associated with a society's attempts to come to terms with a legacy of large-scale past abuses, in order to ensure accountability, serve justice and achieve reconciliation. These may include both judicial and non-judicial mechanisms, with differing levels of international involvement (or none at all) and individual prosecutions, reparations, truth-seeking, institutional reform, vetting and dismissals, or a combination thereof.[2]

Alongside the setting-up of the ad hoc Tribunals, the UN has been instrumental in the establishment and operation of several truth commissions across the globe, initiated by the El Salvador Truth Commission established by the peace accords in 1992. Experiences over time have led to the acknowledgement that 'the United Nations must assess and respect the interests of victims in the design and operation of transitional justice measures. Victims and the organisations that advocate on their behalf deserve the greatest attention from the international community.'[3]

1 Report of the Secretary-General to the General Assembly, 'Investing in the United Nations, for a Stronger Organisation Worldwide', released 7 March 2006, A/60/692 details that: 'in the first 44 years of the history of the UN, only 18 peacekeeping missions were set up. In the 16 years since 1990, 42 new missions have been authorized', para. 4.

2 Report of the Secretary-General to the Security Council, 'The Rule of Law and Transitional Justice in Conflict and Post-Conflict Societies', UN Doc. S/2004/616, 23 August 2004, para. 8.

3 Report of the Secretary-General to the Security Council, 'The Rule of Law and Transitional Justice in Conflict and Post-Conflict Societies', para. 18.

Research conducted on transitional justice mechanisms has started to focus on the issue of reparations only during the past few years and, in particular, since the adoption of the Basic Principles on the Right to Reparation for Victims in 2005.[4] Hayner was among the first to conduct comparative international research on truth commissions.[5] As non-judicial accountability mechanisms such as truth commissions were originally seen as a trade-off regarding accountability, initial debate focused on the dichotomy of 'truth versus justice' and explored issues relating to impunity, amnesties and reconciliation through forgiveness.[6] Wilson underlined the importance that truth commissions should not compromise fundamental human rights norms and the expectations and rights of victims by allowing political interests to take precedence.[7] Cohen emphasised the importance of victims being fully aware and informed about the circumstances of the violations they are expected to forgive.[8] Méndez has firmly and consistently argued in favour of the right to truth for victims.[9]

Over time, critique of international tribunals for their lack of consideration for victims in judicial proceedings and the recognition of the value of victim participation in transitional justice mechanisms,[10] has

[4] Prominent examples of such recent research include K. De Feyter, S. Parmentier, M. Bossuyt and P. Lemmens (eds), *Out of the Ashes, Reparation for Victims of Gross and Systematic Human Rights Violations* (Antwerp: Intersentia, 2005); P. De Greiff (ed.). *The Handbook of Reparations* (Oxford University Press, 2006); C. Ferstman, M. Goetz and A. Stephens (eds), *Reparations for Victims of Genocide, War Crimes and Crimes against Humanity, Systems in Place and Systems in the Making* (Leiden: Martinus Nijhoff, 2009).

[5] Hayner, *Unspeakable Truths*; P. Hayner, 'Fifteen Truth Commissions 1974 to 1994: A Comparative Study', *Human Rights Quarterly*, 16 (1994), 597–655; P. Hayner, 'Commissioning the Truth: Further Research Questions', *Third World Quarterly*, 17 (1996), 19–29. Notable in this regard is also the research by the International Center for Transitional Justice (ICTJ), available at: www.ictj.org.

[6] See further discussion in Rotberg and Thompson (eds), *Truth v. Justice*; Barahona de Brito, Gonzalez Enriquez and Aguilar (eds), *The Politics of Memory*; McAdams (ed.), *Transitional Justice and the Rule of Law in New Democracies*; Kritz (ed.), *Transitional Justice*; Rigby, *Justice and Reconciliation after Violent Conflict*. On the evolution of transitional justice see N. Roht-Arriaza and J. Mariezcurrena (eds), *Transitional Justice in the Twenty-First Century, Beyond Truth versus Justice* (Cambridge University Press, 2006).

[7] Wilson, *The Politics of Truth and Reconciliation in South Africa*.

[8] S. Cohen, 'State Crimes of Previous Regimes: Knowledge, Accountability and the Policing of the Past', *Law and Social Inquiry*, 20(1) (1995), 7–50.

[9] J. Méndez, 'Accountability for Past Abuses', *Human Rights Quarterly*, 19 (1997), 255–82.

[10] Zacklin, 'The Failings of Ad Hoc International Tribunals', pp. 541–5; E. Stover, 'Witnesses and the Promise of Justice in The Hague', in E. Stover and H. Weinstein (eds), *My Neighbour, My Enemy, Justice and Community in the Aftermath of Mass Atrocity* (Cambridge University Press, 2004), pp. 104–20; Haslam, 'Victim Participation at the International

led to a reassessment of the role played by truth commissions. This has been reflected in a gradual recognition that transitional justice measures, consisting of both tribunals for accountability and truth commissions for victim participation, may be complementary in the overall pursuit of justice.[11]

Unlike criminal investigations, truth commissions are set up to establish a comprehensive public record of large-scale abuses that have taken place during a determined period in the past, commonly during a period of internal armed conflict or dictatorship. The findings of truth commissions are presented with an analysis of the instigating factors and circumstances surrounding the violence in order to paint an overall picture and suggest specific as well as comprehensive recommendations. Unlike during prosecutions, the victims and witnesses play a central and interactive role in providing testimony, either in public or in private, of their personal experience of abuses. As such, truth commissions may assist in overcoming the inherent limitations of criminal justice processes,[12] in particular, by addressing the needs of victims and their relatives, by the establishment of a comprehensive historical record and by issuing policy-oriented recommendations for reparations.[13]

Truth commissions initially set out as nationally driven processes and originated from the South Cone of Latin America. While the concept of truth commissions has been adopted as a transitional justice mechanism by the international community, it is essential to note that the establishment of such inquiries requires approval and sanctioning, although this may be conceded reluctantly, by the state concerned in order to gain official status and recognition.[14] In attempting to

Criminal Court', pp. 315–34; L. Fletcher and H. Weinstein, 'Violence and Social Repair: Rethinking the Contribution of Justice to Reconciliation', *Human Rights Quarterly*, 24 (2002), 573–639.

[11] Goldstone, 'Advancing the Cause of Human Rights', ch. 9; Stahn, 'United Nations Peace-building, Amnesties and Alternative Forms of Justice', pp. 191–205; Schabas, 'The Relationship between Truth Commissions and Courts'.

[12] Zacklin, 'The Failings of Ad Hoc International Tribunals', pp. 541–5 states: 'Criminal Courts exist for the purpose of establishing individual accountability – not to uncover the fates and remains of loved ones. Nor is it their purpose to provide an official history ... Even less so is the awarding of compensation for victims ... the Tribunal (ICTY) itself is not sufficient to promote reconciliation. Additional mechanisms, such as functioning national courts and Truth Commissions are needed.'

[13] Report of the Secretary-General to the Security Council, 'The Rule of Law and Transitional Justice in Conflict and Post-Conflict Societies', UN Doc. S/2004/616, 23 August 2004, p. 15.

[14] Hayner, *Unspeakable Truths*, p. 14.

comprehensively address past wrongs in large-scale and complex situations of conflict, it is imperative to assess the extent of the violations and if possible to identify institutional structures and root causes that enabled the violence. To ensure that such an assessment is as neutral and multifaceted as possible, while also ensuring the participation of victims, is a major challenge. Over the past two decades, it has been recognised that the involvement of the international community, notably the UN, in the conduct of commissions of inquiry and truth commissions has been crucial in order to underline their neutrality.[15] Over time, the value of mechanisms such as truth commissions has been recognised, as they have provided a solid basis for the elaboration of reparation measures to deal with past violations comprehensively, specifically taking into account the needs of victims. This is further elaborated in the subsequent case studies in Part II.

Transitional justice mechanisms have often been assessed by scholars by comparing their mandates or according to perceptions of the degree of reconciliation achieved. More recently, studies based on direct interviews with victims of armed conflict demonstrate that reparations are a key priority for those affected by serious violations and an essential element in order to undertake more long-term evaluations of the impact of transitional justice mechanisms.[16] It is of crucial importance that future policy discussions and research on transitional justice be informed by direct consultations with victims.

[15] Examples of truth commissions that the United Nations has assisted in setting up at the national level include: El Salvador, 1992; Guatemala, 1996; East Timor, 2001; and Sierra Leone, 2002. In addition, it should be noted that Member States of the UN are increasingly mandating international commissions of inquiry through the Security Council and the Human Rights Council, with support by OHCHR. Examples of commissions of inquiry to assess serious and systematic human rights violations in the context of internal unrest and armed conflict include: Sudan, 2004; Gaza, 2009; Côte d'Ivoire, 2011; and Libya, 2011. Examples of UN inquiries into serious human rights violations that demonstrate a significant emphasis on reparations include: the DRC Mapping Report, finalised by OHCHR in October 2010 (in particular, paras 1073–125); and the Report of the Secretary-General's Panel of Experts on Accountability in Sri Lanka, released in April 2011 (in particular, paras 276–7, 288 and 444).

[16] The ICC Trust Fund for Victims, Programme Progress Report, Autumn 2010; OHCHR, 'Making Peace Our Own, Victims' Perceptions of Accountability, Reconciliation and Transitional Justice in Northern Uganda', 2007; OHCHR Uganda Office, Annual Report of the Office of the High Commissioner for Human Rights to the Human Rights Council for 2007, UN Doc. A/HRC/7/38/Add.2; ICTJ, 'Unfulfilled Expectations, Victims Perceptions of Justice and Reparations in Timor Leste', February 2010; ICTJ, 'Perceptions and Opinions of Colombians Regarding Truth, Justice and Reconciliation', Survey 2006.

A comprehensive overview and assessment of reparation measures available for victims provides a key indicator of a state's willingness to accept responsibility for past violations, even when such responsibility is incurred through succession. Although the gravity of the harm cannot be undone, certain reparations are a prerequisite in order for victims to be able to resume their lives. The civilians most affected in armed conflict are commonly among the most vulnerable and voiceless in society. Without attempts to repair the harm they have suffered, the violations committed will perpetuate their exclusion in society and become continuous impediments to their ability to enjoy and exercise their rights on an equal footing with others.

While the importance of the issue of reparations is gaining recognition, there is still only limited research and studies on the practical implementation of this right, in particular, after armed conflict.[17] Different stakeholders, important among whom are the victims themselves, are likely to express reservations in relation to transitional justice mechanisms, whether tribunals or truth commissions, as long as their achievements in the area of reparations remain neglected and unmonitored. Part II of this book therefore explores, through case studies, transitional justice measures and the extent to which they have managed to promote state responsibility for providing reparations. The contribution of four specific truth commissions in the realm of reparations is explored through the subsequent case studies: Guatemala, Sierra Leone, East Timor and Colombia over the period of a decade from 1999 to 2009. The selected case studies consider the issue of reparations in peace agreements, as well as in statutes of transitional justice mechanisms, notably truth commissions, and in their final report. The degree to which UN peacekeeping presences or other UN entities have followed up on reparations in consultation with authorities is also studied.

The impact of the truth commission reports is analysed, as well as the degree to which there has been the political will to implement the recommendations of the reports. The case studies note the national developments that have taken place regarding legislation and policies/programmes for reparations and explore practical challenges in developing

[17] Examples of research on the degree of implementation of the right to reparation in post-conflict contexts include Ferstman, Goetz and Stephens (eds), *Reparations for Victims of Genocide, War Crimes and Crimes against Humanity, Systems in Place and Systems in the Making*; De Greiff (ed.), *The Handbook of Reparations*; De Feyter, Parmentier, Bossuyt and Lemmens (eds), *Out of the Ashes*; H. Rombouts, *Victim Organisations and the Politics of Reparation: A Case Study on Rwanda* (Antwerp: Intersentia, 2004).

reparation programmes. The relationship between truth commissions and criminal accountability initiatives is considered. When reparation measures have been adopted, attention is given to which push-and-pull factors were applicable in the national circumstances, such as the degree to which international and regional human rights mechanisms have influenced national reparation policies and the strength of civil society and victims' organisations. The case studies identify the reparations measures provided or deemed to be a priority in future programmes and which victims are most likely to be favoured or excluded. Furthermore, the case studies discuss the obligations of non-state actors and study the degree of responsibility assumed by states for such violations.

As will be documented, truth commissions have made significant contributions to the practical realisation of the right to reparation for victims following armed conflict. However, the follow-up given by states to truth commission recommendations has generally disappointed victims. Nevertheless, the recommendations for reparation measures contained in the truth commission reports remain a comprehensive platform for future action. The case studies indicate that although recognition by the state may not be immediately forthcoming, the truth commission recommendations for reparations continue to carry weight in policy-making and international relations through insistent lobbying by civil society and UN human rights entities.

Notably, the case study of Guatemala illustrates that despite initial government hostility and deliberate efforts to ignore the Truth Commission (CEH) recommendations relating to reparations, subsequent governments have made significant policy changes in this area. The case studies of Sierra Leone and East Timor highlight the challenges involved in undertaking parallel transitional justice initiatives without coordination with regard to the issue of reparations. Colombia illustrates the impact that coordinated international, regional and national pressure can have on the public discourse and domestic legislation on reparations. Thus, as described in the case studies, there is an emerging shift in state practice towards not only recognition in law, but also in implementation with regard to the responsibility of the state to provide reparations for victims of armed conflict.

A common element among the countries selected as case studies is their commitment to international human rights and humanitarian law. Guatemala, Colombia, Sierra Leone and East Timor are all states parties to the following human rights treaties: CERD, CCPR, CESCR, CAT, CEDAW, CRC and its Optional Protocol on the involvement of children in armed conflict (CRC-OPAC). With regard to humanitarian law, the four selected countries are all parties to the Geneva Conventions as well as their Additional Protocols I and II. Three of the countries, Sierra Leone, Colombia and East Timor, have ratified the Rome Statute of the International Criminal Court, while Guatemala has yet to do so. The focus of this study is on reparations for serious violations in armed conflict and the Basic Principles on the Right to Reparation for Victims link to these violations (which in the Principles are referred to as gross and serious violations of human rights and humanitarian law). The states' explicit undertakings, by way of ratifications, in the realms of international human rights, humanitarian and criminal law underline their acceptance of state responsibility for reparations to victims. In all four case studies, the respective truth commission reports have made clear references to applicable human rights and humanitarian law standards. These specific references, as well as their translation into national policy and legislation, are explored in further detail in the case studies. When applicable, attempts to issue national amnesties are observed as well as their impact on the issue of reparations.

Before embarking on the case studies, the following pages give a brief introduction to the unique reparations modalities of the United Nations Compensation Commission (UNCC) as it demonstrates the practical role the UN can play in supporting implementation of the right to reparation. However, the unprecedented operational modalities of the UNCC have not been repeated in other instances. The Security Council failed to endorse subsequent initiatives, notably the recommendation for a compensation commission in Darfur.

6.2 The United Nations Compensation Commission

Although the UNCC[18] was set up under challenging and politicised circumstances, it was an innovative mass claims mechanism and it is worthwhile noting some of its particular features that are of direct relevance to the right of victims to seek reparations for violations that have taken place in the context of armed conflict. Experiences of the UNCC are of relevance for mass claims processes and reparations programmes established at the national level. Furthermore, the practices of the UNCC may also provide useful references in the context of the emerging challenges that face the International Criminal Court and its

[18] Official web page of the United Nations Compensation Commission at: www.uncc.ch.

Trust Fund. The UNCC is also relevant in view of the various trust funds that are being established or considered in conjunction with human rights mechanisms, both at the international and regional level.

The Security Council established the Compensation Commission and the Fund it was to administer in 1991,[19] only a few weeks following the end of the Iraqi occupation of Kuwait. The decision of the Security Council to set up the UNCC followed a series of resolutions underlining the responsibility of Iraq. Security Council Resolution 687 affirmed that: 'Iraq ... is liable under international law for any direct loss, damage, including environmental damage and the depletion of natural resources, or injury to foreign Governments, nationals and corporations as a result of Iraq's unlawful invasion and occupation of Kuwait.'[20]

Despite the political and legal controversy during and after its establishment,[21] the Compensation Commission set a unique precedent in international law as the first mechanism created by the UN whereby individual victims could claim compensation for violations in armed conflict. The Commission was established as a subsidiary organ to the Security Council, its Governing Council mirrored the composition of the Security Council, while the determination of the claims was made by independent and geographically diverse panels of Commissioners for whom a Secretariat reviewed and prepared the claims.[22]

As noted by the Secretary-General in his report of 2 May 1991: 'The Commission is not a court or an arbitral tribunal before which the parties appear, it is a political organ that performs an essentially fact-finding function of examining claims, verifying their validity, evaluating losses, assessing payments and resolving disputed claims.'[23]

[19] Security Council Resolution 687, 3 April 1991 and Security Council Resolution 692, 20 May 1991.

[20] Security Council Resolution 687, para. 16.

[21] D. Caron and B. Morris, 'The UN Compensation Commission, Practical Justice, not Retribution', *European Journal of International Law*, 13(1) (2002), 183–99; Gattini, 'The UN Compensation Commission: Old Rules, New Procedures on War Reparations', pp. 161–81; G. Christenson, 'State Responsibility and UN Compensation Commission: Compensating Victims of Crimes of State', in R. Lillich (ed.), *The United Nations Compensation Commission* (New York: Transnational Publishers, 1995), pp. 311–64; D. Bederman, 'Historic Analogues of the UN Compensation Commission', in R. Lillich (ed.), *The United Nations Compensation Commission* (New York: Transnational Publishers, 1995), pp. 257–308.

[22] H. Van Houtte, H. Das and B. Delmartino, 'The United Nations Compensation Commission', in P. De Greiff (ed.), *The Handbook of Reparations* (Oxford University Press, 2006), pp. 322–89.

[23] Report of the Secretary-General of 2 May 1991 Pursuant to Article 19 of Security Council Resolution 687, UN Doc. S/22559.

The Commission was mandated to offer compensation to individuals, governments, corporations and international organisations. Individuals could not petition the Commission directly, but had to submit their claims through their governments. Importantly, the system was not based on the diplomacy principle as individuals themselves rather than states were considered as beneficiaries. The rules specifically stipulated that states were under an obligation to distribute the compensation awards to individuals. It should be noted that certain governments presented claims on behalf of refugees and asylum-seekers. International organisations, notably the United Nations Development Programme (UNDP), the United Nations High Commissioner for Refugees (UNHCR) and the United Nations Relief and Works Agency for Palestine Refugees (UNRWA) submitted claims, in total some 3,000, on behalf of individuals, in particular of stateless persons.[24]

The Compensation Commission received some 2.7 million claims and defined six categories (A to F) for processing the awards. Categories A to C referred to claims by individuals. More specifically, category A claims were submitted by individuals who were forced to abandon Kuwait or Iraq between August 1990 and March 1991. Category B included claims from individuals for serious personal injury and death. Category C included claims for all types of individual loss, including non-pecuniary losses such as mental pain and anguish, up to US$100,000. The other categories related to claims, primarily large-scale ones, from corporations, governments and international organisations.

The UNCC did not define violations in accordance with human rights or humanitarian law. However, individual claims in the categories A–C were processed as a priority on humanitarian grounds.[25] All category B claims were paid in full by the end of 1996.[26] It has been noted that: 'the first phase of the UNCC's work is one of the most significant and under-reported success stories of the United Nations. Over two and a half million A, B and C claims were filed. The merits

[24] L. Taylor, 'The United Nations Compensation Commission', in C. Ferstman, M. Goetz and A. Stephens (eds), *Reparations for Victims of Genocide, War Crimes and Crimes against Humanity, Systems in Place and Systems in the Making* (Leiden: Martinus Nijhoff, 2009), pp. 197–214; Caron and Morris, 'The UN Compensation Commission, Practical Justice, not Retribution', p. 188.

[25] Decisions of the Governing Council of the UNCC on criteria for expediting urgent claims and definition of personal injury and mental pain and anguish, UN Docs S/AC.26/1991/1, S/AC.26/1991/3.

[26] Van Houtte, Das and Delmartino, 'The United Nations Compensation Commission', p. 360.

in all these claims were determined and the monies awarded were paid to the individual claimants within less than 10 years after the liberation of Kuwait.'[27]

The claims awarded in the above categories were defined according to fixed amounts and were modest given the gravity of the violations. For categories A and B, the sum was set at US$2,500 per individual and category. In category B the total amount for a family was established at US$10,000. Some ninety nationalities, Iraqis excluded, submitted claims to the Commission, and it should be noted that a substantial number of the beneficiaries were foreign workers who were forced to flee during the invasion. The largest number of category A claims came from Egypt, India and Sri Lanka.[28] Fixed amounts and lenient standards of proof were established to provide a speedy and effective remedy based on equal treatment and humanitarian urgency.[29]

In this context, it is worthwhile noting that Kälin, the UN Special Rapporteur on the Situation of Human Rights in Kuwait under Iraqi Occupation, following two investigative missions *in situ*, affirmed in his report in 1992 the responsibility of Iraq for gross and systematic human rights violations during the conflict as well as for breaches of humanitarian norms, including summary and arbitrary executions, widespread and systematic torture and the deportation of large numbers of civilians to Iraq. The Special Rapporteur supported the establishment of the Fund for compensation and urged it to interpret its mandate broadly in order to include compensation for both material and non-material damages, in accordance with the international law principle of compensation for victims of human rights violations.[30]

The funding of the UNCC was a unique characteristic and a major source of controversy which overshadowed its operation. The Security Council, following a recommendation of the Secretary-General, determined that the funding for the UNCC would come from 30 per cent (later 25 per cent) of the annual Iraqi oil export revenue, and as such was

[27] Caron and Morris, 'The UN Compensation Commission, Practical Justice, not Retribution', p. 188.

[28] Caron and Morris, 'The UN Compensation Commission, Practical Justice, not Retribution', p. 188.

[29] Van Houtte, Das and Delmartino, 'The United Nations Compensation Commission', p. 371.

[30] UN Special Rapporteur on the Situation of Human Rights in Kuwait under Iraqi Occupation, Reports to the Commission on Human Rights, 1992, UN Doc. E/CN.4/1992/26, paras 240–62. Discussed in Shelton, *Remedies in International Human Rights Law*, pp. 404–5.

part of the framework of the so-called Oil-for-Food programme.[31] In determining the amount to be diverted to the Commission, a number of considerations regarding the Iraqi economy were taken into account, such as previous military expenditure, foreign debt payments and requirements of the population.[32] Nevertheless, the manner in which the Compensation Fund was financed led to critique on the basis that it formed part of a politically motivated sanctions regime. In particular, the negative impact that the Oil-for-Food programme had on the Iraqi civilian population has been widely criticised as being punitive. It has also been noted that among the large-scale claims by companies to the UNCC, there was a predominance of US and Kuwaiti submissions.[33] This in turn raised critique that the UNCC, although operating under the authority of the Security Council, was a form of victors' justice in violation of due process. Although certain procedural aspects of the UNCC have been subject to critique, the state responsibility of Iraq for compensation has generally not been questioned.[34] It has also been noted as an inconsistency that some states, who raised critique against the UNCC, were also creditors who were pursuing pre-Gulf War debts against Iraq.[35]

It is submitted that although the UNCC was created under particular political circumstances and financed in a controversial manner through Iraqi oil revenues, the UNCC provided an exceptional example which highlighted the Security Council's potential regarding state responsibility to provide victims with reparations. It furthermore demonstrated the capacity of the UN to implement, in a relatively expedient manner and on a large scale, the right to reparation for victims. Despite the lack of clear references to violations of human rights and humanitarian law in the mandate of the Commission, in its practice it interpreted that the remedy of violations affecting individual civilian victims was a priority. It has been noted that 'the privileged position of the individual in the UNCC system is to be welcomed as possibly the

[31] Security Council Resolution 705, 15 August 1991.

[32] Caron and Morris, 'The UN Compensation Commission, Practical Justice, not Retribution', p. 197 and Van Houtte, Das and Delmartino, 'The United Nations Compensation Commission', p. 363.

[33] Shelton, *Remedies in International Human Rights Law*, p. 410.

[34] Christenson, 'State Responsibility and UN Compensation Commission', pp. 311–64; M. Frigessi di Rattalma and T. Treves (eds), *The United Nations Compensation Commission, A Handbook* (The Hague: Kluwer Law International, 1999), pp. 30–7.

[35] Caron and Morris, 'The UN Compensation Commission, Practical Justice, not Retribution', p. 198.

most significant contribution of the UNCC to the development of international law in the field of claims settlement'.[36]

6.3 Compensation in Darfur?

Regrettably, despite the invocation of state responsibility to provide compensation for victims in the creation of the UNCC, the Security Council has not given equal priority to this issue when confronted with subsequent conflicts in other parts of the world. This was most blatantly demonstrated in the case of Darfur in Sudan. The 2005 Report of the Commission of Inquiry, appointed by the Secretary-General, made two specific recommendations regarding measures to be taken by the Security Council.[37] One was referral of the situation in Darfur to the ICC and the other was the establishment of a compensation commission. The Report specifically stated that such a compensation commission should be considered as a complementary measure to that of the referral to the ICC. The Report underlined that 'States have the obligation to act not only against the perpetrators, but also on behalf of victims'.[38]

The Security Council endorsed the referral of the situation in Darfur to the ICC in Resolution 1593, but failed to acknowledge the recommendation from the Commission of Inquiry regarding the establishment of an international compensation commission.[39] Only a timid reference in the preamble of the resolution hints at the issue: 'recalling Articles 75 and 79 of the Rome Statute and encouraging States to contribute to the ICC Trust Fund for Victims'. The indirect mention of the Trust Fund for Victims is the only mention of the word 'victims', while the terms 'compensation' or 'reparation' do not figure at all in the resolution. Scholars' and the public debate at the time mainly focused on the political dimensions of the referral to the ICC, while the recommendation regarding compensation was treated as a peripheral issue.[40]

36 Gattini, The UN Compensation Commission: Old Rules, New Procedures on War Reparations', pp. 170, 181.

37 Report of the Commission of Inquiry on Darfur to the Secretary-General, Submission of the Report to the Security Council, UN Doc. S/2005/60, 1 February 2005, paras 590–603.

38 Report of the Commission of Inquiry on Darfur to the Secretary-General, para. 590.

39 Security Council Resolution 1593 on Referral of the Situation in Darfur to the ICC, UN Doc. S/RES/1593, adopted 31 March 2005.

40 R. Cryer, 'Sudan, Resolution 1593 and International Criminal Justice', *Leiden Journal of International Law*, 19 (2006), 195–222; W. Schabas, 'Darfur and the "Odious Scourge": the Commission of Inquiry's Findings on Genocide', *Leiden Journal of International Law*, 18 (2005), 871–85. Tomuschat is a notable exception; he explicitly argued against the

The continued lack of reparations remains among the pending debts owed to the victims in Darfur. The Darfur Peace Agreement signed on 6 May 2006 makes explicit reference to the creation of a compensation commission; this was an echo from the unheeded recommendations of the 2005 Commission of Inquiry. While the Security Council initially failed to address reparations, it is significant that the mandate of the peacekeeping operation in Darfur, UNAMID, established in 2007 by Security Council Resolution 1769, contains specific reference to the need to focus on compensation.[41] Also in 2007, the Human Rights Council mandated a High Level Mission to assess the human rights situation in Sudan. Their mission report identified compensation for victims in Darfur as one of the six critical areas that needed to be addressed in order to improve the human rights situation.[42] Furthermore, the Human Rights Committee, following its review of Sudan in 2007, identified the lack of reparation and compensation for victims, especially in Darfur, among its principal concerns.[43]

While UNAMID continues to promote compensation for victims in its dialogue with local authorities, progress on the ground in Darfur has been slow. Ongoing conflict and the lack of Sudanese cooperation with the ICC make it impossible for the Trust Fund to access victims in the region. However, experiences in Darfur highlight the importance of state responsibility and reparations being kept squarely on the agenda. While reparations may be slow in coming to Darfur, it is crucial that human rights mechanisms and the international community maintain significant pressure on the issue of reparations in order to signal that victims are no longer considered to be of secondary importance in international justice.

creation of a Compensation Commission, see reference to certain of his arguments in Chapter 1 of this book; Tomuschat, 'Darfur – Compensation for the Victims', pp. 579–89. References on the neglect of victims' rights in Darfur, see 'Outcome of the Expert Consultation on the Issue of Protecting the Human Rights of Civilians in Armed Conflict', Report to the Human Rights Council of the Office of the High Commissioner for Human Rights, A/HRC/11/31, 2 June 2009, para. 39.

41 Security Council Resolution 1769 on the Establishment of UNAMID (African Union and United Nations Hybrid Operation in Darfur), UN Doc. S/RES/1769, adopted 31 July 2007.

42 Report of the High-Level Mission on the Situation of Human Rights in Darfur Pursuant to Human Rights Council Decision S-4/101, UN Doc. A/HRC/4/80, 9 March 2007.

43 CCPR Concluding Observations on Sudan, August 2007, CCPR/C/SDN/CO/3, paras 9 and 11.

7 Case study: reparations in Guatemala

7.1 Introduction

The first case study to be explored in Part II is Guatemala and the recommendations issued in relation to reparations by the Truth Commission (CEH) operating there between 1997 and 1999. The rationale for choosing Guatemala as one of the case studies is that it represents one of the first instances where the international community supported a truth commission and thus provides an opportunity to study the degree of follow-up over the past ten years. The Truth Commission's final report contained a strong and comprehensive set of recommendations. While progress has been made in some areas, the overall implementation of the recommendations has been slow and inadequate.

Nevertheless, despite having been issued over a decade ago, the recommendations of the Truth Commission continue to figure as a platform for action for human rights and victims' organisations. Through legal and political international human rights mechanisms, Guatemala continues to be subjected to pressure to ensure their effective implementation. The aim of this chapter is to look more closely into the extent to which reparations figured in the peace process and transitional justice mechanisms, and which key factors have contributed to advancing the realisation of reparations in practice. Notably, the post-conflict context in Guatemala was marked by a strong UN presence through a UN peacebuilding mission between 1994 and 2004, the continued presence of an OHCHR country office and the gradually increased engagement with international human rights mechanisms. The Inter-American human rights system has played a key catalyst role in promoting reparations for victims of the armed conflict and has had a strong influence in the national debate on this issue.

The Truth Commission in Guatemala built on previous experiences from truth commissions in Latin America, notably in Argentina, Chile and El Salvador.[1] In the cases of El Salvador and Guatemala, the truth commissions were established by the peace accords that ended the internal armed conflicts and the UN played an instrumental role in their establishment and operation. The unprecedented involvement of the UN in the truth commissions in El Salvador and Guatemala represented the first occasions when the UN officially sponsored and set up such commissions as transitional justice mechanisms.

7.2 Brief historical background

The origins of the armed conflict in Guatemala can be traced back to the long-standing racial and social exclusion of the indigenous majority by the ladino minority.[2] To a large extent, the conflict was also a consequence of US Cold War policies. In 1954, a CIA-sponsored coup overthrew the democratically elected president after he attempted to initiate one of the first agrarian land reforms in Latin America. A series of military dictatorships followed, all of which received significant military support from the United States.

Initial popular protest movements by farmers, students, trade unionists and left-wing sympathisers were crushed and turned to clandestine guerrilla activities. State-sponsored death squads persecuted left-wing sympathisers and large-scale offensives were launched against rural indigenous communities. The violence peaked in the 1980s. Indigenous youth were systematically recruited from indigenous communities and forced to participate as paramilitaries, Patrullas de Autodefensa Civil (PAC). A deliberate policy of disintegration of the indigenous peoples was conducted through the PAC, who were responsible for some of the most brutal atrocities against their own communities. The legacy of distrust and division among indigenous communities remains tangible today, decades after the violence occurred. Hundreds of massacres took place

1 M. Popkin and N. Roht-Arriaza, 'Truth as Justice: Investigatory Commissions in Latin America', *Law and Social Inquiry: The Journal of the American Bar Foundation*, 20(1) (1995), 79–116.

2 T. O'Kane, *In Focus Guatemala, A Guide to the People, Politics and Culture* (London: Latin America Bureau, 1999); J. M. Simon, *Guatemala: Eternal Spring, Eternal Tyranny* (New York: W. W. Norton, 1987); P. Ball, P. Kobrak and H. Spirer, *State Violence in Guatemala, 1960–1996; A Qualitative Reflection* (Washington, DC: American Association for the Advancement of Science, 1999).

among indigenous communities, whole villages were exterminated through a scorched-earth policy, women and girls raped on a large scale, pregnant women were tortured to death and children murdered in front of their parents. Around a million people fled across the border to Mexico as refugees. Priests were also targeted due to their participation in the liberation theology movement.

In 1985, a new constitution was adopted and elections brought the first civilian president in two decades. New institutions were created, such as the Congressional Human Rights Commission and the Human Rights Ombudsman; the latter was given a wide-reaching mandate to investigate violations and promote legal action. However, large-scale human rights violations persisted. The Ombudsman initially proved to be a facade intended to placate the international community. Civil society and human rights organisations were repressed, auto censorship ruled in the media and several prominent human rights defenders, such as Myrna Mack, were executed by government agents.

7.3 Peace negotiations

The peace talks between the Guatemalan government and the guerrilla movement, the Guatemalan National Revolutionary Unity (Unidad Revolucionaria Nacional Guatemalteca, URNG), started in the late 1980s. In fact, the guerrilla movement in Guatemala, unlike its counterparts in Colombia, was never a particularly strong force and was only integrated by a few thousand members. During the early 1990s a series of peace accords were negotiated through UN mediation. In 1996, the final agreement was signed and brought all previous accords into force. In total thirteen agreements were signed committing the Guatemalan government to a comprehensive agenda for building a more democratic state. Major issues covered by the separate agreements related to human rights, judicial reforms, resettlement of the displaced, demobilisation of the guerrillas, reduction and restructuring of the army, and the status of the indigenous population.[3] References to human rights are present in several of the agreements and there is a significant overlap of issues relating to the rights of victims of the armed conflict.[4]

[3] Guatemala Peace Agreements, UN, New York, 1998.

[4] International Council on Human Rights Policy, 'Negotiating Justice, Human Rights and Peace Agreements', Geneva, 2006, pp. 28–30.

The Comprehensive Agreement on Human Rights was the only agreement to enter into effect immediately upon signing in 1994. It affirmed a commitment to end impunity and in section VIII recognises 'that it is a humanitarian duty to compensate and/or assist victims of violations. Said compensation shall be effected by means of government measures and programmes of a civilian and socio-economic nature addressed, as a matter of priority, to those whose need is greatest, given their economic and social position.'[5]

The same agreement established a UN verification mission, MINUGUA, which was set up the same year and remained in operation for a decade, during which it played a key role in monitoring and reporting on the implementation of the peace accords. OHCHR, upon invitation of the government, opened a small office in Guatemala in the late 1990s, primarily focused on the provision of technical cooperation. Following the closing of the MINUGUA mission in 2004, OHCHR has been given a more active role in monitoring human rights and retains its presence in the country.

7.4 Establishment and mandate of the Truth Commission

In 1994, a separate agreement to establish the Truth Commission, formally known as the Historical Clarification Commission (CEH), was signed. The Clarification Commission was expected to cover over three decades of internal armed conflict from the early 1960s until the signing of the final peace agreement in 1996.

Furthermore, an agreement on the Basis for the Legal Integration of the URNG was concluded in 1996, which referred to the importance placed on the Clarification Commission to ensure that the truth be known in order to avoid a repetition of events. Paragraph 19 of the same agreement set out that:

> on the principle that any violation of human rights entitles the victim to obtain redress and imposes on the State the duty to make reparation, the (National Reconciliation) Act shall assign to a State body responsibility for implementing a public policy of compensation for and/or assistance for the victims of human rights violations. The body in question shall take into consideration the recommendations to be formulated in this regard by the Clarification Commission.

Thus, the issue of reparations figures prominently in several of the peace agreements that affirm the duty of the state to provide reparations to

[5] *The Guatemala Peace Agreements*, 'Comprehensive Agreement on Human Rights', s. VIII, p. 28.

victims and foresee the establishment of a government programme for this purpose. However, it should be noted that the exact wording refers to 'compensation and/or assistance', which leaves some room for interpretation whether assistance and not compensation would suffice.

With regard to the Clarification Commission, its mandate specifically set out three goals:

1. To clarify with all objectivity, equity and impartiality the human rights violations and acts of violence that have caused the Guatemalan population to suffer, connected with the armed conflict.
2. To prepare a report that will contain the findings of the investigations carried out and provide objective information regarding events during this period covering all factors, internal as well as external.
3. Formulate specific recommendations to encourage peace and national harmony in Guatemala. The Commission shall recommend, in particular, measures to preserve the memory of the victims, to foster a culture of mutual respect and observance of human rights and to strengthen the democratic process.[6]

Unlike other truth commissions previously established, the mandate specified that abuses to be investigated were 'human rights violations causing the population to suffer', without a qualifying element to include only the most serious acts of violence.[7] On the other hand, it set an impossible task for the Commission as it was expected to cover a period of over thirty years. Finally, the Commission determined that priority had to be given to attacks on life and personal integrity, in particular, extrajudicial executions, forced disappearances and sexual violations.[8]

A significant restraint on the work of the Commission was the inclusion of a clause in the agreement specifying that it should 'not attribute responsibility to any individual in its work, recommendations and report, nor shall these have any judicial aim or effect'.[9] In particular, the final phrase severely crippled the expectations of the Commission

[6] *The Guatemala Peace Agreements*, 'Agreement on the Establishment of the Commission to Clarify Past Human Rights Violations and Acts of Violence that Have Caused the Guatemalan Population to Suffer', p. 54.

[7] In contrast, the 1991 Truth Commission in Chile, established while Pinochet was still in power, focused only on victims who had been killed or disappeared, excluding torture victims from its mandate, see Popkin and Roht-Arriaza, 'Truth as Justice', p. 84. Not until 2004 did a revised Chilean Truth Commission inquiry include reference to victims of torture and arbitrary detention.

[8] C. Tomuschat, 'Clarification Commission in Guatemala', *Human Rights Quarterly*, 23(2) (2001), 239.

[9] *The Guatemala Peace Agreements*, 'Agreement on the Establishment of the Commission to Clarify Past Human Rights Violations', p. 55.

and caused significant concern among human rights and victims' organisations. However, the international member of the Commission, Prof. Tomuschat, affirmed upon termination of the report that 'it would be totally inappropriate to maintain that the report can never serve as evidence if and when its findings may determine the outcome of proceedings. It is the relevant rules of procedure that must be used to determine whether such indirect proof can be relied upon in a case.'[10]

7.5 Operational aspects of the Historical Clarification Commission

The Commission was finally set up in 1997 and operated for two years before delivering its final report. The Commission was headed by three members: one was appointed by the Secretary-General of the United Nations and the other two were Guatemalans, one of whom was selected by the national university presidents. In total, more than 250 professionals were contracted by the Commission, about half of them Guatemalan and the other half foreign, from more than thirty different countries. Among the specialists hired were, for example, anthropologists, political scientists, lawyers, military experts, social workers and interpreters. The Commission faced substantial challenges regarding communication as the indigenous communities speak over twenty different languages.

In order to collect testimonies, fourteen regional offices were set up and the investigators visited about 2,000 rural communities and collected more than 8,000 testimonies. The Commission benefited from the presence of the MINUGUA mission and based most of their regional offices at the same locations. The Commission worked in different areas focusing, for example, on thematic studies of violence, legal evaluation, in-depth case studies, historical analysis, foreign involvement and final recommendations. When preparing the recommendations in the report, the Commission invited organisations of civil society to a national forum where they were able to make suggestions. The forum was held in May 1998, with more than 400 participants from 139 organisations.[11] In addition, members of various organisations were asked to submit their suggestions for consideration in the final document. Many human rights organisations expressed satisfaction with regard to the consultation process and the manner in which they were invited to contribute

[10] Tomuschat, 'Clarification Commission in Guatemala', p. 244.
[11] CEH Report, vol. 1, p. 48.

to the Commission.[12] The Commission maintained close contact with non-governmental organisations from whom it received significant documentation on human rights violations, including a comprehensive inquiry done as a parallel civil society initiative (Recuperation of Historical Memory Project, REMHI) by the human rights office of the Catholic Church. In retaliation, Bishop Gerardi was assassinated two days after presenting the REMHI report to the public in 1998.

The Commission furthermore received assistance from three teams of forensic anthropologists who conducted exhumations of mass grave sites and handed over their documentation files. All the interviews recorded by the Commission were kept confidential as there were considerable fears for the safety of victims and witnesses. Unlike, for example, the Truth Commission in South Africa, no testimonies were given in public sessions in Guatemala.

7.6 The Final Report of the Historical Clarification Commission

On 25 February 1999, the final report was finally presented at a public ceremony.[13] Despite the vague mandate of the Commission, excluding the possibility of individualising responsibility, it nevertheless succeeded in releasing a strongly worded report.[14] Based on its findings, the Commission estimated that a total of about 200,000 people had been killed or disappeared. In over 80 per cent of all violations the victims were Mayan, and in more than 90 per cent of all cases the perpetrators were presumed to be state agents.[15] This suggested an extent of violence beyond previous estimations of both international and national human rights organisations. The conclusions stated that 'the violence was fundamentally directed by the State against the excluded, the poor and above all, the Mayan people, as well as against those who fought for

[12] Author's interview with Helen Mack, founder and head of the Myrna Mack Foundation, a leading human rights organisation in Guatemala (Guatemala City, 2 November 1999).

[13] In total, the complete report of the CEH encompasses twelve volumes and consists of more than 4,000 pages.

[14] See assessments in P. Ball and C. Audrey, 'The Truth of Truth Commissions: Comparative Lessons from Haiti, South Africa and Guatemala', *Human Rights Quarterly*, 23 (2001), 13, 28, 33; R. Seider, 'War, Peace and Memory Politics in Central America', in A. Barahona de Brito, C. Gonzalez Enriquez and P. Aguilar (eds), *The Politics of Memory, Transitional Justice in Democratizing Societies* (Oxford University Press, 2001), pp. 161–89; V. Sanford, *Buried Secrets, Truth and Human Rights in Guatemala* (Basingstoke: Palgrave Macmillan, 2003), p. 259.

[15] CEH Report, vol. 5, Conclusions, Articles 2 and 15.

justice and greater social equality'. A significant section of the report was dedicated to historical analysis of the political and socio-economic factors behind the conflict. Among these institutionalised racism was identified as a key factor. Over 600 massacres of Mayan communities were identified; the definition of massacres was applied on cases involving the killing of more than five people. Several of the massacres involved some 200 people, often large numbers of women and children. The majority of the massacres took place in the early 1980s, but some were committed as late as 1995.

An unexpectedly strong conclusion in the report was its affirmation that a state policy of genocide took place during the early 1980s. The Commission analysed the application of the Genocide Convention in four rural regions and found that during the dictatorship of General Ríos Montt between 1981 and 1983, the State of Guatemala was responsible for acts of genocide against the Mayan population.[16]

The section on recommendations in the report established a broad platform for a comprehensive reparations policy as well as for institutional reform. The first recommendation was that parties to the conflict recognise and apologise for the violations committed. The then president of Guatemala, Álvaro Arzú, offered a tactical apology a few months before the Commission report was released, but refused to reiterate it once the full extent of the violence was revealed. It was not until 2004 that the then president, Óscar Berger, recalled the recommendations of the Commission and offered a public apology to the victims of the armed conflict. The guerrillas offered a formal apology in March 1999 and published a full-page apology in the major daily newspapers.[17] Further recommendations related to remembrance of the victims by commemoration by the designation of a national day of dignity for the victims. The construction of monuments in accordance with Mayan culture and reclaiming of Mayan sacred sites was also recommended.

Importantly, a National Reparation Programme was proposed, as foreseen in the peace agreements. The Commission specifically recommended

[16] CEH Report, Conclusions, paras 108–23.

[17] 'El Perdón de URNG', *El Periódico*, 13 March 1999. It may be added that Bill Clinton during a visit to Guatemala in March 1999 apologised in public for the role played by the United States in the conflict. The CIA was instrumental in the military coup in 1954 and provided significant military and intelligence support to the dictatorships during the subsequent decades. The Clarification Commission, on the basis of its mandate to take into account both internal as well as external factors, documented the roles played by the United States and Cuba during the conflict.

that a reparations programme be based on principles relating to restitution, compensation, rehabilitation and satisfaction, and restoration of the dignity of the victims.[18] It is significant that already in 1999 the proposed reparations programme reflected the, at the time draft, Basic Principles on the Right to a Reparation for Victims of Gross Human Rights Violations, which were not formally adopted by the General Assembly until 2005.[19] The fact that these principles were already referred to while still at a draft stage supports their legal value.

Furthermore, it was proposed that the reparatory measures of the programme could be individual and collective; the latter was encouraged for violations that had been suffered collectively by entire communities and care was urged to promote reconciliation and avoid stigmatisation. With regard to the beneficiaries, it was suggested that these be victims or their relatives, and with regard to individual economic indemnification, prioritisation should be given according to economic situation and social vulnerability and by paying particular attention to the elderly, widows, children or those who were found to be disadvantaged in any other way. It was put forward that the victims of cases contained in the annexes of the Commission report be automatically qualified as victims without the need for further documentation.[20] The reparations programme, it was suggested, should be operative for a period of at least ten years.

Further recommendations related to the high incidence of disappearances during the armed conflict and it was specifically recommended that a National Commission for the Search of Disappeared Children be established.[21] It was also recommended that a bill of law be passed whereby the declaration of absence due to forced disappearance would be legally recognised for reparation and succession matters. The government was also urged to establish an active policy on exhumations by providing support to NGOs specialised in forensic anthropology and the national Human Rights Ombudsman. Exhumations should be carried out with due regard to the cultural values of the victims, the majority of whom were indigenous.

Additional recommendations in the report related to measures of satisfaction and non-repetition. Among educational measures proposed

[18] CEH Report, Recommendations, paras 7–21.

[19] UN Basic Principles and Guidelines on the Right to a Remedy and Reparation for Victims of Gross Violations of International Human Rights Law and Serious Violations of International Humanitarian Law, UN Doc. A/RES/60/147.

[20] CEH Report, Recommendations, para. 18(b).

[21] CEH Report, Recommendations, para. 24.

were recommendations relating to the dissemination of the report among the public, its translation into indigenous languages and incorporation into the school curricula. Among proposed measures relating to the administration of justice and human rights was the prosecution of crimes not extinguished by the Law on National Reconciliation of 1996. The law, which in essence contained an amnesty provision, nevertheless excluded amnesties for crimes of genocide, torture, forced disappearances and crimes not subject to prescription or which according to international treaties ratified by Guatemala did not permit extinction of criminal liability.[22] Furthermore, the report recommended recognition of the competency of individual complaints mechanisms of UN human rights treaty bodies, with which Guatemala subsequently complied.[23]

Regarding measures to prevent repetition of events, the report proposed the development and adoption of a new military code, military training in accordance with human rights standards and the creation of a civilian police force (previously part of the military). The report also recommended measures to combat the legacy of institutionalised racism and fiscal reform by adopting progressive taxation. Importantly, the report recommended the creation of an institution responsible for follow-up of the overall implementation of the recommendations, and it was suggested that such a mechanism be composed of representatives of both government and civil society.[24]

7.7 Follow-up and implementation of the recommendations regarding reparations

The initial reception of the CEH report by the government was one of reluctance and there were deliberate attempts to downplay the importance of the report and its findings.[25] As previously mentioned, the

[22] N. Roht-Arriaza, 'The Role of International Actors in National Accountability Processes', in A. Barahona de Brito, C. Gonzalez Enriquez and P. Aguilar (eds), *The Politics of Memory, Transitional Justice in Democratizing Societies* (Oxford University Press, 2001), p. 41.

[23] CEH Report, Recommendations, paras 39, 47. Guatemala subsequently recognised the competency of the Human Rights Committee, the Committee against Torture and the Committee for the Elimination of Discrimination against Women to receive individual complaints.

[24] CEH Report, Recommendations, paras 55, 56, 60, 62–5, 77, 78, 79–84.

[25] The author spent three months in Guatemala in 1999 shortly after the release of the CEH Report to document its impact through extensive interviews with different stakeholders: victims, civil society organisations, government representatives, former

government initially refused to acknowledge the findings and offer an apology. The establishment of the cross-institutional mechanism for follow-up, the Commission for Peace and Harmony, was delayed until 2001. Contrary to the recommendations of the CEH, it was established by executive decree rather than by the adoption of legislation through Congress.[26]

In 2003, a National Programme for Reparations (PNR) was established and similar to the mechanism for follow-up, it was created by an executive decree rather than through a legislative initiative in Congress. The lack of a solid legal basis has rendered the programme volatile with regard to changes to its operation as it depends on the political will of the sitting government, which unilaterally has the power to amend its mandate.[27] In 2005, the then government changed the decree regarding the composition of the National Commission for Reparations, responsible for executing the reparations programme. Previously, it had consisted of equal representation of government officials and representatives of human rights, women's, Maya and victims' organisations. The change of the decree made it exclusively a government entity, without consultation with the affected organisations.[28] The rifts between civil society organisations and their distrust towards government officials has been a major impediment in making the programme operative. OHCHR has consistently insisted that the PNR should have a solid legal basis in order to guarantee its independence and sustainability; however, progress in this regard has been slow. By early 2011, no legislation had yet been adopted.[29]

Commissioners and staff of the CEH, academics, journalists, UN staff and diplomats. See also discussion in J. Tepperman, 'Truth and Consequences', *Foreign Affairs*, 81(2) (2002), 128–45.

[26] MINUGUA, Report on Progress in Implementation of the Peace Accords 2000–2004, November 2004.

[27] Programa Nacional de Resarcimiento (National Programme for Reparations, PNR), *La vida no tiene precio: Acciones y omisiones de resarcimiento en Guatemala*, Guatemala City, 2007, pp. 179, 186; MINUGUA Final Human Rights Assessment Report, November 2004, pp. 22–3; Procuraduría de los Derechos Humanos de Guatemala (National Human Rights Ombudsman), Seguridad y justicia en tiempos de Paz, *Cumplimiento e institucionalizaron de los compromisos contraídos por el Estado en los Acuerdos de Paz*, Guatemala City, 2006, pp. 100–3.

[28] C. Correa, J. Guillerot and L. Magrell, 'Reparation and Victim Participation: A Look at the Truth Commission Experience', in C. Ferstman, M. Goetz and A. Stephens (eds), *Reparations for Victims of Genocide, War Crimes and Crimes against Humanity, Systems in Place and Systems in the Making* (Leiden: Martinus Nijhoff, 2009), pp. 385–414.

[29] OHCHR Guatemala Office, Annual Report to the Human Rights Council for 2007, A/HRC/7/38/Add.1, para. 42; OHCHR Guatemala Office, Annual Report to the Human Rights

The delayed creation of the follow-up mechanism and the reparations programme and the manner in which they were established can in part be explained by the political dynamics. Unlike some other countries that have emerged from periods of armed conflict, in Guatemala this process was not accompanied by a political transition. The former guerrilla movement URNG was, relatively speaking,[30] never a particularly influential actor; their military strength even during the armed conflict was limited. The strong wording of the peace agreements was secured through the active role of the UN and the international community.[31] Following the peace process, the URNG was converted into a minor political party. The conservative regime and the army retained their political positions,[32] illustrated by the fact that the former military dictator Ríos Montt launched himself as a presidential candidate in 1999 and continued to head the Congress during the early 2000s. During this period, considerable debate centred on compensation benefits for the paramilitary PAC.[33] Large numbers of former PAC soldiers united and claimed financial compensation through pensions.[34] While many PAC soldiers carried the dual identity of perpetrator as well as victim, the fact that they received compensation created major resentment among victims' organisations, who had yet to receive any response from the government to their claims.

As noted by Tomuschat, in the first years after the release of the Truth Commission report, civil society and victims' organisations remained too weak to lobby for faithful compliance with the recommendations.[35] The insistence on maintaining reparations for human rights violations on the political agenda has been achieved through a combination of factors such as the presence of the UN mission MINUGUA and an OHCHR

Council for 2009, A/HRC/13/26/Add.1, para. 50; OHCHR Guatemala Office, Annual Report to the Human Rights Council for 2010, A/HRC/16/20/Add.1, para. 79.

30 For example, compared with the FARC-EP guerrillas in Colombia who controlled significant parts of the territory from the 1960s.

31 International Council on Human Rights Policy, 'Negotiating Justice, Human Rights and Peace Agreements', Geneva, 2006, p. 29.

32 Seider, 'War, Peace and Memory Politics in Central America', pp. 161–89.

33 N. Roht-Arriaza, 'Reparations in the Aftermath of Repression', in E. Stover and H. Weinstein (eds), *My Neighbour, My Enemy, Justice and Community in the Aftermath of Mass Atrocity* (Cambridge University Press, 2004), p. 126.

34 Amnesty Report, 'The Civil Defense Patrols Re-emerge in Guatemala', AI Index: AMR 34/053/2002, 4 September 2002.

35 Tomuschat, 'Clarification Commission in Guatemala', p. 245.

country office, support from UNDP, the interest of international donors who contributed towards the Truth Commission,[36] and the significant number of cases brought to the Inter-American human rights system, some 200 cases by 2000.[37] By the early 2000s, the government started to seek friendly settlements through the regional human rights system, and in 2004 decided to accept state responsibility for all cases pre-dating 1996 and appointed persons known for their human rights work to head the Presidential Commission on Human Rights (COPREDEH) to undertake negotiations. The groundbreaking judgment of the Inter-American Court in 2004 regarding the Plan de Sánchez massacre (discussed in Chapter 3), whereby record awards for compensation of nearly US$8 million were ordered, prompted the commitment of the government to make the PNR operational in order to stem the number of cases brought to the regional human rights system.[38] Mr La Rue, the head of COPREDEH at the time of paying the compensation for the Plan de Sánchez massacre, noted that 'given the number of people killed and the atrocities that were committed, I personally believe it was a modest and reasonable decision'.[39]

As noted above, the PNR[40] started its work in difficult political circumstances and its initial steps were slow. The programme was criticised for its ineffectiveness, the initial funding available was limited and it was unable to execute the delivery of reparations due to divisions within victims' organisations, and due to lacking real political support. The Decree that established the programme in 2003 did not define the violations that were to be compensated, the beneficiaries to be prioritised or what kind of reparations were to be distributed.[41] These issues were debated over a period of two years until a revised Decree was adopted in 2005; it defined and clarified in a fairly inclusive manner the above concerns. The revised Decree covered a broad range of serious human rights violations, defined the groups that should be prioritised, according to the recommendations of the CEH, and added some categories such as orphans and the disabled. Women's organisations noted as positive the specific inclusion of sexual violence and rape among the

[36] Principally the Nordic countries, Spain, the European Union and the United States.
[37] Mersky and Roht-Arriaza, 'Case Study Guatemala', pp. 7–32.
[38] Mersky and Roht-Arriaza, 'Case Study Guatemala'.
[39] La Rue, Speech at Conference on Reparations in the Inter-American System, American University, pp. 1459–63.
[40] Official web page of the Guatemalan National Reparations Programme at: www.pnr.gob.gt.
[41] Guatemalan Government Decree 258-2003, revised by Decree 619-2005.

violations.[42] Furthermore, the revised Decree included a comprehensive definition of reparations measures, defined as individual or collective, which took into account the Basic Principles on the Right to Reparation for Victims.

However, the practical implementation of the reparations programme remains a major challenge. A principal obstacle is the difficulty of documenting the victims, as many were never registered at birth, the majority being indigenous and from remote rural areas, also many civil registries were deliberately burned during the war.[43] Names of victims mentioned in the CEH report have been used to include victims in the reparations programme, however, progress towards the establishment of a national registry of victims has been slow.[44] Additional ongoing challenges for the programme include continued uncertainty over funding and that not enough attention has been given to comprehensive reparations measures. So far, the programme has mostly provided individual financial compensation (for some 3,700 persons in 2008), while the provision of psychosocial and rehabilitation measures has been neglected. The programme officially affirms that measures should include support for rehabilitation and satisfaction, for example, through assistance for exhumations and the construction of memorials. In practice, measures have been uncoordinated and victims have complained over the lack of collective reparation measures for their communities.[45] Concerns have also been raised over the lack of consideration for gender aspects and the persistence of racial discrimination. In 2006, the Human Rights Ombudsman made a critical assessment of the PNR and called for legislation to firmly entrench the programme, the establishment of a central database with victim information, harmonised working methods, more attention to psychosocial assistance, and better dialogue with victims and their communities. Regrettably, the majority of these challenges have not been adequately addressed.

While the operation of the programme continues to be criticised and concerns remain over the sustainability of its funding, nevertheless,

[42] C. Paz and P. Bailey, 'Guatemala: Gender and Reparations for Human Rights Violations', in R. Rubio-Marín, *What Happened to the Women? Gender and Reparations for Human Rights Violations* (New York: Social Science Research Council, 2006), pp. 93–135.

[43] Bejarano, C., 'Legalidad versus Conciencia, Implicaciones Jurídicas del Trabajo de PNR', in *La vida no tiene precio: Acciones y omisiones de resarcimiento en Guatemala*, Guatemala City, 2007, pp. 173–91.

[44] OHCHR Guatemala Office, Annual Report to the Human Rights Council for 2006, A/HRC/4/49/Add.1, para. 32.

[45] L. Viaene, 'Life is Priceless: Mayan Qeqchi Voices on the Guatemalan National Reparations Program', *International Journal of Transitional Justice*, 4 (2010), pp. 4–25.

certain progress has been made.[46] The impact of the programme cannot be properly judged until it has been operative over a longer period of time; however, it is crucial that critique be addressed and that reparation measures are carried out in consultation with affected communities. The programme is expected to exist for thirteen years – the number of years was defined with reference to the positive significance of the number thirteen in Maya indigenous culture – however, its continued existence will depend on whether political will can be sustained.

Many victims stress the importance of apologies, public recognition of state responsibility and psychosocial assistance as their key priorities regarding reparations.[47] However, from the perspective of the victims, a main concern is that the attention given to reparations in Guatemala is used to silence calls for criminal accountability. In fact, some victims have abandoned calls for investigations following the receipt of reparations. This may be partly explained by a generalised and deep-seated mistrust of the justice system.[48] Some human rights defenders have warned that advocating for reparations, without simultaneously considering the context of structural poverty in which the most vulnerable victims remain, may in fact offend the victims as they are not provided with long-term solutions to their situation.[49]

While the jurisprudence of the Inter-American human rights system has provided crucial impetus for the national policy on reparations, it has also created some challenges which will be difficult to resolve. As noted in Chapter 3, an aspect that has caused controversy is the discrepancy between the reparation awards by the Inter-American Court (US$25,000 per person for extrajudicial executions in the Plan de Sánchez massacre case), while the same violation only amounts to reparation awards of around US$5,000 through the national scheme. The amounts at the national level may appear excessively low, but given the estimated number of people killed during the conflict, approximately 200,000, this aspect raises issues of equity and that of realistic expectations on the

[46] OHCHR Guatemala Office, Annual Report to the Human Rights Council for 2008, A/HRC/10/31/Add.1, para. 61.

[47] Mersky and Roht-Arriaza, 'Case Study Guatemala', p. 26; Dill, 'Reparation and the Elusive Meaning of Justice in Guatemala', pp. 183–204.

[48] Mersky and Roht-Arriaza, 'Case Study Guatemala', p. 26.

[49] Helen Mack cited in Due Process of Law Foundation, *Después de procesos de justicia transicional ¿cuál es la situación de las victimas? Los casos de Chile y Guatemala*, public conference report, 2008, p. 7.

state's capacity to finance reparations for as many as possible rather than for the select few able to undertake a cumbersome process of litigation at the national and regional level.

7.8 Conclusions

In conclusion, through the insistent mediation of the UN, reparations provisions figured prominently in the peace agreements. The transitional justice mechanism, the Historical Clarification Commission, managed, despite the limitations of its mandate, to provide an important legacy upon which victims' organisations have been able to continue their advocacy for truth, justice and reparations.

While at the national level criminal proceedings have been unsuccessful, it is significant that Guatemala over the last few years has recognised state responsibility for the majority of cases of violations dating back to the armed conflict which have been brought to the Inter-American human rights system.[50] In total, this relates to more than 200 cases filed, and in many of them the Guatemalan government has negotiated a settlement with the petitioners. Furthermore, the reparations orders in Guatemalan cases that have been decided by the Inter-American Court on Human Rights have by and large been complied with and the award of reparations by the court has provided key impetus to the establishment of a large-scale reparations scheme at the national level. In a number of cases, the report of the CEH was submitted to the IACtHR as evidence.[51] As noted by Mersky and Roht Arriaza, the recognition of state responsibility for crimes committed during the armed conflict has had a cumulative effect, and the Inter-American human rights system has complemented the work of the CEH and the REMHI reports in order to reverse state denial of the role of the state in the crimes.[52] Thus, the experience in Guatemala highlights the reciprocity between efforts by transitional justice initiatives and human rights jurisprudence in order to advance in the realm of reparations.

[50] Mersky and Roht-Arriaza, 'Case Study Guatemala'.

[51] Some sentences of the Inter-American Court on Guatemalan human rights cases which refer to the report of the CEH include: *Plan de Sánchez Massacre* v. *Guatemala*, IACtHR, Judgment, Merits, 29 April 2004, Ser. C, No. 105; *Maritza Urrutia* v. *Guatemala*, IACtHR, Judgment (Merits, Reparations and Costs), 27 November 2003, Ser. C, No. 103; *Myrna Mack-Chang* v. *Guatemala*, IACtHR, Judgment (Merits, Reparations and Costs), 25 November 2003, Ser. C, No. 101.

[52] Mersky and Roht-Arriaza, 'Case Study Guatemala', p. 28.

At the international level, human rights treaty bodies have also contributed to the promotion of the implementation of the recommendations of the CEH regarding reparations and continue to do so a decade after its completion.[53] During the Universal Periodic Review of Guatemala by the Human Rights Council in May 2008, following questions from other states regarding reparations, the Guatemalan government representatives publicly affirmed the commitment of the state to recognise responsibility for human rights violations committed during the armed conflict, and noted that the state budget had been restructured to allow for comprehensive compensation in financial, cultural, legal and psychosocial terms through the National Reparations Programme.[54] These examples illustrate the importance of the interplay between transitional justice mechanisms and human rights bodies, both at the international and regional level, in order to advance in the implementation of reparations.

The establishment of the PNR may have been motivated as a measure to prevent further human rights complaints from being brought to the Inter-American human rights system. Nevertheless, the programme has gradually made progress and offers a measure of resort for the large number of victims who have yet to receive any reparations after the conflict. While international and regional human rights jurisprudence set important precedents regarding reparations, it is nevertheless impossible for the majority of victims to access such mechanisms, thus the establishment of comprehensive national reparations programmes will remain crucial in order to ensure that the maximum number of victims benefit. While the amounts offered by the programme will remain in stark contrast to the reparation orders of the IACtHR, they will provide a degree of equity among victims. In this sense, the Guatemalan government has taken significant steps. However, challenges remain, such as ensuring that the programme includes psychosocial measures and carries out its activities in a culturally sensitive manner, that sustainable and adequate funds are provided, and that its mandate becomes entrenched in legislation, rather than executive decree.

[53] CAT, Concluding Observations on Guatemala 2006, CAT/C/GTM/CO/4, para. 15; CRC, Concluding Observations on Guatemala under OPAC 2007, CRC/C/OPAC/GTM/CO/1, paras 20–1.

[54] Report on Guatemala of the Working Group on the Universal Periodic Review of the Human Rights Council, A/HRC/8/38, 29 May 2008, paras 19 and 78. However, it should be noted that the UPR of Guatemala focused primarily on the issues of impunity and racial discriminations, while the issue of reparations featured more dominantly, for example, during the UPR of Colombia; see reference in case study of Colombia.

The role of national civil society and its ability to invoke the attention of the international community to the Guatemalan state's reparations policy is vital. Unfortunately, civil society organisations in Guatemala continue to be relatively weak and divided compared with, for example, civil society in Colombia (see subsequent case study on Colombia). The OHCHR office in Guatemala has contributed to maintaining focus on reparations for violations committed during the conflict; it has, however, played a less prominent role regarding this issue than the OHCHR office in Colombia. This in part is a reflection of the varying public debate on reparations and the difference in strength of the civil society. The public debate on reparations may be less strong in Guatemala than in Colombia, however, the government does engage in a largely constructive manner, unlike, for example, in East Timor where the debate on reparations is stigmatised and opposed by the government (see subsequent case study on East Timor).

While attempts have been made to address aspects of truth and reparations in Guatemala, it is nevertheless clear that the third element of justice, that of accountability, remains absent. Despite that, the amnesty provisions specifically exclude serious human rights violations; the Guatemalan judiciary has been unable and unwilling to break the impunity of the past and this is reflected in the reluctance to ratify the Statute of the International Criminal Court.[55] Human rights and victims' groups fear that the issue of reparations may overshadow the need to make progress in establishing accountability for the past. The delicate balance between these elements represents the principal challenge facing the Guatemalan State in order to comprehensively assume its responsibility for the violations of the past.

[55] Human Rights Watch, Annual Report on Guatemala, released in January 2008, stated that only two of the 626 massacres documented by the CEH have been successfully prosecuted in the domestic criminal justice system, see www.hrw.org.

8 Case study: reparations in Sierra Leone

8.1 Introduction

The transitional justice process in Sierra Leone was characterised by the unprecedented parallel operation of the ad hoc Special Court and the Truth Commission, both mixed with international as well as national elements. The two mechanisms were established in separate processes and operated without much regard for each other, which resulted in confusion among victims as well as perpetrators. The Truth Commission originated in the Lomé Peace Agreement of 1999, while the Special Court was created after violence reignited in 2000, following a request by the government. While the term reparations did not specifically figure in the Lomé Agreement, there was ample reference to victims, rehabilitation and the creation of a Special Fund for War Victims. The Truth Commission, while not always victim-oriented in public hearings, did focus its final report on the rights of victims and expounded at length a comprehensive set of recommendations to ensure non-repetition of events as well as detailed proposals for a reparations programme. The Special Court, on the other hand, interpreted its mandate as essentially retributive, did not replicate the provisions relating to victims and reparations in the Rome Statute of the International Criminal Court, and to date has declined to order restitution in its judgments.[1] The two transitional justice institutions regrettably did not take advantage of the momentum to leave a coordinated legacy in favour of victims.

The United Nations peacekeeping mission in Sierra Leone and OHCHR played a key role in supporting national civil society actors and in highlighting the rights of victims throughout the process. Despite the

[1] Details of the provisions of the Special Court for Sierra Leone are contained in Chapter 4 on reparations in international criminal law.

existence of a regional human rights system in Africa, this was regrettably largely inactive during both the conflict and post-conflict period. Furthermore, Sierra Leone lacked a national human rights institution (NHRI) for independent monitoring and follow-up to human rights obligations at the domestic level; however, such an entity was created in 2006.

8.2 Brief historical background

The armed conflict in Sierra Leone started in 1991 when an armed group, the Revolutionary United Front (RUF) led by Foday Sankoh, commenced to attack with support from Liberia. Their stated objective was to overthrow the one-party government that had been ruling the country for three decades.[2] The RUF soon gained international notoriety for its brutal practices of amputation, child recruitment and sexual violence. During the armed conflict, Civil Defence Forces (CDF) were set up in support of the national armed forces, and they also engaged in brutal war crimes against the civilian population. In 1996, attempts were made to broker peace and an accord was signed between the government and the RUF in Abidjan. In 1997, a military coup overthrew the government and the affiliation of the different armed groups and forces became increasingly difficult to distinguish as the country descended into chaos. 'Sobels' was a commonly used term at the time, indicating the transient nature of fighters' shifting allegiances between rebels and government soldiers.

Meanwhile, the international community was slow to react. In early 1998, forces of the Economic Community of the West African States Monitoring Group (ECOMOG) intervened against the military regime and reinstated the exiled government. In 1998, a small unarmed UN mission (UNOMSIL) was established to oversee demobilisation.[3] Yet, in January 1999, the RUF and the AFRC, a group of disaffected soldiers who had adopted the characteristics of rebels, led a major attack against the capital, Freetown, causing large losses of civilian lives and leaving the city in ruins.[4] Faced

[2] W. Schabas, 'The Sierra Leone Truth Commission', in N. Roht-Arriaza and J. Mariezcurrena (eds), *Transitional Justice in the Twenty-First Century, Beyond Truth versus Justice* (Cambridge University Press, 2006), p. 22.

[3] M. O'Flaherty, 'Case Study: The United Nations Human Rights Field Operation in Sierra Leone', in M. O'Flaherty (ed.), *The Human Rights Field Operation; Law Theory and Practice* (Farnham: Ashgate, 2007), pp. 287–315.

[4] Hayner, 'Negotiating Peace in Sierra Leone', pp. 1–37.

with the situation that rebels controlled approximately two-thirds of the country, the government again initiated talks with the RUF.

8.3 Lomé Peace Agreement

The peace negotiations took place over several months in Togo and concluded in the signing of the Lomé Peace Agreement in July 1999. Similar to the previous negotiations, there was a general presumption that the rebels had to be awarded a degree of amnesty and the final text of the agreement included reference to a blanket amnesty.[5] However, the United Nations participated in the negotiations and the representative of the organisation attached a handwritten disclaimer upon signing the accords whereby he noted that 'the agreement shall not apply to international crimes of genocide, crimes against humanity, war crimes and other serious violations of international humanitarian law'.[6]

The Lomé Agreement included reference to the establishment of a Truth and Reconciliation Commission. As O'Flaherty notes, national human rights groups played an important role in lobbying for the inclusion of the Truth Commission during the negotiations, which they had been invited to observe.[7] Article XXVI of the Agreement states that:

> A Truth and Reconciliation Commission shall be established to address impunity, break the cycle of violence, provide a forum for both the victims and perpetrators of human rights violations to tell their story, get a clear picture of the past in order to facilitate genuine healing and reconciliation ... the Commission shall deal with the question of human rights violations since the beginning of the Sierra Leonian conflict in 1991 ... this Commission shall, among other things, recommend measures to be taken for the rehabilitation of victims of human rights violations ... and shall, not later than 12 months after the commencement of its work, submit its report to the Government for immediate implementation of its recommendations.

The Lomé Agreement thus foresaw a truth commission with an open-ended and broad mandate to address human rights violations. The far-reaching objective of breaking the cycle of violence was attributed

[5] Lomé Peace Agreement, Article IX. See discussion in International Council on Human Rights Policy, 'Negotiating Justice, Human Rights and Peace Agreements', pp. 32–3, 78–9.

[6] Report of the Secretary-General on the Establishment of a Special Court for Sierra Leone, UN Doc. S/2000/915, 4 October 2000, paras 22–4; Hayner, 'Negotiating Peace'.

[7] M. O'Flaherty, 'Sierra Leone's Peace Process: The Role of the Human Rights Community', *Human Rights Quarterly*, 26(1) (2004), 29–62.

to the Truth Commission. It was also expected to address impunity, yet the Agreement gave few clues as to how this should be done in concrete terms.

While the Lomé Agreement unfortunately contained no direct reference to the specific term reparations, it did refer to rehabilitation in Article XXVIII which stated that: 'The Government, through the National Commission for Resettlement, Rehabilitation and Reconstruction and with the support of the International Community, shall provide appropriate financial and technical resources for post-war rehabilitation, reconstruction and development.' The same Article referred to women as a group particularly victimised during the armed conflict.[8] There was, however, no mention of other groups of vulnerable victims who were targeted, such as children.

It is significant that the Agreement made specific reference to compensation for 'incapacitated war victims', financed by proceeds from natural resources, notably gold and diamonds, exportation of which was to be state-controlled and licensed.[9] Furthermore, Article XXIX refers to rehabilitation and a specific Fund for War Victims: 'The Government, with the support of the International Community, shall design and implement a programme for the rehabilitation of war victims. For this purpose, a special fund shall be set up.'

National human rights organisations advocated for the establishment of a reparations fund for victims of serious human rights violations during the negotiations.[10] All parties to the Agreement were in favour of such a fund, as there were victims on all sides. However, the language of the provision has been criticised for its vagueness as it contains no clear definition of who would be considered a war victim (civilians as well as demobilised?), nor does it contain any reference to state responsibility.[11]

[8] Lomé Peace Agreement, Article XXVIII, '2. Given that women have been particularly victimized during the war, special attention shall be accorded to their needs and potentials in formulating and implementing national rehabilitation, reconstruction and development programmes, to enable them to play a central role in the moral, social and physical reconstruction of Sierra Leone.'

[9] Lomé Peace Agreement, Article VII. See discussion in W. Schabas, 'Reparation Practices in Sierra Leone and the Truth and Reconciliation Commission', in K. De Feyter, S. Parmentier, M. Bossuyt and P. Lemmens (eds), *Out of the Ashes, Reparation for Victims of Gross and Systematic Human Rights Violations* (Antwerp: Intersentia, 2005), p. 293.

[10] O'Flaherty, 'Case Study: The United Nations Human Rights Field Operation in Sierra Leone', p. 306.

[11] US Ambassador Melrose cited in Hayner, 'Negotiating Peace', p. 20.

The Peace Agreement also foresaw the creation of a more long-term body for monitoring human rights violations through an 'autonomous quasi-judicial National Human Rights Commission'.[12] Both the Truth Commission and the National Human Rights Commission were supposed to be set up, with technical assistance from the international community, within ninety days of signing the Agreement. In practice, their establishment was postponed due to a variety of factors, including continued instability, delays in adopting relevant national legislation and insufficient technical and financial support from donors, who had pledged to support the process. The lack of a monitoring body for implementation of the human rights components of the Peace Agreement was a significant shortcoming. National human rights organisations, with UN support, created a follow-up mechanism coordinated among themselves.[13] While national NGOs played a prominent role, the absence of an independent NHRI was a lacuna, especially for monitoring the implementation of recommendations from the Truth Commission. The National Human Rights Commission Act was only adopted by Parliament in 2004 and the institution gradually set up in 2006.[14]

In October 1999, a new UN mission, UNAMSIL, with a stronger mandate was established by the Security Council; however, the deployment of troops was slow.[15] The RUF refused to demobilise and fighting continued despite the signing of the Lomé Peace Agreement. Hundreds of peacekeepers were taken hostage by the RUF and its allies in early 2000, which prompted the rapid deployment of British armed forces to regain control of the capital area.[16] Foday Sankoh was arrested in May 2000 and the government of Sierra Leone formally requested the assistance of the United Nations to bring RUF members to justice, leading to the agreement on the Special Court for Sierra Leone in 2002.[17] The provisions relevant to reparations in the Statute of the Special Court are referred to in Chapter 4, while this chapter focuses on the issue of reparations in

[12] Lomé Peace Agreement, Article XXV.

[13] International Council on Human Rights Policy, Negotiating Justice, Human Rights and Peace Agreements, p. 33.

[14] Hayner, 'Negotiating Peace', p. 29.

[15] J. Poole, 'Post-Conflict Justice in Sierra Leone', in C. Bassiouni, *Post Conflict Justice* (New York: Transnational Publishers, 2002), pp. 563–92.

[16] O'Flaherty, 'Case Study: The United Nations Human Rights Field Operation in Sierra Leone', p. 292.

[17] Report of the Secretary-General on the Establishment of a Special Court for Sierra Leone, UN Doc. S/2000/915, 4 October 2000; Horovitz, 'Transitional Criminal Justice in Sierra Leone', pp. 43–69.

relation to the Truth Commission and how the relationship between and the parallel operation of the Special Court and the Truth Commission were perceived from a victim's perspective.

Following the instability and arrest of Sankoh in May 2000, new negotiations were undertaken with the RUF and additional agreements signed, essentially reaffirming the validity of the Lomé Agreement.[18] In January 2002, the civil war was officially declared by the government to be over. The armed conflict in Sierra Leone killed between 50,000 and 75,000 people and rendered almost half the country's population of 5 million either internally displaced or refugees.[19]

8.4 The Truth and Reconciliation Commission Act of 2000

As Sierra Leone is a state with a dualist legal system, domestic legislation creating the Truth and Reconciliation Commission (TRC) was required. This was, following consultations with civil society, enacted by Parliament in February 2000.[20] The Act, section 6.1, specifically mandated the TRC with five principal tasks, namely:

- to create an impartial historical record of violations and abuses of human rights and international humanitarian law related to the armed conflict in Sierra Leone, from the beginning of the conflict in 1991 to the signing of the Lomé Peace Agreement;
- to address impunity;
- to respond to the needs of the victims;
- to promote healing and reconciliation; and
- to prevent a repetition of the violations and abuses suffered.

As indicated above, the mandate of the Truth Commission was quite ambitious and thus from the outset created expectations which were impossible to fulfil. In contrast, the Truth Commission in Guatemala, as noted in Chapter 7, set out somewhat more modest objectives that indicated that the recommendations put forward in its final report, rather than the actual Truth Commission process itself, would simply seek to 'encourage peace and observance of human rights'.

With regard to the first objective of establishing an 'impartial historical record', this wording has been the subject of considerable critique

[18] Hayner, 'Negotiating Peace', p. 24.
[19] Horovitz, 'Transitional Criminal Justice in Sierra Leone', pp. 43–69.
[20] O'Flaherty, 'Case Study: The United Nations Human Rights Field Operation in Sierra Leone', p. 311.

by historians and sociologists in various countries where truth commissions have had such an aim. Following scrutiny of the operation and final reports of several truth commissions, these have sometimes demonstrated certain biases and, in some cases, clear influences of national political considerations which have overshadowed the voices of victims.[21] A more modest expectation has been suggested by Ignatieff, who stated that: 'all that a truth commission can achieve is to reduce the number of lies that circulate unchallenged'.[22] In fact, the Final Report of the Sierra Leone Truth Commission recognises that:

> Parliament was surely ambitious in thinking that the Commission could create anything resembling a comprehensive historical record of the conflict in Sierra Leone. In any event, the proximity of the events to the writing of the historical record makes any aspiration to a thorough study troublesome and possibly unrealistic. While it may be illusory to think that bodies like Truth Commissions can establish a complete historical record, they can nevertheless discredit and debunk certain lies about conflicts.[23]

Regarding the second objective of the Commission to 'address impunity', the attribution of such an aim was clearly at odds with the blanket amnesty provisions of the Lomé Agreement, yet can be explained by the fact that it pre-dates the violence in May 2000 that prompted the request for prosecutions. As the national political environment changed through the negotiations for the Special Court, the retention of such an objective for the Truth Commission highlights the incongruity of the two institutions and became the source of confusion among both victims and perpetrators.

The third objective, that of 'addressing the needs of victims', presented another significant challenge to the Commission. The Commission had little available means to actually address the needs of victims as it lacked resources for psychosocial counselling and support and had no reparation measures to offer. All the Commission could do was take note of the needs and concerns expressed by victims and suggest overall recommendations for their benefit. Unfortunately, the vague wording

[21] For critical analysis of the aim of establishing an impartial historical record see, e.g., Ball and Audrey, 'The Truth of Truth Commissions', pp. 1–43; C. Maier, 'Doing History, Doing Justice: The Narrative of the Historian and of the Truth Commission', in R. Rotberg and D. Thompson (eds), *Truth v. Justice, The Morality of Truth Commissions* (Princeton University Press, 2000), pp. 261–78.

[22] M. Ignatieff, *The Warrior's Honor* (New York: Vintage, 1999), p. 173.

[23] Final Report of the Sierra Leone Truth Commission, ch. 1, para. 26, available at: www.sierra-leone.org/TRCDocuments.html.

in its mandate led many victims to believe that the Commission would be able to award them reparations, as evidenced by observers to the public sessions of the Commission.[24]

A questionable aspect of the Commission was the treatment of victims in public hearings. Some commentators have noted that, contrary to the mandate of the Commission, the hearings tended to focus more on perpetrators and their reintegration rather than on victims and their suffering. At times, victims were interrogated in public in a court-like manner. While clearly fearful of reprisals, many victims were reluctantly prompted into participating on the understanding that they would receive some benefits in return, rather than motivated by a desire to relate their personal experience. In this context, it is of note that in Guatemala there were no public sessions or hearings. Rather, for safety reasons, the interviews with victims, witnesses and perpetrators were conducted in private sessions, although sometimes in groups with up to fifteen victims.[25] The modality of public hearings was a feature that was transferred from the Truth Commission in South Africa, where the unique political shift allowed for these to take place without major fears of retaliation. In retrospect, the use of public hearings in Sierra Leone without conditions or guarantees that victims could participate safely risked undermining the process and constitutes an important lesson learnt for the future.

With regard to the fourth objective of reconciliation, the setting up of the Truth Commission in Sierra Leone again drew largely from the experience in South Africa and came to repeat some of its controversial aspects, such as the disproportional emphasis on the promotion of national reconciliation with religious undertones[26] and the presumption that public hearings with victims and perpetrators would, in Desmond Tutu's words, 'cleanse wounds in order for them to not fester but heal'. As explored by Wilson, the equation of human rights with reconciliation and amnesty by the South African Truth Commission caused damage to the understanding of human rights and served to de-legitimise the concept of justice.[27]

[24] T. Kelsall, 'Truth, Lies, Ritual: Preliminary Reflections on the Truth and Reconciliation Commission in Sierra Leone', *Human Rights Quarterly*, 27 (2005), 361–91; R. Shaw, 'Rethinking Truth and Reconciliation Commissions, Lessons from Sierra Leone', United States Institute for Peace, Special Report 130, February 2005.

[25] Ball and Audrey, 'The Truth of Truth Commissions', pp. 1–43.

[26] Kelsall, 'Truth, Lies, Ritual', pp. 361–91; Shaw, 'Rethinking Truth and Reconciliation Commissions'.

[27] For a detailed analysis and critique of the South African Truth Commission, see Wilson, *The Politics of Truth and Reconciliation in South Africa*, pp. 228–30; B. Hamber and

Regarding the final objective of the mandate to 'prevent a repetition of the violations and abuses suffered', this phrasing again placed an unfair burden on the Truth Commission. A more realistic objective would have been to issue recommendations, the implementation of which would contribute to the prevention of a repetition of violations. In any case, the Final Report of the Truth Commission dedicated significant efforts to suggesting recommendations for concrete measures to avoid a repetition of violence. Unfortunately, as will be further explored below, the degree of implementation of these recommendations has been modest and many of the structural factors that caused the origins of the conflict remain unchanged.

8.5 Operational aspects of the Truth and Reconciliation Commission

The Truth Commission was not established until 5 July 2002, when the seven Commissioners appointed by the President were formally sworn in during a public ceremony. Among the seven Commissioners, three were internationals. The Special Representative of the Secretary-General and the OHCHR were responsible for recommending the non-Sierra Leonean members of the Commission to the President for his endorsement.[28]

The Truth Commission in Sierra Leone, similar to those of Guatemala and East Timor, benefited from the presence of a UN peacekeeping mission. UNAMSIL provided considerable logistical support and conducted awareness-raising activities on the mandate of the Truth Commission.[29] However, unlike the Truth Commission in Guatemala, which was created directly through the peace agreements and run by UN administration, the Truth Commission in Sierra Leone was constituted under domestic law and was considered a national institution. Nevertheless, the OHCHR played a significant role in fundraising among donors, who paid the majority of the costs of the Commission. The Truth Commission faced delays that were caused in part by a lack of clarity as to the responsibility for its administration and due to fears of national political

R. Wilson, 'Symbolic Closure Through Memory, Reparation and Revenge in Post-Conflict Societies', *Journal of Human Rights*, 1(1) (2002), 35–53.

[28] The Chairman of the TC was Bishop Humper (Sierra Leone). The three international Commissioners were Ms Yasmin Sooka (South Africa), Ms Satang Jow (Gambia) and Prof. William Schabas (Canada).

[29] OHCHR Annual Report on the Situation of Human Rights in Sierra Leone to the Commission on Human Rights for 2001, E/CN.4/2002/37, p. 17.

interference.[30] This in turn resulted in donor fatigue. In the end, the Truth Commission received less than half the amount budgeted for its operation and had difficulties in fulfilling its activities and completing its report.[31] It is relevant to note that the Special Court, which was set up in parallel, over a three-year period cost more than twenty times as much as the Truth Commission.[32] As victims' provisions were weak and almost non-existent in the mandate of the Special Court, it is submitted that the disproportionate allocations of funding for the court in relation to that of the Truth Commission indicate the failure of the international community to recognise victims and their rights in the transitional justice process in Sierra Leone.

The Truth Commission worked in three stages. It only had approximately forty core staff, the majority of whom were nationals. Between December 2002 and March 2003, focus was on statement-taking. With the assistance of civil society organisations, some 7,700 statements from victims were compiled throughout the country. A deliberate effort was made to ensure that a significant percentage of the statement-takers were women.[33] This was followed by public hearings in several regions between April and August 2003. The descriptions of the public hearings vary, and as noted above, certain observers raised considerable critique against the manner in which they were conducted and the way in which victims were treated. In principle, the hearings with women and children who had suffered sexual violence were held in private. Unfortunately, the hearings phase concluded with a rather poor performance by President Kabbah, who publicly refused to recognise responsibility or apologise for his own role in the conflict.[34] The final stage of writing up the report took more than a year as it was not publicly presented until October 2004.

[30] International Crisis Group, 'Sierra Leone's Truth and Reconciliation Commission: A Fresh Start?', Africa Briefing, 20 December 2002; International Center for Transitional Justice, 'The Sierra Leone Truth and Reconciliation Commission, Reviewing its First Year', Case Study Series, January 2004.

[31] The Sierra Leone Truth Commission was originally budgeted at US$10 million, however, it received only approximately US$4 million. In contrast, the Guatemalan Truth Commission operated on a budget of approximately US$10 million and the South African Truth Commission's budget was around US$33 million. See Schabas, 'The Sierra Leone Truth Commission', p. 23; Ball and Audrey, 'The Truth of Truth Commissions', pp. 16–17.

[32] Between 2002 and 2005 some US$80 million were spent on the Special Court, see Horovitz, 'Transitional Criminal Justice in Sierra Leone', p. 60.

[33] Schabas, 'The Sierra Leone Truth Commission', p. 25; International Center for Transitional Justice, 'The Sierra Leone Truth and Reconciliation Commission', p. 3.

[34] Schabas, 'The Sierra Leone Truth Commission', p. 26.

8.6 The relationship between the Truth Commission and the Special Court

The Special Court for Sierra Leone became operational in mid 2002 and thus coincided with the setting up of the Truth Commission. Much speculation surrounded the unprecedented parallel existence of the two transitional justice initiatives. A clear challenge was the fact that they were set up at different times with little regard for each other. The Statute of the Special Court showed no recognition of the previously established Truth Commission despite their overlapping mandates. A letter from the Secretary-General Kofi Annan to the Security Council in 2001 expressed concern that 'care must be taken to ensure that the Special Court and the Truth and Reconciliation Commission will operate in a complementary and mutually supportive manner, fully respectful of their distinct but related functions'.[35] Considerable analysis was done by NGOs regarding the overlaps between the two mandates and the need for them to conclude an agreement to clarify their relationship and possible ways of cooperation. Most of the debate centred on technical and procedural aspects and whether the Special Court would be able to request confidential information from the Truth Commission.[36]

Finally, no agreement was concluded between the two institutions. The Prosecutor publicly announced that he would not request information from the Truth Commission.[37] However, disagreement prevailed over the hierarchy of power between the institutions and it became apparent that perpetrators were hesitant to cooperate with the Truth Commission for fear that their testimonies might end up in the Special Court, which was simultaneously issuing

[35] Letter dated 12 January 2001 from the Secretary-General to the President of the Security Council, UN Doc. S/2001/40, para. 9. See also discussion in Schabas, 'The Sierra Leone Truth Commission', p. 34.

[36] Human Rights Watch, 'Policy Paper on the Interrelationship Between the Sierra Leone Special Court and the Truth and Reconciliation Commission', 18 April 2002; International Center for Transitional Justice (Wierda, Hayner and van Zyl), 'Exploring the Relationship between the Special Court and the Truth and Reconciliation Commission of Sierra Leone', Paper of 24 June 2002; W. Schabas, 'The Relationship between Truth Commissions and Courts: The Case of Sierra Leone', *Human Rights Quarterly*, 25 (2003), 1035–66.

[37] Prosecutor Crane of the Special Court announced this publicly, e.g., in national media in Sierra Leone and at international conferences, including at a conference held at the Irish Centre for Human Rights on the Inter-Relationship between Truth Commissions and Courts, Galway, 4–5 October 2002 (attended by author).

indictments.[38] Schabas, a former Commissioner in the Truth Commission, has insisted that the 'relationship between the two mechanisms was synergistic' and proved the 'usefulness of a genuinely complementary approach by which international prosecutions coexist with alternative accountability mechanisms'.[39] Horovitz, a former staff member of the Special Court, has, on the other hand, suggested that for the future it may be wise to prevent the simultaneous existence of such institutions. Rather, it would be preferable to sequence them; had the Truth Commission been completed prior to the establishment of the Special Court, there would have been less confusion among the general public, more willingness to cooperate with the Truth Commission and its Final Report could subsequently have been used as evidence during prosecutions.[40]

In retrospect, it seems that much of the attention given to the parallel existence of the two transitional justice institutions focused on technicalities and paid insufficient attention to the importance of coordinating the legacy they would leave, not least among the victims. Although public awareness campaigns were conducted separately on their respective mandates, they both neglected the crucial aspect of clarifying their relationship and the implications this would have for victims as well as perpetrators. A particular area which would have merited coordination was that of reparations. A united position on this issue would have strengthened the possibilities of pursuing the effective implementation of reparations for victims and contributed to the credibility of the respective institutions. Despite the precedents set by the International Criminal Court in this area, in Sierra Leone the issue of reparations was perceived by the Special Court to have been delegated to the Truth Commission, which in turn only had a mandate to propose recommendations. As a result, victims were surrounded by two significant and costly international transitional justice initiatives, neither of which was able to provide them with any concrete reparation measures. In this context, it is of note that the Truth Commission in East Timor managed to implement an Urgent Reparations Scheme, albeit small scale, which was able to provide some interim reparations, mostly aimed at medical and psychosocial care for the most vulnerable victims (see Chapter 9).

38 International Crisis Group, 'Sierra Leone's Truth and Reconciliation Commission', p. 4; Kelsall, 'Truth, Lies, Ritual', p. 381; Shaw, 'Rethinking Truth and Reconciliation Commissions', p. 4.

39 Schabas, 'The Sierra Leone Truth Commission', p. 39.

40 Horovitz, 'Transitional Criminal Justice in Sierra Leone', p. 56.

8.7 The Final Report of the Truth Commission and its Recommendations

The Truth Commission publicly presented its Final Report to the President of Sierra Leone in October 2004. The Report dedicated a considerable section to analysis of the root causes of the conflict. A common perception both within Sierra Leone and abroad was that the RUF were the principal culprits and that the diamond industry was the main triggering factor. The Commission did, indeed, find the RUF to be responsible for the majority of the serious violations committed.[41] However, the Commission, when exploring the root causes of the conflict, underlined the failure of governance and accountability, the interplay of poverty, social marginalisation and endemic corruption, in addition to years of denial of basic human rights, as key factors that caused and sustained the war.[42] As noted by Schabas, the Sierra Leonian Truth Commission operated under very different circumstances than in South Africa, where there was a clear political transition and the root evil of apartheid was unquestionable. In Sierra Leone, the depressing conclusion was a lack of real political change after the civil war, despite elections.[43] Unlike in Guatemala, the Truth Commission in Sierra Leone was not restricted from indicating names of persons in authority who bore responsibility for violations and decided to do so in its Final Report.[44] This aspect was considered necessary among the Commissioners, however, it hardly endeared the Report within the government, where key figures remained the same as during the internal armed conflict.

The Final Report dedicated specific chapters to analysis of the violations which affected women and children. Former Commissioner Sooka has highlighted that: 'contrary to the belief that amputations had been the main violation carried out, the Commission was able to establish that, in fact, rape and sexual violence were the most prevalent crime. Rape had been the silent crime that most women and girls in Sierra Leone had suffered during the conflict.'[45] The Commission analysed gender-based violence and its origins in detail and, following extensive consultations with women's rights

[41] Sierra Leone Truth Commission Final Report, vol. 1, Introduction, para. 16.
[42] Sierra Leone Truth Commission Final Report, vol. 1, para. 11 and vol. 2, p. 6.
[43] Schabas, 'The Sierra Leone Truth Commission', pp. 28, 39.
[44] Schabas, 'The Sierra Leone Truth Commission', pp. 24, 28.
[45] Sooka, 'Dealing with the Past and Transitional Justice', p. 319.

organisations,[46] set forth broad-ranging recommendations which touched on root causes, including, for example, customary practices, such as female genital mutilation. The Final Report furthermore proposed concrete measures, such as repealing discriminatory legislation and providing gender-specific reparations to deal with the stigma and medical complications that female victims suffered after the extensive sexual violence during the conflict.[47] Surveys and estimates by NGOs indicated that approximately one-third of the female population was subjected to rape, sexual slavery and other forms of sexual violence during the conflict.[48]

Unlike certain other truth commissions, such as in South Africa, in Sierra Leone the mandate of the Commission did not delimit it to investigating only the most serious violations.[49] Consequently, the Commission was able to interpret its mandate broadly and analysed violations of civil and political rights and their linkages to structural violations by the denial of economic, social and cultural rights as well. The interrelationship between these rights was strongest in the section of the report that dealt with recommendations and reparations. The majority of the victims who had suffered serious physical violence expressed a yearning to have improved access to economic and social rights. The Commission based its recommendations on the needs and requests expressed by victims and indicated these clearly in the Final Report in order of the expressions of priority: housing, education and medical care.[50] The Report set out extensive recommendations, many of them structural, institutional and legislative, and ranked

[46] H. Millar, 'Facilitating Women's Voices in Truth Recovery: An Assessment of Women's Participation and the Integration of a Gender Perspective in Truth Commissions', in H. Durham and T. Gurd (eds), *Listening to the Silences, Women and War* (Leiden: Martinus Nijhoff, 2005), pp. 171–222.

[47] Sierra Leone Truth Commission Final Report, vol. 2, ch. 3, Recommendations, ch. 4, Reparations; J. King, 'Gender and Reparations in Sierra Leone', in R. Rubio-Marín (ed.), *What Happened to the Women? Gender and Reparations for Human Rights Violations* (New York: Social Science Research Council, 2006), pp. 247–83; Schabas, 'The Sierra Leone Truth Commission', p. 32.

[48] Physicians for Human Rights, *War-Related Sexual Violence in Sierra Leone; A Population-Based Assessment*, 2002 quoted in Amnesty International, 'Sierra Leone: Getting Reparations Rights for Survivors of Sexual Violence', Report AI Index AFR51/005/2007, 1 November 2007, pp. 1–36.

[49] Truth and Reconciliation Act 2000, s. 6.

[50] The Report demonstrated that among the 7,700 statements given to the Commission, 49 per cent requested assistance with housing/shelter, 41 per cent with education and 27 per cent with medical care. See Sierra Leone Truth Commission Final Report, vol. 2, ch. 4, Reparations, paras 30–1.

them according to importance and urgency as 'imperative', 'work towards' and 'seriously consider'.

In addition to a comprehensive chapter on recommendations, the Final Report dedicated a whole separate chapter specifically to recommendations for reparations. The Report identified the consequences of the violations, specifically in cases where these continued to have an impact on the lives of victims, notably permanent physical disability, stigma and social exclusion. For many victims, the lack of assistance and reparations after the conflict meant that they were not able to resume their lives and move beyond the trauma of the violence. Many victims, especially women, continued to be re-victimised.[51] The report identified five specific groups of victims who were especially vulnerable: amputees, war-wounded with physical disabilities, victims of sexual violence, children and war widows.[52] The Commission argued that these groups of victims should be the beneficiaries of a reparations programme primarily aimed at rehabilitation, restoring their dignity, reduction of their dependency and at bringing them on an equal footing with a larger category of victims.[53] While the Commission considered all victims to be entitled to some form of reparations, the proposed delimitation was essentially pragmatic in view of very limited resources. The Commission set out that the reparations programme should consist of health care, pensions, education, skills training and micro-credit projects, as well as community and symbolic reparations. Importantly, the Report did not restrict the beneficiaries to those who had cooperated with the Commission, unlike in South Africa where this had been an eligibility criteria.[54] Such delimitation would primarily have had a negative impact on women, many of whom had been reluctant to give testimonies due to fears of stigma and rejection in the community.[55]

As foreseen by the Lomé Agreement, Article XXIV, the programme should be financed by the setting up of a Special Fund for War Victims,

[51] The continuing impact of sexual violence on women is, e.g., documented by Amnesty International, 'Sierra Leone: Getting Reparations Rights for Survivors of Sexual Violence'.

[52] Amnesty International, 'Sierra Leone: Getting Reparations Rights for Survivors of Sexual Violence', paras 53–99.

[53] Amnesty International, 'Sierra Leone: Getting Reparations Rights for Survivors of Sexual Violence', paras 42–6, 57. See also Schabas, 'Reparation Practices in Sierra Leone and the Truth and Reconciliation Commission', p. 300.

[54] Sierra Leone Truth Commission Final Report, para. 54; Schabas, 'Reparations Practices in Sierra Leone and the Truth and Reconciliation Commission', p. 301.

[55] King, 'Gender and Reparations in Sierra Leone', p. 261.

and the Commission proposed that its funding should come from the state budget, revenue from mineral resources (also foreseen in the Lomé Agreement) and donor support. Another potential source of funding identified was that of seized assets from convicted persons, with indirect reference to Article 19 of the Statute of the Special Court on restitution. Unfortunately, to date the Special Court has not referred to restitution in any of its judgments.[56]

In giving their testimonies to the Commission, victims clearly indicated that they wanted to see state responsibility for reparations. Many victims were simply unable to identify the perpetrators due to the at times blurred distinction between soldiers and rebels and therefore had no other recourse than the state. With regard to state responsibility, the Report affirmed the following:

> The Commission took the view that the State has a legal obligation to provide reparations for violations committed by both State actors and private actors. The Commission is of the opinion that all victims should be treated equally, fairly and justly. Given the nature of the conflict in Sierra Leone, it was not always possible to identify the perpetrators or the groups they belonged to. States have an obligation to guarantee the enjoyment of human rights ... and that reparations are made to victims ... If governments fail to apply due diligence in responding adequately to, or in structurally preventing human rights violations, then they are legally and morally responsible.[57]

In formulating its position on the issue, the Commission cited reparation awards in human rights provisions and jurisprudence, including, for example, in the Inter-American human rights system. Although the Basic Principles on the Right to Reparation[58] were still in draft form at the time, the Commission stated that they were 'indicative of the current status of international law of the right to redress from victims of such violations'[59] and explicitly endorsed them.[60] An additional

[56] Article 19 of the Statute of the Special Court for Sierra Leone provides for possible restitution: 'the Trial Chamber may order the forfeiture of the property, proceeds and any assets acquired unlawfully or by criminal conduct, and their return to their rightful owner or to the State of Sierra Leone'. See details in Chapter 4 on reparations in international criminal law.

[57] Sierra Leone Truth Commission Final Report, vol. 2, ch. 4, Reparations, para. 21.

[58] UN Basic Principles and Guidelines on the Right to a Remedy and Reparation for Victims of Gross Violations of International Human Rights Law and Serious Violations of International Humanitarian Law, UN Doc. A/RES/60/147.

[59] Sierra Leone Truth Commission Final Report, vol. 2, ch. 4, Reparations, para. 19.

[60] Schabas, 'Reparation Practices in Sierra Leone and the Truth and Reconciliation Commission', p. 299.

consideration given by the Commission was that the majority of victims expressed discontent over the assistance provided to about 50,000 perpetrators through DDR programmes. The Report notes that 'the widely held perception that the State had taken better care of ex-combatants than victims ... created an onus on the government to replicate these efforts on behalf of victims'.[61] Schabas underlines the point that although the term 'reparation' did not appear either in the Lomé Peace Agreement or in the Truth and Commission Act, the Commission clearly understood its mandate to be centred on the needs and rights of victims and that these could best be promoted through a reparations programme.[62]

8.8 Follow-up and implementation of the recommendations regarding reparations

The Report underlined that the Truth and Reconciliation Commission Act set forth a clear obligation on the government to implement the recommendations of the Commission:

> Section 17 of the Act requires that Government shall faithfully and timeously implement the recommendations of the report that are directed to State bodies and encourage or facilitate the implementation of any recommendations that may be directed to others.

Despite the commitment to give effect to the recommendations of the Commission, in practice the response of the government was reluctant. As noted previously, during the hearings phase of the Commission, the President refused to recognise and apologise for the role played by himself and the government during the conflict. It took almost a year for the government to officially respond to the Commission report, and this was done by the issuing of a White Paper in mid 2005, which accepted the recommendations in principle, but without demonstration of a clear commitment to advance their implementation.[63]

[61] Sierra Leone Truth Commission Final Report, vol. 2, ch. 4, Reparations, paras 36–7.

[62] Schabas, 'Reparation Practices in Sierra Leone and the Truth and Reconciliation Commission', p. 293.

[63] Hayner, 'Negotiating Peace', p. 27; OHCHR Annual Report on the Situation of Human Rights in Sierra Leone to the Commission on Human Rights for 2005, E/CN.4/2006/106, para. 52; Amnesty International, 'Sierra Leone Government Urged to Implement the Recommendations of the Truth and Reconciliation Commission', Public Statement, AFR 51/012/2005, 29 November 2005.

Human rights' and women's NGOs applauded the comprehensive recommendations set out in the Truth Commission Report and their persistent lobbying has been instrumental in maintaining attention and pressure on the government to implement the recommendations. In the area of legal reform, some progress has gradually been achieved as several bills relating to women's and children's rights were, after considerable delay, approved by Parliament in 2007.[64] The National Human Rights Commission, as noted above, was only established in 2006 following considerable technical advice from OHCHR.[65] The Human Rights Commission should play a prominent role in monitoring implementation of the recommendations from the Truth Commission and it has been officially designated as the 'Follow-Up Committee' for this purpose. The Human Rights Section of the successor of the peacekeeping mission, the UN Integrated Office in Sierra Leone (UNIOSIL), has continued to support the Human Rights Commission and jointly organised a national consultative conference with stakeholders regarding implementation of the Truth Commission recommendations in 2008, which concluded that twenty of the fifty-six overall recommendations had been fully or partially implemented.[66]

An area where the government showed little interest in implementing recommendations was disappointingly, although not unexpectedly, that of reparations. The Truth Commission Report recommended that an already existing government body, the National Commission for Social Action (NaCSA), be given responsibility to implement the reparations programme. The government was reluctant to set up the Special Fund for War Victims, but in 2006 established a task force to advise on a reparations programme and conceded that the NaCSA could be the implementing entity of such a programme.[67] One negative aspect of the Truth Commission's Final Report was that it was not able to estimate an approximate total number of victims.[68] The government was initially

[64] OHCHR Annual Report on the Situation of Human Rights in Sierra Leone to the Human Rights Council for 2007, A/HRC/7/66, para. 59.

[65] OHCHR Annual Report on the Situation of Human Rights in Sierra Leone to the Human Rights Council for 2006, A/HRC/4/96, para. 45; Hayner, 'Negotiating Peace', p. 29.

[66] OHCHR Annual Report on the Situation of Human Rights in Sierra Leone to the Human Rights Council for 2008, A/HRC/10/52, para. 38.

[67] OHCHR Annual Report on the Situation of Human Rights in Sierra Leone to the Human Rights Council for 2007, para. 61; Amnesty International, 'Sierra Leone: Getting Reparations Rights for Survivors of Sexual Violence', p. 23.

[68] King, 'Gender and Reparations in Sierra Leone', p. 273.

disinclined to document the number of victims, in part due to the financial implications involved with reparation claims.

Critique has also been raised regarding the role of the UN in relation to the issue of reparations. Schabas has noted that at the time when the Truth Commission Report was published, references to reparations were suspiciously absent from UN reports and documents.[69] However, as is revealed by a review of the more recent OHCHR human rights reports on Sierra Leone to the Human Rights Council and of reports of UNIOSIL to the Security Council, the issue of reparations has become a central concern and a focus for follow-up.[70] In fact, the attention given to the issue and the explicit criticism voiced by the UN regarding the lack of national political will and resource allocation has been a major contributing reason as to why the spotlight has been kept on the issue of reparations.

While progress has been slow, some important progress has taken place. Sierra Leone remains at the very bottom of the UNDP development index (ranked as number 179 in 2008[71]), and thus it is necessary that state funds for a reparations programme be supplemented by international assistance. The Sierra Leone Poverty Reduction Strategy (PRSP), adopted in 2005, made reference to the implementation of the recommendations of the Truth Commission as one of its priorities. However, the World Bank Country Assistance Strategy for Sierra Leone 2006–2009 failed to reflect the issue of reparations, but rather centred on the DDR of former combatants.[72] Sooka has underlined that the disproportionate investment by the international community in DDR programmes stands in stark contrast to the lack of support for victims and signalled that failure to sustain support for Truth Commission recommendations relating to reparations may result in a crisis of legitimacy of transitional justice processes.[73]

[69] Schabas, 'Reparation Practices in Sierra Leone and the Truth and Reconciliation Commission', p. 294.

[70] For example, see references to reparations in OHCHR Annual Report on the Situation of Human Rights in Sierra Leone to the Human Rights Council for 2007, para. 59; OHCHR Annual Report on the Situation of Human Rights in Sierra Leone to the Commission on Human Rights for 2005, para. 54; Sixth Report of the Secretary-General to the Security Council on the United Nations Integrated Office in Sierra Leone, S/2008/281, 29 April 2008, para. 44; OHCHR Report on Assistance to Sierra Leone in the field of Human Rights in Sierra Leone to the Human Rights Council for 2010, A/HRC/16/78, para. 49.

[71] UNDP Human Development Report 2008, available at: http://hdr.undp.org/en.

[72] World Bank country page Sierra Leone, available at: http://go.worldbank.org/COWMCN2VS0.

[73] Sooka, 'Dealing with the Past and Transitional Justice', pp. 324–5.

In 2005, the UN Peace Building Commission was established. One of its principal objectives, and of its accompanying Peace Building Fund (PBF), is to support long-term strategies for post-conflict peace-building.[74] Sierra Leone was selected among the first countries to qualify for assistance. In July 2008, a project grant allocated US$3 million specifically to create a Reparations Unit within the NaCSA and to provide initial funding for the establishment of the Special Fund for War Victims and the setting up of a database on victims. Data collection was done on the estimated number of victims (presumed to be around 55,000) and some 30,000 victims came forward to register themselves. The Special Fund for War Victims was finally established in December 2009. Some 20,000 victims received reparations in the form of medical assistance and a minor grant of US$100. The majority of these were children, war widows and victims of sexual abuse.[75] The funding from the Peace Building Commission provided an important momentum to advance concrete progress in the area of reparations for victims in Sierra Leone, yet concerns remain over the sustainability of the reparations programme.[76] OHCHR warned in early 2011 that 'there is a dire need for further support from the international community. Failure to continue the reparations entails the risk of fuelling anger, as the victims' fate is in contrast to that of former combatants (apparent perpetrators) who have received financial assistance and training as part of demobilisation and reintegration programmes.'[77] Ultimately, continued international support combined with national political will and a degree of allocation of state resources will be essential in order to sustain and demonstrate a genuine commitment to implement the right to reparation in practice.

8.9 Conclusions

The issue of reparations in the transitional justice process in Sierra Leone illustrates some important lessons. The references to victims' rights and a fund for rehabilitation in the Lomé Peace Agreement set an important framework. The active involvement and presence of the

74 Official UN web pages of the Peace Building Commission, available at: www.un.org/peace/peacebuilding and the Peace Building Fund at: www.unpbf.org.

75 International Center for Transitional Justice (ICTJ) (Suma and Correa), 'Report and Proposals for the Implementation of Reparations in Sierra Leone', December 2009.

76 ICTJ, 'Report and Proposals for the Implementation of Reparations in Sierra Leone'.

77 OHCHR Report on Assistance to Sierra Leone in the field of Human Rights in Sierra Leone to the Human Rights Council for 2010, para. 49.

United Nations throughout the setting up of the transitional justice initiatives contributed to enhancing their impartiality and also provided essential support for the national human rights movement, particularly in the context of an ineffective regional human rights system and the absence of a national human rights institution. The Truth Commission, although underfunded and at times criticised for lacking a victim's perspective in its hearings, provided a Final Report with in-depth analysis of human rights violations, their consequences for victims, elements of state responsibility and clear proposals for the establishment of a reparations programme.

The Special Court regrettably did little to advance reparations and has so far failed to even explore aspects of restitution in its judgments. Despite the limitations in the Statute of the Court, it is unfortunate that it did not take greater advantage of its presence in the country to promote the issue of reparations and the recommendations of the Truth Commission. While it may be noted that the judgments issued by the Special Court provide victims with a kind of reparation in the form of 'satisfaction', this measure alone does not change their situation in practice.

The lack of coordination between the two transitional justice institutions was a missed opportunity to leave a stronger legacy in favour of victims. Ultimately, this raises questions at the national level concerning the credibility of transitional justice, as the absence of reparations effectively blocks the ability of many victims to restart their lives and re-establish their dignity. Sierra Leone challenges the solidarity of the international community to replicate the assistance given to demobilised perpetrators with equal support for the victims. Despite wavering political will and scarce resources, the recommendations of the Truth Commission provide a solid basis for progress on victims' rights. Attention should remain focused on the degree of state allocations for the newly established Special Fund for War Victims and also on sustaining the support by the international community.

9 Case study: reparations in East Timor

9.1 Introduction

The transitional justice process in East Timor[1] was, similar to that in Sierra Leone, characterised by two parallel mechanisms, one aimed at prosecutions and the other at establishing a narrative overview of violations during the conflict based on testimonies of victims. In Sierra Leone, the mandate of the Truth Commission was drafted in a hurry, while significant reflection was dedicated to, and political support was ensured for, the Special Court. The scenario was the opposite in East Timor. The unprecedented mandate awarded to the UNTAET mission by the Security Council raised expectations that it would deal with criminal accountability as an urgent priority. However, the result of the Serious Crimes Process remains questioned as it only managed to establish accountability for a small number of low- and mid-level perpetrators, while those bearing the greatest responsibility remain sheltered in Indonesia. Overall, the Serious Crimes Process in East Timor was critically under-resourced and lacked a victim's perspective.

On the other hand, in East Timor the Commission for Truth, Reception and Reconciliation (CAVR) was developed through a process of consultation, enjoyed local ownership and received international support, which resulted in considerable financial and human resources. The Truth Commission was specifically designed to complement the Serious Crimes Process and developed a number of victim-oriented measures, including the provision of psychosocial support and interim reparations, as well as victim participation in community reconciliation processes.

[1] Although the name was changed from East Timor to Timor Leste after independence on 20 May 2002, this chapter uses the term East Timor for the sake of consistency.

The Asian region has lacked a regional human rights system to promote accountability,[2] and East Timor did not have an independent national human rights institution until 2006, both factors that have played important roles in promoting victims' rights in other case studies. On the positive side, the creation of transitional justice initiatives in East Timor was facilitated by the extensive mandate awarded to the UN administration. However, the outcome with regard to accountability and reparations remains seriously compromised due to the lack of cooperation by Indonesia, which bears primary state responsibility for the violations committed and the principal obligation to provide reparations.

9.2 Brief historical background

The armed conflict in East Timor was set in the context of decolonisation. In 1974, Portugal was in the process of withdrawing from East Timor after four centuries of colonial rule. Following a brief civil war, in late 1975 Indonesia invaded and occupied East Timor. The following twenty-four years were characterised by military suppression, whereby those suspected of supporting the East Timorese liberation movement were systematically tortured and killed. Forced displacements took place, under the pretext of dislodging guerrillas, and this policy resulted in extensive famine. The Indonesian military strategically sought local militia allies among opponents of the main independence movement in order to divide the local population. It has been estimated that one-quarter of the East Timorese population, around 200,000 people, died during the occupation.[3]

The country was largely closed to foreign media during Indonesian rule. Following the fall of the Indonesian President Suharto in 1998, the subsequent interim President Habibi allowed a referendum to be held in East Timor in 1999. The referendum was arranged by the UN in August 1999, however, the security remained the responsibility of the Indonesian military (TNI). The turnout was over 99 per cent of those registered to vote, of whom an overwhelming majority, 78.5 per cent, of the East Timorese voted for independence, much to the surprise of the Indonesians

[2] However, in December 2008 the ASEAN Charter entered into effect and in late 2009 the ASEAN Intergovernmental Commission on Human Rights was established by eleven states in south-east Asia; see the official web page of ASEAN at: www.asean.org.

[3] P. Burgess, 'A New Approach to Restorative Justice – East Timor's Reconciliation Process', in N. Roht-Arriaza and J. Mariezcurrena (eds), *Transitional Justice in the Twenty-First Century, Beyond Truth versus Justice* (Cambridge University Press, 2006), pp. 178–80.

who prior to the ballot had arranged a campaign of intimidation.[4] Leaving security arrangements to the Indonesian police and military was a fatal mistake as they refused to accept the result of the vote. Many East Timorese anticipated the reaction and immediately took to the hills as soon as they had cast their vote. The Indonesian army, in collaboration with East Timorese militia groups, instigated a massive revenge campaign against the civilian population. The majority of the population, around half a million, was displaced, large numbers of them to West Timor. Some 1,400 people were killed and hundreds of women were raped. Approximately 60,000 houses were burned and 75 per cent of government buildings and infrastructure were destroyed.[5]

In response to the violence, the Security Council adopted Resolution 1272 under Chapter VII of the UN Charter on 25 October 1999, whereby the peacekeeping mission, UNTAET, was created and given an unprecedented (although similar to the parallel mandate in Kosovo) complete administrative and executive authority in the territory, including for the administration of justice.[6]

A number of inquiries issued late 1999 or early 2000 identified a systematic pattern of serious violations against the civilian population and called for prosecution of the TNI. Among the reports were a joint UN Special Rapporteurs' fact-finding mission,[7] an International Commission of Inquiry on East Timor of the Secretary-General[8] and, somewhat surprisingly, an investigation by the Indonesian independent national human rights institution KomnasHam.[9] The International Commission of Inquiry underlined the importance of the issue of reparations as it stated that: 'The Commission believes it has a special responsibility to speak out on behalf of the victims who may not have easy access to international forums. They must not be forgotten in the rush of events

[4] Chesterman, 'East Timor', p. 195.

[5] P. Burgess, 'Justice and Reconciliation in East Timor, the Relationship between the Commission for Reception, Truth and Reconciliation and the Courts', *Criminal Law Forum*, vol. 15 (Amsterdam: Kluwer, 2004), pp. 135–58.

[6] Security Council Resolution on the Situation in East Timor, S/RES/1272, adopted 25 October 1999. Discussed in Chesterman, 'East Timor', pp. 192–216.

[7] Joint UN Special Rapporteurs' of the Commission on Human Rights Fact-Finding Mission to East Timor (Arbitrary Detention, Torture and Violence against Women), December 1999, A/54/660.

[8] Report of the International Commission of Inquiry on East Timor to the Secretary-General, UN Doc. A/54/726-S/2000/59, 31 January 2000.

[9] See further discussion regarding the reports and their findings in Reiger and Wierda, *The Serious Crimes Process in Timor Leste*, pp. 8–10; Linton, 'Cambodia, East Timor and Sierra Leone', pp. 207–8.

to redefine relations in the region, and their basic human rights to justice, compensation and the truth must be fully respected.'[10]

9.3 Prosecutions and the Truth Commission

As noted in Chapter 4 on reparations in international criminal law, the first measure undertaken by UNTAET to establish accountability was the adoption of Regulation No. 2000/15 in June 2000, which created the Special Panels for Serious Crimes.[11] It soon became apparent that the Special Panels faced an insurmountable task for a number of legal, practical and political reasons. While the mandate of the Special Panels was modelled on the Rome Statute of the International Criminal Court, their temporary jurisdiction was limited from 1 January to 25 October 1999 and thereby excluded violations that had occurred during more than two decades of Indonesian occupation. The Special Panels and the Serious Crimes Unit within the Public Prosecutor were seriously underfunded and critique was raised in relation to the number of prosecutions of serious crimes that took place as part of a widespread and systematic pattern of violations, but where the charges were presented individually as single homicide cases without linking them to related crimes.[12]

Among the practical obstacles were the nearly complete lack of qualified national staff and nearly non-existent infrastructure. During the occupation, professionals were specifically brought in from Indonesia and the majority of the East Timorese lacked the training and skills necessary to take over the administration of justice. The number of concurrent working languages, in many cases four, caused significant difficulties during the proceedings. Political considerations constituted additional obstacles as those who carried the main responsibility remained in Indonesia which, in response to repeated calls for prosecutions and the threat of an international tribunal, decided to set up its own ad hoc human rights court to investigate incidents during the referendum. However, the Indonesian prosecutions of atrocities in East Timor are generally considered to have been a sham, seriously criticised by the UN High Commissioner for Human Rights,[13] and described by a

[10] Report of the International Commission of Inquiry on East Timor to the Secretary-General, para. 146.

[11] UN Doc. UNTAET/REG/2000/15, adopted 6 June 2000.

[12] Linton, 'Cambodia, East Timor and Sierra Leone', p. 218.

[13] Report of the United Nations High Commissioner for Human Rights on the Situation of Human Rights in Timor Leste to the Commission on Human Rights, E/CN4/2004/107, paras 50–1.

subsequent International Commission of Experts in 2005 as 'manifestly deficient'.[14] Senior military commanders in Indonesia were not indicted and of the eighteen people tried, all but one, an East Timorese militia member, were acquitted upon appeal.[15]

Following independence, President Xanana Gusmao indicated that he did not intend to pursue calls for criminal accountability of the Indonesian military. Conscious of the geo-strategic location of East Timor, he decided to favour friendly relations with their giant neighbour. As will be explored below, this political position of the East Timorese government had considerable implications both for the possibility of conducting prosecutions as well as for the work of the Truth Commission.

9.4 Establishment of the Commission for Reception, Truth and Reconciliation

In view of considerable obstacles to prosecutions, including those mentioned above, other transitional justice measures were contemplated to address the legacy of the conflict and a truth commission was proposed. In some ways, the scenario was the opposite of that in Sierra Leone, as described in Chapter 8, where the Truth Commission was included as a rushed measure in the peace agreement, while the Special Court was more carefully elaborated and benefited from considerably more funding. In East Timor, the hasty establishment of, and difficulties faced by, the Serious Crimes Panels prompted reflection on the need for complementary measures which could offer a comprehensive overview of the violations during the occupation, promote reconciliation and address victims' rights.

The idea of a truth commission was supported by the CNRT (a coalition of the East Timorese pro-independence groups) and was developed by a steering committee consisting of representatives of East Timorese groups and the United Nations.[16] Following consultations in the National Council, UNTAET adopted Resolution 2001/10 on 13 July 2001,

[14] Report of the UN Commission of Experts to Review the Prosecution of Serious Violations of Human Rights in East Timor (appointed by the Secretary-General) to the Security Council, S/2205/458, 24 June 2005, Annex II, para. 371.

[15] De Bertodano, 'East Timor: Trials and Tribulations', pp. 92–4; Reiger, 'Hybrid Attempts at Accountability for Serious Crimes in East Timor', p. 156; Burgess, 'A New Approach to Restorative Justice', p. 200.

[16] See introduction in CAVR, *Chega!*, Final Report of the East Timorese Commission for Reception, Truth and Reconciliation (CAVR), Dili, October 2005, available at: www.cavr-timorleste.org; Burgess, 'Justice and Reconciliation in East Timor', p. 143.

whereby the Commission for Reception, Truth and Reconciliation (known as CAVR, the Portuguese acronym) was established.[17]

The mandate of the Commission included a broad range of objectives, namely:

a. inquiring into human rights violations in the political conflicts in East Timor;
b. establishing the truth regarding past human rights violations;
c. reporting the nature of the human rights violations and identifying the factors that may have led to such violations;
d. identifying practices and policies, whether of state or non-state actors, which need to be addressed to prevent future recurrences of human rights violations;
e. the referral of human rights violations to the Office of the General Prosecutor with recommendations for the prosecution of offences where appropriate;
f. assisting in restoring the human dignity of victims;
g. promoting reconciliation; and
h. supporting the reception and reintegration of individuals who caused harm to their communities through the commission of minor criminal offences through the facilitation of community based mechanisms for reconciliation.

The mandate of the Truth Commission is more specific than most previous such inquiries and included novel features, such as quasi-judicial powers and a clear relationship with prosecutions as well as a provision for community reintegration for low-level perpetrators.[18] Unlike Sierra Leone, the regulation for the Truth Commission in East Timor stipulated that the Prosecutor General could request access to its information in practice and a detailed Memorandum of Understanding (MoU) between the institutions was drawn up to clarify procedures for witness and victim protection. In practice, this did not hamper the work of the Commission, but rather clarified the relationship and respective roles of the two entities.[19]

[17] Regulation on the Establishment of a Commission for Reception, Truth and Reconciliation in East Timor, UNTAET/REG/2001/10, 13 July 2001.

[18] C. Stahn, 'Accommodating Individual Criminal Responsibility and National Reconciliation: The UN Truth Commission for East Timor', *American Journal of International Law*, 95(4) (2001), 952–66.

[19] UNTAET/REG/2001/10, 13 July 2001, s. 44. See discussion in B. Lyons, 'Getting Untrapped, Struggling for Truths; the Commission for Reception, Truth and Reconciliation (CAVR) in East Timor', in C. Romano, A. Nollkaemper and J. Kleffner (eds), *Internationalized Criminal Court, Sierra Leone, East Timor, Kosovo and Cambodia* (Oxford University Press, 2004), p. 117; Burgess, 'Justice and Reconciliation in East Timor', pp. 144–6.

While the objectives of the mandate did not make specific reference to the issue of reparations, the Commission clearly considered this an integral aspect of restoring the dignity of victims.[20] Within its mandate to work with victims, the Commission established a dedicated victim support division and, as will be described below, undertook a range of measures specifically focused on victims.

In contrast to the Serious Panels Process, which was limited to events during 1999, the Truth Commission was established to cover the time period between 25 April 1974 and 25 October 1999 and also included the internal conflict prior to the occupation. The mandate expressly covered state as well as non-state actors and referred to 'persons, authorities, institutions and organisations'.[21] The Commission was vested with significant powers of inquiry, similar to that of the Truth Commission in Sierra Leone.[22] Following independence, the new Constitution of Timor Leste adopted in March 2002 included recognition in section 162 of the Commission for Reception, Truth and Reconciliation (CAVR).

9.5 Operational aspects of the Commission for Reception, Truth and Reconciliation

The CAVR was established as an independent national authority and not subject to the control or direction of any member of Cabinet. While formally approved by the UN transitional authority, the Commission members were nominated by a selection panel, consisting of national political parties and civil society organisations following a process of public consultations.[23] Although a provision of the mandate allowed for two members to be internationals, the final selection of members was exclusively East Timorese.[24] Among the seven commissioners, there were five men and two women. Another novel feature of the CAVR in East Timor was the nomination of twenty-nine regional commissioners at district level, which allowed for more grassroots contact and community accessibility. The Commission started its work in April 2002 and was initially given two years to operate, however, this was extended to a total of thirty-nine months. Nearly 8,000 individual statements were collected,

[20] CAVR, *Chega!*, Final Report, Part 11.12, Recommendations, p. 36.

[21] Regulation on the Establishment of a Commission for Reception, Truth and Reconciliation in East Timor, UNTAET/REG/2001/10, 13 July 2001, s. 13.

[22] Lyons, 'Getting Untrapped, Struggling for Truths', p. 106.

[23] CAVR, *Chega!*, Final Report, Part 1.3, Introduction, Formation of the Commission, p. 16.

[24] Lyons, 'Getting Untrapped, Struggling for Truths', pp. 99–124.

the overwhelming majority from victims, and eight thematic public hearings were held and broadcast live through media.

The Commission had significantly more resources, both human and financial, than the Serious Crimes Unit and Panels as it benefited from earmarked funding from a range of international donors. At the peak of the work of the Commission, it had some 278 staff. While the human rights unit of UNTAET and OHCHR played an important role during the starting-up phase,[25] staff in the Truth Commission were primarily national. The Commission decided that internationals would not hold management positions, but rather act as advisers or short-term consultants on specific areas of work.[26] This contrasts with the Serious Crimes Unit, which was dominated by internationals, resulting in subsequent difficulties regarding national ownership. In comparison with the Truth Commission in Sierra Leone, its contemporary counterpart in East Timor benefited from significantly more staff, a longer period to work, a much smaller country to cover and a broader and more carefully drafted mandate.

The innovation of the Community Reconciliation Process (CRP) of the CAVR has received significant attention. In essence, it was devised to promote reconciliation and some limited accountability among low-level perpetrators of minor offences, such as, for example, theft and destruction of property. Those suspected of serious crimes were excluded from the process. Applicants would approach the Commission and deposit a statement, which was forwarded to the Office of the Prosecutor General, who would decide if it would be an appropriate case to be dealt with in a CRP. If approved, a community panel would conduct a public hearing, in which victims and traditional leaders participated and where the offender publicly admitted wrongs and apologised. Collectively, the community would agree on conditions on the basis of which the offender could be reintegrated into the community. Interestingly, despite being a community decision, the approval of the affected victims was crucial and in practice victims could veto the process, which occurred in some instances.[27]

The conditions with which the offenders were obliged to comply were described as 'acts of reconciliation', and were in many cases symbolic

[25] Report of the United Nations High Commissioner for Human Rights on the Situation of Human Rights in Timor Leste to the Commission on Human Rights, E/CN4/2004/107, paras 38–43.

[26] CAVR, *Chega!*, Final Report, Part 1.3, Introduction, Formation of the Commission, pp. 39–42.

[27] Burgess, 'A New Approach to Restorative Justice', p. 191.

and limited to a public apology. They could, however, also consist of community service, such as participation in reconstruction work, or include reparations measures, such as restitution by returning stolen property or the payment of a minor amount.[28] Once the 'act of reconciliation' was complied with, the offender received immunity from criminal liability. While an innovative process and largely viewed favourably according to initial assessments, there were drawbacks. One of them was the pressure that communities placed on individual victims to forgive perpetrators in the interest of 'the greater good'.[29] While the system contemplated a mechanism for reparations, these were largely symbolic, which in turn related to the fact that the majority of the offenders were destitute.

In total some 1,400 offenders participated in CRPs, however, it was estimated that double that number would have been willing to do so. As indicated by Burgess, the high degree of community participation in CRPs across the country, in total estimated between 30,000 and 40,000 people, indicated a relatively high degree of approval of the process, which was specifically designed to be in accordance with local customs.[30]

While having received less attention than the CRP process, innovative practices were also applied by the Truth Commission with regard to victims. A Victim Support Division was set up within the CAVR, and it established a network throughout the various districts in order to implement grassroots activities.[31] During a three-month period, the process of statement-taking was coupled with a range of other community activities organised in a participatory manner with victims. Among these were Community Profile Workshops at village level to discuss the impact of the conflict. At district level, each statement-taking period was completed with a public Victims Hearing, which focused entirely on victims. The Victims Hearing was an opportunity for the Commission staff to report back to the community about its activities and it allowed victims, who had chosen to participate and previously made a statement to the CAVR, to give their testimony in public. The Commission followed

[28] Regulation on the Establishment of a Commission for Reception, Truth and Reconciliation in East Timor, UNTAET/REG/2001/10, 13 July 2001, s. 27. Discussed in Burgess, 'Justice and Reconciliation in East Timor', pp. 150–2.

[29] Burgess, 'A New Approach to Restorative Justice', p. 194.

[30] Burgess, 'A New Approach to Restorative Justice', p. 187. Also noted in D. Grenfell, 'When Remembering Isn't Enough: Reconciliation and Justice in Timor-Leste', *Arena Magazine*, Issue 80, December–January 2005–6, pp. 32–5.

[31] CAVR, *Chega!*, Final Report, Part 10, Acolhimento and victim support.

up with a survey in 2004 among victims who had participated in district Victims Hearings (in total fifty-two hearings were conducted) and the overwhelming response was that it had been a positive experience and an important step for victims to regain their dignity.[32] The Commission also arranged a widely broadcast National Public Hearing exclusively focused on victims.

Towards the latter stage of the Commission's work, in 2003 an internal evaluation determined that it would be important to provide additional assistance to victims who were particularly vulnerable and had been severely affected by violations during the conflict. Therefore, the Victim Support Division identified a minor group of victims and arranged for them to participate in a number of small 'healing' workshops, one of which was arranged for women only. In partnership with local NGOs, the Commission arranged for professional mental health workers to conduct the workshops.[33] Although the number of beneficiaries was very limited, in total only around 150 people, this initiative of the CAVR in East Timor should be heralded as recognition of the importance of counselling and psychosocial support, an aspect generally overlooked by previous Truth Commissions as well as international courts.

Another unprecedented measure undertaken by the Truth Commission in East Timor was its initiative to provide, within its own mandate, some degree of reparations directly to victims. No previous Truth Commission had carried out such an undertaking and although the measures provided were very limited, and reached only a small category of beneficiaries, they are of significant symbolic importance for the affirmation of victims' right to reparation. The Truth Commission simply considered that it was 'not enough to tell survivors to wait until the recommendations of the Final Report had been acted on for help to come'.[34] An Urgent Reparations Scheme was established to assist victims 'who were clearly vulnerable and whose need was severe, immediate and related directly to human rights violations which had occurred between 1974 and 1999'. The majority of the beneficiaries were survivors of torture or rape or had suffered indirectly through the disappearance or killing of family members. Many of those selected were widows, orphans, persons with a disability or who had suffered stigmatisation within the community.

32 CAVR, *Chega!*, Final Report, Part 10, Acolhimento and victim support, pp. 26–30.
33 CAVR, *Chega!*, Final Report, Part 10, Acolhimento and victim support, pp. 30–8.
34 CAVR, *Chega!*, Final Report, Part 10, Acolhimento and victim support, pp. 38–9. See further discussion in Linton, 'Putting Things into Perspective', p. 56.

The reparations provided were modest and primarily consisted of urgent medical and psychosocial care, equipment for the disabled and an emergency grant of US$200. The financing of the scheme was provided through the Trust Fund for East Timor, administered by the World Bank. In total 712 people participated in the Urgent Reparations Scheme, of these 516 were men and 196 women.[35] Considering the attention that the Truth Commission placed on gender-based violence, it is surprising that its Report does not comment on why men were over-represented among the beneficiaries of urgent reparations. A likely explanation is that many fewer women than men approached the Truth Commission to make statements, despite attempts to hire female staff and the application of gender-sensitive working methods.[36] The Report underlined that the Urgent Reparations Scheme was 'developed as a temporary measure and does not prejudice in any way any right of victims to full reparations as part of a long-term settlement ... [and] was not to be regarded as full restitution. Nor was it considered to extinguish the duty of the State to provide reparations for victims of human rights violations.'[37]

9.6 The Final Report of the Truth Commission and its Recommendations

The Final Report of the CAVR was handed to President Xanana Gusmao in a formal ceremony in Dili on 31 October 2005. The title of the report was *Chega!*, which roughly means 'no more, stop, enough!' in Portuguese.[38] In total the report consisted of some 2,000 pages and was published in three languages, Indonesian, English and Portuguese, with a partial version being produced in Tetum.[39] A 200-page Executive Summary was also

[35] CAVR, *Chega!*, Final Report, Part 10, Acolhimento and victim support, p. 41. All those who participated in healing workshops also received emergency reparations.

[36] G. Wandita, K. Campbell-Nelson and M. Pereira, 'Learning to Engender Reparations in Timor-Leste: Reaching Out to Female Victims', in R. Rubio-Marín (ed.), *What Happened to the Women? Gender and Reparations for Human Rights Violations* (New York: Social Science Research Council, 2006), pp. 285–334.

[37] Wandita, Campbell-Nelson and Pereira, 'Learning to Engender Reparations in Timor-Leste', p. 39.

[38] CAVR, *Chega!*, Final Report, Foreword, p. 6.

[39] CAVR, *Chega!*, Final Report, Introduction, p. 21. See discussion in Chesterman, 'East Timor', p. 210. The language issue was (and remains) a major challenge in East Timor. The Constitution adopted upon independence in 2002 recognised two official languages, Tetum and Portuguese. For political reasons Indonesian was not chosen, although this was the dominant language spoken among the population. Less than 10 per cent of the population could understand Portuguese and among them virtually nobody under the age of thirty.

made available. The Final Report explored in significant detail the causes of the conflict and unsurprisingly focused to a large extent on the responsibility of Indonesia in conjunction with the 1975 invasion, the twenty-four-year occupation and the 1999 referendum. The Report specifically studied the role played by the Indonesian military and police, studied command responsibility for specific periods and events, and named a number of senior military officials. The report estimated that 18,600 killings and disappearances took place during the occupation and that the Indonesian military bore responsibility for approximately 85 per cent of the violations. The Report concluded that the serious and systematic nature of the violations amounted to crimes against humanity.[40]

The Report also studied the internal conflict and the responsibility of East Timorese armed groups prior to the Indonesian occupation. The role of Portugal towards the end of the colonial period and the passive reaction of Western countries, among them the United States and Australia, to the occupation was also brought forth in the report. As in Sierra Leone, the Report dedicated specific attention to analysis of violations which affected women and children.[41]

The Final Report, like previous truth commissions in other countries, contained a comprehensive set of recommendations.[42] The recommendations can be broadly identified according to three categories. The first category of recommendations explored a range of human rights violations and set out measures that should be taken to address specific groups of victims and to establish an institutional framework to promote respect for human rights. Many of the recommendations of the CAVR were forward-looking and provided a platform for a future national human rights policy.[43] The second category of recommendations related to responsibility and squarely placed the principal duty upon Indonesia to ensure accountability and reparations. In a controversial move, the Report dedicated a specific section of recommendations relating to justice and commented in depth on the failure of the Serious Crimes Panels to hold accountable those carrying the greatest responsibility and underlined that a majority of the Indonesians indicted figured, listed by name and institutional affiliation, in the Truth

[40] CAVR, *Chega!*, Final Report, ch. 8, Responsibility.
[41] Millar, 'Facilitating Women's Voices in Truth Recovery', pp. 171–222.
[42] CAVR, *Chega!*, Final Report, ch. 11, Reparations.
[43] OHCHR Report on Technical Cooperation in the Field of Human Rights in Timor Leste to the Commission on Human Rights for 2004, E/CN4/2005/115, para. 38.

Commission Report. At the time of the publishing of the Report, the Serious Crimes Panels had recently been discontinued. The Report recommended that their mandate be renewed by the United Nations and, should Indonesia persist in the obstruction of justice, the possibility of establishing an international tribunal should be considered.

The third category of recommendations related specifically to reparations and contained a detailed proposal for a national reparations programme, which the Government was urged to implement and finance through the establishment of a trust fund. Like in Sierra Leone, the proposal identified particularly vulnerable groups of victims and underlined 'we are all victims – but not all victims are equal'.[44] The Report identified six categories of victims: namely, individuals who had suffered torture, sexual violence, disabilities (mental and physical), widows and single mothers, children, and also communities particularly affected by a high concentration of violence.[45] The Final Report highlighted the experiences from the Urgent Reparations Scheme implemented by the Commission, the focus on victims upon whom the violations was having a continuing effect and the humble nature of what the majority of survivors sought, simply to enable them and their children to participate on a more or less equal footing in society. The Commission report therefore urged that the main aim of the reparations programme should be rehabilitation through social services and medical and psychosocial care, scholarships for children, as well as symbolic measures aimed at restoring dignity, such as commemorations and honouring of victims through grave memorials. At the time of the presentation of the Report, the Basic Principles on the Right to Reparation for Victims had recently been adopted by the Commission on Human Rights in April 2005, and the Report specifically endorsed them as an applicable human rights standard for reparations.[46]

With regard to funding for a reparations programme, the Final Report noted that a fixed allocation should be designated from the East Timorese national budget, however, it underlined repeatedly that reparations should be the prime obligation and state responsibility of Indonesia. The Report also suggested that permanent members of the Security Council who had given backing to the Suharto regime, particularly the United States, but also the United Kingdom and France, should

[44] CAVR, *Chega!*, Final Report, p. 35. [45] CAVR, *Chega!*, Final Report, p. 41.

[46] UN Basic Principles and Guidelines on the right to a remedy and reparation for victims of gross violations of international human rights law and serious violations of international humanitarian law, UN Doc. A/RES/60/147.

contribute to the provision of reparations for victims. Portugal was also recommended to provide financial support, as were business corporations that profited from the sale of weapons to Indonesia during the occupation. Finally, the Report suggested that international agencies, foundations and civil society provide support based on the principle of social justice.

9.7 Follow-up and implementation of the recommendations regarding reparations

The reaction of the President upon receiving the Report was predictable. The government led by Xanana Gusmao had determined to steer clear of a collision course with Indonesia, and out of geo-strategic considerations was conducting a policy of reconciliation with their giant neighbour. The insistence of the CAVR report on accountability and prosecutions and the responsibility of Indonesia to provide reparations was deemed by the President to be counterproductive to the country's foreign policy interests and described as 'grandiose idealism'.[47] Consequently, the President refused to officially endorse the report and deliberately delayed its official publication and the nomination of a follow-up institution.[48]

In anticipation of the findings of the CAVR, the East Timorese Government approached Indonesia and in late 2004 established a bilateral alternative inquiry, The Commission of Truth and Friendship (CTF), which was launched under the pretext of supporting restorative justice. The CTF was established without any public consultation, its Terms of Reference (ToR) lacked legal basis and there was no provision that its commissioners from both countries act independently of the governments that appointed them. The mandate of the CTF contained provisions that permitted amnesty for human rights violations, allowed it to focus only on events in 1999, omitted mentioning victims and specifically excluded references to reparations. Although the CAVR report was supposed to be taken into account, the final CTF report showed no recognition of the CAVR recommendations.[49]

[47] J. Kingston, 'Regaining Dignity: Justice and Reconciliation in East Timor', *Brown Journal of World Affairs*, 13(1) (2006), 227–40.

[48] Grenfell, 'When Remembering Isn't Enough', p. 32.

[49] International Center for Transitional Justice (M. Hirst), 'Too Much Friendship, Too Little Truth, Monitoring Report on the Commission of Truth and Friendship in Indonesia and Timor Leste', January 2008; International Center for Transitional Justice (M. Hirst), 'An Unfinished Truth: An Analysis of the Commission of Truth and Friendship's Final Report on the 1999 Atrocities in East Timor', March 1999; Reiger, 'Hybrid Attempts at Accountability for Serious Crimes in Timor Leste', pp. 157–8.

The UN specifically refused to collaborate with the CTF initiative and vigorously objected to its amnesty provisions. In June 2005, another inquiry, the International Commission of Experts (CoE), appointed by the UN Secretary-General, made public its report to the Security Council.[50] The CoE Report underlined the lack of accountability and reparations for East Timorese victims and strongly criticised Indonesia's lack of cooperation and its attempts to divert international justice through the setting up of a domestic ad hoc human rights court and the CTF. The CoE expressed renewed calls for justice and urged that the Serious Crimes Process be continued and, in the absence of progress towards establishing accountability, recommended that the Security Council again consider the possibility of establishing an international tribunal. The report of the CoE was rejected by both East Timor and Indonesia and a lack of political support within the international community resulted in an absence of action. As described by Kingston: 'Gusmao's dilemma is being caught between high public expectations for justice and insufficient international support to make this happen.'[51] Burgess notes that 'the unlikely prospect of a Security Council mandate targeting those responsible in the world's largest Islamic nation has become even more remote in the post September 11 world'.[52]

The civil unrest in East Timor in May and June 2006 provided another 'distraction' from the need to establish accountability for the 1999 events. In July 2006, the Secretary-General submitted a report on justice and reconciliation in East Timor to the Security Council.[53] In view of the political opposition to further accountability measures, the report toned down recommendations on prosecution, but highlighted the issue of reparations for victims and encouraged the creation of a solidarity fund in order to provide victims of serious crimes with 'collective and individual restorative measures'. The report was cautiously drafted and replaced the term 'reparations' with 'restorative measures', although in effect it recommended the same type of reparations as the CAVR report.

In this context, it is also worth noting that in comparison with Sierra Leone, OHCHR played a less prominent role in East Timor and, after 2005,

[50] Letter from the Secretary-General to the Security Council containing the Report of the UN Commission of Experts to Review the Prosecution of Serious Violations of Human Rights in East Timor, S/2205/458, 24 June 2005.

[51] Kingston, 'Regaining Dignity', p. 238.

[52] Burgess, 'Justice and Reconciliation in East Timor', p. 139.

[53] Report of the Secretary-General to the Security Council on Justice and Reconciliation in Timor-Leste, UN Doc. S/2006/580, 26 July 2006.

the annual OHCHR report on the human rights situation to the Human Rights Commission, and later the successor Council on Human Rights, was discontinued. International NGOs, notably Amnesty International and Human Rights Watch, played an important role in promoting and maintaining focus on the CAVR and its recommendations.[54] National civil society organisations, on the other hand, have kept a relatively low profile and on the issue of reparations there has been much less public debate than, for example, in Sierra Leone. One of the main reasons for this was the hesitation to publicly challenge a government that consisted of key resistance leaders. As noted by Wandita, Campbell-Nelson and Pereira: 'Those who believe that reparations are part of the international tribunal package and who fear the social stigma in Timor Leste currently associated with calls for justice are, therefore, reluctant to discuss reparations.'[55]

Similarly as in Guatemala and Sierra Leone, the independent national human rights institution has come to play a significant role in following up on the implementation of the recommendations of the Truth Commission. Legislation establishing a Human Rights *Provedoria* was passed in 2004, however, the institution was only set up in 2006. The Provedoria has gradually been advocating for follow-up to the CAVR recommendations.[56] The Final Report of the CAVR identified the Parliament as the national entity for follow-up. Parliamentary debate on the Report was delayed, and not until 2008 was a resolution adopted in Parliament which expressed support for the CAVR recommendations and endorsed the proposal of setting up a reparations scheme for victims. However, the establishment of a reparations scheme remains outstanding and partly relates to the political sensitivities that make civil society organisations reluctant to promote the issue. In June 2010, draft legislation on reparations was finally submitted to Parliament, however, the process was halted as certain political elements insisted that support for war veterans first be defined before victims' rights and reparations were

[54] Joint letter from Amnesty International and Human Rights Watch to the President of the Timor Leste National Parliament, 'Honoring the Report of the Commission for Reception, Truth and Reconciliation', 14 March 2007, available at: www.hrw.org.

[55] Wandita, Campbell-Nelson and Pereira, 'Learning to Engender Reparations in Timor-Leste', p. 318.

[56] OHCHR Report on Technical Cooperation in the Field of Human Rights in Timor Leste to the Commission on Human Rights for 2004, E/CN4/2005/115, paras 21–2; Provedoria for Human Rights and Justice, 'Report to the Asia Pacific Forum of National Human Rights Institutions', 2010.

discussed.[57] The Security Council referred to the draft legislation on reparations in the resolution it adopted on the situation in East Timor in February 2011 and encouraged progress in finalising the legislation.[58]

9.8 Conclusions

As in the other case studies, the experiences in East Timor indicate the difficulties of harmonising measures for accountability with consideration of victims' rights and the difficulties implied in conceptually linking reparations with retributive measures. East Timor, unlike the other case studies explored in this book, has undergone a fundamental transition through its political independence. The violations that occurred during the Indonesian occupation were documented by a number of internationally supported transitional justice initiatives and inquiries. However, ultimately the progress made towards establishing accountability remains weak. Only East Timorese perpetrators carrying a relatively low degree of responsibility were held accountable through the Serious Crimes Process and Community Reconciliation Processes. Those bearing the greatest responsibility remain sheltered in Indonesia and are unlikely to stand trial. The international community failed to establish an effective accountability mechanism in 1999 and did not provide adequate resources and political support to the Serious Crimes Process. The result was characterised by an almost complete lack of consideration for victims and, in particular, their needs for protection and counselling.

The Truth Commission, on the other hand, applied several novel features in its operational work. It enjoyed a high degree of political support both internationally and domestically and was well supported with financial and human resources. It resorted to a grassroots approach to its work and had a high percentage of local staff, which enhanced its legitimacy and sense of national ownership. Its mandate was detailed and the relationship with prosecutions was relatively clear, thereby largely avoiding the confusions that marred the process in Sierra Leone. Importantly, the Truth Commission worked closely with victims at the

[57] Report of the Secretary-General on the United Nations Integrated Mission in Timor-Leste to the Security Council (September 2010–January 2011), UN Doc. S/2011/32, para. 8; Report of the Secretary-General on the United Nations Integrated Mission in Timor-Leste to the Security Council (January–September 2010), UN Doc. S/2010/522, para. 35.

[58] Security Council Resolution 1969 on the Situation in Timor-Leste, UN Doc. S/RES/1969, adopted 24 February 2011.

community level, involved them in CRPs, provided psychosocial support and symbolic efforts were undertaken by the actual Commission to provide a limited degree of reparations for victims as an interim measure.

Despite considerable documentation supporting the right to reparation for victims in East Timor, the primary hurdle resides in the fact that Indonesia declines to collaborate with such efforts despite clear evidence of its state responsibility for violations. Victims have been let down as the national political leadership in East Timor has failed to promote their rights vis-à-vis Indonesia, instead favouring a 'restorative justice' approach which omits reparations. As noted by several commentators, despite the geo-strategic location of East Timor, it is surprising and unfortunate that an inter-state compensation process has not been initiated.[59] This indicates, as noted in Chapter 1, the weakness of making victims dependent on the initiation and outcome of such a political process.

The impetus for providing reparations is temporarily stalled due to political factors; however, the national political climate may well change in the near future, and East Timor has a solid basis for requesting compensation from Indonesia. While Indonesia is unlikely to proceed with prosecutions against TNI military officials, it may well concede to the provision of financial compensation as a measure to placate the international community, pending the application of political pressure applied. While reparations without accountability provide an incomplete measure of justice, it may provide an important stepping stone for victims in East Timor to move beyond past violations.

[59] Linton, 'Putting Things into Perspective: the Realities of Accountability in East Timor, Indonesia and Cambodia', pp. 55–7, also notes the ironic fact that Indonesia is seeking compensation for Indonesian individuals and companies in East Timor who sustained damages during post-referendum violence in 1999. See also Lyons, 'Getting Untrapped, Struggling for Truths', p. 115.

10 Case study: reparations in Colombia

10.1 Introduction

Colombia is the final case study to be elaborated in this study. The rationale for selecting Colombia is based on the particular set of circumstances that have conditioned the application of transitional justice mechanisms at the national level, and the considerable degree of attention given to the issue of reparations in this context. Unlike the other country case studies, Colombia is characterised by the absence of a comprehensive peace process as only one of the armed groups has demobilised: the paramilitary United Self-Defense Forces of Colombia (Autodefensas Unidas de Colombia, AUC). As part of the negotiation and demobilisation process, which started in 2003, the Colombian government resorted to transitional justice measures by adopting specific legislation for reducing the accountability of perpetrators, the establishment of a kind of national truth commission (La Comisión Nacional de Reparación y Reconciliación, CNRR) and reparations measures for victims. The United Nations never had a peace mission in Colombia; however, OHCHR has had a significant country office there for over a decade and together with other actors, notably the Inter-American Commission on Human Rights (IACHR), advocates vigorously for compliance with minimum human rights standards and the consideration of victims' rights.

The route initially chosen by the government was strongly flavoured with restorative justice elements, resulting in *de facto* amnesties for serious violations. Criticism has been raised against the government for failing to comply with its international obligations adhered to through human rights instruments and the Rome Statute of the International Criminal Court, and for using the issue of reparations in order to distract attention from the duty to establish accountability of perpetrators.[1] An important factor that has yet to fully demonstrate its impact at the national level is the entry into force of the full jurisdiction of the ICC in 2009 and the requirement that Colombia counteract claims that it is unwilling or unable to carry out genuine investigations or prosecutions.[2]

Despite its failure to establish accountability for serious violations, the transitional justice process in Colombia stands apart for its unprecedented focus on victims' rights; achieved by a vibrant civil society and the involvement of the international community. The active engagement of Colombia with human rights mechanisms has provided additional impetus, for example, the emphasis on reparations was particularly tangible during the debate at the Universal Periodic Review (UPR) of Colombia in the Human Rights Council in 2008 and in treaty body reviews in 2009 and 2010.[3]

10.2 Brief historical background

Colombia stands out as one of the countries in the Latin American region having a long democratic tradition, relatively uninterrupted by military dictatorships apart from a brief period in the 1950s. However,

1 Among the principal critics are the UN Office of the High Commissioner for Human Rights, the Inter-American Commission on Human Rights, Human Rights Watch, Amnesty International, the International Crisis Group and the Colombian Commission of Jurists. See discussion in International Crisis Group, 'Correcting Course; Victims and the Justice and Peace Law in Colombia', 30 October 2008.

2 The Rome Statute of the International Criminal Court, Article 17(a). Upon ratification in November 2002, Colombia submitted a declaration requesting exemption from the category of war crimes during a seven-year period, as provided for in Article 124 of the Statute. However, the temporary exemption of war crimes does not apply to the other categories specified with the jurisdiction of the court, notably crimes against humanity. OHCHR, within its mandate of observation of international human rights and humanitarian law, has in its annual reports to the UN Commission on Human Rights and its successor the Human Rights Council repeatedly affirmed that crimes against humanity have occurred in Colombia due to the systematic nature of the violence. See OHCHR Colombia, Annual Report to the Commission on Human Rights for 2002, UN Doc. E/CN.4/2003/13, para. 42; OHCHR Colombia, Annual Report to the Commission on Human Rights for 2003, UN Doc. E/CN.4/2004/13, para. 67; OHCHR Colombia, Annual Report to the Commission on Human Rights for 2005, UN Doc. E/CN.4/2006/9, para. 17; OHCHR Colombia, Annual Report to the Human Rights Council for 2006, UN Doc. A/HRC/4/49, paras 62–7.

3 Report on Colombia of the Working Group on the Universal Periodic Review of the Human Rights Council, UN Doc. A/HRC/10/82, 9 January 2009; Human Rights Committee Concluding Observations on Colombia, 2010, UN Doc. CCPR/C/COL/CO/6; Committee against Torture Concluding Observations on Colombia, 2009, UN Doc. CAT/C/COL/CO/4.

Colombia continues to experience one of the longest civil wars in the world, ongoing since the 1960s, and has for decades had one of the highest homicide rates in the world. The country is marked by significant polarisation and inequity, coupled with a historically weak state apparatus, which was unable to control the national territory.[4] The 1980s saw the gains from the narcotics trade filter into the financial and political sphere, resulting in a corrupt and paralysed judiciary and deepened socio-economic divisions.[5]

The principal left-wing guerrilla groups in Colombia, the Revolutionary Armed Forces of Colombia (Fuerzas Armadas Revolucionarias de Colombia, FARC) and the National Liberation Army (Ejército de Liberación Nacional, ELN), were both founded in the 1960s and had ties with other agrarian reform movements and communist parties in Latin America. In the late 1990s, the government initiated negotiations with FARC, which included the granting of a demilitarised zone in the south of the country. The peace talks collapsed in 2002 and FARC were largely considered to be at fault for not having adhered to a ceasefire.[6]

During the 1990s, the paramilitaries consolidated their power in various parts of the country, and in 1997 the AUC was formed with support from the elite of the business and large-scale farming sectors. Lack of faith in the state military and the justice system are factors that partly explain the political support for private armed forces. Like FARC, paramilitaries built their power base on funds from cocaine production and sought to dominate regions with natural resources, in particular, petroleum and minerals. [7]

[4] OHCHR Colombia, Annual Report to the Human Rights Council for 2007, UN Doc. A/HRC/7/39, para. 75: 'The GINI coefficient [in Colombia] is the third worst in Latin America'.

[5] UNDP National Development Report on Colombia 2003; El Conflicto, Callejón con Salida, Bogotá, 2003, p. 32; N. Richani, *Systems of Violence, The Political Economy of War and Peace in Colombia* (New York: SUNY, 2002), p. 25; G. Livingston, *Inside Colombia, Drugs, Democracy and War* (London: Latin American Bureau, 2003), p. 8.

[6] Reasons for the collapse of the negotiations can also be traced to the simultaneous signing by the government of Plan Colombia, whereby large-scale military support from the United States was secured. Furthermore, scepticism also relates to Union Patriotica (UP), a political party formed by FARC in the mid 1980s. Within a period of approximately five years more than 3,000 members were assassinated, including two presidential candidates, leaving little faith in political negotiations. The case of the UP is currently subject to 'friendly settlement' negotiations in the Inter-American Human Rights system.

[7] Richani, *Systems of Violence*, pp. 93–109. The political support for paramilitary units dates back several decades. In the mid 1960s the Congress enacted legislation which authorised the forming of paramilitary units in order to promote public order.

The paramilitaries acted with varying levels of complicity with the armed forces, which allowed their gradual strengthening throughout the country. In numerous regions during the 1990s, the reduction in the number of human rights violations committed by the army related to the transfer of power to paramilitary groups. In the areas controlled by paramilitaries, extrajudicial killings became commonplace and targeted left-wing sympathisers, social leaders, civil society organisations and trade unionists. According to the Colombian Commission of Jurists, 953 massacres were committed between July 1996 and June 2001, and the responsibility for 66 per cent of these was attributed to paramilitaries.[8]

The power play over territorial control between several armed groups caused a humanitarian crisis, and the number of civilians displaced annually rose from 27,000 in 1985 to over 300,000 in 2002.[9] The internally displaced population in Colombia is one of the largest in the world, and according to the UN High Commissioner for Refugees (UNHCR) amounted to approximately one million people in 2002, while in 2006 the number had risen to an estimated three million people, an estimate which remained valid in 2010.[10] The guerrillas as well as the paramilitary groups both demonstrated their disregard for international humanitarian law and, in particular, the principle of distinction. According to estimates by Amnesty International, around 60,000 people died due to the internal armed conflict in Colombia between 1985 and 2003, approximately 80 per cent of whom were civilians.[11]

Colombia is distinguished by a significant discrepancy between its sophisticated legal framework and its dysfunctional operation in practice. The high rate of impunity is aggravated by the extreme congestion in the justice system of some one million cases and by the constant threats directed against members of the judiciary.[12] Additional difficulties arise due to continuous clashes of jurisdiction between the ordinary justice system and the military justice system. However, with regard to

[8] Colombian Commission of Jurists, 'A Growing Absence of Guarantees, Situation of HR and IHL in Colombia 1997–2003', Bogotá, 2003, p. 25; G. Gallon, 'Human Rights – a Path to Democracy and Peace in Colombia', in C. Welna and G. Gallon (eds), *Peace, Democracy and Human Rights in Colombia* (University of Notre Dame Press, 2007), pp. 353–410.

[9] UNDP National Development Report on Colombia 2003, p. 122.

[10] UN High Commissioner for Refugees, at: www.unhchr.org.

[11] Livingstone, *Inside Colombia*, p. 8.

[12] UNDP National Development Report on Colombia 2003, p. 167; Livingstone, *Inside Colombia*, p. 32; International Crisis Group, 'Colombia, Negotiating with the Paramilitaries', Report, September 2003, p. 24.

international legal obligations, Colombia is a state party to the majority of the regional and international human rights treaties.

While Colombia has no UN peacekeeping mission, there is significant UN presence in the country through twenty different UN agencies and entities; of particular relevance are OHCHR and UNHCR.[13] OHCHR's mandate entails monitoring of human rights and humanitarian law and providing advice to the government on human rights matters. During the peace negotiations with FARC, the Secretary-General appointed a Special Adviser on Colombia to mediate, however, the government requested this mandate to be terminated in 2005.[14] The ICRC is widely present throughout the country.

10.3 Negotiations with the paramilitaries

In August 2002, Álvaro Uribe Vélez assumed the presidency with a hard-line campaign to fight the war on internal terrorism by implementing a policy of 'democratic security'. The policy resulted in increased presence of police and armed forces throughout the country; however, the territorial gains were not accompanied by an increased presence of civilian authorities.[15] The Uribe government initiated a dialogue with the AUC shortly after coming into power and he became the first president to negotiate with the paramilitaries.[16] The AUC saw a favourable political momentum in Uribe's right-wing government,[17] and in December 2002 a unilateral ceasefire was announced by the AUC. The impetus for the AUC to seek negotiations originated partly due to pressure caused by its international classification as a terrorist organisation and partly

[13] Both OHCHR and UNHCR have been present in Colombia since the signing of bilateral agreements with the government in 1996.

[14] UN Press release SG/A/823, 1 November 2002. The termination of the mandate by the government in 2005 was in response to critical comments by the Special Adviser, Mr LeMoyne, on the government negotiations with the paramilitaries.

[15] OHCHR Colombia, Annual Report to the Commission on Human Rights for 2003, UN Doc. E/CN.4/2004/13, paras 18–19.

[16] L. Laplante and K. Theidon, 'Transitional Justice in Times of Conflict: Colombia's Ley de Justicia y Paz', *Michigan Journal of International Law*, 28(49) (2006), pp. 49–108.

[17] After Uribe's re-election in 2006, the Colombian Supreme Court initiated investigations against, e.g., numerous right-wing politicians belonging to Uribe's coalition parties for links with paramilitary groups. In 2007 investigations were formally opened against forty-five parliamentarians and by 2011 the Supreme Court had filed 120 cases against current or former parliamentarians. OHCHR Colombia, Annual Report to the Human Rights Council for 2007, UN Doc. A/HRC/7/39, para. 15; OHCHR Colombia, Annual Report to the Human Rights Council for 2010, UN Doc. A/HRC/16/22, paras 45–6.

because of the increasing demands from the United States to extradite leaders on drug trafficking charges. An additional factor seen as a concern by paramilitary leaders was that the ICC could have jurisdiction in Colombia after November 2002. The ratification of the Rome Statute was done during the last days of the previous government and the Uribe administration was faced with the looming threat of the ICC invoking its jurisdiction. As will be explored below, however, both the paramilitaries and the government underestimated the reaction of the international community and the legal implications of initiating the demobilisation process, in particular, in relation to the international norms that restrict the application of amnesties and provide victims with the right to claim reparations.

Among the first challenges the government faced was open questioning by human rights organisations, among them Amnesty International, with regard to the contradictory concept of a peace process between the government and the paramilitaries. This contradiction is illustrated by the long-standing and close links between the security forces and paramilitaries, whose raison d'être was the defence of the Colombian State. As discussed by Gallon, the Colombian government has persuasively counterargued by resorting to the 'fallacy of the State as victim' theory, whereby the government eschews responsibility by shifting it to the narcotics trade and armed groups, without acknowledgement of entwined links with political and financial interests.[18]

The first step taken by the government to facilitate the negotiation process with the paramilitaries was the adjustment of the legal framework for demobilisations, previously based on Law 418 of 1997, by adopting modifications through Law 782 of 2002 and Decree 128 of 2003. In brief terms, through these measures the government sought to apply amnesty provisions to the paramilitaries. The legislation excluded pardons for certain violations; namely, atrocious and barbaric acts, terrorism, genocide, kidnappings, homicide committed in non-combat situations or by placing the victim in a state of defencelessness.[19] Furthermore, it set out that no benefits would be offered to anyone who 'when demobilising is being prosecuted or has been condemned for crimes contrary to the Colombian Constitution or international treaties ratified by Colombia'.[20] The above provisions are, however, inadequate as the list of violations for which pardons cannot be given is too brief and only covers certain war

[18] Gallon, 'Human Rights – a Path to Democracy and Peace in Colombia', pp. 353–410.
[19] Law 782 of 2002, Article 19. [20] Decree 128 of 2003, Article 21.

crimes, in contravention of Colombia's international obligations, and the exclusion would apply only if the person was actually being prosecuted or had been sanctioned. In practice, persons who sought to be demobilised according to Decree 128 of 2003 were assessed by the Operational Committee for Disarmament (CODA), which upon review of the applicant's criminal record determined whether to issue a certificate and approve incorporation into the reintegration programme of the Ministry of the Interior and Justice, which enabled the demobilised person to receive socio-economic benefits.[21] The widespread impunity for serious human rights and humanitarian law violations in Colombia rendered this provision practically useless, in particular, when applied to collective demobilisations to which the judiciary did not have the capacity to respond. Furthermore, the legislative framework was criticised for entirely omitting the rights of victims.[22]

In July 2003, the government and the AUC signed an agreement, the pact of Santa Fé de Ralito, to demobilise and publicly declared that 13,000 men would demobilise by the end of 2005. The process quickly drew additional international and domestic criticism for a number of reasons. The declared ceasefire, a stated pre-condition of the government to conduct negotiations with any illegal armed group, was openly breached and hundreds of violations were recorded by national and UN human rights monitors.[23] Furthermore, it became apparent that the legal framework described above and the resources of the Attorney General's office were completely inadequate, as several of the initial demobilisation initiatives, paraded on television, resulted in mass

[21] Inter-American Commission on Human Rights, Report on the Implementation of the Justice and Peace Law: Initial Stages in the Demobilisation of the AUC and the First Judicial Proceedings, OEA/Ser.L/V/II, Washington, 2 October 2007, p. 10; R. Uprimny Yepes and L. Lasso Lozano, 'Verdad, Reparación y Justicia para Colombia: Algunas Reflexiones y Recomendaciones', in Friedrich Ebert Stiftung (ed.), *Conflicto y Seguridad, Democracia en Colombia, Temas Críticos y Propuestas* (Bogotá: Fundación Social, 2004), p. 165.

[22] OHCHR Colombia, Annual Report to the Commission on Human Rights covering 2003, annex 3, para. 8.

[23] OHCHR Colombia, Annual Report to the Commission on Human Rights covering 2003, para. 54; Colombian Human Rights Ombudsman (Defensoria del Pueblo), Report on Breaches of the Ceasefire, September 2004. The report documents 342 cases of violations by the AUC between January and August 2004, see at: www.defensoria.org.co/pdf/informes/informe_107.pdf; Amnesty International, Annual Human Rights Report on Colombia for 2003.

pardons, including for numerous paramilitaries under preliminary investigation for having committed serious human rights violations.[24]

In an attempt to improve the legitimacy of the process, the government requested the Organization of American States (OAS) to verify the demobilisation. In February 2004, the General Assembly of the OAS passed a resolution establishing the mandate of the OAS verification mission in Colombia.[25] At the last minute, a reference was included in the resolution, inviting the IACHR to advise the OAS verification mission. The OAS mission in Colombia adopted a low profile and limited its mandate to passively reporting on violations to the ceasefire.[26] The IACHR, on the other hand, vigorously stepped up its monitoring role and, in parallel with OHCHR in Colombia, made numerous public calls for the adoption of a legal framework for demobilisations in line with international obligations.

10.4 The 'Alternative Justice' bill

In the face of mounting controversy and critique, the government attempted to pass legislation which could be applied to demobilised paramilitaries responsible for serious violations. The first attempt was launched in August 2003 and was known as the 'Alternative Justice' bill. It claimed to be inspired by restorative justice theory and proposed alternative justice sanctions, which basically translated into amnesty provisions without excluding those responsible for gross human rights violations. The bill was sent to Congress without prior consultations with civil society and considerable objections were raised by members of the judiciary, the NGO community, academia and the international community. OHCHR in Colombia analysed the proposed bill and raised a number of concerns: the bill did not make any reference to human rights obligations; and the sanctions proposed were clearly lacking proportionality to the violations committed, in breach of the state duty to investigate and sanction gross violations. Particular concern was

24 Procuraduría General de la Nación, cited in Laplante and Theidon, 'Transitional Justice in Times of Conflict', p. 65.

25 It should be noted that the OAS Secretary-General at the time, Mr Cesar Gaviria, was a former Colombian president. Queries were raised in respect of the incentive behind the OAS commitment to the verification mission, which was strongly promoted by Mr Gaviria himself. Mr Gaviria subsequently returned to national politics in Colombia.

26 M. Camilleri, 'The OAS in Colombia; MAPP/OEA, Paramilitary Demobilisation and Civil Society', *Revista CEJIL*, 2 (2006), 156–8.

expressed over the provision establishing presidential discretion regarding pardons, as this would interfere with the independence of the judiciary. Furthermore, the references to reparations for victims were unclear, there was no implementation mechanism contemplated and, importantly, the obligation of the state to guarantee reparations for victims was absent.[27]

The draft 'Alternative Justice' bill illustrated an example whereby the concept of restorative justice was deliberately distorted to justify impunity. The bill displayed a notion of victims as passive beneficiaries and its drafting excluded the participation of victims' groups. This runs contrary to the concept of restorative justice as 'a process whereby all the stakeholders come together to resolve collectively how to deal with the aftermath of the offence and its implications for the future' and 'involves the victim, the offender and the community in a search for solutions which promote repair and reconciliation'.[28] As noted by the Constitutional Court Judge Uprimny, any attempt to apply restorative justice in the Colombian context is complicated due to a number of reasons, including the consideration that restorative justice is aimed at addressing 'ordinary' crimes and not gross violations and, therefore, implies sanctions that are disproportionately lenient in relation to the seriousness of the crimes. Furthermore, from a practical perspective, finding a suitable and safe modality to bring together victims and perpetrators in Colombia is a significant challenge.[29]

10.5 Law 975 of 2005: La Ley de Justicia y Paz

During 2004 and 2005 there was intense debate in Colombia concerning the legal framework for demobilisation of the paramilitaries. Due to significant international pressure from OHCHR,[30] IACHR, as well as the

[27] For OHCHR's analysis see OHCHR Colombia, Annual Report to the Commission on Human Rights for 2003, annex 3, paras 9–11 and the public statement made by the OHCHR Director in Colombia at the Colombian Senate, 23 September 2003, available at: www.hchr.org.co.

[28] Zehr, *Changing Lenses*, p. 181. On restorative justice theory, see mention in Chapter 4 and also IDEA, *Reconciliation after Violent Conflict, A Handbook* (Stockholm: IDEA, 2003), pp. 111–13; Braithwaite, *Restorative Justice and Responsive Regulation*; T. Marshall, *Restorative Justice: An Overview* (London: Home Office. Research Development and Statistics Directorate, 1999), p. 5.

[29] Uprimny Yepes and Lasso Lozano, 'Verdad, Reparación y Justicia para Colombia: Algunas Reflexiones y Recomendaciones', p. 125.

[30] During 2004 and 2005, OHCHR presented and published six public statements, widely echoed in national media, with considerable analysis of the international norms for

academic and NGO community, the government was forced to rework its draft legislation proposal for 'Alternative Justice'. In total nine bills were debated in Congress prior to the adoption on 21 June 2005 of Law 975/2005, re-named the Justice and Peace Law (La Ley de Justicia y Paz). As indicated in the title of the law, the government strategically changed the name following the controversy of the Alternative Justice bill.

The Justice and Peace Law 975 indicated a significant shift in recognition of human rights standards and cited at length provisions relating to truth, justice and reparations, making indirect references to the Rome Statute of the International Criminal Court as well as to UN Principles on Action to Combat Impunity, the Basic Principles on the Right to Reparation for Victims, and the Declaration of the Basic Principles of Justice for Victims of Crime and Abuse of Power. The first Article of Law 975 stated that its objective was to 'facilitate peace processes and reincorporation, collective or individual, into civilian life by members of armed groups while guaranteeing the rights of the victims to truth, justice and reparations'. Furthermore, Law 975, through Articles 4–8, 44 and 46–9, expounded on the definition of victims and on the content of the right to truth, justice and reparations.

Regarding reparations, Law 975 affirmed that this right should be comprehensive and cited the same components as the Basic Principles on the Right to Reparation: namely, restitution, compensation, rehabilitation, satisfaction and guarantees of non-repetition. In this sense Law 975 demonstrated a progressive approach by embracing and enshrining the emerging concept of reparations in international law. Law 975 (Article 5) also contained an inclusive definition of victims, which encompasses family members affected by the killing or disappearance of the victim. On the other hand, one of the drawbacks of the law was the expansion of the definition of victims to include members of the armed forces, which was heavily criticised by victims' organisations.

Although Law 975 attempted to give the impression that the victims were to be given due consideration, it nevertheless retained its core element: namely, that of alternative sentences for perpetrators (Articles 3 and 29). The law, which was intended to be applied only to perpetrators who had committed crimes of such severity that they could not be pardoned by Law 782 of 2002 and Decree 128 of 2003, foresaw

truth, justice and reparations, in particular, calling for their inclusion in the negotiation process with the paramilitaries. All statements are available in Spanish on OHCHR's Colombian web page at: www.hchr.org.co.

deprivation of liberty of between five and eight years (Article 29). The location where the prison sentence was to be carried out would be determined by the government and the period during which the demobilisation took place deducted from the sentence (Article 30).

The lack of proportionality of the proposed sentences in relation to the gravity of the crimes was the key propellant behind a number of legal challenges presented against Law 975 for being unconstitutional. In addition to concerns regarding disproportional sentences, the law was challenged on a number of procedural aspects regarding the participation of victims in the proceedings and in relation to the funding of reparations.[31] The principal lawsuit against Law 975 was submitted by the Colombian Commission of Jurists and it was supported by extensive *amici curiae* briefs by, among others, the International Center for Transitional Justice (ICTJ) and the Center for Justice and International Law (CEJIL).[32] The subsequent ruling of the Constitutional Court C-370 of 19 May 2006 required Law 975 to be amended in a number of areas, although essentially it conceded that alternative penalties could be applied in the interest of achieving peace.[33]

10.6 Reparations in Law 975 of 2005

In relation to the issue of reparations, Law 975 contained, and retained after the Constitutional Court ruling, a number of problematic aspects. Although the right to reparation is affirmed at length, upon closer inspection it is clear that the law presents serious drawback clauses and major practical challenges. A key problem relates to the issue of state responsibility.[34] Article 42 states that it is the duty of members of

[31] See extensive discussion of the Colombian Constitutional Court sentence C-370/2006 in Laplante and Theidon, 'Transitional Justice in Times of Conflict', pp. 81–108.

[32] CEJIL, *Amicus Curiae* brief to Colombian Constitutional Court regarding Law 975, 2006; ICTJ, *Amicus Curiae* brief to Colombian Constitutional Court regarding Law 975, 2006.

[33] For extensive discussion of Law 975 and the Colombian Constitutional Court sentence C-370/2006 see Laplante and Theidon, 'Transitional Justice in Times of Conflict', pp. 81–108; M. J. Guembre and H. Olea, 'No Justice, No Peace, Discussion of a Legal Framework Regarding the Demobilisation of Non-State Armed Groups in Colombia', in N. Roht-Arriaza and J. Mariezcurrena (eds), *Transitional Justice in the Twenty-First Century, Beyond Truth versus Justice* (Cambridge University Press, 2006), pp. 120–47; F. Gomez Isa, 'Justicia, Verdad y Reparación en el Proceso de Desmovilización Paramilitar en Colombia', in F. Gomez Isa (ed.), *Colombia en Su Laberinto, una Mirada al Conflicto* (Madrid: Catarata, 2008), pp. 87–166.

[34] International Crisis Group, Colombia: Towards Peace and Justice?, Latin America Report No. 16, 14 March 2006, pp. 11–12; Guembre and Olea, 'No Justice, No Peace', p. 134.

armed groups to provide reparations following their judicial sanctioning. Thus, despite lengthy affirmations of the right to reparation for victims, it is clear that the government sought to use politically correct terminology regarding reparations as 'window dressing', while denying the core element of state responsibility vis-à-vis the victims. The absence of state responsibility stands in stark contrast to the fact that the Colombian State between 2004 and 2007 was condemned and sanctioned by the Inter-American Court on Human Rights for its responsibility in relation to five major massacres committed by paramilitary groups against civilians. In all five cases, the IACtHR explored at length the extent of state responsibility through active participation by state agents and collusion with paramilitaries or by deliberate omission to prevent the violations.[35] As clearly set out in the Basic Principles on the Right to Reparation for Victims: 'a State shall provide reparation to victims for acts or omissions which can be attributed to the State and constitute gross violations'.[36]

A second major obstacle to making the right to reparation operational was the requirement of prosecutions. Reparations were to be paid pursuant to individual convictions, or if there was proof of the responsibility of the particular paramilitary group of the perpetrator, then the victim could apply to the Reparation Fund for Victims (Articles 42 and 54). These provisions made the award of reparations conditional upon a number of factors, among them: (1) the outcome of the investigation; (2) the ability of the victim to present proof to support his or her claim;[37] (3) if property was relinquished by the perpetrator to the Reparations Fund;[38] and (4) whether the Reparations Fund held sufficient resources

[35] For further reference, see Chapter 3 regarding reparations in human rights jurisprudence. The sentences of the Inter-American Court on Human Rights are *19 Comerciantes* v. *Colombia*, IACtHR, Judgment, 5 July 2004, Ser. C, No. 109; *Mapiripán Massacre* v. *Colombia*, IACtHR, Judgment, 15 September 2005, Ser. C, No. 134; *Pueblo Bello Massacre* v. *Colombia*, IACtHR, Judgment, 31 January 2006, Ser. C, No. 140; *Ituango Massacre* v. *Colombia*, IACtHR, Judgment, 1 July 2006, Ser. C, No. 148; *La Rochela Massacre* v. *Colombia*, IACtHR, Judgment, 11 May 2007, Ser. C, No. 163.

[36] UN Basic Principles and Guidelines on the Right to a Remedy and Reparation for Victims of Gross Violations of International Human Rights Law and Serious Violations of International Humanitarian Law, 2005, para. 15.

[37] Critique was raised as victims were forced to carry the burden of proof in court and present evidence of filed complaints and residence, see Fundación Ideas para la Paz, *Siguiendo el Conflicto, Hechos y Análisis*, Bogotá, No. 50, June 2007, p. 5.

[38] The demobilised paramilitaries were generally unwilling to relinquish their assets and few contributed to the Reparations Fund, see International Crisis Group, 'Correcting Course, Victims and the Justice and Peace Law in Colombia', Latin America Report No. 29, 30 October 2008, p. 10.

to distribute. Linking the award of reparations to prosecutions significantly limited the prospects of making this part of the law operational, especially given the judiciary's entrenched structural difficulties in breaking impunity in Colombia. Although Law 975 foresaw the setting up of a specific unit within the Attorney General's Office (Article 33), in practice insufficient additional resources were allocated for investigations. By mid 2006, some 31,000 paramilitaries had demobilised and of those approximately 3,000 requested to be judged according to Law 975, an implicit recognition of their responsibility for serious crimes. However, only twenty-three prosecutors were assigned to investigate all the cases.[39] Meanwhile, some 300,000 victims filed claims for reparations under Law 975. By the end of 2010, only two convictions had been handed down, effectively rendering reparations provisions inoperative. Furthermore, an additional concern was that several people who presented themselves as victims in the legal proceedings were killed in retaliation attacks.[40]

10.7 National Commission on Reparations and Reconciliation

As described above, Law 975 set out a transitional justice process primarily based on judicial procedures, which allowed perpetrators to dominate while victims were left dependent on the outcome of the investigations. During the debate regarding the law, there was significant discussion of establishing a form of a truth commission as a complement to a process otherwise limited to a strictly 'judicial truth', without victim participation or a comprehensive overview of the factors causing the conflict.[41] OHCHR, with reference to the UN Principles on Combating Impunity, stressed the need to establish a commission for the clarification of historical and sociological factors, that is, an initiative similar to truth commissions previously established in other

[39] Comisión Nacional de Reparación y Reconciliación, Informe al Congreso, 'Proceso de reparación a las victimas, balance actual y perspectivas futuras', 2007, pp. 156–8; International Crisis Group, 'Correcting Justice', p. 8.

[40] OHCHR Colombia, Annual Report to the Human Rights Council for 2007, A/HRC/7/39, para. 50; OHCHR Colombia, Annual Report to the Human Rights Council for 2009, A/HRC/13/72, para. 81; Annual Report 2009 of the Inter-American Commission on Human Rights, OEA/Ser.L/V/II, 30 December 2009.

[41] On the experience of victims in international criminal procedures, see Stover, 'Witnesses and the Promise of Justice in the Hague', pp. 104–20. On the need to balance judicial accountability with mechanisms for the establishment of a comprehensive record of truth, see Goldstone, 'Advancing the Cause of Human Rights', pp. 195–221.

transitional or post-conflict countries.[42] There was significant support for the creation of a truth commission from leading NGOs, such as the Colombian Commission of Jurists,[43] academics and members of the judiciary.[44] However, among the key features of the initiatives presented by civil society organisations and discussed in public was significant involvement of the international community, notably the UN, and it was suggested that a truth commission, following examples in other countries such as Guatemala and Sierra Leone, be composed of both nationals and internationals in order to establish a degree of impartiality. The government responded by discarding the involvement of the international community in the setting up of such a mechanism and at first openly rejected the concept of a truth commission in Colombia.[45] However, the law did finally provide for the establishment of a kind of truth commission, yet with an atypical mandate and composition. Article 50 of Law 975 created the National Commission for Reparations and Reconciliation (La Comisión Nacional de Reparación y Reconciliación, CNRR) and provided it with a sprawling mandate. Among the multitude of tasks, the CNRR should: (1) guarantee the rights of victims and their participation in judicial proceedings; (2) present a public report about the emergence of illegal armed groups; (3) conduct follow-up and verify the process of reincorporation and the work of local authorities to ensure the full demobilisation of members of illegal armed groups; (4) recommend criteria for reparations, conduct follow-up of their implementation and present a report to government on the issue after two years; and (5) coordinate the activities of Regional Commissions for

[42] Public statement made by the OHCHR Director in Colombia, 'Para Lograr la Paz en Colombia Se Necesitan Justicia, Verdad y Reparation', at the International Seminar on Alternative Justice in Barcelona, 28 February 2004; UN Principles on Combating Impunity (Joint principles of 1997), paras 17–24 note that as an extra element to prosecutions of perpetrators of human rights violations, extrajudicial commissions of inquiry fulfil the 'objective of the right to know as a collective right'. For some further reflections on truth commissions and prosecutions, see J. Dugard, 'Possible Conflicts with Truth Commissions', in A. Cassese, P. Gaete and J. Jones (eds), *The Rome Statute of the International Criminal Court, A Commentary* (Oxford University Press, 2002), p. 693.

[43] The Colombian Commission of Jurists was a long-standing supporter of the creation of a truth commission and conducted an alternative inquiry in 2000, together with eighteen other NGOs, entitled the *Nunca más* project (named after previous investigations in South America, which created the concept of truth commissions in the 1980s).

[44] Constitutional Court magistrate, Uprimny Yepes and Lasso Lozano, 'Verdad, reparación y justicia para Colombia: algunas reflexiones y recomendaciones', pp. 128–35.

[45] The Colombian government negotiator, the High Commissioner for Peace, Luis Carlos Restrepo, publicly opposed the proposal, 'Colombia No Necesita Comisiones de Verdad' (Colombia does not Need Truth Commissions), press release, 16 February 2004.

Property Restitution. The CNRR should be composed of twelve members, all nationals, of whom only two represented victims' organisations, one represented the Human Rights Ombudsman's office and the rest were representatives of various government entities. The CNRR was established in 2005 for a period of eight years and differed significantly from previous models of truth commissions,[46] as it would not take victims testimonies or work with the aim of publicly presenting a consolidated and impartial report with an analysis of causes of the conflict and a comprehensive set of recommendations. As evidenced by the selection of members to form part of the CNRR, there was no attempt to establish neutrality as the vast majority of members are government representatives.

It seems unclear what the government intended the prime objective of the CNRR to be, as it was required to undertake an incompatible number of tasks to simultaneously guarantee the rights of victims in proceedings, verify the reintegration process of perpetrators, as well as recommend and simultaneously evaluate the policy for reparations. Victims' organisations, notably among them MOVICE,[47] and human rights NGOs openly rejected collaborating with the CNRR, which they considered politicised and incapable of undertaking the tasks assigned to it.[48] The lack of support from civil society organisations has contributed to undermining the work and credibility of the CNRR.

10.8 Administrative reparations programme

Despite the controversy surrounding the creation of the CNRR, several of its members spoke out publicly against the ineffectiveness of the reparations provisions of Law 975 and called for the state to assume a clearer responsibility towards the victims by allocating resources from the national budget and by establishing an alternative process to claim reparations outside judicial proceedings.[49] The IACHR supported this position and strongly advocated for the establishment of an administrative

[46] See Hayner, *Unspeakable Truths*; Hayner, 'Fifteen Truth Commissions 1974 to 1994', pp. 597–655.

[47] MOVICE, Movimiento de Crimenes de Estado, a major NGO representing large numbers of victims of state and paramilitary violence, was set up in 2005 in the context of the adoption of the Justice and Peace Law.

[48] Laplante, 'Transitional Justice in Times of Conflict', p. 94; International Crisis Group, 'Correcting Justice', p. 4; Fundación Ideas para la Paz, *Siguiendo el Conflicto, Hechos y Análisis*.

[49] Comisión Nacional de Reparación y Reconciliación, Informe al Congreso, 'Proceso de reparación a las victimas, balance actual y perspectivas futuras', 2007, pp. 10 and 109.

reparations process, independent of judicial proceedings, accessible to victims and expedient at processing claims. Furthermore, the IACHR reiterated the central and principal responsibility of the state to ensure that victims have effective access to reparations.[50]

Faced by growing discontent among victims' organisations and the evident ineffectiveness of Law 975, the government issued Decree 1290 in April 2008, whereby an administrative programme for individual reparations was created. The programme was aimed at providing reparations, primarily financial compensation, to victims without requirements of resorting to the judicial system or dependency on the funds handed over by perpetrators. Decree 1290 repeatedly underlined (Articles 2–5) that the programme was based on the principle of solidarity and that the state assumed only subsidiary responsibility. Victims of violations committed by state agents were deliberately excluded. Decisions on the claims were to be made by an Administrative Reparations Committee, which, similar to the CNRR, consisted principally of government representatives.

NGOs and victims' organisations reacted by criticising Decree 1290 for lacking public consultations during its drafting stage and for the continued attempts to deny state responsibility.[51] Critique was also raised against excluding victims who had suffered violence directly at the hands of state agents, as this created discrepancy in the treatment of victims and confusion over available mechanisms.[52] Further criticism was raised over the deliberate exclusion of restitution of land, a key contentious issue due to the high incidence of displacement. The Decree also failed to indicate awareness of the specific needs of persons who may be more vulnerable, such as women and children who constitute a majority of victims, as well as those who live in rural areas or belong to a minority or indigenous group. Finally, concerns were raised that the programme attempted to dissuade victims from continuing to claim reparations through judicial procedures and that it deliberately confused reparations with humanitarian assistance. By early 2010, about 10,500 individual requests for

[50] Inter-American Commission on Human Rights, Report on Principal Guidelines for a Comprehensive Public Policy on Reparations, OEA/Ser.L/V/II.131, Washington, 19 February 2008.

[51] Colombian Commission of Jurists, Position Paper on Decree 1290 of 2008, Reparación o Revictimizacion, Bogotá, 19 June 2008.

[52] Victims of serious violations committed directly by state agents can seek compensation only through civil litigation, la jurisdicción contenciosa-administrativa, which is notoriously difficult to resort to in practice.

compensation had been paid and priority was given to three specific categories of victims: children who had been recruited or used in conflict; victims of landmines; and victims of sexual violence.[53] While the programme claimed to apply a comprehensive approach, the reparation measures provided were primarily financial compensation.

Decree 1290 inevitably draws parallels with Law 387 of 1997, which provided victims of forced displacement with the right to seek three months of humanitarian assistance from the state. Law 387 offered an important legal basis for the rights of the displaced population and, from an international comparative perspective, in many ways constitutes a best practice. However, the experience of implementing the law presented significant challenges, documented by UNHCR, as only 50 per cent of the displaced population registered between 2002 and 2004 received any assistance.[54]

There are few studies on the attitude of the general population regarding the issue of reparations, however, in early 2006 the ICTJ conducted a survey among 2,000 persons in Colombia (selected as being representative, although the study was limited to urban areas that were less likely to have been affected by the armed conflict than rural areas). The study revealed a certain scepticism regarding the application of penalties in the framework of Law 975 (68 per cent), however, 89 per cent of the participants in the survey wanted victims to receive reparations and among them, it is significant to note that 68 per cent wished to see state responsibility for paying reparations.[55]

10.9 The Law on Victims' Right to Comprehensive Reparation and Land Restitution: Law 1448

While the establishment of the administrative reparations programme by Decree 1290 indicated a positive step towards gradual recognition of state responsibility for reparations, civil society organisations continued to

[53] Written replies of Colombia to the Human Rights Committee, April 2010, UN Doc. CCPR/C/COL/Q/6/Add.1.

[54] UNHCR Colombia, 'Balance de la política publica de prevención, protección y atención al desplazamiento interno forzado en Colombia 2002–2004', Bogotá 2004, p. 30. For detailed critique of the lack of implementation of Law 387 see Constitutional Court sentence T-025 of 2004. Richani, *Systems of Violence*, p. 122, noted that the 'application and effectiveness of the law remains at best a shy attempt to redress the injustices committed'.

[55] ICTJ, 'Perceptions and Opinions of Colombians regarding truth, justice and reconciliation', Survey 2006.

advocate for a comprehensive law on victims' rights. While several such attempts failed to gain political support, the new President Juan Manuel Santos Calderón, following his designation in August 2010, declared that a comprehensive law on victims' rights was a political priority and personally presented a draft bill to Congress in September 2010. In June 2011, Law 1448 on Victims' Right to Comprehensive Reparation and Land Restitution was adopted by Parliament and signed by the President in the presence of the UN Secretary-General Ban Ki-Moon. The Law addressed several aspects that had been identified as flaws in previous legislation: it affirmed the responsibility of the state to provide administrative reparations irrespective of the identity of the perpetrators, including state agents; specific and differential attention should be dedicated to vulnerable victims; humanitarian assistance should be clearly separated from administrative reparation; and it clearly stipulated that victims who claim reparation under the programme may still resort to judicial remedies. The Law also placed specific emphasis on the right to land restitution for victims, a historically contentious issue in Colombia. OHCHR and several human rights organisations, including Human Rights Watch and Amnesty, welcomed the law, however, they noted the significant challenges in ensuring that the law becomes operative, such as guaranteeing the security of the claimants and coordination between government entities.

10.10 Conclusions

The transitional justice process in Colombia has so far produced little progress in the realm of accountability. However, the public debate surrounding the paramilitary demobilisation process set focus on international legal obligations in an unprecedented manner and resulted in recognition of the right of victims to receive reparation. Among the elements that will continue to influence developments in Colombia is the jurisdiction of the ICC. The Prosecutor of the ICC has visited the country several times and issued warnings that the implementation of the Justice and Peace Law 975 is under the scrutiny of the ICC. In 2006, the Prosecutor of the ICC publicly informed Colombia that it was under preliminary investigation.[56] The threat of the ICC invoking its jurisdiction will continue to be a concern for the government of Colombia, and

[56] International Crisis Group, 'Correcting Justice', p. 4. Additionally, in early 2005 the Prosecutor of the ICC sent a letter to the Colombian Senate signalling that he was following closely the debate over a legal framework for the demobilisations.

it is apparent that Law 975 was designed to seek to ward off admissibility of cases under Articles 17 and 20 of the Rome Statute.[57]

During 2008 a number of paramilitary leaders were extradited to the United States on charges of narcotics trafficking. Resorting to extradition was an escape route for the Colombian government and sent the unfortunate signal that drug trafficking is a more serious offence than war crimes against civilians. Furthermore, the authorisation by the executive of the extraditions in effect questioned the ability of the national judiciary and deprived victims of the possibility of demanding justice and reparations.

Regarding the element of truth, the Truth Commission created in Colombia, the CNRR, lacks independence, suffers from an unclear mandate and has been publicly discredited by victims' organisations and national civil society actors. Being burdened with unrealistic and incompatible tasks, the CNRR is unlikely to play a significant role in advancing its stated objectives of promoting reparations and reconciliation. Nor is it likely that the CNRR will be considered a useful model for the establishment of truth commissions in other countries. The future creation of a truth commission with an impartial mandate remains a possibility. In November 2009, both OHCHR and the Committee against Torture renewed calls for a truth commission in Colombia, as such a mechanism would favour the rights of victims.[58]

While the outcome of prosecutions under Law 975 remains pending, the transitional justice framework set up has been strongly influenced by debate over the participation and rights of victims. The issue of reparations has, through extensive public debates, become a core focus of the process. This is evident in the gradual push for recognition of the right to reparation through adjustments in the applicable legal framework. The consistent pressure by international and regional human rights mechanisms, as well as by national civil society organisations, has played a major role in highlighting concerns relating to reparations and will be crucial to sustain calls for implementation. The active

[57] K. Ambos and F. Huber, 'The Colombian Peace Process and the Principle of Complementarity of the International Criminal Court: Is there sufficient willingness and ability on the part of the Colombian authorities or should the Prosecutor open an investigation now?', Conference paper at ICC OTP–NGO roundtable, 19–20 October 2010, The Hague.

[58] Public statement made by the OHCHR Director in Colombia, 'Intervención en el XII Encuentro de la Jurisdicción Ordinaria de la Corte Suprema de Justicia', 6 November 2009, available at: www.hchr.org.co; Committee against Torture (CAT), Concluding Observations on Colombia 2009, UN Doc. CAT/C/COL/CO/4, para. 26.

engagement of the Colombian government with human rights mechanisms is positive as it provides important momentum to retain focus on the issue of reparations.

From an international legal perspective, the Colombian case sets an unprecedented example of a legal framework affirming acceptance of state responsibility for cases where violations have occurred due to collusion between state agents and armed groups, and omission by the state to prevent violations. The recognition of the Basic Principles on the Right to Reparation for Victims in domestic legislation is significant as it indicates support for this norm and acceptance of a comprehensive concept of reparations. However, the effectiveness of the legislation and its accompanying programme for reparations has yet to be assessed. Key challenges include the need to sustain political and financial will, to provide protection for claimants, and to ensure adequate coordination between the various government entities responsible for implementation and that victims are aware of the mechanisms they should resort to, given the complexity of the legal and institutional structures. In addition, to what extent psychosocial and rehabilitation measures will be available for victims remains unclear.

In conclusion, Colombia has made considerable progress through the adoption of a remarkable legal framework for victims' rights. However, the long-term outcome of the transitional justice process will depend on the continued advocacy by the international community for the state to comply, in law as well as in practice, with international human rights norms.

11 Conclusions Part II – reparations in practice: comparative analysis of practice, lessons learnt and future challenges

Part II of this book set out to study the degree of implementation of reparations in four different national contexts: Guatemala, Sierra Leone, East Timor and Colombia over the period of a decade from 1999 to 2009. The objective was to assess to what degree the right to reparation for victims of armed conflict exists in practice and to what extent state practice supports the argument that the right to reparation has attained customary status in international law.

The case of the UNCC was briefly mentioned as it highlights the Security Council's position on state responsibility to provide victims with reparations. While not explicitly based on human rights and humanitarian law, the UNCC demonstrated the potential of the UN to implement, in a relatively expedient manner and on a large scale, the right of victims to reparations. Without negating the point that the principal obligation to provide reparations is that of the state, the UNCC illustrates the possibility that the UN could play a more proactive role in promoting the right in practice. The Security Council has, however, not approached the issue in a consistent manner, as evidenced in the situation of Darfur.

As stated in the introduction to Part II, the case studies were selected because they illustrate a variety of factors that have affected the degree of developments regarding reparations during one decade in different geographic regions that have experienced armed conflict. Given the key role of the UN in advocating for greater state responsibility vis-à-vis victims, a main factor in the selection of the case studies has been the ability of the UN to promote accountability and transitional justice initiatives. Thus, the second part of the study identifies some of the principal factors that have enabled progress towards the recognition of the right to reparation in transitional justice, notably through the establishment of truth commissions, and which aspects have been decisive in promoting state responsibility and responsiveness to victims' claims for reparations. The case studies consider the degree to which reparations have been addressed in national legislation and policies as well as in practice. Conditions and factors that have contributed to attaining progress, especially as they coincide in the case studies, are highlighted with a view to further promoting the right in practice. Furthermore, some of the principal obstacles to the practical realisation of the right are identified, in particular, as they coincide in the case studies. Based on the findings of the study, it is submitted that truth commissions have made important contributions to the right of victims to receive reparation, especially when compared with justice initiatives aimed primarily at criminal accountability such as ad hoc tribunals.

All four case studies illustrate a varying degree of state practice in favour of reparations. Clear and explicit references to reparations for victims can be found in UN-mediated peace agreements for Guatemala and Sierra Leone. In both countries, the establishment of UN-supported truth commissions were directly linked to peace agreements. In the case of Sierra Leone, the peace agreement specifically referred to the setting up of a Special Fund for War Victims. In East Timor, the Truth Commission was established during the UN administration. The mandates of the truth commissions studied had in common that they clearly aimed at providing a comprehensive analysis of violations during the armed conflict, their impact on victims and also authorised the commissions to emit recommendations regarding reparations for victims. While the legal standing of international peace agreements may remain subject to debate, it is clear that human rights provisions therein, including those on reparation for victims, provide examples of evolving state practice. All truth commission mandates in this study were clearly established on the basis of the obligations of international human rights and humanitarian law and their reports cited the Basic Principles on the Right to Reparation for Victims, although these at the time were in draft form.[1]

The truth commission reports in the countries studied (except in Colombia where the mandate differs) identified categories of victims who were particularly affected by violations and who have continued to suffer stigma, social exclusion and re-victimisation as a consequence

[1] Bell, *Peace Agreements and Human Rights*, p. 290: 'The UN Basic Principles and Guidelines on the right to a remedy and reparation evidences a beginning to how the broader demands of a peace process can be accommodated in international legal frameworks.'

of the lack of reparations and assistance in order to overcome the impact of the armed conflict. All the reports specifically identified women, children and victims of torture and sexual violence among the victims most affected. For a majority of these victims, the absence of reparations has impeded their ability to restart their lives and move beyond the trauma they have endured. For these groups of victims, the reports affirmed that they should be priority beneficiaries of reparation programmes aimed primarily at rehabilitation, restoring their dignity, reduction of their dependency and at bringing them on an equal footing with other members of society. The urgency, yet scarcity, of rehabilitation and psychosocial assistance measures for victims has been identified as a general challenge. All reports underlined the importance of fair treatment of victims irrespective of whether the perpetrators were known or whether the violations occurred under state control. In all instances, the reports documented omissions of the state in preventing violations, which in turn incurred a degree of obligation as states should provide reparation to victims of acts or omissions that may be attributed to the state. Victims are entitled to non-discriminatory treatment and the truth commission reports recommended, in line with the Basic Principles on the Right to Reparation for Victims, that states should endeavour to establish national programmes for reparation and other assistance for victims in the event that the party liable for the harm is unable or unwilling to meet his or her obligation. Significantly, after years of delay, such reparations programmes have been established in Guatemala, Colombia and Sierra Leone, and debate on legislation for reparations is taking place in East Timor.

The case studies illustrate some of the tensions between criminal accountability, truth and reparations. While justice requires all these elements to be fulfilled, the links between these components of justice are rarely clear. As has been documented in Part I, most transitional justice initiatives aimed at establishing criminal accountability of perpetrators have disregarded victims. This lacuna in international criminal law has been recognised and progress has been made, notably through the victims and reparations provisions in the Statute of the International Criminal Court. However, in the case studies herein, it remains true that the rights of victims largely remained overlooked in the Special Court in Sierra Leone and the Special Panels for Serious Crimes in East Timor. The truth commissions in these countries played an imperative role in setting focus on the rights of victims and in promoting their right to reparation. The mandate of the Truth

Commission in Guatemala limited its ability to point to criminal accountability; however, it made the strong affirmation that a state policy of genocide has existed. Compared with the other case studies described, the experience to date in Guatemala is characterised by an absence of criminal accountability for responsibility of violations during the armed conflict. The attention to the issue of reparations in Guatemala has dual implications: it has led to greater acknowledgement of state responsibility for violations and thereby retained awareness that criminal accountability remains outstanding. On the other hand, the Guatemalan government has resorted to the discourse of reparations in order to dissuade victims' organisations from further legal action. In Colombia, the government has applied a similar emphasis on reparations in an attempt to dissuade calls for criminal accountability.

In East Timor, the Truth Commission issued recommendations that advocated for criminal accountability for those responsible, not only for the post-referendum violence, but generally for the violations that occurred during Indonesian rule. The closely linked calls for criminal accountability and reparations for victims in East Timor, also echoed in several UN reports and inquiries, prompted the government to initially refute and disregard reparations and resulted in stigmatisation of human rights defenders seeking to pursue such claims.

In Guatemala, the recommendations of the Truth Commission emitted in 1999 regarding reparations remained dormant for years, however, they have gradually re-emerged following government changes. International human rights monitoring mechanisms and the presence of the UN verification mission, MINUGUA, and the subsequent OHCHR office sustained and echoed victims' claims for reparations. The Inter-American human rights system has played a particularly important standard-setting role in the area of reparations for gross human rights violations by developing comprehensive reparation awards for entire communities. The jurisprudence of the Inter-American Court on Human Rights entrenched the notion of state responsibility and provided the key impetus for the establishment of the National Reparations Programme in Guatemala. While the design of the Guatemalan reparations programme applied an ample concept of victims and reparations, the progress made so far has been limited. This is partly explained by divisions within victims' groups and civil society rather than the lack of state funding. The time lapse since the armed conflict has perpetuated the social exclusion of the most vulnerable victims, who remain mired in the divisions created among them during the conflict.

In Sierra Leone, the establishment of the Truth Commission (2000) predated the creation of the Special Court (2002), which was a contributing factor as to why the Statute of the Court largely omitted references to reparations, despite the precedents already established by the reparations provisions in the Rome Statute of the International Criminal Court. The Special Court declined to act on its ability to order restitution; rather, it was presumed that the Truth Commission would address aspects of reparations. The discrepancies in relation to the resources available to the Truth Commission compared with the significant financial support for the Special Court resulted in an overall process that prioritised retributive justice over the rights of victims.

In the case of East Timor, the issue of reparations figured already in the Report of the International Commission of Inquiry on East Timor to the Secretary-General (2000). However, the subsequent establishment of the Serious Crimes Panels (2000) demonstrated little consideration of victims in the criminal proceedings. On the other hand, the Truth Commission in East Timor (2001) was carefully designed to address the concerns of victims and undertook innovative reparations measures as part of its mandate. The Truth Commission facilitated small-scale restitution through community reconciliation processes, and established and implemented an urgent reparations scheme, albeit on a small scale, primarily in order to provide medical and psychosocial care.

The three Truth Commission reports of Guatemala, Sierra Leone and East Timor have in common that they were reluctantly received by the respective national governments, who in turn delayed the designation of authorities responsible for follow-up and implementation of recommendations. Notably, in the cases of Guatemala and Sierra Leone, the post-conflict political leadership was integrated by persons who retained their position since before (and during) the armed conflict. The case of East Timor is unique because of the creation of a government consisting of leaders who had spearheaded the independence movement. Nevertheless, the government in East Timor was among those most opposed to the recommendations of the CAVR and explicitly appointed an additional parallel inquiry, which to some degree undermined its findings. Despite the successor obligation of Indonesia with regard to reparations for victims in East Timor, progress has so far been blocked by geopolitical considerations.

Colombia represents an anomaly among the case studies, as a comprehensive peace agreement is still lacking and the so-called Truth Commission established in 2005 is a government entity. However, it provides an extraordinary example of state practice in light of the extensive references to reparations for victims in national legislation. Although initially legislation sought to refute the obligation to provide reparation to victims, revised legislation set important precedents by acknowledging state responsibility and seeking consistency with the Basic Principles on the Right to Reparation for Victims, whereby, as noted above, the state should provide reparation to victims for acts or omissions that may be attributed to the state. Similarly to the case of Guatemala, the existence of considerable case law from the Inter-American Court of Human Rights affirming the responsibility of the state for large-scale human rights violations, including massacres, either by direct participation of state agents or by omission to prevent, prompted the adoption of domestic legislation on reparations for victims.

While the existence of progressive legislation on reparations in Guatemala and Colombia sets valuable examples internationally, it should be recognised that initial legislation was adopted by the Executive by decree. Parliamentary debates on the adoption of legislation on victims' rights remain ongoing in Guatemala as well as in East Timor. It is essential that future legislation be entrenched by parliamentary approval in order to ensure that its implementation is sustained. Despite certain loopholes in legislation and the inadequacies in national reparation programmes, their existence is still significant. The fact that in three of the four case studies national reparation programmes for victims have been established, albeit after certain delays, demonstrates important examples of state practice in favour of reparations for victims of human rights and humanitarian law violation in armed conflict.

The degree of strength among civil society in the different case studies varies significantly. Without doubt, civil society organisations in Colombia, despite the fact that they continue to be virulently persecuted, stand out as the strongest example. While they may have been unable to exert faithful compliance with their demands, the state nevertheless engages with them as well as with international human rights mechanisms and the debate on reparations, while legalistic, is more sophisticated than in many other contexts. In Guatemala, as noted above, civil society organisations have made considerable progress in advancing their compensation claims; however, their internal divisions remain an obstacle to achieving concrete advances. In Sierra Leone and East Timor, civil society organisations depended and largely continue to reply on support from international NGOs, UN agencies and the donor community. In the Latin

American context, the regional human rights system has catalysed the national human rights organisations. In Africa, the presence of the regional human rights system has been significantly weaker, while in Asia the absence of an effective regional system has meant that national human rights organisations have no regional mechanisms to which to resort. The existence of independent national human rights institutions (NHRI) is another factor that has played an important role in advancing reparations claims from victims. In Guatemala, Sierra Leone and East Timor, the NHRIs played a role in following up on the implementation of the recommendations of the Truth Commission. In the case of Colombia, the NHRI has played a somewhat ambivalent role.

An aspect of particular contention is that of funding for reparations. Many states that have experienced armed conflict wish to focus on future development rather than pay attention to aspects of the past, in particular, when these have financial implications. However, as previously mentioned, unless victims of serious human rights violations receive reparations, they are likely to continue to suffer social exclusion and stigma. States have a general obligation to implement economic, social and cultural rights to the maximum extent of their available resources. However, the right to reparation goes beyond the need to ensure that victims of serious human rights violations are given an opportunity to participate in society on an equal footing with others. Reparations for victims should not be viewed as a gesture of solidarity in the interest of development, but rather as a fundamental state responsibility based on human rights and, in particular, on the principles of non-discrimination and equality. The right to reparation for serious violations is an indispensable corollary to an effective remedy for the injuries suffered. Unless victims receive reparations, this obligation will not be fulfilled and perpetrators will retain a more powerful standing over victims in society.

In addition, the case studies illustrate the challenges regarding funding for demobilisation (DDR) of former combatants versus funding for victims. To date, the disproportionate investment by the international community in DDR programmes stands in stark contrast to the lack of support for victims.[2] Furthermore, failure to sustain support for truth commission recommendations relating to reparations undermines trust among victims and may result in a crisis of legitimacy of

[2] Sooka, 'Dealing with the Past and Transitional Justice', pp. 324–5; De Geiff, 'Contributing to Peace and Justice'; Roht-Arriaza, 'Reparations in the Aftermath of Repression', p. 126.

transitional justice processes. On a more hopeful note, the case studies illustrate growing recognition by the international community of the need to re-prioritise the rights of victims. Among the positive examples are support from the Peace-building Fund for Sierra Leone and World Bank financing of the urgent reparations scheme in East Timor. While the obligation to provide reparations is that of the state, in certain instances it is clear that the international community bears positive obligations to assist poorer states in fulfilling their responsibilities.[3]

In conclusion, significant challenges remain in relation to the implementation of the right to reparation for victims. In general terms, the contribution of truth commissions for the advancement of reparations claims is yet to be fully appreciated.[4] However, the case studies of this study indicate progressive state practice and the impact of the growing number of truth commissions across the world indicates that they have played, and will continue to play, a significant role in promoting the practical implementation of the right to reparation for victims of armed conflict.

[3] M. E. Salomon, *Global Responsibility for Human Rights, World Poverty and the Development of International Law* (Oxford University Press, 2007).

[4] Bassiouni, 'International Recognition of Victims' Rights', pp. 203–79.

12 Final remarks: the right to reparation and implementation of the legal norm: emerging convergence of law and practice?

The overall aim of this book was to analyse the international legal standing of the right to reparation for victims of serious human rights and humanitarian law violations, and to assess the degree of practical implementation of the right at the national level through case studies on post-conflict and transitional justice measures. The central objective was to chart and evaluate developments in law and practice in order to substantiate arguments in favour of an emerging customary right for individuals to receive reparations for serious violations of human rights and the corresponding responsibility of states.

To this end, Part I of the study explored the customary nature of human rights and humanitarian provisions, outlined the basic premise of state responsibility in relation to violations and identified the general international norms that establish the obligation to provide reparations. Analysis of the jurisprudence of the ICJ, the ILC Articles on State Responsibility (2001) and the convergence of norms in different branches of international law, notably human rights law, humanitarian law and international criminal law, as well as extensive human rights jurisprudence, international and regional, supports and consolidates the position that the right to reparation is gaining customary recognition.

The adoption by the UN General Assembly of the Basic Principles on the Right to Reparation for Victims in 2005 further strengthens this claim. The Principles reflect the normative connection between international humanitarian and human rights law, and stress the importance of, and obligation to, implement domestic reparations for victims of armed conflict. The Principles explicitly state in the preamble that they 'identify mechanisms, modalities, procedures and methods for the implementation of existing legal obligations under international human rights and international humanitarian law, which are complementary though different as to their norms'.

Following the legal analysis, Part II of the study explored state practice in relation to reparations through illustrating developments in four case studies: Guatemala, Sierra Leone, East Timor and Colombia during the period of a decade between 1999 and 2009. The case studies represented different geographic regions that have experienced armed conflict and where the UN has played a significant role in promoting transitional justice initiatives. Emphasis was placed on the extent to which it has been possible to provide reparations in practice through UN-supported transitional justice processes, notably truth commissions, and which factors have been decisive in promoting state responsibility and responsiveness to victims' claims for reparations. A detailed examination was undertaken of relevant reparations provisions in peace agreements, mandates and reports of truth commissions, national legislation and government policies on reparations for victims of armed conflict.

While the legal standing of international peace agreements may remain subject to debate, it is clear that human rights provisions therein, including those on reparations for victims, provide examples of evolving state practice. All the Truth Commission mandates in the case studies were clearly established on the basis of international human rights and humanitarian law and their reports cited the Basic Principles on the Right to Reparation for Victims, although these were in draft form at the time.

The outcome of the study indicates that significant progress has been made in relation to the right to reparation for victims who have endured violations in armed conflict. The normative basis of the right has developed through significant convergence in different branches of law, yet the principal lacuna remains in transferring the right into reality for victims. Nevertheless, the selected case studies are indicative of important progress in practice and illustrate a degree of *opinio juris* in favour of the right as progressive legislation and reparation policies have been adopted at the national level.

The study envisaged using the right to reparation for victims, established as an international legal norm, as a yardstick to measure implementation of the right in practice at the national level. The study, however, reveals a dynamic and reciprocal process with considerable synergies between a number of factors, including international legal developments, human rights mechanisms at the international and regional level, transitional justice mechanisms and the creation of constituencies in favour of victims' rights and their interaction with the international community, in particular, international organisations such as the UN, but also wider actors, such as donors and international financial institutions.

The creation of a global constituency for victims' rights has been a determining factor that has brought the right to reparation to the forefront of the debate on international justice. The constituency that specifically advocates in favour of reparations is intrinsically linked to the human rights movement and the growth of a global civil society with ready access to and exchange of advocacy information. Engagement was furthermore triggered as a reaction against how victims were treated in international criminal justice mechanisms. The ad hoc Tribunals underscored the disproportional efforts dedicated to pursuing retributive justice, while victims were largely neglected. The adoption of the Rome Statute of the International Criminal Court galvanised victims' organisations, and the successful incorporation of provisions on victims' rights inspired further attention to the practical implementation of the right to reparation and to the potential of the ICC Trust Fund for Victims. The accountability of perpetrators and access to a judicial remedy for victims remain core objectives of justice. However, there is growing recognition that the absence of reparations for victims raises fundamental questions about the credibility of international law and international organisations and, if not addressed, could potentially undermine the concept of international justice.

The expansion of transitional justice mechanisms brought a more victim-oriented approach and has gradually emphasised the effect of violations upon victims and the perpetuation of such consequences, unless concerted efforts are made to provide reparations. A particularly strong impetus has come from women's organisations and has emerged alongside greater awareness of sexual violence in armed conflict and of the stigmatisation of the civilians most vulnerable in conflict: women and children. Significant contributions from human rights organisations and transitional justice initiatives in Latin America were brought into the human rights systems of the UN and supported the development of increased international awareness of victims' rights.

The UN in turn has gradually brought attention to victims' rights in post-conflict and transitional justice initiatives at the global level and has played a vital role in supporting national efforts for victims' rights, including in countries with a weak civil society, such as Sierra Leone and

East Timor. Victim-oriented transitional justice measures, many supported by the United Nations, have spread across continents during the past decade and have been established in a significant number of countries. Some of these measures have been volatile to political circumstances and designed without sufficient attention to victims' perspectives. However, there is growing recognition of the value of transitional justice measures such as truth commissions, precisely because they enable large-scale consultations with the affected victims and allow their voices to be heard and their needs expressed. The recent increase in the establishment of international commissions of inquiry has provided additional valuable fora for advocating for reparations for victims. As stated in the Guidance Note of the Secretary-General on the United Nations Approach to Transitional Justice, adopted on 10 March 2010: 'successful transitional justice programmes recognise the centrality of victims and their special status in the design and implementation of such processes. The UN must respect and advocate for the interest and inclusion of victims where transitional processes are under consideration.'

Truth commissions have played a particularly valuable role in identifying vulnerable groups of victims and their needs in relation to reparations. The reports of truth commissions provide compelling evidence of the effects that armed conflicts have on vulnerable civilians and they underscore the importance of a comprehensive reparations concept, which should include rehabilitation and measures that seek to restore the dignity of victims. However, as illustrated in this study, an element of the Basic Principles on the Right to Reparation for Victims that remains particularly neglected, both in human rights jurisprudence and transitional justice measures, is the provision of medical and psychological rehabilitation for victims.

The influence that human rights jurisprudence from the Inter-American region has had at the international level cannot be underestimated. While it remains true that human rights mechanisms were *per se* not designed to deal with large-scale violations in the context of armed conflict, a rapidly expanding number of such cases have challenged the traditional litigation of human rights cases, which primarily related to individual violations. The regional systems are increasingly seeking to develop modalities in order to deal with complaints of violations affecting large numbers of victims in conflict situations. Efforts have been made to analyse such violations with reference to humanitarian law, which in turn is yet another indication of the convergence of victims' rights in international law. Furthermore, attempts have been made to respond to such violations by awarding collective reparations. The Inter-American Court of Human Rights has been particularly prominent in this regard and issued comprehensive reparations for the benefit of affected communities, including measures that have taken into account cultural aspects, such as the preferences of victims of indigenous origin. The European Court of Human Rights is gradually also developing judgments that seek to address systematic violations. The judgments of regional courts are binding and the compliance rate is relatively high. While the jurisprudence of human rights courts can benefit only a limited number of victims, it nevertheless sets a benchmark for reparations and has played an important role in influencing the national discourse on reparations. Impetus from the regional human rights system in Latin America has contributed to consolidating a normative framework for reparations. This is particularly evident in Guatemala and Colombia, where national legislation and policies for reparations have been adopted.

Awareness has increasingly focused on the need to ensure that reparations reach as many victims as possible. Over the past few years, several trust funds have been established by human rights mechanisms and notably also by the ICC. However, expectations are likely to exceed the potential of such trust funds, which, while they offer a clear indication of the commitment of the international community, will be able to reach only a limited number of beneficiaries. The challenge of reaching the victims also points to the need to ensure that reparation measures are not unduly tied to judicial processes, as this severely restricts the number of potential beneficiaries. Practical measures, such as the establishment of trust funds and national reparations programmes that operate independently of judicial procedures, are essential. Only a small percentage of victims of serious violations will ever be likely or able to undertake litigation or seek assistance from international or regional trust funds. Therefore, in the interest of non-discrimination and equity for victims, the primary measures should be taken through reparation programmes at the national level. Furthermore, this is a particularly important signal that state responsibility, even if for a successor government, is being assumed. While national administrative reparation programmes can provide a significant change in victims' lives and indicate a certain willingness of the state to assume responsibility for the violations committed, such programmes should never be used to impede victims from resorting to judicial proceedings.

Individual perpetrators may be held responsible for reparations in international criminal procedures, yet experiences to date demonstrate this to be an unlikely avenue for the majority of victims. Many victims may never have known the perpetrator's identity or be able to link responsibility for the violations they have suffered to those indicted for carrying the greatest responsibility for war crimes. It is submitted that responsibility for reparations should maintain an element of state responsibility, as those considered to have carried the greatest responsibility for serious violations may, and indeed are likely to, have exercised functions of state authority. There are inherent dangers in shifting responsibility from states towards individuals, as this may ultimately leave victims without redress. While the shift towards recognising victims and their right to reparation in international criminal law is welcome and positive, this should operate alongside measures to establish state responsibility vis-à-vis victims. The concurrent application of individual and state responsibility and its practical implications for reparations is an area of international law that requires significant further consideration.

This book concludes that the state should bear primary responsibility to provide reparations for victims of armed conflict. This argument can be supported both on legal grounds as well as on general moral obligations to promote and ensure equity, fairness and non-discrimination. Based on the analysis of the current state of international law, it is clear that the state has positive duties to prevent violations and demonstrate due diligence. It has become increasingly frequent that states have been found to carry a degree of responsibility for omission to protect civilians when the perpetrators have been non-state actors. To this effect, there is a convergent approach in international law on state responsibility. This is illustrated in Article 2 of the ILC Articles on State Responsibility which define that 'there is an international wrongful act of a State when conduct consisting of an action or omission … constitutes a breach of an international obligation when arising from a breach of an international obligation of the State'. The Official Commentary of the ICRC on Article 91 of the Additional Protocol I to the Geneva Conventions also affirms that state responsibility may be incurred by omission when due diligence to prevent violations from taking place has not been demonstrated. The Human Rights Committee, in its General Comment No. 31, concurs:

There may be circumstances in which a failure to ensure Covenant rights as required by Article 2 would give rise to violations by States Parties of those rights, as a result of States Parties' permitting or failing to take appropriate measures or to exercise due diligence to prevent, punish, investigate or redress the harm caused by such acts by private persons or entities.

Jurisprudence from regional human rights courts has further consolidated positive obligations of the state to prevent violations and demonstrate due diligence, including in the context of armed conflict; examples of such cases are *Mahmut Kaya* v. *Turkey* and *Mapiripán Massacre* v. *Colombia*. The consistent and convergent affirmation of positive obligations of the state translates into an obligation to assume responsibility for such violations, including reparations.

As for moral grounds, the difficulties victims face in seeking reparations have been extensively documented in relation to international criminal law and the transitional justice initiatives in the selected case studies. It is immoral, unfair and discriminatory that disproportionate amounts of resources are spent on offenders and the demobilisation of former combatants, while their victims are left empty-handed. As noted in the Report of the Secretary-General on the Rule of Law and Transitional Justice in Conflict and Post-Conflict Societies: 'States have an obligation to act not only against perpetrators, but also on behalf of victims, including through the provision of reparations.'[1]

The international community plays a key role in advocating for a balanced approach in post-conflict measures and should assume positive obligations in assisting developing states to fulfil their obligations and support the effective implementation of reparation measures. While the state where violations occurred carries the principal responsibility, it is foreseeable that the international community will continue to be called upon to support post-conflict measures and reparation programmes where state institutions are weak and resources are scarce. As this study indicates, there is growing recognition of this obligation through numerous states' support for a variety of trust funds and for providing donor contributions to national reparation programmes. The sustainability and commitment of the international community to support such efforts and to ensure that due consideration is given to victims' rights in this context will remain a vital challenge.

[1] Report of the Secretary-General on the Rule of Law and Transitional Justice in Conflict and Post Conflict Societies, S/2004/616, 23 August 2004, para. 54.

It is pertinent to recall the preamble of the Basic Principle on the Right to Reparation for Victims, which reminds us of the path forward:

> In honouring the victim's right to benefit from remedies and reparation, the international community keeps faith with the plight of victims, survivors and future human generations, and reaffirms the international principles of accountability, justice and the rule of law.[2]

The right to reparation is gaining customary recognition in international law and significant progress has been made, however, the effective practical implementation of the right at the global level remains the principal challenge. Progress will depend on vigilant scrutiny of the obligations of states and the degree of solidarity of the international community in order to prove that victims of the most serious violations, irrespective of where they are in the world, are no longer an afterthought and that their rights are ensured not only in law, but also in practice.

[2] UN Basic Principles and Guidelines on the Right to a Remedy and Reparation for Victims of Gross Violations of International Human Rights Law and Serious Violations of International Humanitarian law, UN Doc. A/RES/60/147.

Bibliography

Books

Abtani, H. and Webb, P., *The Genocide Convention, the Travaux Preparatoires*, vol. 1 (Leiden: Martinus Nijhoff, 2008).

Alfredsson, G., Grimheden, J., Ramcharan, B. and de Zayas, A. (eds), *International Human Rights Monitoring Mechanisms* (The Hague: Kluwer Law International, 2001).

Alston, P. and Crawford, J. (eds), *The Future of UN Human Rights Treaty Monitoring* (Cambridge University Press, 2000).

An-Naim, A. and Amadiume, I. (eds), *The Politics of Memory: Truth, Healing and Social Justice* (London: Zed Books, 2000).

Arnold, R. and Quenivet, N. (eds), *International Humanitarian Law and Human Rights Law, Towards a New Merger in International Law* (Leiden: Martinus Nijhoff, 2008).

Ball, P., Kobrak, P. and Spirer, H., *State Violence in Guatemala, 1960–1996: A Qualitative Reflection* (Washington, DC: American Association for the Advancement of Science, 1999).

Barahona de Brito, A., Gonzalez Enriquez, C. and Aguilar, P. (eds), *The Politics of Memory, Transitional Justice in Democratizing Societies* (Oxford University Press, 2001).

Bassiouni, C., *International Protection of Victims, Nouvelle Etudes Penales*, Association International de Droit Penal (Toulouse: Eres Publications, 1988).

(ed.), *Post-Conflict Justice* (New York: Transnational Publishers, 2002).

Bayfesky, A., *The UN Human Rights Treaty System in the 21st Century* (The Hague: Kluwer Law, 2001).

Bell, C., *Peace Agreements and Human Rights* (Oxford University Press, 2000).

Berdal, M. and Economides, S. (eds), *United Nations Interventionism 1999–2004* (Cambridge University Press, 2007).

Bigger, N., *Burying the Past; Making Peace and Doing Justice after Civil Conflict* (Washington, DC: Georgetown University Press, 2003).

Boraine, A. and Levy, J. (eds), *The Healing of a Nation?* (Cape Town: Justice in Transition, 1995).

Bottigliero, I., *Redress for Victims of Crimes under International Law* (Leiden: Martinus Nijhoff, 2004).

Bracken, P. and Petty, C. (eds), *Rethinking the Trauma of War* (London: Save the Children, 1998).

Braithwaite, J., *Restorative Justice and Responsive Regulation* (Oxford University Press, 2002).

Brownlie, I., *Principles of Public International Law*, 6th edn (Oxford: Clarendon Press, 1990).

Cassese, A., *International Criminal Law* (Oxford University Press, 2003).

International Law (Oxford University Press, 2006).

Cassese, A., Gaeta, P. and Jones, J. (eds), *The Rome Statute of The International Criminal Court* (Oxford University Press, 2002).

Clapham, A., *Human Rights Obligations of Non-State Actors* (Oxford University Press, 2006).

Cohen, D., 'Indifference and Accountability: The United Nations and the Politics of International Justice in East Timor', *East West Center Special Report*, No. 9, June 2006.

Cohen, S., *States of Denial, Knowing about Atrocities and Suffering* (Cambridge: Polity Press, 2001).

Crawford, J., *The International Law Commission's Articles on State Responsibility; Introduction, Text and Commentaries* (Cambridge University Press, 2002).

Cryer, R. (ed.), *An Introduction to International Criminal Law and Procedure* (Cambridge University Press, 2007).

De Feyter, K., Parmentier, S., Bossuyt, M. and Lemmens, P. (eds), *Out of the Ashes, Reparation for Victims of Gross and Systematic Human Rights Violations* (Antwerp: Intersentia, 2005).

De Greiff, P. (ed.), *The Handbook of Reparations* (Oxford University Press, 2006).

Dixon, R. and Khan, K., *Archbold, International Criminal Courts, Practice, Procedure and Evidence* (London: Sweet & Maxwell, 2005).

Durham, H. and Gurd, T. (eds), *Listening to the Silences, Women and War* (Leiden: Martinus Nijhoff, 2005).

Dutertre, G., *Key Case Law Extracts European Court of Human Rights* (Strasbourg: Council of Europe Publishing, 2003).

Elias, R., *The Politics of Victimization, Victims, Victimology and Human Rights* (Oxford University Press, 1986).

Evans, M. and Murray, R., *The African Charter on Human and Peoples' Rights, the System in Practice 1986–2000* (Cambridge University Press, 2002).

Fattah, E. (ed.), *Towards a Critical Victimology* (London: St. Martin's Press, 1992).

Ferstman, C., Goetz, M. and Stephens, A. (eds), *Reparations for Victims of Genocide, War Crimes and Crimes against Humanity, Systems in Place and Systems in the Making* (Leiden: Martinus Nijhoff, 2009).

Forsythe, D., *Human Rights in International Relations* (Cambridge University Press, 2000).

Friedrich Ebert Stiftung, 'Conflicto y Seguridad, Democracia en Colombia, Temas Críticos y Propuestas', Conference Report, Bogotá, 2004.

Frigessi di Rattalma, M. and Treves, T. (eds), *The United Nations Compensation Commission, A Handbook* (The Hague: Kluwer Law International, 1999).

Gaeta, P. (ed.), *The Genocide Convention, A Commentary* (Oxford University Press, 2009).
Gardam, J. and Jarvis, M., *Women, Armed Conflict and International Law* (The Hague: Kluwer Law International, 2001).
Gomez Isa, F. (ed.), *Colombia en su laberinto, una mirada al conflicto* (Madrid: Catarata, 2008).
Gomien, D., *Short Guide to the European Convention on Human Rights*, 2nd edn (Strasbourg: Council of Europe Publishing, 1998).
Harris, D., O'Boyle, M. and Warbrick, C., *Law of the European Convention on Human Rights* (London: Butterworths, 1995).
Harris, D. and Livingstone, S. (eds), *The Inter-American System of Human Rights* (Oxford: Clarendon Press, 1998).
Harris, J. W., *Legal Philosophies* (London: Butterworths, 1980).
Hayner, P., *Unspeakable Truths: Confronting State Terror and Atrocity, How Truth Commissions around the World are Challenging the Past and Shaping the Future* (New York: Routledge, 2001).
Henckaerts, J-M. and Doswald-Beck, L., *Customary International Humanitarian Law*, 3 vols (Cambridge University Press, 2005).
Henkin, A. (ed.), *The Legacy of Abuse – Confronting the Past, Facing the Future* (Washington, DC: The Aspen Institute, 2002).
Heyns, C. (ed.), *Compendium of Key Human Rights Documents of the African Union* (Pretoria University Law Press, 2005).
Higgins, R., *Problems and Process, International Law and How We Use It* (Oxford: Clarendon Press, 1994).
Hoyle, C. and Young, R., *New Visions of Crime Victims* (Oxford: Hart Publishing, 2002).
Ignatieff, M., *The Warrior's Honor* (New York: Vintage, 1999).
Johnson, J., *Morality and Contemporary Warfare* (New Haven, CT: Yale University Press, 1999).
Joseph, S., Schultz, J. and Castan, M., *The International Covenant on Civil and Political Rights: Cases, Material and Commentary*, 2nd edn (Oxford University Press, 2004).
Kalshoven, F. (ed.), *The Centennial of the First International Peace Conference* (The Hague: Kluwer Law, 2000).
Kalshoven, F. and Zegveld, L., *Constraints on the Waging of War, An Introduction to IHL* (Geneva: ICRC, 2001).
Kozma, J., Nowak, M. and Scheinin, M., *A World Court of Human Rights – Consolidated Statute and Commentary* (Vienna: Neuer Wissenschaftlicher Verlag, 2010).
Kritz, N. (ed.), *Transitional Justice: How Emerging Democracies Reckon with Former Regimes*, 3 vols (Washington, DC: US Institute of Peace Press, 1995).
Lee, S. (ed.), *The International Criminal Court: the Making of the Rome Statute, Issues, Negotiations, Results* (The Hague: Kluwer Law International, 1999).
Lepard, B., *Customary International Law: A New Theory and Practical Applications* (Cambridge University Press, 2010).
Linton, S., *Putting Things into Perspective: the Realities of Accountability in East Timor, Indonesia and Cambodia*, Maryland Series in Contemporary Asian Studies, School of Law, University of Maryland, No. 3, 2005.

Livingston, G., *Inside Colombia, Drugs, Democracy and War* (London: Latin American Bureau, 2003).

MacDonald, A., 'Rights to Legal Remedies for Victims of Serious Violations of IHL', Doctoral thesis, Queen's University of Belfast, 2003.

Malanczuk, P., *Akehurst's Modern Introduction to International Law*, 7th edn (London: Routledge, 1997).

Mani, R., *Beyond Retribution, Seeking Justice in the Shadows of War* (Cambridge: Polity Press, 2002).

Marshall, T., *Restorative Justice: An Overview* (London: Home Office. Research Development and Statistics Directorate, 1999).

May, L., *Crimes against Humanity, A Normative Account* (Cambridge University Press, 2005).

May, R. (ed.), *Essays on ICTY Procedure and Evidence* (The Hague: Kluwer Law International, 2001).

McAdams, A. J. (ed.), *Transitional Justice and the Rule of Law in New Democracies* (University of Notre Dame Press, 1997).

McGoldrick, D., Rome, P. and Donnelly, E. (eds), *The Permanent International Criminal Court, Legal and Policy Issues* (Oxford: Hart Publishing, 2004).

Meron, T., *Human Rights in Internal Strife, Their International Protection* (Cambridge: Grotius Publications, 1987).

Minow, M., *Between Vengeance and Forgiveness: Facing History after Genocide and Mass Violence* (Boston, MA: Beacon Press, 1998).

Morris, V. and Scharf, M., *An Insider's Guide to the International Criminal Tribunal for the Former Yugoslavia* (New York: Transnational Publishers, 1995).

Mowbray, A., *Cases and Materials on the European Convention on Human Rights* (London: Butterworths, 2001).

Murray, R., *Human Rights in Africa: From OAU to AU* (Cambridge University Press, 2004).

Neuffer, E., *The Key to My Neighbour's House, Seeking Justice in Bosnia and Rwanda* (London: Picador, 2002).

Nowak, M., *Introduction to the International Human Rights Regime* (Leiden: Martinus Nijhoff, 2003).

UN Covenant on Civil and Political Rights, CCPR Commentary, 2nd edn (Kehl: N. P. Engel, 2005).

Nowak, M. and McArthur, E., *The United Nations Convention against Torture, A Commentary* (Oxford University Press, 2008).

O'Donnell, D., '*Derecho Internacional de los Derechos Humanos, Normativa, Jurisprudencia y Doctrina de los Sistemas Universal e Interamericano*', OHCHR, Bogotá, 2004.

O'Flaherty, M. (ed.), *The Human Rights Field Operation; Law Theory and Practice* (Farnham: Ashgate, 2007).

O'Kane, T., *In Focus Guatemala, A Guide to the People, Politics and Culture* (London: Latin America Bureau, 1999).

Osiel, M., *Mass Atrocity, Collective Memory and the Law* (London: Transaction Publishers, 1997).

Ovey, C. and White, R., *The European Convention on Human Rights*, 3rd edn (Oxford University Press, 2002).

Pasqualucci, J., *The Practice and Procedure of the Inter-American Court of Human Rights* (Cambridge University Press, 2003).
Procurador de los Derechos Humanos de Guatemala, 'Seguridad y Justicia en Tiempos de Paz, Cumplimiento e institucionalizaron de los compromisos contraídos por el Estado en los Acuerdos de Paz', Guatemala City, 2006.
Programa Nacional de Resarcimiento, 'La vida no tiene precio: Acciones y omisiones de resarcimiento en Guatemala', Guatemala City, 2007.
Provost, R., *International Human Rights and Humanitarian Law* (Cambridge University Press, 2002).
Ragazzi, M. (ed.), *International Responsibility Today, Essays in Memory of Oscar Schachter* (Leiden: Martinus Nijhoff, 2005).
Rawls, J., *The Law of Peoples* (Cambridge, MA: Harvard University Press, 1999).
Rehn, E. and Johnson Sirleaf, E., 'Women, War and Peace: The Independent Experts' Assessment on the Impact of Armed Conflict on Women and Women's Role in Peace-building', UNIFEM, 2002.
Richani, N., *Systems of Violence, The Political Economy of War and Peace in Colombia* (New York: SUNY, 2002).
Rigby, A., *Justice and Reconciliation after Violent Conflict* (Boulder, CO: Lynne Rienner, 2001).
Robertson, G., *Crimes against Humanity, The Struggle for Global Justice* (London: Penguin, 2002).
Roche, D., *Accountability in Restorative Justice* (Oxford University Press, 2003).
Rock, P. (ed.), *Victimology* (Aldershot: Dartmouth Publishing, 1994).
Roht-Arriaza, N., (ed.), *Impunity and Human Rights in International Law and Practice* (Oxford University Press, 1995).
Roht-Arriaza, N. and Mariezcurrena, J. (eds), *Transitional Justice in the Twenty-First Century, Beyond Truth versus Justice* (Cambridge University Press, 2006).
Romano, C., Nollkaemper, A. and Kleffner, J. (eds), *Internationalized Criminal Court, Sierra Leone, East Timor, Kosovo and Cambodia* (Oxford University Press, 2004).
Rombouts, H., *Victim Organisations and the Politics of Reparation: A Case Study on Rwanda* (Antwerp: Intersentia, 2004).
Rotberg, R. and Thompson, D. (eds), *Truth v. Justice, The Morality of Truth Commissions* (Princeton University Press, 2000).
Rubio-Marín, R., *What Happened to the Women? Gender and Reparations for Human Rights Violations* (New York: Social Science Research Council, 2006).
Salomon, M. E., *Global Responsibility for Human Rights, World Poverty and the Development of International Law* (Oxford University Press, 2007).
Sánchez, G., *Guerras, Memoria e Historia* (Bogatá: ICANH, 2003).
Sanford, V., *Buried Secrets, Truth and Human Rights in Guatemala* (Basingstoke: Palgrave Macmillan, 2003).
Schabas, W., *Genocide in International Law, the Crime of Crimes* (Cambridge University Press, 2000).
An Introduction to the International Criminal Court, 2nd edn (Cambridge University Press, 2004).

An Introduction to the International Criminal Court, 3rd edn (Cambridge University Press, 2007).
Schacter, O., *International Law in Theory and Practice* (Dordrecht: Martinus Nijhoff, 1991).
Shelton, D. (ed.), *International Crimes, Peace and Human Rights: The Role of the International Criminal Court* (New York: Transnational Publishers, 2000).
Remedies in International Human Rights Law, 2nd edn (Oxford University Press, 2005).
Shklar, J., *Legalism: Law, Morals and Political Trials* (Cambridge, MA: Harvard University Press, 1986).
Simon, J. M., *Guatemala; Eternal Spring, Eternal Tyranny* (New York: W. W. Norton, 1987).
Simpson, G., *Law, War and Crime* (Cambridge: Polity Press, 2007).
Stover, E., *The Witnesses, War Crimes and the Promise of Justice in The Hague* (Philadelphia, PA: University of Pennsylvania Press, 2005).
Stover, E. and Weinstein, H. (eds), *My Neighbour, My Enemy; Justice and Community in the Aftermath of Mass Atrocity* (Cambridge University Press, 2004).
Tebbit, M., *Philosophy of Law* (London: Routledge, 2000).
Teitel, R., *Transitional Justice* (Oxford University Press, 2000).
Thakur, R., *The United Nations, Peace and Security* (Cambridge University Press, 2006).
Tomasevski, K., *Responding to Human Rights Violations 1946–1999* (Leiden: Martinus Nijhoff, 2000).
Tomuschat, C., *Human Rights, Between Idealism and Realism*, 2nd edn (Oxford University Press, 2008).
Van Dijk, P. and Van Hoof, G., *Theory and Practice of the European Convention on Human Rights* (The Hague: Kluwer Law International, 1998).
Welna, C. and Gallon, G. (eds), *Peace, Democracy and Human Rights in Colombia* (University of Notre Dame Press, 2007).
Wilson, R. A., *The Politics of Truth and Reconciliation in South Africa, Legitimising the Post-Apartheid State* (Cambridge University Press, 2001).
Zappala, S., *Human Rights in International Criminal Proceedings* (Oxford University Press, 2003).
Zegveld, L., *Accountability of Armed Opposition Groups in International Law* (Cambridge University Press, 2002).
Zehr, H., *Changing Lenses: A New Focus for Crime and Justice* (Scottsdale, PA: Herald Press, 1990).
The Little Book of Restorative Justice (Intercourse, PA: Good Books, 2002).

Articles and chapters

Akhavan, P., 'Justice in The Hague, Peace in the Former Yugoslavia?', *Human Rights Quarterly*, 22 (1998), 737–816.
'Beyond Impunity: Can International Justice Prevent Future Atrocities?', *American Journal of International Law*, 95(7) (2002), 7–31.
Askin, K., 'Women's Issues in International Criminal Law: Recent Developments and the Potential Contribution of the ICC', in D. Shelton (ed.), *International*

Crimes, Peace and Human Rights: The Role of the International Criminal Court (New York: Transnational Publishers, 2000), pp. 47–63.

Ball, P. and Audrey, C., 'The Truth of Truth Commissions: Comparative Lessons from Haiti, South Africa and Guatemala', *Human Rights Quarterly*, 23 (2001), 1–43.

Barria, L. and Roper, S., 'Providing Justice and Reconciliation: The Criminal Tribunals for Sierra Leone and Cambodia', *Human Rights Review*, October–December (2005), 4–25.

Bassiouni, C., 'International Crimes: *Jus Cogens and Obligatorio Erga Omnes*', *Law and Contemporary Problems*, 59 (1996), 63–74.

'Accountability for Violations of International Humanitarian Law and other Serious Violations of Human Rights', in C. Bassiouni (ed.), *Post-Conflict Justice* (New York: Transnational Publishers, 2002), pp. 3–54.

'International Recognition of Victims' Rights', *Human Rights Law Review*, 6 (2006), 203–79.

Bederman, D., 'Historic Analogues of the UN Compensation Commission', in R. Lillich (ed.), *The United Nations Compensation Commission* (New York: Transnational Publishers, 1995), pp. 257–308.

Bejarano, C., 'Legalidad versus Conciencia, Implicaciones Jurídicas del Trabajo de PNR', in Programa Nacional de Resarcimiento (PNR), *La vida no tiene precio: Acciones y omisiones de resarcimiento en Guatemala*, Guatemala City, 2007, pp. 173–91.

Beresford, A. S., 'The Special Court for Sierra Leone: An Initial Comment', *Leiden Journal of International Law*, 14 (2001), 635–51.

Biegon, J. and Killander, M., 'Human Rights Developments in the African Union during 2009', *African Human Rights Law Journal*, 10 (2010), 212–28.

Bitti, G. and Gonzalez Rivas, G., 'The Reparations Provisions for Victims Under the Rome Statute of the International Criminal Court', in International Bureau of the Permanent Court of Arbitration (ed.), *Redressing Injustices Through Mass Claims* (Oxford University Press, 2006), pp. 299–322.

Buergenthal, T., 'The United Nations Truth Commission for El Salvador', *Vanderbilt Journal of Transnational Law*, 27 (1994), 497–544.

Burgess, P., 'Justice and Reconciliation in East Timor, the Relationship between the Commission for Reception, Truth and Reconciliation and the Courts', *Criminal Law Forum*, vol. 15 (Amsterdam: Kluwer Academic, 2004), pp. 135–58.

'A New Approach to Restorative Justice – East Timor's Reconciliation Process', in N. Roht-Arriaza and J. Mariezcurrena (eds), *Transitional Justice in the Twenty-First Century, Beyond Truth versus Justice* (Cambridge University Press, 2006), pp. 176–205.

Camilleri, M., 'The OAS in Colombia; MAPP/OEA, paramilitary demobilisation and civil society', *Revista CEJIL*, 2 (2006), 156–8.

Cançado Trindade, A., 'The Operation of the Inter-American Court of Human Rights', in D. Harris and S. Livingstone (eds), *The Inter-American System of Human Rights* (Oxford: Clarendon Press, 1998), pp. 133–49.

'Complementarity between State Responsibility and Individual Responsibility for Grave Violations of Human Rights, The Crime of State Revisited', in

M. Ragazzi (ed.), *International Responsibility Today, Essays in Memory of Oscar Schachter* (Leiden: Martinus Nijhoff, 2005), pp. 253–69.

Caron, D. and Morris, B., 'The UN Compensation Commission, Practical Justice, not Retribution', *European Journal of International Law*, 13(1) (2002), 183–99.

Carrillo, A., 'Justice in Context: The Relevance of Inter-American Human Rights Law and Practice to Repairing the Past', in P. De Greiff (ed.), *The Handbook of Reparations* (Oxford University Press, 2006), pp. 504–38.

Cerna, C., 'The Inter-American Commission on Human Rights', in D. Harris and S. Livingstone (eds), *The Inter-American System of Human Rights* (Oxford: Clarendon Press, 1998), pp. 65–114.

Charlesworth, H., 'Feminist Methods in International Law', *American Journal of International Law*, 93(2) (1999), 379–94.

Chesterman, S., 'East Timor', in M. Berdal and S. Economides (eds), *United Nations Interventionism 1999–2004* (Cambridge University Press, 2007), pp. 192–216.

Chetail, V., 'The Contribution of the International Court of Justice to International Humanitarian Law', *International Review of the Red Cross*, 85(850) (2003), 235–69.

Chinkin, C., 'The Protection of Victims and Witnesses', in K. McDonald and S. Goldman (eds), *Substantive and Procedural Aspects of International Criminal Law* (The Hague: Kluwer Law International, 2000), pp. 451–77.

Chinkin, C. and Charlesworth, H., 'Building Women into Peace, the International Legal Framework', *Third World Quarterly*, 27(5) (2006), 937–57.

Christenson, G., 'State Responsibility and UN Compensation Commission: Compensating Victims of Crimes of State', in R. Lillich (ed.), *The United Nations Compensation Commission* (New York: Transnational Publishers, 1995), pp. 311–64.

Clark, J. N., 'The Limits of Retributive Justice, Findings of an Empirical Study in Bosnia and Hercegovina', *Journal of International Criminal Justice*, 7 (2009), 463–87.

Cohen, D., 'Hybrid Justice in East Timor, Sierra Leone and Cambodia: Lessons Learnt and Prospects for the Future', *Stanford Journal of International Law*, 43(1) (2007), 1–38.

Cohen, S., 'State Crimes of Previous Regimes: Knowledge, Accountability and the Policing of the Past', *Law and Social Inquiry*, 20(1) (1995), 7–50.

Correa, C., Guillerot, J. and Magrell, L., 'Reparation and Victim Participation: A Look at the Truth Commission Experience', in C. Ferstman, M. Goetz and A. Stephens (eds), *Reparations for Victims of Genocide, War Crimes and Crimes against Humanity, Systems in Place and Systems in the Making* (Leiden: Martinus Nijhoff, 2009), pp. 385–414.

Couillard, V., 'The Nairobi Declaration: Redefining Reparations for Women Victims of Sexual Violence', *International Journal of Transitional Justice*, 1 (2007), 444–53.

Crawford, J. and Olleson, S., 'The Continuing Debate on a UN Convention on State Responsibility', *International and Comparative Law Quarterly*, 54 (2005), 959–71.

Cryer, R., 'Sudan, Resolution 1593 and International Criminal Justice', *Leiden Journal of International Law*, 19 (2006), 195–222.

De Bertodano, S., 'East Timor: Trials and Tribulations', in C. Romano, A. Nollkaemper and J. Kleffner (eds), *Internationalized Criminal Court, Sierra Leone, East Timor, Kosovo and Cambodia* (Oxford University Press, 2004), pp. 80–97.

De Brouwer, A., 'Reparation to Victims of Sexual Violence: Possibilities at the International Criminal Court and the Trust Fund for Victims and Their Families', *Leiden Journal of International Law*, 20 (2007), 207–37.

De Wet, E., 'The Protection Mechanism under the African Charter and the Protocol on the African Court of Human and Peoples' Rights', in G. Alfredsson, J. Grimheden, B. Ramcharan and A. de Zayas (eds), *International Human Rights Monitoring Mechanisms* (The Hague: Kluwer Law International, 2001), pp. 713–30.

De Zayas, A., 'The Examination of Individual Complaints by the United Nations Human Rights Committee under the Optional Protocol of the CCPR', in G. Alfredsson, J. Grimheden, B. Ramcharan and A. de Zayas (eds), *International Human Rights Monitoring Mechanisms* (The Hague: Kluwer Law International, 2001), pp. 67–121.

Dill, K., 'Reparation and the Elusive Meaning of Justice in Guatemala', in B. Johnston and S. Slyomovics (eds), *Waging War, Making Peace, Reparations and Human Rights* (Walnut Creek, CA: Left Coast Press, 2009), pp. 183–204.

Dixon, R., 'Rape as a Crime in International Humanitarian Law. Where to From Here?', *European Journal of International Law*, 13(3) (2002), 697–719.

Donnat-Cattin, D., 'Article 75', in O. Triffterer (ed.), *Commentary on the Rome Statute of the International Criminal Court – Observers' Notes, Article by Article* (Baden Baden: Nomos Verlag, 1999), pp. 965–78.

Droege, C., 'Elective Affinities? Human Rights and Humanitarian Law', *International Review of the Red Cross*, 90(871) (2008), 501–48.

Drumbl, M., 'Restorative Justice and Collective Responsibility: Lessons For and From the Rwandan Genocide', *Contemporary Justice Review*, 5(1) (2002), 5–22.

Dugard, J., 'Possible Conflicts with Truth Commissions', in A. Cassese, P. Gaete and J. Jones (eds), *The Rome Statute of The International Criminal Court, A Commentary* (Oxford University Press, 2002), pp. 693–704.

Dupuy, P-M., 'A General Stocktaking of the Connections between the Multilateral Dimension of Obligations and Codification of the Law of Responsibility', *European Journal of International Law*, 13(5) (2002), 1053–81.

Echeverria, G., 'Redressing Torture, A Genealogy of Remedies and Enforcement', *Torture (IRCT Journal)*, 16(3) (2006), 152–81.

Ferstman, C. and Goetz, M., 'Reparations before the International Criminal Court: The Early Jurisprudence on Victim Participation and its Impact on Future Reparations Proceedings', in C. Ferstman, M. Goetz and A. Stephens (eds), *Reparations for Victims of Genocide, War Crimes and Crimes against Humanity, Systems in Place and Systems in the Making* (Leiden: Martinus Nijhoff, 2009), pp. 313–50.

Fletcher, L. and Weinstein, H., 'Violence and Social Repair: Rethinking the Contribution of Justice to Reconciliation', *Human Rights Quarterly*, 24 (2002), 573–639.

Friman, H., 'The International Criminal Court and the Participation of Victims: A Third Party to the Proceedings?', *Leiden Journal of International Law*, 22 (2009), 485–500.

Gaja, G., 'Obligations *Erga Omnes*, International Crimes and *Jus Cogens*, A Tentative Analysis of Three Related Concepts', in J. Weiler, A. Cassese and M. Spinedi (eds), *International Crimes of States, A Critical Analysis of the ILC's Draft Article 18 on State Responsibility* (Berlin: Walter de Gruyter, 1998), pp. 151–60.

Gallon, G., 'Human Rights – A Path to Democracy and Peace in Colombia', in C. Welna and G. Gallon (eds), *Peace, Democracy and Human Rights in Colombia* (University of Notre Dame Press, 2007), pp. 353–410.

Gardam, J. and Charlesworth, H., 'Protection of Women in Armed Conflict', *Human Rights Quarterly*, 22 (2000), 148–66.

Garkawe, S., 'Victims and the International Criminal Court: Three Major Issues', *International Criminal Law Review*, 3 (2003), 345–67.

Gattini, A., 'The UN Compensation Commission: Old Rules New Procedures on War Reparations', *European Journal of International Law*, 13(1) (2002), 161–81.

Gillard, E-C., 'Reparation for Violations of International Humanitarian Law', *International Review of the Red Cross*, 85(851) (2003), 529–53.

Goldstone, R., 'Advancing the Cause of Human Rights: The Need for Justice and Accountability', in S. Power and G. Allison, *Realizing Human Rights, Moving from Inspiration to Impact* (New York: St. Martin's Press, 2000), pp. 195–221.

Gomez Isa, F., 'Justicia, Verdad y Reparación en el Proceso de Desmovilización Paramilitar en Colombia', in F. Gomez Isa (ed.), *Colombia en Su Laberinto, una Mirada al Conflicto* (Madrid: Catarata, 2008), pp. 87–166.

Greco, G., 'Victims' Rights Overview under the ICC Legal Framework: A Jurisprudential Analysis', *International Criminal Law Review*, 7 (2007), 531–47.

Greenwood, C., 'International Humanitarian Law', in F. Kalshoven (ed.), *The Centennial of the First International Peace Conference* (The Hague: Kluwer Law, 2000), pp. 161–259.

Grenfell, D., 'When Remembering Isn't Enough: Reconciliation and Justice in Timor-Leste', *Arena Magazine*, Issue 80, December–January 2005–6, pp. 32–5.

Guembe, M. J. and Olea, H., 'No Justice, No Peace; Discussion of a Legal Framework Regarding the Demobilisation of Non-State Armed Groups in Colombia', in N. Roht-Arriaza and J. Mariezcurrena (eds), *Transitional Justice in the Twenty-First Century, Beyond Truth versus Justice* (Cambridge University Press, 2006), pp. 120–42.

Hae Bong, S., 'Compensation for Victims of Wartime Atrocities, Recent Developments in Japan's Case Law', *Journal of International Criminal Justice*, 3 (2005), 187–206.

Hall, C. K., 'The Duty of States Parties to the Convention against Torture to Provide Procedures Permitting Victims to Recover Reparations for Torture Committed Abroad', *European Journal of International Law*, 18(5) (2008), 921–37.

Hamber, B. and Wilson, R., 'Symbolic Closure through Memory, Reparation and Revenge in Post-Conflict Societies', *Journal of Human Rights*, 1(1) (2002), 35–53.

Hampson, F., 'The Relationship between International Humanitarian Law and Human Rights Law from the Perspective of a Human Rights Body', *International Review of the Red Cross*, 90(871) (2008), 549–72.

Haslam, E., 'Victim Participation at the International Criminal Court: A Triumph of Hope over Experience', in D. McGoldrick, P. Rome and E. Donnelly (eds), *The Permanent International Criminal Court, Legal and Policy Issues* (Oxford: Hart Publishing, 2004), pp. 315–34.

Hayner, P., 'Fifteen Truth Commissions 1974 to 1994: A Comparative Study', *Human Rights Quarterly*, 16 (1994), 597–655.

'Commissioning the Truth: Further Research Questions', *Third World Quarterly*, 17 (1996), 19–29.

'The Sierra Leone Truth and Reconciliation Commission: Reviewing its First Year', *ICTJ Case Studies Series*, January 2004.

'Negotiating Peace in Sierra Leone, Confronting the Justice Challenge', Study of the Humanitarian Dialogue project 'Negotiating Justice', December 2007, pp. 1–37.

Hayner, P., Wierda, M. and van Zyl, P., 'Exploring the Relationship between the Special Court and the Truth Commission of Sierra Leone', *ICTJ Case Studies Series*, June 2002.

Henckaerts, J-M., 'Study on Customary International Humanitarian Law: A Contribution to the Understanding and Respect for the Rule of Law in Armed Conflict', *International Review of the Red Cross*, 87(857) (2005), 175–212.

'Concurrent Application of International Humanitarian Law and Human Rights Law: A Victim Perspective', in R. Arnold and N. Quenivet (eds), *International Humanitarian Law and Human Rights Law, Towards a New Merger in International Law* (Leiden: Martinus Nijhoff, 2008), pp. 237–67.

Heyns, C., 'Civil and Political Rights in the African Charter', in M. Evans and R. Murray (eds), *The African Charter on Human and Peoples' Rights, the System in Practice 1986–2000* (Cambridge University Press, 2002), pp. 137–77.

Heyns, C. and Viljoen, F., 'The Impact of United Nations Human Rights Treaties on the Domestic Level', *Human Rights Quarterly*, 23(3) (2001), 483–535.

Heyns, C., Padilla, D. and Zwaak, L., 'A Schematic Comparison of Regional Human Rights Systems', *African Human Rights Law Journal*, 5(2) (2005), 308–20.

Higgins, R., 'The International Court of Justice and Human Rights', in K. Wellens (ed.), *International Law: Theory and Practice* (The Hague: Kluwer Law International, 1998), pp. 691–705.

Horovitz, S., 'Transitional Criminal Justice in Sierra Leone', in N. Roht-Arriaza and J. Mariezcurrena (eds), *Transitional Justice in the Twenty-First Century, Beyond Truth versus Justice* (Cambridge University Press, 2006), pp. 43–69.

Ingadottir, T., 'The Trust Fund of the ICC', in D. Shelton (ed.), *International Crimes, Peace and Human Rights: The Role of the International Criminal Court* (New York: Transnational Publishers, 2000), pp. 149–61.

Ingadottir, T., Ngendahayo, F. and Sellers, P., 'The Victims and Witnesses Unit', in T. Ingadottir (ed.), *The International Criminal Court: Recommendations on Policy and Practice* (New York: Transnational Publishers, 2003), pp. 1–45.

Jeong, H-W. and Lerche, C., 'Reconciliation and Its Social and Political Dimensions', *International Politics*, 39 (2002), 329–39.

Jorda, C. and Hemptinne, J., 'The Status and Role of the Victim', in A. Cassese, P. Gaete and J. Jones (eds), *The Rome Statute of The International Criminal Court* (Oxford University Press, 2002), pp. 1387–419.

Kalshoven, F., 'State Responsibility for Warlike Acts of the Armed Forces', *International and Comparative Law Quarterly*, 40 (1991), 827–58.

Katzenstein, S., 'Hybrid Tribunals: Searching for Justice in East Timor', *Harvard Human Rights Journal*, 16 (2003), 245–78.

Kelsall, T., 'Truth, Lies, Ritual: Preliminary Reflections on the Truth and Reconciliation Commission in Sierra Leone', *Human Rights Quarterly*, 27 (2005), 361–91.

King, J., 'Gender and Reparations in Sierra Leone', in R. Rubio-Marín (ed.), *What Happened to the Women? Gender and Reparations for Human Rights Violations* (New York: Social Science Research Council, 2006), pp. 247–83.

Kingston, J., 'Regaining Dignity: Justice and Reconciliation in East Timor', *Brown Journal of World Affairs*, 13(1) (2006), 227–40.

Kristjansdottir, E., 'International Mass Claims Processes and the ICC Trust Fund for Victims', in C. Ferstman, M. Goetz and A. Stephens (eds), *Reparations for Victims of Genocide, War Crimes and Crimes against Humanity, Systems in Place and Systems in the Making* (Leiden: Martinus Nijhoff, 2009), pp. 167–95.

La Rue, F., Speech at Conference on Reparations in the Inter-American System, American University, Washington, 6 March 2007, published in *American University Law Review*, 56 (2007), 1459–63.

Laplante, L. and Theidon, K., 'Transitional Justice in Times of Conflict: Colombia's Ley de Justicia y Paz', *Michigan Journal of International Law*, 28(49) (2006), 49–108.

Linton, S., 'Cambodia, East Timor and Sierra Leone: Experiments in International Justice', *Criminal Law Forum*, 12 (2001), 185–246.

'Putting Things into Perspective: the Realities of Accountability in East Timor, Indonesia and Cambodia', *Maryland Series in Contemporary Asian Studies*, School of Law, University of Maryland, No. 3, 2005, pp. 1–90.

Loucaides, L., 'Reparation for Violations of Human Rights under the European Convention and Restitutio in Integrum', *European Human Rights Law Review*, 2 (2008), 182–92.

Lubell, N., 'Challenges in Applying Human Rights Law to Armed Conflict', *International Review of the Red Cross*, 87(860) (2005), 737–54.

Lyons, B., 'Getting Untrapped, Struggling for Truths; the Commission for Reception, Truth and Reconciliation (CAVR) in East Timor', in C. Romano, A. Nollkaemper and J. Kleffner (eds), *Internationalized Criminal Court, Sierra Leone, East Timor, Kosovo and Cambodia* (Oxford University Press, 2004), pp. 99–124.

MacDonald, A., 'Sierra Leone's Shoestring Special Court', *International Review of the Red Cross*, 84 (2002), 121–42.

Maier, C., 'Doing History, Doing Justice: The Narrative of the Historian and of the Truth Commission', in R. Rotberg and D. Thompson (eds), *Truth v. Justice, The Morality of Truth Commissions* (Princeton University Press, 2000), pp. 261–78.

Malmström, S., 'Restitution of Property and Compensation to Victims', in R. May (ed.), *Essays on ICTY Procedure and Evidence* (The Hague: Kluwer Law International, 2001), pp. 373–84.

Marshall, D., 'The Human Rights Field Operation in Partnership for Transitional Justice', in M. O'Flaherty (ed.), *The Human Rights Field Operation; Law Theory and Practice* (Farnham: Ashgate, 2007), pp. 141–57.

Martín, I., 'The High Commissioner's Field Presences', in G. Alfredsson, J. Grimheden, B. Ramcharan and A. de Zayas (eds), *International Human Rights Monitoring Mechanisms* (The Hague: Kluwer Law International, 2001), pp. 403–14.

McCarthy, C., 'Human Rights and the Laws of War under the American Convention on Human Rights', *European Human Rights Law Review*, 6 (2008), 762–80.

McKay, F., 'Are Reparations Appropriately Addressed in the ICC Statute?', in D. Shelton (ed.), *International Crimes, Peace and Human Rights: The Role of the International Criminal Court* (New York: Transnational Publishers, 2000), pp. 163–78.

McLaughlin, C., 'Victim and Witness Measures of the International Criminal Court: A Comparative Analysis', *The Law and Practice of International Courts and Tribunals*, 6 (2007), 189–220.

Méndez, J., 'Accountability for Past Abuses', *Human Rights Quarterly*, 19 (1997), 255–82.

Meron, T., 'On the Inadequate Reach of Humanitarian and Human Rights Law and the Need for a New Instrument', *American Journal of International Law*, 77(3) (1983), 589-606.

'The Continuing Role of Custom in the Foundation of International Humanitarian Law', *American Journal of International Law*, 90(2) (1996), 238–49.

Mersky, M. and Roht-Arriaza, N., '"Case Study Guatemala" in Due Process of Law Foundation', *Victims Unsilenced: The Inter-American Human Rights System and Transitional Justice in Latin America* (Washington, DC: DPLF, 2007), pp. 7–32.

Millar, H., 'Facilitating Women's Voices in Truth Recovery: An Assessment of Women's Participation and the Integration of a Gender Perspective in Truth Commissions', in H. Durham and T. Gurd (eds), *Listening to the Silences, Women and War* (Leiden: Martinus Nijhoff, 2005), pp. 171–222.

Murray, R., 'Current Developments, Recent Decisions of the African Commission on Human and Peoples' Rights', *South African Journal on Human Rights*, 17 (2001), 119–70.

'Recent Developments in the African Human Rights System 2007', *Human Rights Law Journal*, 8(2) (2008), 356–76.

Muttukumaru, C., 'Reparations to Victims', in S. Lee (ed.), *The International Criminal Court: the Making of the Rome Statute, Issues, Negotiations, Results* (The Hague: Kluwer Law International, 1999), pp. 262–70.

Naldi, G., 'Reparations in the Practice of the African Commission on Human and Peoples' Rights', *Leiden Journal of International Law*, 14 (2001), 681–93.

Naqvi, Y., 'The Right to the Truth in International Law, Fact or Fiction?', *International Review of the Red Cross*, 88(862) (2006), pp. 245–73.

Nollkaemper, A., 'Concurrence between Individual Responsibility and State Responsibility in International Law', *International and Comparative Law Quarterly*, 2(3) (2003), 615–30.

Nowak, M., 'The Right of Victims of Gross Human Rights Violations to Reparation', in F. Coomans (ed.), *Rendering Justice to the Vulnerable* (The Hague: Kluwer Law International, 2000), pp. 203–24.

'The Right to Reparation for Victims of Gross Human Rights Violations', in G. Ulrich and L. Krabbe Boserup (eds), *Human Rights in Development Yearbook 2001* (The Hague: Kluwer Law International, 2002), pp. 277–308.

'Reparations by the Human Rights Chamber for Bosnia Herzegovina', in K. De Feyter, S. Parmentier, M. Bossuyt and P. Lemmens (eds), *Out of the Ashes, Reparation for Victims of Gross and Systematic Human Rights Violations* (Antwerp: Intersentia, 2005), pp. 245–88.

'The Need for a World Court of Human Rights', *Human Rights Law Review*, 7(1) (2007), 251–9.

O'Flaherty, M., 'Sierra Leone's Peace Process: The Role of the Human Rights Community', *Human Rights Quarterly*, 26(1) (2004), 29–62.

'Case Study: The United Nations Human Rights Field Operation in Sierra Leone', in M. O'Flaherty (ed.), *The Human Rights Field Operation; Law Theory and Practice* (Farnham: Ashgate, 2007), pp. 287–315.

Orentlicher, D., 'Settling Accounts: The Duty to Prosecute Human Rights Violations of a Prior Regime', in N. Kritz (ed.), *Transitional Justice: How Emerging Democracies Reckon with Former Regimes*, 3 vols (Washington, DC: US Institute of Peace Press, 1995), pp. 375–415.

Osiel, M., 'Why Prosecute? Critics of Punishment for Mass Atrocity?', *Human Rights Quarterly*, 22 (2000), 118–47.

Padilla, D., 'An African Human Rights Court: Reflections from the Perspective of the Inter-American System', *African Human Rights Law Journal*, 2(2) (2002), 185–94.

Pasqualucci, J., 'Victim Reparations in the Inter-American Human Rights System: A Critical Assessment of Current Practice and Procedure', *Michigan International Law Journal*, 18 (1996), 1–58.

Paz, C. and Bailey, P., 'Guatemala: Gender and Reparations for Human Rights Violation', in R. Rubio-Marín (ed.), *What Happened to the Women? Gender and Reparations for Human Rights Violations* (New York: Social Science Research Council, 2006), pp. 93–135.

Pieter van der Mei, A., 'The New African Court on Human and Peoples' Rights; Towards an Effective Human Rights Protection Mechanism for Africa?', *Leiden Journal of International Law*, 18 (2005), 112–29.

Pisillo Mazzeschi, R., 'Reparation Claims by Individuals for State Breaches of Humanitarian Law and Human Rights: An Overview', *Journal of International Criminal Justice*, 1 (2003), 339–47.

Poole, J., 'Post-Conflict Justice in Sierra Leone', in C. Bassiouni (ed.), *Post Conflict Justice* (New York: Transnational Publishers, 2002), pp. 563–92.

Popkin, M. and Roht-Arriaza, N., 'Truth as Justice: Investigatory Commissions in Latin America', *Law and Social Inquiry: The Journal of the American Bar Foundation*, 20(1) (1995), 79–116.

Ratner, S., 'The Schizophrenias of International Criminal Law', *Texas International Law Journal*, 33 (1998), 237–56.

Reiger, C., 'Hybrid Attempts at Accountability for Serious Crimes in East Timor', in N. Roht-Arriaza and J. Mariezcurrena (eds), *Transitional Justice in the Twenty-First Century, Beyond Truth versus Justice* (Cambridge University Press, 2006), pp. 143–70.

Reiger, C. and Wierda, M., 'The Serious Crimes Process in Timor Leste: In Retrospect', *Prosecution Case Studies Series*, International Center for Transitional Justice, March 2006, pp. 1–41.

Roche, D., 'Gluttons for Restorative Justice', *Economy and Society*, 32(4) (2003), 630–43.

Rodriquez Pinzon, D., Speech at Conference on Reparations in the Inter-American System, American University, Washington, 6 March 2007, *American University Law Review*, 56 (2007), 1390–6.

Roht-Arriaza, N., 'The Role of International Actors in National Accountability Processes', in A. Barahona de Brito, C. Gonzalez Enriquez and P. Aguilar (eds), *The Politics of Memory, Transitional Justice in Democratizing Societies* (Oxford University Press, 2001), pp. 40–64.

'Reparations in the Aftermath of Repression', in E. Stover and H. Weinstein (eds), *My Neighbour, My Enemy, Justice and Community in the Aftermath of Mass Atrocity* (Cambridge University Press, 2004), pp. 121–39.

Rombouts, H. and Vandeginste, S., 'Reparation to Victims in Rwanda: Caught between Theory and Practice', in K. De Feyter, S. Parmentier, M. Bossuyt and P. Lemmens (eds), *Out of the Ashes, Reparation for Victims of Gross and Systematic Human Rights Violations* (Antwerp: Intersentia, 2005), pp. 309–41.

Rosenstock, R., 'The ILC and State Responsibility', *American Journal of International Law*, 96 (2002), 792–7.

Sandoval-Villalba, C., 'The Concepts of "Injured Party" and "Victim" of Gross Human Rights Violations in the Jurisprudence of the Inter-American Court of Human Rights: A Commentary on their Implications for Reparations', in C. Ferstman, M. Goetz and A. Stephens (eds), *Reparations for Victims of Genocide, War Crimes and Crimes against Humanity, Systems in Place and Systems in the Making* (Leiden: Martinus Nijhoff, 2009), pp. 243–82.

Sarkin, J., 'The Necessity and Challenges of Establishing a Truth and Reconciliation Commission in Rwanda', *Human Rights Quarterly*, 21(3) (1999), 767–823.

'The Tension between Justice and Reconciliation in Rwanda', *Journal of African Law*, 45(2) (2001), 143–73.

'The Role of Regional Systems in Enforcing State Human Rights Compliance: Evaluating the African Commission on Human and Peoples' Rights and the New African Court of Justice and Human Rights with Comparative Lessons from the Council of Europe and the Organization of American States', *Inter-American and European Human Rights Journal*, 1(2) (2008), 199–242.

Sassoli, M., 'The Victim-oriented Approach of International Humanitarian Law and of the International Committee of the Red Cross', in C. Bassiouni, *International Protection of Victims*, Nouvelle Etudes Penales, Association International de Droit Penal (Paris: Eres, 1988), pp. 147–80.

Schabas, W., 'The Relationship between Truth Commissions and Courts: The Case of Sierra Leone', *Human Rights Quarterly*, 25 (2003), 1035–66.

'Darfur and the "Odious Scourge": the Commission of Inquiry's Findings on Genocide', *Leiden Journal of International Law*, 18 (2005), 871–85.

'Reparation Practices in Sierra Leone and the Truth and Reconciliation Commission', in K. De Feyter, S. Parmentier, M. Bossuyt and P. Lemmens (eds), *Out of the Ashes, Reparation for Victims of Gross and Systematic Human Rights Violations* (Antwerp: Intersentia, 2005), pp. 289–307.

'The Sierra Leone Truth Commission', in N. Roht-Arriaza and J. Mariezcurrena (eds), *Transitional Justice in the Twenty-First Century, Beyond Truth versus Justice* (Cambridge University Press, 2006), pp. 21–42.

Scharf, M., 'The Case for a Permanent International Truth Commission', *Duke Journal of Comparative and International Law*, (1997), 375–405.

Schmidt, M., 'Follow-up Procedures to Individual Complaints', in G. Alfredsson, J. Grimheden, B. Ramcharan and A. de Zayas (eds), *International Human Rights Monitoring Mechanisms* (The Hague: Kluwer Law International, 2001), pp. 201–15.

Seider, R., 'War, Peace and Memory Politics in Central America', in A. Barahona de Brito, C. Gonzalez Enriquez and P. Aguilar (eds), *The Politics of Memory, Transitional Justice in Democratizing Societies* (Oxford University Press, 2001), pp. 161–89.

Shaw, R., 'Rethinking Truth and Reconciliation Commissions, Lessons from Sierra Leone', United States Institute for Peace, Special Report 130, February 2005.

Shelton, D., 'Righting Wrongs: Reparations in the Articles on State Responsibility', *American Journal of International Law*, 96(4): (2002), 833–56.

Simma, B. and Alston, P., 'The Sources of Human Rights Law: Custom, *Jus Cogens* and General Principles', *Australian Yearbook of International Law*, (1988–9), 82–108.

Simma, B. and Paulus, A. L., 'The Responsibility of Individuals for Human Rights Abuses in Internal Conflicts: A Positivist View', *American Journal of International Law*, 93(2) (1999), 302–16.

Sluiter, G., 'The ICTR and the Protection of Witnesses', *Journal of International Criminal Justice*, 3 (2005), 962–76.

Sooka, Y., 'Dealing with the Past and Transitional Justice: Building Peace through Accountability', *International Review of the Red Cross*, 88(862) (2006), 311–25.

Stahn, C., 'Accommodating Individual Criminal Responsibility and National Reconciliation: The UN Truth Commission for East Timor', *American Journal of International Law*, 95(4) (2001), 952–66.

'United Nations Peace-building, Amnesties and Alternative Forms of Justice: A Change in Practice', *International Review of the Red Cross*, 84(845) (2002), 191–205.

Stover, E., 'Witnesses and the Promise of Justice in the Hague', in E. Stover and H. Weinstein (eds), *My Neighbour, My Enemy, Justice and Community in the Aftermath of Mass Atrocity* (Cambridge University Press, 2004), pp. 104–20.

Taylor, L., 'The United Nations Compensation Commission', in C. Ferstman, M. Goetz and A. Stephens (eds), *Reparations for Victims of Genocide, War Crimes and Crimes against Humanity, Systems in Place and Systems in the Making* (Leiden: Martinus Nijhoff, 2009), pp. 197–214.

Tepperman, J., 'Truth and Consequences', *Foreign Affairs*, 81(2) (2002), pp. 128–50.

Tolbert, D. and Swinnen, F., 'The Protection of, and Assistance to, Witnesses at the ICTY', in H. Abtahi and G. Boas (eds), *The Dynamics of International Criminal Justice* (Leiden: Martinus Nijhoff, 2006), pp. 193–229.

Tomuschat, C., 'Clarification Commission in Guatemala', *Human Rights Quarterly*, 23(2) (2001), 233–58.

'Reparation for Victims of Grave Human Rights Violations', *Tulane Journal of International and Comparative Law*, 10 (2002), 157–84.

'Darfur – Compensation for the Victims', *Journal of International Criminal Justice*, 3 (2005), 579–89.

Udombana, N., 'So Far So Fair: The Local Remedies Rule in the Jurisprudence of the African Commission of Human and Peoples' Rights', *American Journal of International Law*, 97(1) (2003), 1–37.

Umozurike, O., 'The Complaint Procedures of the African Commission on Human and Peoples' Rights', in G. Alfredsson, J. Grimheden, B. Ramcharan and A. de Zayas (eds), *International Human Rights Monitoring Mechanisms* (The Hague: Kluwer Law International, 2001), pp. 713–30.

Uprimny Yepes, R. and Lasso Lozano, L., 'Verdad, Reparación y Justicia para Colombia: Algunas Reflexiones y Recomendaciones', in Friedrich Ebert Stiftung (ed.), *Conflicto y Seguridad, Democrática en Colombia, Temas Críticos y Propuestas* (Bogotá: Fundación Social, 2004).

Van Boven, T., 'Victims' Rights to a Remedy and Reparation: The New United Nations Principles and Guidelines', in C. Ferstman, M. Goetz and A. Stephens (eds), *Reparations for Victims of Genocide, War Crimes and Crimes against Humanity, Systems in Place and Systems in the Making* (Leiden: Martinus Nijhoff, 2009), pp. 19–40.

Van Houtte, H., Das, H. and Delmartino, B., 'The United Nations Compensation Commission', in P. De Greiff (ed.), *The Handbook of Reparations* (Oxford University Press, 2006), pp. 322–89.

Viaene, L., 'Life is Priceless: Mayan Qeqchi Voices on the Guatemalan National Reparations Program', *International Journal of Transitional Justice*, 4 (2010), 4–25.

Viljoen, F., 'Admissibility under the African Charter', in M. Evans and R. Murray (eds), *The African Charter on Human and Peoples' Rights, the System in Practice 1986–2000* (Cambridge University Press, 2002), pp. 61–99.

Waldorf, L., 'Goats and Graves: Reparations in Rwanda's Community Courts', in C. Ferstman, M. Goetz and A. Stephens (eds), *Reparations for Victims of Genocide, War Crimes and Crimes against Humanity, Systems in Place and Systems in the Making* (Leiden: Martinus Nijhoff, 2009), pp. 515–39.

Wandita, G., Campbell-Nelson, K. and Pereira, M., 'Learning to Engender Reparations in Timor-Leste: Reaching Out to Female Victims', in R. Rubio-Marín (ed.), *What Happened to the Women? Gender and Reparations for Human Rights Violations* (New York: Social Science Research Council, 2006), pp. 285–334.

Wildhaber, L., 'Article 41 and Just Satisfaction in the European Convention on Human Rights', *Baltic Yearbook of International Law*, 3 (2003), 1–18.

Wyler, E., 'From State Crime to Responsibility for Serious Breaches of Obligations under Peremptory Norms of General International Law', *European Journal of International Law*, 13(5) (2002), 1147–60.

Zacklin, R., 'The Failings of Ad Hoc International Tribunals', *Journal of International Criminal Justice*, 2 (2004), 541–5.

Zalaquett, J., 'Balancing Ethical Imperatives and Political Constraints: The Dilemma of New Democracies Confronting Past Human Rights Violations', *Hastings Law Journal*, 43 (1992), 1425–38.

Zegveld, L., 'Remedies for Victims of Violations of International Humanitarian Law', *International Review of the Red Cross*, 85 (2003), 497–526.

'Victims' Reparations Claims and International Criminal Courts, Incompatible Values?', *Journal of International Criminal Justice*, 8 (2010), 79–111.

Reports and publications of NGOs, professional associations, unpublished papers and academic seminar proceedings

Amnesty International, Annual Human Rights Reports, 2003, 2004, 2005, 2006.

'End Impunity, Justice for the Victims of Torture', Amnesty International Publications, 2001.

'The Civil Defense Patrols Re-emerge in Guatemala', AI Index AMR 34/053/2002, 4 September 2002.

'Sierra Leone Government Urged to Implement the Recommendations of the Truth and Reconciliation Commission', Public Statement, AFR 51/012/2005, 29 November 2005.

'Sierra Leone: Getting Reparations Rights for Survivors of Sexual Violence', Report AI Index AFR51/005/2007, 1 November 2007, pp. 1–36.

Colombian Commission of Jurists, 'A Growing Absence of Guarantees, Situation of HR and IHL in Colombia 1997–2003', Bogotá, 2003.

De Geiff, P., 'Contributing to Peace and Justice, Finding a Balance between DDR and Reparations', Paper presented at conference 'Building a Future on Peace and Justice', Nuremberg, 25–27 June 2007.

Due Process of Law Foundation (DPLF), 'Victims Unsilenced: The Inter-American Human Rights System and Transitional Justice in Latin America', DPLF, Washington, 2007.
'Después de Procesos de Justicia Transicional, Cual es la situación de las victimas? Los casos de Chile y Guatemala', Public conference report, 2008.
Friedrich Ebert Stiftung, 'Conflicto y Seguridad, Democracia en Colombia, Temas Críticos y Propuestas', Conference Publication, Bogotá, 2004.
Fundación Ideas para la Paz, 'Siguiendo el Conflicto, Hechos y Análisis', Bogotá, No. 30, September 2005.
'Siguiendo el Conflicto, Hechos y Análisis', Bogotá, No. 50, June 2007.
Harvard Law School Human Rights Program, 'Truth Commissions: A Comparative Assessment', Report of an interdisciplinary discussion held at Harvard Law School in May 1996, Harvard Law School Human Rights Program, 1997.
Human Rights Watch, Annual Human Rights Reports, 2003–9.
Policy Paper on the Interrelationship between the Sierra Leone Special Court and the Truth and Reconciliation Commission, 18 April 2002.
IDEA, *Reconciliation after Violent Conflict, A Handbook* (Stockholm: IDEA, 2003).
International Center for Transitional Justice (P. Wierda, M. Hayner and P. van Zyl), 'Paper Exploring the Relationship between the Special Court and the Truth and Reconciliation Commission of Sierra Leone', 24 June 2002.
'The Sierra Leone Truth and Reconciliation Commission, Reviewing its First Year', Case Study Series, January 2004.
(M. Hirst), 'Too Much Friendship, Too Little Truth', Monitoring Report on the Commission of Truth and Friendship in Indonesia and Timor Leste, January 2008.
'An Unfinished Truth: An Analysis of the Commission of Truth and Friendship's Final Report on the 1999 Atrocities in East Timor', March 2009.
(M. Suma and C. Correa), Report and Proposals for the Implementation of Reparations in Sierra Leone, December 2009.
'Unfulfilled Expectations, Victims Perceptions of Justice and Reparations in Timor-Leste', February 2010.
International Council on Human Rights Policy, 'Negotiating Justice, Human Rights and Peace Agreements', Geneva, 2006.
International Crisis Group, 'Sierra Leone's Truth and Reconciliation Commission: A Fresh Start?', *Africa Briefing*, 20 December 2002.
'The Special Court for Sierra Leone, Promises and Pitfalls of a "New Model"', *Africa Briefing*, No. 16, 4 August 2003.
'Colombia: Towards Peace and Justice?', Latin America Report No. 16, 14 March 2006.
'Correcting Justice: Victims and the Justice and Peace Law in Colombia', Latin America Report No. 29, 30 October 2008.
Magarrell, L., 'Reparaciones por Violaciones de los Derechos Humanos y al Derecho Internacional Humanitario', unpublished paper presented by the

International Center for Transitional Justice, Seminar on International Criminal Law, Bogotá, April 2004.
No Peace without Justice, 'Lawyers' Guide to the Special Court for Sierra Leone', 2004.
Open Society Justice Initiative, 'From Judgment to Justice, Implementing International and Regional Human Rights Decisions', New York, 2010.
Redress, 'Reparation, A Sourcebook for Victims of Torture and Other Violations of Human Rights and Humanitarian Law' (London: The Redress Trust, 2003).
'Enforcing Reparations, Enforcement of Awards for Victims of Torture and Other International Crimes' (London: The Redress Trust, 2006).
'Victims' Central Role in Fulfilling the ICC's Mandate', Paper prepared for the 8th Assembly of States Parties, The Hague, 18–26 November 2009, available at: www.redress.org.
'Considering Reparations for Victims of the Khmer Rouge Regime', Discussion Paper, November 2009.
'Report on the Impact of the Rome Statute System on Victims and Affected Communities', The Redress Trust, London, 22 March 2010.
Schabas, W., 'The Relationship between Truth Commissions and Courts: The Case of Sierra Leone', Paper presented at 'Conference on the Inter-Relationship between Truth Commissions and Courts', Galway, 4 October 2002.
Stockholm International Forum, 'A Conference on Truth, Justice and Reconciliation', Stockholm, 23–24 April 2002.

United Nations documents

Reports of the UN Secretary-General

Draft Convention on the Crime of Genocide, UN Doc. E/447, report presented 26 June 1947 by the Secretary-General upon request by the General Assembly.
Report of the Secretary-General to the Security Council on the Establishment of a Special Court for Sierra Leone, UN Doc. S/2000/915, 4 October 2000.
Report of the Secretary-General to the Security Council, 'The Rule of Law and Transitional Justice in Conflict and Post-Conflict Societies', UN Doc. S/2004/616, 23 August 2004.
Report of the Commission of Inquiry on Darfur to the Secretary-General, Submission of the Report to the Security Council, UN Doc. S/2005/60, 1 February 2005.
Report of the Secretary-General to the General Assembly, 'In Larger Freedom, Towards Development, Security and Human Rights for All', UN Doc. A/59/2005, 25 March 2005, para. 132.
Letter from the Secretary-General to the Security Council containing the Report of the UN Commission of Experts to Review the Prosecution of Serious Violations of Human Rights in East Timor, UN Doc. S/2205/458, 24 June 2005.

Report of the Secretary-General to the General Assembly, 'Investing in the United Nations, for a Stronger Organisation Worldwide', UN Doc. A/60/692, 7 March 2006.

Report of the Secretary-General to the Security Council on Justice and Reconciliation in Timor-Leste, UN Doc. S/2006/580, 26 July 2006.

Report of the Secretary-General to the General Assembly and the Security Council, Uniting our Strengths: Enhancing United Nations Support for the Rule of Law, UN Doc. A/61/636-S/2006/980, 14 December 2006.

Report of the Secretary-General on the United Nations Voluntary Fund for Victims of Torture, UN Doc. A/63/220, 5 August 2008.

Guidance Note of the Secretary-General on the United Nations Approach to Transitional Justice, adopted on 10 March 2010.

Report of the Secretary-General on the United Nations Integrated Mission in Timor-Leste to the Security Council, January–September 2010, UN Doc. S/2010/522.

Report of the Secretary-General on the United Nations Integrated Mission in Timor-Leste to the Security Council, September 2010–January 2011, UN Doc. S/2011/32.

UN General Assembly

Resolutions

UN Declaration of the Basic Principles of Justice for Victims of Crime and Abuse of Power, UN Doc. A/RES/40/34, adopted by the General Assembly 29 November 1985.

UN Basic Principles and Guidelines on the Right to a Remedy and Reparation for Victims of Gross Violations of International Human Rights Law and Serious Violations of International Humanitarian Law, UN Doc. A/RES/60/147, adopted by the General Assembly 16 December 2005.

Reports

Joint UN Special Rapporteurs' of the Commission on Human Rights Fact-Finding Mission to East Timor (Arbitrary Detention, Torture and Violence against Women), Report to the General Assembly, UN Doc. A/54/660, December 1999.

Report of the International Commission of Inquiry on East Timor to the Secretary-General, UN Doc. A/54/726-S/2000/59, 31 January 2000.

Report of the Special Rapporteur on Torture and Other Cruel, Inhuman or Degrading Treatment or Punishment, Sir Nigel Rodley, Report to the General Assembly, UN Doc. A/55/290, 11 August 2000.

Report of the Special Rapporteur on Torture and Other Cruel, Inhuman or Degrading Treatment or Punishment, Theo van Boven, Report to the General Assembly, UN Doc. A/58/120, 23 December 2003.

Report of the Special Rapporteur on Torture and Other Cruel, Inhuman or Degrading Treatment or Punishment, Theo Van Boven, Report to the General Assembly, UN Doc. A/59/324, 1 September 2004.
Report of the Committee against Torture to the General Assembly, UN Doc. A/65/44, 14 May 2010.
Report of the Human Rights Committee to the General Assembly, UN Doc. A/65/40, 19 October 2010.

UN Security Council

Resolutions

Security Council Resolution 827 establishing the ICTY, UN Doc. S/RES/827, adopted 25 May 1993.
Security Council Resolution 955 establishing the ICTR, UN Doc. S/RES/955, adopted 8 November 1994.
Security Council Resolution 1272 on the Situation in East Timor, UN Doc. S/RES/1272, adopted 25 October 1999.
Security Council Resolution 1315, Requesting the Secretary-General to Negotiate an Agreement with the Government of Sierra Leone to Create an Independent Special Court, UN Doc. S/RES/1315, adopted 14 August 2000.
Security Council Resolution 1325 on Women, Peace and Security, UN Doc. S/RES/1325, adopted 31 October 2000.
Security Council Resolution 1593 on Referral of the Situation in Darfur to the ICC, UN Doc. S/RES/1593, adopted 31 March 2005.
Security Council Resolution 1769 on the Establishment of UNAMID, UN Doc. S/RES/1769, adopted 31 July 2007.
Security Council Resolution 1888 on Sexual Violence and Armed Conflict, UN Doc. S/RES/1888, adopted 30 September 2009.
Security Council Resolution No. 1969 on the Situation in Timor-Leste, UN Doc. S/RES/1969, adopted 24 February 2011.

UN Commission on Human Rights/Human Rights Council

Resolutions

UN Basic Principles and Guidelines on the right to a remedy and reparation for victims of gross violations of international human rights law and serious violations of international humanitarian law, UN Doc. E/CN.4/RES/2005/35, adopted 19 April 2005.

Reports

First Consultative Meeting on the Right to a Remedy and Reparation for Victims of Violations, Report to the Commission on Human Rights, 2003, UN Doc. E/CN.4/2003/63.

Second Consultative Meeting on the Right to a Remedy and Reparation for Victims of Violations, Report to the Commission on Human Rights, 2004, UN Doc. E/CN.4/2004/57.

Third Consultative Meeting on the Right to a Remedy and Reparation for Victims of Violations, Report to the Commission on Human Rights, 2005, UN Doc. E/CN.4/2005/59.

OHCHR Annual Report on the Situation of Human Rights in Sierra Leone to the Commission on Human Rights for 2001, UN Doc. E/CN.4/2002/37.

Annual Report on the Situation of Human Rights in Timor Leste to the Commission on Human Rights for 2003, UN Doc. E/CN.4/2004/107.

Annual Report on the Situation of Human Rights in Sierra Leone to the Commission on Human Rights for 2005, UN Doc. E/CN.4/2006/106.

Annual Report on the Situation of Human Rights in Sierra Leone to the Human Rights Council for 2006, UN Doc. A/HRC/4/96.

Annual Report on the Situation of Human Rights in Sierra Leone to the Human Rights Council for 2007, UN Doc. A/HRC/7/66.

Annual Report on the Situation of Human Rights in Sierra Leone to the Human Rights Council for 2008, UN Doc. A/HRC/10/52.

OHCHR Colombia Office, Annual Report to the Commission on Human Rights for 2003, UN Doc. E/CN.4/2004/13.

Annual Report to the Commission on Human Rights for 2004, UN Doc. E/CN.4/2005/10.

Annual Report to the Commission on Human Rights for 2005, UN Doc. E/CN.4/2006/9.

Annual Report to the Human Rights Council for 2006, UN Doc. A/HRC/4/48.

Annual Report to the Human Rights Council for 2007, UN Doc. A/HRC/7/39.

Annual Report to the Human Rights Council for 2009, UN Doc. A/HRC/13/72.

Annual Report to the Human Rights Council for 2010, UN Doc. A/HRC/16/22.

OHCHR Guatemala Office, Annual Report to the Human Rights Council for 2006, UN Doc. A/HRC/4/49/Add.1.

Annual Report to the Human Rights Council for 2007, UN Doc. A/HRC/7/38/Add.1.

Annual Report to the Human Rights Council for 2008, UN Doc. A/HRC/10/31/Add.1.

Annual Report to the Human Rights Council for 2009, UN Doc. A/HRC/13/26/Add.1.

Annual Report to the Human Rights Council for 2010, A/HRC/16/20/Add.1.

OHCHR Uganda Office, Annual Report of the Office of the High Commissioner for Human Rights to the Human Rights Council for 2007, UN Doc. A/HRC/7/38/Add.2.

OHCHR Report on Technical Cooperation in the Field of Human Rights in Timor Leste to the Commission on Human Rights for 2004, UN Doc. E/CN.4/2005/115.

OHCHR Report on Assistance to Sierra Leone in the field of Human Rights in Sierra Leone to the Human Rights Council for 2010, UN Doc. A/HRC/16/78.

Report to the Commission on Human Rights submitted by the Subcommission on Prevention of Discrimination and Protection of Minorities, 'The Question of the Right to Restitution, Compensation and Rehabilitation for Victims of Gross Violations of Human Rights and Fundamental Freedoms', 1993, UN Doc. E/CN.4/Sub.2/1993/8.

Report of the High-Level Mission on the Situation of Human Rights in Darfur Pursuant to Human Rights Council Decision S-4/101, UN Doc. A/HRC/4/80, 9 March 2007.

Report to the Human Rights Council of the Office of the High Commissioner for Human Rights, 'Outcome of the Expert Consultation on the Issue of Protecting the Human Rights of Civilians in Armed Conflict', UN Doc. A/HRC/11/31, 2 June 2009.

'Analytical Study on Human Rights and Transitional Justice', A/HRC/12/18, 6 August 2009, Addendum, 'Inventory of Human Rights and Transitional Justice Aspects of Recent Peace Agreements', UN Doc. A/HRC/12/18/Add.1, 21 August 2009.

Sixth Report of the Secretary-General to the Security Council on the United Nations Integrated Office in Sierra Leone, 29 April 2008, UN Doc. S/2008/281.

Special Rapporteur on the Situation of Human Rights in Kuwait under Iraqi Occupation, Reports to the Commission on Human Rights, 1992, UN Doc. E/CN.4/1992/26.

Special Rapporteur on Torture and Other Cruel, Inhuman or Degrading Treatment or Punishment, Manfred Nowak, Report to the Human Rights Council 2007, UN Doc. A/HRC/4/33.

Special Rapporteur on Violence Against Women, Rashida Manjoo, Report to the Human Rights Council 2010, UN Doc. A/HRC/14/22.

Special Rapporteur on Torture and Other Cruel, Inhuman or Degrading Treatment or Punishment, Juan E. Méndez, Report to the Human Rights Council 2011, UN Doc. A/HRC/16/52.

UN set of principles for the protection and promotion of human rights through action to combat impunity, adopted in 1997, UN Doc. E/CN.4/Sub.2/1997/20/Rev.1, annex II, and updated in 2005, UN Doc. E/CN.4/2005/102/Add.1.

Various UN or OHCHR documents and reports

OHCHR, 'Making Peace Our Own, Victims' Perceptions of Accountability, Reconciliation and Transitional Justice in Northern Uganda', Research Report, 2007.

OHCHR, 'Rule of Law Tools for Post-Conflict States; Reparations Programmes', 2008.

UN, Guatemala Peace Agreements, New York, 1998.

UNDP, 'El Conflicto, Callejón con Salida', National Development Report on Colombia, 2003.

UNDP, 'Human Development Report', 2008.

ICC related documents and reports

Regulations of the Trust Fund for Victims, Resolution ICC-ASP/4/Res. 3, adopted 3 December 2005.

Report of the International Criminal Court to the General Assembly of the United Nations, 2005/2006, A/61/217.

Report of the International Criminal Court to the General Assembly of the United Nations, 2007/2008, A/63/323.

Report of the International Criminal Court to the General Assembly of the United Nations, 2008/2009, A/64/356.

Report of the International Criminal Court on the Strategy in Relation to Victims, ICC-ASP/8/45, 10 November 2009.

Report of the International Criminal Court to the General Assembly of the United Nations, 2009/2010, A/65/313.

The ICC Trust Fund for Victims, Programme Progress Report, Autumn 2010.

Prosecutor v. *Lubanga* ICC-01/04-01/06, pending open investigation.

Prosecutor v. *Katanga and Chui* ICC-01/04-01/07, pending open investigation.

International Law Commission

International Law Commission, Draft Articles on Responsibility of States for Internationally Wrongful Acts, adopted 2001 (extract of ICL Report to the GA, A/56/10, ch. IV.E.1).

Commentaries on the Draft Articles on Responsibility of States for Internationally Wrongful Acts, 2001 (extract of ICL to the GA, A/56/10, ch.IV.E.2).

'Fragmentation of International Law: Difficulties Arising from the Diversification and Expansion of International Law', Report of the Study Group of the International Law Commission, A/CN.4/L.702, 2006.

'Seventh Report on Diplomatic Protection by Special Rapporteur John Dugard', A/CN.4/567, 2006.

Draft Articles on Diplomatic Protection, adopted 2006, Official Records of the General Assembly, 61st session, Supplement No. 10 (A/61/10).

Commentaries on the Draft Articles on Diplomatic Protection, 2006, Official Records of the General Assembly, 61st session, Supplement No. 10 (A/61/10).

Reports from regional human rights organisations

Committee of Ministers of the Council of Europe, Supervision of the Execution of Judgments, 2nd Annual Report, 2008.

Monitoring of the Payment of Sums Awarded by Way of Just Satisfaction, 15 January 2009.

European Court of Human Rights, Annual Report 2008, Strasbourg.

Inter-American Commission on Human Rights, Report on the Implementation of the Justice and Peace Law: Initial Stages in the Demobilisation of the AUC and the First Judicial Proceedings, OEA/Ser.L/V/II, Washington, 2 October 2007.

Report on Principal Guidelines for a Comprehensive Public Policy on Reparations, OEA/Ser.L/V/II.131, Washington, 19 February 2008.

Annual Report 2009, OEA/Ser.L/V/II, Washington, 30 December 2009.

National truth commission reports

East Timor/Timor Leste

CAVR, *Chega!* Final Report of the Commission for Reception, Truth and Reconciliation of Timor-Leste (CAVR), Dili, October 2005, available at: www.cavr-timorleste.org.

Guatemala

Memoria del Silencio, Final Report of the Historical Clarification Commission (CEH) in Guatemala, Guatemala City, January 1999, available at: http://shr.aaas.org/guatemala/ceh/report/english/toc.html.

Sierra Leone

Final Report of the Truth and Reconciliation Commission of Sierra Leone, Freetown, October 2004, available at: www.trcsierraleone.org and www.sierra-leone.org/TRCDocuments.html.

Index